# Models, Methods, and Progress
# in World Politics

# Models, Methods, and Progress in World Politics

——————— ■ ———————

## A Peace Research Odyssey

## J. DAVID SINGER

**University of Michigan**

**Westview Press**
BOULDER, SAN FRANCISCO, & OXFORD

Published in 1990 in the United States of America by Westview Press, Inc., 5500 Central Avenue, Boulder, Colorado 80301, and in the United Kingdom by Westview Press, Inc., 36 Lonsdale Road, Summertown, Oxford OX2 7EW

Library of Congress Cataloging-in-Publication Data
Singer, J. David (Joel David), 1925–
  Models, methods, and progress in world politics.
  Includes bibliographical references.
    1. International relations—Research. 2. Peace—
Research. 3. United States—Foreign relations—
1945–    . I. Title.
JX1291.S398    1990    327'.072    89-70510
ISBN 0-8133-0640-X
ISBN 0-8133-0641-8 (pbk.)

Printed and bound in the United States of America

The paper used in this publication meets the requirements
of the American National Standard for Permanence of Paper
for Printed Library Materials Z39.48-1984.

10    9    8    7    6    5    4    3    2    1

# Contents

Introduction     1

**PART ONE**
**Traditional Policy Analysis and Prescription**

    Introduction     7

1   The Error Term and Accident in Nuclear War     9

2   Armaments, Security, and Prosperity:
    An Imaginary Congressional Speech     17

3   Arms Control Negotiations and the Third World     24

4   Negotiation by Proxy: A Proposal     46

5   Negotiations, Initiatives, and Arms Reduction     50

**PART TWO**
**Beyond Policy Prescription**

    Introduction     57

6   Conflict Research, Political Action, and
    Epistemology     58

7   Social Science and Social Problems     67

8   Campaign for a U.S. Peace Academy     83

9   A Manhattan Project for War Prevention Research     88

**PART THREE**
**The Research Outlook and Options**

    Introduction     93

10   The Incompleat Theorist: Insight Without
    Evidence     94

**11**   Variables, Indicators, and Data: The Measurement
       Problem in Macro-political Research                          110

**12**   The Historical Experiment as a Research Strategy
       in the Study of World Politics                              134

**13**   Cumulativeness in the Social Sciences: Some
       Counter-Prescriptions                                       151

**PART FOUR**
**The Research Program and Some Results**

       Introduction                                                157

**14**   Alliance Aggregation and the Onset of War,
       1815–1945                                                   159

**15**   Capabilities, Allocations, and Success in
       Militarized Disputes and War, 1816–1976                     201

**16**   Periodicity, Inexorability, and Steersmanship
       in International War                                        220

**17**   System Structure, Decision Processes, and the
       Incidence of International War                              238

**PART FIVE**
**Implications and Recapitulation**

       Introduction                                                257

**18**   Research, Policy, and the Correlates of War               260

**19**   The Responsibilities of Competence in the
       Global Village                                              272

*Notes*                                                            293
*References*                                                       307

# Introduction

THE GENESIS OF THIS VOLUME might be of interest to the reader. Invited to speak for political science in the University of Colorado lecture series on the Behavioral Sciences, I chose to focus on the promise of the discipline and its failures to fulfill that promise. In the audience was Fred Praeger, that wise and thoughtful publisher whom I had known for years but with whom, somehow, I'd never worked. One reason was methodological; my strong commitment to the scientific mode was surely not convergent with the long and distinguished, but largely nonscientific, list of his authors in either his New York or Boulder incarnations. In any event, we met at his suggestion the next day, talked of history, politics, philosophy, and science, and he then broached the possibility of his publishing a volume or two of my collected papers.

Naturally, I was flattered, not only because of my respect for Fred as an intellectual and literary figure but also because the invitation suggested that he found persuasive my argument for a closer bond between social ethics and scientific method and between the policy process and reproducible evidence. Thus, I agreed in principle on the spot and returned to Michigan to mull over the proper criteria for inclusion, exclusion, and organization. Having already anthologized a good many of my papers in *Correlates of War I & II*, there was the question of redundancy, further complicated by the happy fact that another thirty of my papers are also to be found in one or more other anthologies. But that still left a fair supply and strengthened my preference for concentrating on those that were somewhat less readily available in book form and for emphasizing the more recent writings, while nevertheless offering a coherent and representative sampling of my best work.

Considering the matter of theme and organization, and faced with the reminder—via several recent requests for autobiographical essays as well as the impending appearance of a twenty-fifth anniversary *festschrift* for the Correlates of War project—that I was no longer among the youngest of the Turks, I was attracted to the historical overview. And while that thread is visible in the table of contents, the flow is perhaps more logical than chronological.

In this connection, a few words about my checkered career might be appropriate. Although there have been good times and bad times for the

1

likes of myself over the past three decades or so, the picture that emerges is hardly flattering to my country, its universities, and the political science discipline. I recognize, of course, that part of the problem might be my improbable mix of humor and irascibility but see no good case for going the conventional route; almost every "successful" scholar paints a rather rosy picture of his/her career, thereby misleading the innocent and enticing the weak of heart. The cold war may well have made me into an ardent peace researcher, but it also made for a damned erratic and often inhospitable environment in which to ply that trade with any degree of ethical and scientific consistency. For a more complete—if subjective—picture, one may turn to my chapter in the Kruzel and Rosenau collection *Journeys Through World Politics*. And for the more specific and positive experiences in my role as initiator and principal investigator of the Correlates of War project, there is "One Man's View" in *Prisoners of War?* edited by Charles Gochman and Alan Sabrosky.

What emerges in this book, then, is a carefully chosen sample of my work intended to illuminate the three-way connection amongst policy problems, normative values, and reproducible evidence, emphasizing the extent to which progress toward the acquisition and codification of such evidence rests upon a combination of theoretically insightful models and rigorous systematic methods. The audience I have in mind is quite general, but with particular attention to the graduate student preparing for a career in teaching, research, journalism, or government service in world affairs. I especially hope, given what passes for "theory" these days, that the collection will find wide use in graduate and undergraduate seminars on that general topic. Worth noting in this context is my strong sense that scientific method must be relevant not only to the substantive question at hand, but also accessible to the many students who have not yet had much formal training in methodology. Thus, I pride myself in attending to the literary lyrics as well as to the numerical music. As I tell my students, a serious concern with social phenomena requires that we be both literate and numerate; neither mode of expression by itself will suffice.

From the title onward, it is evident that my research and teaching has unambiguously been problem-driven. Obviously, expression of and search for self are present in the work of all of us, myself included, and I deny neither the anger at being labeled difficult and abrasive nor the warmth on reading epithets like creative or courageous, along with the sheer ego-kick in earshot of enthusiasm for my turn of phrase or oratorical style. But more powerful for most of us is the drive to create and/or solve, and for most scientists it is the latter: a preoccupation with some class of theoretical or practical problems.

And for the reasons that I struggle to articulate, the problem has been, and remains, that of war. My motives may or may not be honestly and accurately divined and portrayed, but there should be no ambiguity about what emerges from them. First, that the problem is both a theoretical-scholarly one and a practical-political one: I am in pursuit of applicable knowledge or, in the pretentious language of the academy, "the theory of war," such that we might discover something as to which policies are most and least likely to culminate in crisis or war under particular sets of conditions. One way or another, each paper is intended to move us closer to the point at which we—political elites, counter-elites, and the rest—might generate, evaluate, integrate, and apply knowledge as to the "causes of war and conditions of peace," to use Quincy Wright's felicitous phrase.

The origins of peace research can be traced back to the work of Bloch (1899), Richardson (1919), Sorokin (1937), and Wright (1942), but they are treated here as relatively recent, post–World War II phenomena. That is, those four scholars did indeed try to bring scientific methods to bear on the search for an explanation of war, but not in the same self-conscious political activist sense of the word that came to characterize the movement as we know it today. The social scientists who banded together in the middle and late 1950s were, like their predecessors, driven by intellectual curiosity, but they also thought of themselves as applied scientists who could possibly "make a difference" through rigorous research, public education, and political action.

They were also a disparate group, from a variety of disciplines, and quite interdisciplinary as individuals. Not surprisingly, there were more psychologists and sociologists than political scientists or economists among these "founding fathers"; naturally, the former would tend to see the problem of war in terms of misperception and miscommunication on the part of the attentive public and elites, and they did not find it painful to recognize that our own nation's policies were no less culpable than those of the Soviet Union. But those few economists and political scientists in this peculiarly American enterprise were not only reluctant to see the symmetry in the East-West struggle but tended in addition to interpret the danger of nuclear war as a function of incompatible national objectives and/or flawed strategies. In other words, the distribution of outlooks in the peace research community was shaped not only by the theoretical paradigm dominant in the separate disciplines but also by their different selection-socialization processes.

In the three decades since the peace research movement became institutionalized—marked perhaps by the first publication of the *Journal of Conflict Resolution* at Michigan in 1956, and the Center of the same name a year or so later—it has undergone some important changes. And it has experienced some important divisions. Briefly stated, most political scientists were reluctant to become involved in the early days on three grounds: (a) the movement was strongly oriented toward the methodological rigor of the behavioral sciences, in which few of us were schooled; (b) it attended more to micro-level explanations of war, about which most of us were quite skeptical, focusing as we did on such realpolitik variables as "national interest" and "balance of power" considerations; and (c) it took an insufficiently patriotic view of the U.S.-Soviet cold war and arms race.

But while political scientists tended to remain aloof—if not hostile—the behavioral scientists soon experienced some important disappointments.

In addition to the gradual realization that public opinion and elite perception were hardly sufficient to account for international tension, conflict, and war, the younger and newer recruits to the fold were an increasingly radicalized cohort. Joined by a growing number of like-minded colleagues from West European and Japanese universities and institutes, these North Americans, partly in response to the brutality of the war in Vietnam, Cambodia, and Laos, turned in droves from systematic research to philosophic speculation, ideological polemics, and direct political action—not always peaceful.

In due course, there were three discernible international groupings: (a) the Peace Research Society (later, if prematurely, Peace Science Society), which tended toward the mathematical in methodology and the pro-West in ideology; (b) the International Peace Research Association, largely an-tiscientific in method and anti-West in ideology; and (c) the Peace and Conflict Research Committee of the International Political Science Asso-ciation (IPSA), which sought to serve as a bridge between the other two groups, attentive to methodological rigor as well as to a more diverse range of ideological and theoretical perspectives. Unfortunately, this committee has been recently abolished by the IPSA leadership for its reluctance to invest limited resources and energy into more conferences and conference publications, thus eliminating for the moment any group that might serve to bring together the members of these disparate groups.

This decision is especially unfortunate because over the past two decades serious and systematic peace research has fallen increasingly within the political science discipline. That is, with the decline in radical social science and the attendant resurgence of more conventional definitions of the roles of the several disciplines, many—but not all—psychologists and sociologists have moved away from both radical activism and those problem areas such as international conflict that have been seen traditionally as outside their empirical domain. The same holds for some of the more unconventional economists and historians who had gravitated toward peace research. While scholars from these disciplines will continue to play a modest role in the study of war and peace, and some political scientists will try to remain partially au courant vis-à-vis those disciplines, there is little doubt that this "applicable science" problem will be largely in our court. The question, therefore, is whether we are adequately prepared to take on this important responsibility.

Given this trend, let me outline here a few of the more salient issues with which we in political science have yet to come to terms, beginning with those of a methodological sort. I take these to be more serious than our theoretical problems, even while recognizing their intimate interde-pendence. That is, in any relatively new field, there is plenty of room for theoretical tolerance. We need all the hunches, orientations, and insights we can get, on the assumption that wide diversity increases the probability of coming up with the "right" one. Further, when the amount of systematic research is small, and thus the evidence for or against any given explanation for some particular class of phenomena is close to nil, there are few grounds for either accepting or rejecting a given theoretical model. There are, however, some *meta*theoretical issues, and these are treated in several of the papers in this book, indicating that Feyerabend's (1975) preference for anarchy may go a bit too far. Whereas *theoretical* tolerance is now, and always will remain, something of a virtue, when such tolerance spills over into the *methodological* sector, we have a sure-fire guarantee that theoretical progress will be slow or nonexistent.

Thus, the pages that follow will clearly reflect my *theoretical* biases as well as the empirical and ethical assumptions on which these biases rest, and I trust that my readers will find them interesting, suggestive, and perhaps even compelling. If not, the loss is probably small. But these papers also reflect my *methodological* and epistemological biases, and I trust that these will be *more* than interesting and suggestive. That is, if the reader finds these orientations less than compelling, he or she will be rejecting an intellectual strategy that is not merely a matter of taste; although far from being totally satisfactory, the fact is that it is the only strategy that has worked, leading to the extraordinary advances that have occurred in the physical and biological sciences in recent centuries.

# PART ONE

■

# Traditional Policy Analysis and Prescription

*In the introduction to the book, I briefly mention some of the pioneering efforts to bring scientific method to bear on matters of war and peace. Among the propositions that I derive from that particular tale is the dual conviction that (a) a major research effort might well lead to a body of knowledge that could appreciably reduce the incidence of international war; but (b) we dare not accept political passivity while waiting for all those important discoveries to emerge and then to be properly utilized by national security elites around the world. Rather, I conclude that prudence and patriotism require that we act on the basis of what is known at the moment along with our best scholarly judgments, even when they rest on little more than one's admittedly subjective understanding of "how things work."*

*This is not to suggest that one man's views are no better than another's; after all, the scientific mode is designed not only to generate findings, test rival hypotheses, and strengthen or weaken the case for a given theoretical explanation of war or other phenomena. Those of us who take that mode of inquiry seriously may also benefit from its additional strengths in the shorter run: sensitivity to alternate perspectives on a given issue, awareness of the need to generalize—however impressionistically—from a large and representative aggregation of similar or comparable cases, attention to conceptual and verbal precision, and the like. All of these are more fully illuminated in subsequent parts of the book, but it seems useful at the outset to delineate some of the major policy issues confronting the world in general and Americans in particular, to indicate their significance to peace research, and to offer some tentative analyses and prescriptions as to how best to address them. By and large, Chapters 1 through 5 rest on that familiar mix that is long on trained intuition and short on reproducible evidence, but they nevertheless help put the balance of the book into perspective and serve to alert the reader to my political biases.*

*Chapter 1 is a rather unconventional analysis of the probability of nuclear war, reflecting no systematic historical-empirical findings but suggest-*

7

ing that greater conceptual precision might lead to a more accurate understanding of the problem. Chapter 2 looks at the strategic arms race and
points to a few specific changes in the U.S. strategy that could be proposed
by a newly elected (or any other) member of Congress. In Chapter 3 we
look more closely at the U.S.-Soviet armed rivalry, but more in terms of its
deleterious impact on those whose nations lie outside the major power or-
bits. In the latter part of that chapter and in the shorter Chapters 4 and
5, I lay out several approaches to the negotiation of arms reduction and
elimination that to date have received very little attention.

As I write these lines in the opening days of the 1990s, the probability
of general war between the major powers and their allies would seem to be
considerably lower than when the papers were originally written between
1965 and 1986. Despite the dramatic changes in Eastern Europe and the
temporary improvement in Soviet-American relations, it is important to remember that the most menacing weapons remain in place, as do the command and control systems, the strategic doctrines, the organizations, and
the people who control these weapons; the human race is still in considerable jeopardy and will remain so until some of the policies outlined here
begin to take hold and set in train the necessary changes in world politics.
Too many of our recent gains can be too readily reversed. Further, most of
my analyses apply equally to the problem of "conventional" war, and it is
worth noting that the frequency of international and civil war remains as
it has been for nearly two centuries; only the locale has changed. In sum,
systematic peace research will be as crucial in the decades ahead as it has
been in the bloody and violent past.

# CHAPTER ONE

■

# The Error Term and Accident in Nuclear War

## INTRODUCTION

As we look out on an international system that appears all too ripe for war, an examination of the historical record might well be in order. That record can, of course, offer comfort and reassurance to the optimistic as well as fear and trembling to the pessimistic; one of the virtues of casually-studied history is that we can find in it almost anything for which we are searching. A favorite past-time of politicians, concerned citizens, and all too many scholars is to ransack the historical record, pulling out those cases that meet our intellectual or emotional needs of the moment, and overlooking (or rejecting) those that do not quite fit. Recognizing the political and scientific futility of anecdotal history, my colleagues and I in the Correlates of War project have been systematically examining all international wars from the Napoleonic period to the present in order to see whether there are indeed certain regularities and whether the conditions and events surrounding the onset of these wars might offer any guidance to those of us now living in the shadow of the most terrible one of them all. While few of our systematically data-based findings will be reported here (see *Correlates of War I and II* as well as *Explaining War* for a sampling, 1, 2, 3), certain of the more impressionistic generalizations will be applied to the question at hand.

There are, of course, many criticisms not only of such quantitative historical research, but more generally of *all* efforts to apply the "lessons of history" to the present or future. Perhaps the most salient of these criticisms is the technological: that no armed rivalry of the past unfolded in a world of such devastating weapons, long range delivery vehicles, and

This chapter originally appeared in Alan Newcombe (ed.), "The Nuclear Time Bomb," *Peace Research Reviews Journal*, vol. 10, no. 4 (May 1986), pp. 58–67. © 1984 *Peace Research Reviews*. Reprinted by permission. Occasional phrases reflecting changes that have occurred since the original publication date are shown in brackets.

rapid communications. While factually correct, two considerations help put this allegedly disabling argument into context. First, almost every pre-war period over the past century or so was seen, at the time, as unlike any that had preceded it in terms of weapons technology, and correctly so. Further, in each period there were those who argued that the destructiveness of the new weapons would bring the nations to their senses and make war obsolete, and incorrectly so (4, 5). Second, and equally depressing, the behavior patterns of nations (especially the major powers) in disputes have shown amazing consistency from one pre-war epoch to the next, over and over, right up to the current pre-World War III era. There is, however, one possibly reassuring difference this time: While governments show the same dysfunctional tendency toward demonstrating resolve, hanging tough, and seeking escalation dominance as in the past, when both sides are nuclear capable, they have—so far—always backed away at the very brink. (6)

## CLARIFYING THE CONCEPT

Given the ambiguities that are inherent in the notion of accidental war, let me turn first to some definitional implications before addressing the scientific and epistemological ones. To begin, the many synonyms for accident include fortuitous, adventitious, unintended, unexpected, unforeseen, inadvertent, by chance, and arising out of sources remote or unknown. These all suggest that accidents occur as a result of factors outside of the actors' control. But another side of the concept is associated with negligence, inattention, mistake, oversight, folly, or lack of care. While there could easily be some overlap between these two sets of associations, it is clear that the first set convey the idea of competent and responsible people producing an unexpected outcome as a result of forces beyond their control, whereas the second set suggests incompetence and negligence.

This is certainly a distinction worth making, but it nevertheless begs at least two important questions. First, there are few events that surprise *everybody*; some will have suspected and others may have predicted a given outcome, be it happy or tragic. Thus, it makes sense to restrict our definition to those who made the decisions culminating in the unexpected outcome. This raises, in turn, the second question: why some people are surprised and others are, to a greater or lesser extent, not surprised. The answer lies largely in the domain of knowledge—factual, correlational, or explanatory. While some predictions of generally unexpected events may well be fortuitous, the more usual explanation is that some people understood the situation, know that Z usually follows X, or picked up a piece of factual intelligence that was both appropriate to the prediction and not generally known.

All of this suggests, then, that the unexpected war is one that comes as a surprise to some or many, but not all, of those who participate in, or study, the policy process. It also suggests that this population cannot be divided neatly into those who were/will be surprised by war and those who were/will not be surprised. Recognizing that even the most pre-scientific of us think, however crudely, in terms of the odds, likelihoods, and probabilities, it follows that surprise is a matter of degree rather than a dichotomous matter of yes or no. That degree will, in turn, be a function of the knowledge that has been generated and codified, its accuracy and relevance, and of course, the ability and willingness of the decisional elites to put that knowledge to use.

Closely related to the use of relevant knowledge and common prudence is another aspect of unexpected war: negligence and carelessness. The distinction is between ignorance and irresponsibility, but it should not be exaggerated: often we "didn't know it was loaded" (ignorance) merely because we didn't bother to look (negligence). Similarly, and for a variety of emotional, ideological, bureaucratic, and political reasons, practitioners fail to seek, evaluate, or apply information that could mean life or death for scores or for hundreds of millions. This is sometimes referred to as miscalculation.

Thus far, we have examined the relationship between the unexpected war which comes out of ignorance and that which comes out of negligence. Let us turn now to a third dimension of unexpected war: that which is unintended. Surely all unintended wars are also unexpected, and all unexpected wars are unintended, but in each case we must again distinguish between the parties. In some rare cases, some of the parties may possibly seek war, and for them, the event when it comes is hardly a surprise; it is both intended and expected. But we can readily note that this is an extremely rare event. For most strata and sectors in most societies, war is far from cost-effective and thus is rarely the intended outcome of a rivalry or dispute. On the other hand, elites and publics have, over and over, stepped onto the road to war and knowingly passed up a good many well-marked exit ramps along the way, believing or hoping that steadfastness and resolve would produce the desired outcome without war. To take perhaps the most extreme case, the evidence is that neither Hitler nor most of the general staff preferred or intended war, but each successful act of intimidation strengthened their conviction that all could be had without it. In almost every major power dispute or rivalry (defined as an enduring and repeated sequence of disputes), we find many escalatory acts usually intended to produce compliance in the adversary, but our evidence shows how delusory that intent can be. Even if such compliance is produced in the first or second confrontation between two majors, it typically leads to the "never again" reaction, with the temporarily intimidated power coming back again, better armed and with greater resolve (7). As a result, each successive episode is more severe, and the probability of each one ending in war is greater than the prior one. In sum, our reading of these cases strongly suggests that neither the 28 major wars since the Congress of Vienna, nor WW III if it comes, was or will be intended.

## ACCIDENT AND EPISTEMOLOGY

Turning to the "accidental" side of the coin, the picture is more interesting and more complicated. One way of looking at the notion of accident is the probabilistic one, and since no social event is ever either totally predetermined or totally accidental, we are faced with a question of degree (8). To back up a bit, we can think of every action or event as arising out of three sets of phenomena. First are the *voluntaristic* acts of the immediate participants, which we will refer to as human choice for the moment. Second, there are the conditions—material, structural, and cultural—within which such choices are made; while these inherited and pre-existing elements will influence the choices that are made, they do not fully determine those choices, but regardless of the perceptions, predictions, and preferences of the decision makers, those conditions *will* play a dominant role in the results of those decisions. In this sense, such conditions can be thought of as *deterministic* inputs into the sequence of events that culminates in war—or compromise, capitulation, or stalemate.

But, as already noted, no event or outcome is totally determined by the preconditions and/or the human choices made in their context. There is, then, not only the voluntaristic and the deterministic input, but the *probabilistic* input as well, and this element is the source not only of philosophical confusion but of human grief as well. The confusion stems from our inability to distinguish among—or measure the potency of—four sources of the probabilistic element in our understanding of our subject: (a) imprecision in our observation and measurement of the phenomena of interest; (b) the limits of and errors in our current "knowledge"; (c) the inherent intractability and unknowability of the "causal" processes; and (d) closely related, the essential randomness of the universe, making the search for law-like regularity an allegedly fruitless enterprise. While the first two sources of the probabilistic are often beyond the comprehension of policy makers and others of a pre-scientific orientation, they are widely appreciated in the scientific community and typically subsumed under "e", or the "error term" in our explanatory equations.

It is the third and fourth source, however, that resists scholarly consensus and becomes entangled with one's religious and ontological preconceptions. The issue is partially illuminated by the contradiction between Heisenberg's "uncertainty principle" and Einstein's contention that "God does not play dice with the universe," and while few scientists (physical, biological, or social) embrace either the inherent knowability or the inherent unknowability extreme, most of us lean toward the Heisenberg end of the spectrum. Where we come out philosophically is, however, of less consequence than the strategies by which we pursue scientifically validated knowledge, and most of us proceed on the premise that whether or not some phenomena lie inherently beyond the reach of human investigation, or are fundamentally random, we are nowhere near that boundary, and that a great deal of further research is both possible and necessary, especially in the social sciences.

## THE POTENCY OF PROBABILISM

So much, then, for the epistemology of the probabilistic, stochastic, and random element in our search for explanation in general. Bearing these points in mind, let us return to the notion of accidental war. Clearly, there are powerful factors of a deterministic and voluntaristic sort (and these latter are, of course, themselves a function of both deterministic and probabilistic factors) affecting the outcome of international rivalries, and some modest progress has been made in identifying them and estimating their potency in accounting for the war, stalemate, compromise, or capitulation result (9).

But, as already made clear, the probabilistic component of the error term remains all too large, with ominous consequences. One ominous aspect is that of ignorance: if we just do not know which policy choices are most likely to lead to which outcomes under which conditions—or if the decision makers operate in ignorance of solid research findings—we will continue to make those choices in response to the familiar and deadly extra-rational considerations of personal and factional interests, about which we have considerably more knowledge. The other implication, equally dangerous, is that we will continue to act on the basis of superstition, folklore, and naive faith that the fates are on "our side." In traveling by air, for example, it is reasonable to "play the odds"; we know pretty well what they are, and the consequences of the rare disaster are limited to a few hundred people. But if we play the odds not knowing what they are, and the consequences are near-obliteration of humanity, this is another matter indeed.

## THE ERROR TERM: CONFLICTING TENDENCIES

In the accidental or probabilistic war problem today, the situation is doubly compounded. First, the international system is considerably more complex today than in the past, and apparently becoming more so decade by decade. One indicator of this is that the statistical goodness of fit between our postdictive models and the actual historical outcomes is consistently much lower for twentieth century rivalries and disputes than for the nineteenth century (10). To put it another way, researchers have a far weaker understanding of the dynamics of contemporary international conflict than we do of the simpler epochs gone by; and since national security elites—understanding as much about war and peace as the Dutch boy with his finger in the dike did about hydraulics—are even more ignorant of what leads to what, the frequency of error-induced surprise is appreciably greater. As the saying goes, they didn't know "it was loaded!"

The second compounding factor, is, of course, the increasing complexity of weapon systems. While the "fog of war" has always been exacerbated by weapons failures and transport breakdown, the electronic battlefield offers uncertainties of dramatically greater magnitude. This is not only because the systems are far more complex and considerably more prone to failure, but also because few of the components—and almost none of the integrated systems—have been adequately field tested.

While the increasing complexity of the political dynamics and the man-machine systems through which we seek to control our weaponry both tend to increase the error term, and thus reduce our ability to understand and predict the consequences of a given decision or sequence of decisions, the upward tendency need not be inexorable. Some counter-vailing tendencies are also at work, via research and application. That is, to the extent that systematic research on the dynamics of international conflict in an evolving complex of domestic and global politics goes forward—and is effectively communicated to the national security elites—the rising magnitude of the error term can at least be slowed down. For that effect to be reversed, however, we would need a research initiative comparable to that of the Manhattan project or the current Strategic Defense Initiative, but given the scientific ignorance and political indolence of major power elites, this self-correcting effort is hardly likely to be undertaken in time.

Similarly, competent research on the technological side and at the man-machine interface could help to inhibit the growing propensity toward error in the hardware and software sector. While somewhat more likely than in the political and diplomatic areas, research that is intended to make the systems less error-prone will continue to get less attention than efforts to make them more attractive to those who buy and deploy these gold-plated gadgets. The values and mentality that characterize the U.S. automobile industry seem to obtain in the military-industrial sector as well.

Another aspect of the conflicting tendencies issue is that of cumulative probabilities, typically presented in formal mathematical or statistical terms, devoid of the empirical context. As often expressed, even a very low objective probability of nuclear war (let us say 2 percent) in a given month or year will increase by one or another arithmetical function until, at some later date (let us say 15 years) that probability approaches 100 percent. While this might be true of some mechanical systems in which no learning or adaptation takes place, it seems inapplicable to the international system or the command and control man-machine systems to which we have abdicated so much of our security. There is, after all, some degree of independence from one trial or roll of the dice to the next, and for two reasons.

One is that these systems are in a state of flux and change, and no matter how small the change in only a few of the components from month to month, the cumulative effect is one of nearly continuous change; this is not to suggest that these systems become more dependable and less error-prone over time. The net effect might well be in the other direction, but either way the probability of error—especially in the sense of a false positive—is neither constant nor cumulative; perhaps the most plausible assumption is that there is a fair amount of short-run perturbation around a long-run trend toward increasing error-proneness. A second consideration is that, while most mechanical and electronic systems have almost no learning capacity, human systems manifest some modest signs of that capacity. Admittedly, a fair fraction of that learning may well be mal-adaptive (11, 12), making the decisional system more likely to launch on erroneous grounds, but again, it hardly seems constant and/or cumulative.

## CONCLUSION

Having examined the role of the error term in the context of international rivalry from a fairly abstract perspective, let me close with some brief observations of a more concrete sort. If the problem, as suggested, is not *unintended* war, but *unexpected* war, and the problem is one of reducing the magnitude and potency of the error term in our predictive models (be they explicit, implicit, or an unholy mix of the two), are there some short-run and mid-run corrections that might consciously be introduced? From Quincy Wright (13) through Reagan-Gorbachev (1985) there has been a recurrent interest in early warning and crisis monitoring arrangements, and though the idea merits high priority, the prospects are far from encouraging. While "hotlines" could be useful in extremes, it is more important to be alerted to and able to head off impending crises at an earlier stage, but that would require—inter alia—a step-function increase in our knowledge as to which moves are more likely to produce what consequences under certain conditions. Despite isolated efforts to illuminate the problem and to describe our limited progress on this front (14, 15), neither the Soviets, the West, nor the Office of the U.N. Secretary-General [until very recently] has shown much interest. Our national and international decision makers continue to show a touching faith in their bureaucratic intuition, as did their predecessors in earlier pre-war periods.

Second, as noted above, if we continue to design and deploy weapons and control systems of excessive complexity and high error-proneness, the least we can do is try to also design far better fail-safe mechanisms for reducing the frequency and magnitude of these inherent threats to our survival. Third, we need to train those who use and rely upon these systems to better understand how they work, where they are particularly error-prone, and how to identify and respond to such periodic system failure.

More significant, however, would be a major shift away from hair-trigger, error-prone, and fundamentally provocative weapons and controls. As several of the other papers in this volume make clear, there is little sense in entrusting our security to weapons that *must* go first, that are vulnerable, accurate, and lethal beyond need, and to strategic doctrines that ask of the technology more than it can possibly deliver. The nuclear-missile marriage was menacing enough to this fragile planet, but tactical nuclears, MIRV, MX, Trident, and SDI have all contributed to making the state of affairs more parlous still. If we want to avoid accidental fires, we do not place buckets of gasoline, sticks of dynamite, and long criss-crossing fuses all over town and then distribute butane lighters to most of the inhabitants.

We have gone far to making the northern hemisphere hard-wired for nuclear detonation, and rapid dismantling is clearly the order of the day. The error term is menacingly large, and even in our current sorry state of ignorance, it is clear what needs to be done. With good sense, moral prudence, and political courage, we could begin to reduce it back to a safer and more acceptable magnitude as we move, with a mix of knowledge, concern, and good fortune, to construct a global system that is at least safe for conflict.

# CHAPTER TWO

■

# Armaments, Security, and Prosperity: An Imaginary Congressional Speech

LIKE MOST OF THE POLITICAL CAMPAIGNS in our country since World War II, that of 1980 has added nothing to the electorate's understanding of national security policy. To the contrary, the candidates, their spokesmen, and the media once again offered up the familiar evasions, misinformation, and simplistic interpretation, assuring that we are no more capable of rational choice now than we were *before* the election. There is, however, one small ray of hope. Whether incumbent or challenger, Democrat or Republican, the conventional candidate is always eager to assert—in defense of his or her mindless campaign—that "you can't do a thing unless elected." Regardless of the accuracy of that bromide, it has an interesting implied corollary: that, if elected, one *can* do all sorts of wonderful things for the country. With this implied responsibility in mind, let me propose here the possible text of a speech on the floor of the House or Senate; the speaker may not be greeted with a standing ovation, but he or she might just possibly begin the formidable task of turning us away from a path that is pregnant with disaster.

Mr. Speaker (etc). I rise this morning to address an issue that was somehow neglected during my recent and successful campaign for this revered office. Preoccupied as I was with those bread and butter issues so dear to my constituents, I seldom ventured into the more risky waters of foreign and military policy. And when I did, it was usually to assure the voters that I would bend every effort to make our armed forces leaner and meaner, our nation second to none in military strength, and our policies firm but just. Like most of my colleagues in this chamber, my primary concern was to win the election, and having succeeded in that enterprise,

---

This chapter, written for a congressional candidate in 1980, originally appeared in the *Scandinavian Journal of Development Alternatives*, June 1987, pp. 37–44. Reprinted by permission. Occasional phrases reflecting changes that have occurred since the original publication date are shown in brackets.

I would hope to vindicate my constituents' faith in my judgement, patriotism, and integrity. To do so, it is clear that I can no longer ignore these fundamental questions of war and peace, survival and prosperity, and I thus turn now to what may be the most urgent and pressing issue facing this great nation of ours. I refer, of course, to the dangerous and costly arms race in which we and the Soviet Union have been engaged for more than 30 years.

## THE ARMS RACE AND ITS DANGERS

For a third of a century, both societies have been pouring their resources into one new weapon system after another, along with the treasure that goes just to keep the military establishment fed, housed, and maintained. Let none think that these resources have been well invested. Our land and homes and factories are less secure today than ever before in the nation's history. Even though I would heavily discount some of the assertions we hear today from the militarists of both political parties regarding Soviet capabilities and the vulnerability of our land-based missiles, there is no doubting the fact that we cannot—no matter how much we spend and what weapons we deploy—protect ourselves from a nuclear attack. As a matter of fact, as long as we continue to test, build, and deploy just about every new weapon system that is technologically feasible, the chances are that we will become even *less* secure.

This is for two reasons. One is that our Russian rivals, despite their inferior technology and weaker industrial base, have the capacity and the will to pretty much keep up with our weaponry in quality and quantity. Some may believe that we can out-distance the adversary and thus regain the military superiority we "enjoyed" in the 1950s and 1960s, but they are dead wrong. Modern weapons technology, while it is inherently provocative and destabilizing, has one important virtue: it makes numerical or qualitative superiority difficult to achieve. And even if it *could* be achieved, it would have no value in terms of physical security or political influence or diplomatic leverage. "Throwing money" at our national security problems is not only as wasteful, corrupting and inflationary as throwing money at our domestic problems; it is also much more dangerous because it alarms and provokes our adversaries, leading them to give ever greater power and resources to *their* military establishment. And virtually every increase in so-called preparedness on their part similarly strengthens the case for giving more resources and power to *our* military establishment. Certain sectors and groups on both sides may temporarily benefit, but the net result is an increasingly dangerous arms race and decreasing availability of resources for the serious domestic problems that each society faces.

There is, of course, a second reason for opposing this continuing madness. Each new round of expenditures threatens our security in the *domestic* and *social* sense of the word as well. Not only does it strengthen the "hawks" on both sides and weaken the forces of prudence and reason in foreign affairs; it also weakens the claims of those here at home whose basic needs are just not being met. And how much longer these people— here and in the Soviet empire—are going to tolerate this misallocation is anybody's guess. The disadvantaged among us—be they in Detroit or Danzig (Gdansk), Los Angeles or Leningrad—will eventually claim their due, and appeals to patriotism will hardly suffice to pacify them. Those who, in asking for social justice, threatened the domestic tranquility of our society, looted our shops, burned down our cities, and paralyzed our police and fire departments in the 1960s are relatively no better off today than they were then. It is not only a matter of decency and fairness that we respond to their very legitimate demands for jobs, housing, health, and education. It is *essential* that we do so if we value our domestic security.

There is yet a third set of reasons for urging a slowdown and then a reversal of the arms race. It is increasingly clear, even to the most conventional economists, that military spending is a major factor in our double digit inflation rates, and has been for over a decade. This is because it puts substantial income into the hands of the military sector without providing those commensurate goods and resources that could be purchased with that income. Furthermore, the weapons producers need a great deal of capital, natural resources, manufactured components, and skilled labor, and in competing for these scarce items with civilian production firms, they help drive the prices up. This is, in turn, amplified by the fact that military production is generously reimbursed and cost over-runs often tolerated, making it easy to outbid the producers of the more competitive civilian goods. Plentiful money "chasing" scarce goods and services is the classic mechanism for driving prices upward. Military spending is also a major factor in unemployment; this is because money for strategic weapons development and production goes into the more capital-intensive sector where a *few* people (highly specialized and well-paid) work with a *lot* of machinery, rather than into the more labor-intensive sectors. For example, every million dollars spent on housing provides nearly twice as many jobs as the same amount spent on nuclear weaponry. Similarly, if the tax revenues used to finance our military growth were returned to the private sector, this too would create more employment, not to mention more capital for improving industrial efficiency.

Then there is the balance of payments problem, which affects the world-wide value of the dollar as well as American economic and political influence around the globe. The inflation generated by the arms race drives up the prices of our goods and makes them less attractive abroad. Also, as a large fraction of the research and development (R & D) expenditures in this country are devoted to the military, as is engineering talent as well, American industrial innovation has deteriorated dramatically. As a result, our productivity per worker has declined vis-à-vis that of our European and Asian competitors, making their products on the world market appreciably cheaper and often *better* than ours. Moreover, they now come out with more new and innovative exportable goods than we do, further reducing American sales abroad and further increasing our trade deficit.

## GETTING INTO THE ARMS RACE

Now some will contend that "we have no choice" and that the U.S.S.R. *compels* us to engage in this spiraling expenditure. I find this a rather dubious line of argument. First of all, it takes two (or more) to get an arms race going, and since the end of World War II, our own country has pursued—and maintained—an overall superiority in strategic capabilities. At no time have the Soviets been ahead in the strategic categories that matter (such as accuracy or the number of deliverable bombs and warheads), and it is only under the very sensible SALT arrangements of the past decade that they have approached approximate parity.

Nor is the trend toward parity a result of negligence or treason, as the big military spenders would have us believe. Partly it was the result of a sustained Soviet drive to achieve a rough equality on the strategic weapons front, and partly it was the result of intelligent American planning plus meticulous, hard bargaining over the provisions of the SALT I and SALT II agreements. Our negotiators knew very well what they were doing, and nothing has been given away; as a matter of fact, the U.S. has come out of these negotiations in a better position than the other side, largely because the Soviets have been extremely eager to get an agreement. While there is no question that the Kremlin can and will keep up with the U.S. in strategic preparedness, their leaders strongly prefer to stay more or less abreast of us at *lower* levels. And their reasons are essentially the same as the ones that should guide us: the realization that higher levels—qualitative and quantitative—make for a more provocative, unstable, and dangerous relationship, plus the need to attend to pressing social and economic problems at home.

A second reason for doubting the assertion that we are compelled by Soviet policies to perpetuate the arms race is that even if they *sought* strategic superiority *and* were able to achieve it, the overall deterrence picture would not change. They realize that it would take an overwhelming superiority—perhaps a three- or four-to-one-ratio—in deliverable nuclear warheads to make a credible first strike threat. Anything less than a massive preponderance would not only *not intimidate* American strategists, but would rather serve to *provoke* us. We should, similarly, understand that there is no military or political payoff in our striving for strategic superiority. Unless one side can credibly threaten to wipe out *virtually all* of the other's retaliatory force, there is no justification in seeking a numerical advantage. Although today's weapons technology is highly dangerous in that: (a) it creates strong incentives to go first in a crisis; and (b) the actual use would be catastrophic, it does offer one virtue, if that is the appropriate word; as I noted earlier, one side can fall *very* far behind the other and still not be any less secure. To the contrary, it may even be *preferable* to be behind, because your deterrent effect remains relatively high and your provocation effect relatively low, and the rational objective is to have a maximum deterrence-to-provocation ratio.

Of course, all of this assumes that both parties have accepted the rather obvious proposition that nuclear war is to be considered only as a last dismal resort, entered into only if the other does so. But if there are voices, even minority voices, arguing that nuclear war is not so bad, and that it can be initiated, fought, and won, then we have a rather different situation. Tragically enough, such voices have existed since the 1950s on both sides, and their influence has gone up and down as the technology advanced or stabilized, as political relations between the superpowers have fluctuated, and as domestic politics waxed and waned. Today, thanks to the technology that gives higher "kill probabilities" to both side's offensive forces, and thanks to a wide range of domestic and foreign moves on both sides, those voices have become louder, more insistent, and more influential. Now, sadly enough, advocates of the "credible first strike" strategy on the U.S. side have been able to get their views embodied in last July's [1979] Presidential Directive 59. While this document need not constitute an irreversible commitment to a whole new round of weapon acquisitions, dictated by the logic of trying to destroy the Soviet missiles in their silos, it is indeed an ominous step. It legitimizes the drive for the MX and cruise missile systems, for example, and it shifts the burden of the strategic argument. The more prudent and far-sighted among defense analysts are now on the defensive, and the quality and tone of the policymaking process will be increasingly determined by those whose virility and patriotism cannot be questioned. They, after all, have the courage to think about the unthinkable, and to face nuclear holocaust without flinching.

One could, of course, go into much greater detail as to how we got into this highly dangerous situation, and why it *is* so dangerous, but my point should be quite clear: we must find a route out of this mess, and quickly. *Is* there a range of moves by which the U.S. might seize the initiative, and begin to extricate the world from this imbecilic state of affairs?

## GETTING OUT OF THE ARMS RACE

In my view, there *is*. My examination of the problem, and my consultation with people who are competent foreign policy analysts and world politics specialists, leads me to a sense that there may still be time. All is not yet lost, although there is little question that the Soviet-American momentum toward showdown will not easily be stopped in time. While this occasion does not permit much attention to detail, let me—despite the risks of being misunderstood and/or misquoted—suggest some steps that might possibly head off the final plunge into nuclear oblivion.

I would begin by having our government accept as promptly as possible the standing offer from the U.S.S.R. for a formal agreement on "no first use" of nuclear weapons of any size or shape. On the heels of that critical move, we should shift back to a strategic doctrine that in both word and deed reflects the "no first use" commitment, and accepts the proposition that mutual assured destruction—however flimsy and irrational it may be as the foundation of a nation's security—is preferable to a first strike, counter-force, silo-busting, pre-emptive doctrine.

From this, the abandonment of the MX system is the logical consequence, and the same holds for the cruise missile and the newly-revived plans for an anti-ballistic missile system. Then, as we move—in doctrine and in deployment—away from the "we might go first" doctrine toward a "retaliation only" doctrine, the SALT II treaty becomes relevant once again. Thus, I would urge the President to reactivate its passage through the Senate as rapidly as possible. At the same time, to eliminate any serious economic losses to firms and communities that have been associated with military growth, the federal and state governments should encourage, and aid in the conversion, from military production to production for civilian needs. A crash program of economic conversion could indeed be a major element in turning America away from its obsession with military force.

Once we are back on the road to a sane and prudent strategic policy, my prediction is that the U.S.S.R. will, in due course, begin to emulate us. Even if it takes a while for them to get things sorted out at home, and to bring the skeptics on board and begin to comprehend that we have indeed decided to move back from the brink, our security is not jeopardized. To reiterate my earlier point, even if we were well *behind* the adversary, there is no way that the Soviets can contemplate a rational first strike any more than we can. True, either side could, in the months and years ahead, wipe out a fair fraction of the other's *land*-based ICBM weapons, but to what purpose? Even the Soviets, whose sea-based and air-based retaliatory forces are dramatically weaker than ours, would still be able to ride out an American first strike and then retaliate with devastating swiftness and destruction. In my judgement, there is absolutely no question of the survivability of our retaliatory forces. Even if our *entire* ICBM force were destroyed, the retaliatory blow delivered by our submarine, aircraft, and European-based systems would lay waste to Russia—and most of Eurasia to boot.

Since there is so much talk these days of current or impending Soviet superiority, let me summarize my understanding of the balance of terror, and on the basis of official Pentagon figures, indicate why I consider this talk to be ill-informed—and because it inhibits serious considerations of arms control and disarmament measures—pernicious as well.

Yes, the U.S.S.R. is ahead [as of 1980] in inter-continental missiles by 2,350 to 1,700, but if manned bombers are included to arrive at a total of strategic delivery vehicles, the gap is a somewhat smaller 2,500 to 2,058. Too many of our propagandists stop here, as if the number of *delivery vehicles* were a valid indicator of relative capability. More relevant is the number of *deliverable warheads*, and here the U.S. has an advantage of about 9,200 to 6,000.

Then there is the notorious "throw weight" figure, which reflects the total tonnage that can be delivered via missiles, and in this case the U.S.S.R.

holds an advantage of 9,036,000 to 4,326,000 for the U.S. This figure, however, is crude and misleading; a more valid indicator is that of stockpiled megaton equivalents, in which the Soviet edge is a more modest 5,900 to 3,600. But even this is too crude, as it says little about the ability to hit military targets. Thus, many analysts use a "lethality index," reflecting total numbers of warheads, their megaton equivalents, and their accuracy, and on this index the U.S. has an edge of about 44,800 to 33,500.

One could go on and itemize the estimated results of all sorts of nuclear war scenarios, but my point should be clear. The U.S. is *not* behind the U.S.S.R. in nuclear strength categories that matter, nor do the current trend lines point toward any weapon ratios that would enable the Soviets to launch an effective "disarming first strike." Moreover, the SALT II agreements, despite their very limited scope, will make it impossible for them to achieve such superiority without obvious—and easily detected— violation of the production bans.

Finally, and most important, I do not suggest that Americans or Russians or any others are more secure with a superiority in deliverable warheads or in an overall lethality score. Both sides today are dangerously overarmed in strategic weapons (conventional weapons are another matter), and if both follow current production and deployment plans, they will soon be even more dangerously overarmed.

One reason, unfortunately, is that both governments still have people who believe that nuclear wars can be initiated, fought, and won, and that having some first-strike components is militarily and politically desirable. In my view, this borders on insanity, and it bodes ill for everyone's security. Nuclear weapons should be looked upon in purely second-strike and retaliatory terms, and the sooner we cut back to the levels needed for that more prudent role, the sooner we can begin the imperative but delicate task of nuclear disarmament.

In sum, despite the dangers to us that are inherent in today's strategic balance, the adversary is in an even more vulnerable position all across the board. It would be not only responsible, but good politics, for the more powerful of the rivals to make the first move back to sanity. We may never be friends with the Russians politically, but if we could merely try to do business with them in a clear-headed fashion, all of us would be better off.

Mr. Speaker, I thank you for your attention, and trust that these remarks will strike my colleagues as both reasonable and reassuring, and that this body will move quickly to implement the policies that they imply.

# CHAPTER THREE

———————— ■ ————————

# Arms Control Negotiations and the Third World

IT IS INDEED A DISTINCT PLEASURE to be here in Ahmedabad, a city graced by the memory of our great peace maker, Mahatma Gandhi, as well as the home of the distinguished centre of learning named for that renowned English scholar, Harold Laski. Let me, however, combine my appreciation and gratitude to your Director, Professor P. G. Mavalankar, with a minor quarrel vis-à-vis one of Professor Laski's more notorious epigrams. I refer to his touching faith in democratically-elected politicians to whom he urged that the professional specialists be kept "on *tap*, not on *top!*" While it is clear that our elected leaders *should* have the last word, there is nevertheless an implied corollary that we specialists must keep our places, give professional and technical guidance to the elites, but not challenge them on general policy matters.

A moment's reflection suggests that all too large a fraction of humanity's grief may well be a result of taking that advice too literally. Just as the military professionals under Stalin and Hitler might have saved Europe from the scourge of World War II, and Truman's foreign service officers might have prevented the confrontation with China and the expansion of the Korean War, today's social scientists may yet save the people of the world from the holocaust of World War III. To date, however, all too many of us have been all too willing to advise our governments on *how* to conduct and manage the arms races that menace our freedom and our welfare, not to mention our very survival as a species. Thus, I come here not as an *adviser* to my own government, but as—I trust—a constructive but vigorous *critic* of that government. My mission—and that of my counterparts in Russia or France or Pakistan or India—is not to serve as a coach and a cheer-leader, but to urge in the strongest possible terms that we should not even be *playing* the armed rivalry game.

This chapter originally appeared in *Arms Control Negotiations and the Third World*, 1986. Reprinted by permission of the Harold Laski Institute of Political Science, Ahmedabad, India.

## THE ARMS RACE AND ITS IMPACT
## ON THIRD WORLD SOCIETIES

Let me begin this critical analysis by expressing great pleasure at the recent shifts in opinion among third world intellectuals, who, for far too long, have focussed so intensively on the struggle *against* neo-colonialism and *for* economic development that the implications and dangers of global militarization have been all but ignored. But in recent years, one finds an increasing awareness of, and concern for, the interdependence between the development problem and the disarmament problem. We must put an end to war, and we must put an end to poverty and starvation. Some of us believe that we cannot solve the development problem until we solve the security problem, and *vice versa*, and all too often one's view depends on which of them is most immediately threatening. Those who experience (or, more precisely, speak for those who experience) the tragedies of poverty, whether in the third and fourth worlds or in the first and second worlds, tend to give highest priority to the development problem. And those for whom an adequately high material quality of life is no longer a concern tend to give highest priority to the security problem. As the immediate threat of death or disablement from grinding poverty begins to recede, one can begin to attend to the threat of death and disablement from war.

But there may be more to the question than the immediate situation of the observer. A good many observers accept the proposition that poverty is a major "cause" of international conflict, much of which ultimately escalates to war. And while one can make a plausible argument as to why this should be so, the empirical evidence reveals a negative correlation between the poverty levels of nations (aggregated as well as per capita) and their war-proneness. Even if we look at civil war, there tends to be a curvilinear relationship, with very few cases occurring in the extremely poor or the extremely wealthy societies; the very poor are too weak, physically as well as politically, nor do they have the incentive for violent change that typically requires both the hope based upon a small taste of economic progress and the aggressiveness based on a frustration of that hope. The rich, of course, have even fewer incentives.

If poverty seldom leads to war, it follows that its elimination or amelioration will have almost no effect on the incidence of war; we may want to give development the highest priority for normative or ideological reasons, but not because we expect it to reduce the incidence of international war.

Recognizing the possibility that, as a white male, middle class and middle age, well-fed and healthy, in a relatively prosperous society, my concern for the poor and starving might not be as strong as it should be, let me nevertheless summarize the counter-arguments. A useful point of departure is an itemization of the ways in which the search for security among the industrial powers inhibits and corrupts the search for development among the pre-industrial societies. The most obvious, of course, is the deflection to military preparedness of funds that *might* have gone into development assistance programs. While there is no assurance that the annual world military spending that *could* meet the essential food and health needs of the developing countries for two decades *would* indeed go to that purpose, it is clear that the funds that *do* go to the military in the north *cannot* go to development in the south.

But military preparedness programs mobilize more than money; they mobilize the minds of their citizens in a way that is destructive at home and abroad. As the financial resources of a major power go to the military sector over a long period of time, two important consequences develop. One is the incremental shift in political power away from those who *might* be fairly cosmopolitan, far-sighted, and humane, and toward those who *seldom* give high priority to such considerations. The policies of that nation become increasingly militarized, and with that shift, the resources that *could* have gone to economic development go instead to the military buildup, arms transfers, and other military assistance programs; the other developmental implications of this shift will be considered in a moment.

The second consequence of this mobilization is an ethical and emotional one. Governments, however centralized they may be, cannot milk the public economically, intrude into their political freedom, and conscript their sons, unless there is a sufficiently widespread and strong belief in the legitimacy of these depredations. That requires a propaganda and socialization program of some magnitude and duration, and the more successful that program, the more xenophobic the public and the opinion makers will become; with these cognitive and affective trends, we should not be surprised to find two attendant shifts. One is the obvious shift toward greater belief in the importance of military force as an instrument of national security; even in the most autocratic of societies, cognitive dissonance is uncommon. The other is an increasing indifference to those whom Fanon called "the wretched of the earth." Persuaded of the threat to the nation from enemies at home and abroad, and acquiescing in the use of mass murder as a legitimate instrument of national survival, there is little room for concern, altruism, or generosity, not to mention far-sighted self-interest. (For the present, we will ignore the effects of military preparedness programs on the domestic scene and on the moral integration of the citizens and their society.)

Another dysfunctional linkage between the major power rivalry and economic development is found in their struggle for influence in the underdeveloped regions, and while less obvious, the effects may be equally pernicious. First, there is the eagerness to put and to keep friendly regimes in power, and it seems that—along with economic and military aid—no ploy is beneath them; from bribery and subversion to assassination and insurgency, all are used by the leaders of the "free world" and the "socialist camp" to depose less-than-friendly regimes. And to maintain these staunch supporters of democracy and/or socialism, no amount of terrorism, torture, repression, and intimidation seems excessive. Without suggesting that these instruments of political influence are entirely the creation of Washington and Moscow, Paris and Prague, the initiative, the training, and the resources typically originate in the first and second worlds. That it is easy to find indigenous elites and counter-elites to carry out these unsavory deeds should come as no surprise. How many political leaders and their opponents in the third world have come to power or to opposition without outside support? And even when the struggle for power in the developing countries is not violent, brutal, and evil, it is heavily burdened by the East-West rivalry. This is not to say that essentially domestic issues are of no consequence in the struggle for power, but that the super-power rivalry is so pervasive that the money, the men, and the methods can usually be traced back to the Soviets, the Americans, or their allies.

This corruption of the political process in the underdeveloped nations has, in turn, a disquieting effect on their economies and their foreign policies. Given the ubiquitousness of a regional standoff between East-leaning and West-leaning regimes, the high incidence of rivalry, conflict, and war in these areas is virtually foreordained; all too often, there are proxy wars between regimes and armies that are financed, trained, equipped, and sometimes even led by the super power rivals. Such externally-stimulated conflict not only leads to death, devastation, brutality, flight, and famine, and to a steady drain on the financial resources of the regional economies, but to the incurring of high opportunity costs as well. External funds that might have gone to development go to the military. Occasional surpluses in the balance of payments that might have gone to investment in agricultural infrastructure often go to pay for training of military personnel in overseas war colleges and military academies. In addition, military expenditures typically (not always) inhibit economic growth, generate inflationary pressures, enhance the rate of debt accumulation, exercise an upward push on interest rates, mortgage the nation's economic future, and encourage more attention to short-run considerations.

Then there is the competition for human resources; third world economies need a fairly large cadre of trained public administrators, foreign ministry personnel, commercial managers, industrial technicians, mining engineers, harbor pilots, agricultural specialists, and health care professionals, to name but a few. But if the educational facilities are limited, off-shore training expensive, and armed forces salaries (not to mention related personal and political perquisites) high, it comes as no surprise that there will be insufficient talent for development purposes. Further, because the resources are greater, the recruiting incentives less idealistic, and the role of the military often more of a domestic constabulary than a national defense force, one typically finds rather higher levels of corruption in the military than in other sectors of developing societies, and the larger the military the more pervasive its corrupting influence.

Closely related is the problem of negotiating equitable terms of trade or reasonable roles for their nationals in the multi-national corporations resident in their countries. Addiction to military "preparedness" and dependence on the supplier are hardly conducive to a strong bargaining stance.

There are other ways, more political, in which the militarization of these nations, through cold war incentives and blandishments, turns out to be counter-productive. One is the increasing boldness of major power interference in the domestic political process: those who pay the piper *expect* to call the tune, and in order to ingratiate themselves with the donors, local parties and functionaries are inclined to put domestic issues into the terms of their patrons to the north, often distorting and submerging bona fide questions in a sea of ideological rhetoric. One extension of this pressure, of course, is in the foreign policy realm. Rather than address the very real security and economic interests of their nations vis-à-vis regional neighbors, eagerness for funds and equipment along with dependence on the donors for spare parts and technical support, makes these regimes frequently inclined to do their master's bidding.

This arraignment should suffice. As long as the East-West rivalry continues, the possibilities for highly symbiotic relations between local elites and one or another of the major powers are extraordinary. And to the extent that these possibilities are exploited, misallocation of material, demographic, and psychic resources will be endemic, and the processes of economic, social, and political development will be stultified. Short run considerations will overwhelm those of long run health.

## THE CALCULUS OF MILITARY PREPAREDNESS

In the preceding section, I have outlined a number of ways in which the Soviet-American rivalry intrudes upon the nations of the third and fourth worlds, strongly suggesting that a dramatic amelioration and reorientation of that contest must occur before any appreciable progress can be achieved on the development front. It follows, of course, that those of us who are committed to the independence and evolution of the non-industrial societies have a powerful incentive to do what we can to slow and reverse the super powers arms race, and to direct the associated competition into less costly and destructive channels.

Let me shift now to the incentives that should be, but seldom are, at work in the nations more directly caught up in an armed rivalry. What are some of the calculations that might lead those of us in the two dominant coalitions to take a harder look at the policies of our governments? To what extent are world affairs specialists, East and West, contributing to or acquiescing in policies that make little sense in either the ethical or the pragmatic sense?

To begin, we in the northern hemisphere are even more vulnerable to mass destruction, widespread devastation, and horrible death than our neighbours to the south, if nuclear deterrence should fail. One can understand why people in third and fourth world countries might underestimate the damage they might sustain in the event of nuclear war, but for those in the first and second worlds such denial is literally a death-defying act. Before identifying the many costs, economic and otherwise, of military preparedness, let us try to look objectively at the alleged benefits.

First, preparedness is supposed to provide the basic ingredient of national security, which can be thought of as a simple two-dimensional concern. Primarily, it is to *minimize* the extent to which one rival can control, dominate, or influence the other's external behaviour or domestic processes. Secondarily, it is to *maximize* one's own ability to influence and shape the external behaviour and domestic processes of the other. Power, we might say, is the ability to both exercise and to inhibit influence. The extreme case, to which the elites refer obliquely and infrequently, would see American troops parading through Red Square and Soviet forces marching up Pennsylvania Avenue. These scenarios are so outlandish as to be relegated to the fantasy life of the deranged and the misinformed. More serious for some and less serious for others is a disarming strategic assault that is so devastating that no nuclear retaliation is possible. Given the technologies of delivery and destruction today and in the decades ahead, this must be classed as an equally improbable event, even though the Dr. Strangeloves on each side may dream and work in terms of such an obsession.

Somewhat more realistic, and thus more objectively dangerous, is the scenario in which one of the rivals is able to launch a nearly-disarming first strike, and with an extraordinarily massive mix of active and passive defenses, keep the retaliatory damage low enough to be politically "acceptable." This obscene hope or psychotic fear must rest on the worst conceivable combination of worst-case and best-case analysis, defying the calculations of virtually all who are not either at the public trough or well-nourished on the more exotic hallucinogens. Of course, the possible credibility of such a scenario is what drives the American, and to a lesser extent, the Soviet investment in one or another version of the "strategic defense initiative." Staying with the strategic problem and the more exotic weapons, the feasibility—and thus the possibility—of a bacteriological, chemical, or radiological attack on the USA, USSR, or their European allies cannot be quite as readily dismissed. Nevertheless, the inadequacy of any known or projected delivery systems, the near certainty of retaliation in one form or another, and the limitations of potential defensive measures all suggest strategic use of BCR weapons as sufficiently suicidal to rule out a viable threat to major power security.

Remaining for the moment with the threats to security via intentional attack, we next examine the non-strategic scenarios, meaning primarily the use of nuclear, exotic, or conventional forces within the European theatre. Here, of course, the Soviet-American symmetry breaks down because the USSR is for the relevant future markedly more vulnerable than is North America. On the other hand, the NATO allies, in whose security the Americans have invested heavily in the military, political, and psychological senses, are about as vulnerable as the Soviet Union or its Warsaw Pact allies. But the first use of nuclear or BCR weapons on the Continent in either direction is so pregnant with sure retaliation, regionally and intercontinentally, as to be hardly more credible than the original strategic scenarios.

We come, then, to the purely conventional (or more accurately, sub-exotic) weapon case, in which tactical air, massed armor, and mobile infantry could conceivably be employed in Europe. But despite the numerical superiorities of the Soviet bloc in some categories and the NATO forces superiority in others, military analysts are nearly unanimous in agreeing that neither side has anything approaching a preponderance sufficient for an offensive assault against the other. And if extra-conventional forces are introduced to provide the necessary preponderance, we are back to the stalemate described earlier. In other words, given the character of today's military technology combined with the force levels on both sides, the likelihood of a calculated attack in either direction must be considered extremely low.

This brings us, then, to the oft-heard argument that it is not so much the objective threat to basic security on each side, but the *perceived* threat. Of course, in a sane world there would be a fairly close relationship between the *objective* and the *subjective* threats, but if we lived in a sane world, no one would have permitted the arms race to proceed juggernaut-like to such mutually destructive and destabilizing heights. In the insane and obscene world of military analysts and national security elites, this discrepancy need not surprise us. Those who seek to generate perceptions of missile and bomber gaps, asymmetric windows of vulnerability, and impending enemy breakthroughs in weapons technology, for purposes of budgetary and political mobilization or career advancement, have little difficulty doing so. A press corps that is ill-trained and easily seduced—if not indistinguishable from those who shape, make, and enunciate security policy—is usually all too ready to provide such a service.

Once the legitimacy of such misperceptions has been established, the case for military preparations against them can more easily be made. Sometimes the perceived threat is a current one, as when Americans were being told that their nation's land-based missiles were in jeopardy via a window of vulnerability, but more typically, the alleged threat is a *projected* one. For recent examples, there is the U.S. argument that a strategic defense initiative is essential to defend against a dramatic buildup in Soviet land based ICBM forces, or the Soviet argument that the further deployment of SS-20 Euro-missiles would be necessary to "counter" the NATO deployment of Pershing II missiles.

In these, and others that come to mind, one might wonder whether the alleged perception is not only intentionally generated, but a self-fulfilling one—in two senses—as well. The first sense is the more immediately dangerous in that it could conceivably lead the adversary to *believe* such statements of its superiority and then seek to exploit it. For decades, the Western line has emphasized a critical Warsaw Pact superiority in conventional capabilities, but fortunately Moscow has either not accepted such an appraisal or has, at least, not sought to exploit it in an effective way. The second is more remote in time, but it is also more dangerous, as the earlier examples suggest. In the East-West arms race, the worst-case analysis, anticipating the rival's intention *and* capability to develop and deploy a given offensive or defensive weapon system typically provides the justification for going ahead on the next available system of its own; with the exception of ABM, one is hard-pressed to identify any case in which the worst case did not thus come to fruition.

To return to the basic question of genuine military threats to either superpower or its European allies, we have so far been unable to identify a single compelling example. The qualities of the weapons, and to a lesser extent, the quantities, are more than adequate to deter all but the most ill-advised attack. This is not to say that the military deterrent is always sufficient, nor is it to say that it is always necessary. As already noted, misperception of capabilities and/or intentions are by no means rare in history. Similarly, there may well be less costly and more reliable instruments of national security.

This then leaves us with only two sectors in which a case might be made in today's world, (or that of the past three decades) for a continuing buildup of the superpowers' military capabilities. The first, already alluded to, is that of intimidation via the brandishing of military force. But as already seen, if the threat of force is far from credible, there is little political mileage in seeking to exploit it. The second is, however, a more legitimate concern, and reference is to the so-called gray areas: regions outside of North America and Europe. Most salient is North Asia, where both China and Japan are relatively vulnerable to the USSR. As to China, its conventional forces are probably sufficient to deter a non-nuclear threat, and even its limited "force de frappe" should be adequate to head off a nuclear threat. The Japanese case, along with that of Taiwan, the Philippines, and the Koreas, could be more troublesome, but local capabilities and superpower commitments should probably suffice to keep the peace, at least in the short run.

As we cross the equator, however, the military configurations are considerably more ambiguous. But the relative tenuousness of that state of affairs should raise two important questions for the U.S. and the USSR. One concerns the centrality of these regions to the vital security interests of the superpowers, and the evidence is that both sides are, wisely, increasingly inclined to recognize both the marginality of their interests in the third and fourth worlds (especially if the Western Hemisphere is excluded) and the volatility of their dominance at a given point of time and place. The ability to keep commitments limited in these regions, would, on balance, serve to enhance the security of both. The other question, closely related, is whether military force, be it deployed rapidly or slowly, is indeed the appropriate instrument of superpower security or influence in the third and fourth worlds. By converting their struggle for influence in these regions into a non-military one, with heavier reliance on diplomatic, psychological, economic, and other political instruments, the U.S. and the USSR could not only enhance their own security, but that of the peoples over whom they now seek to establish some degree of hegemony.

Having gone into considerable detail regarding the possible relevance of high levels of military preparedness to the security of the superpowers, and concluding that the *benefits* are probably much lower than we tend to believe, let me shift briefly to the *costs*. First are the obvious economic opportunity costs: government revenues that might go to constructive activities at home or abroad are diverted instead to the creation, growth, and maintenance of the military machine. To arouse the slumbering sensibilities that often accompany professional involvement, let me be more specific as to where those funds could be used: pre-natal care of a welfare mother, adequately educated teachers in adequate school buildings, public transport that does not foul the human nest, programs in health maintenance, including sex, drug, and alcohol education, adequate housing for marginal families, job re-training for the potentially unemployed before they become unemployed, enforcement of laws against exploitation, pollution, and all the myriad forms of abuse that the strong impose on the weak, legal aid for those so abused, decent housing for those too poor, economic development programs to put an end to poverty at home and abroad—and of particular concern to our profession—funds for research and education on the correlates, causes, and possible cures for war, poverty, and the other indignities and deprivations that we inflict upon one another.

A second cost—less immediate and less uniform—is the weakening of the nation's economic, industrial, and agricultural foundations. In most economies at most stages of development, military spending can sometimes serve as a pump-primer, but more often it tends to reduce gainful employment, inhibit sound investment, deflect innovation away from constructive activities, encourage stockpiling of "strategic materials," exacerbate protectionist tendencies, discourage sound agricultural practices, and generate inflationary pressures. To the extent that these generalizations are correct, we perpetuate all those deprivations and indignities noted above.

A third set of costs are those associated with what Lasswell called "the garrison state," in which we mobilize and misallocate not only material resources but our moral and psychic resources as well. We even allocate resources to the creation of propaganda production, so that those who benefit from these misallocations can help persuade us to continue feeding the war machine: a classic example of the self-amplifying mechanism. We go on to acquiesce in government and party intrusion into our lives; the press, usually with adequate incentives, typically accepts and/or embraces censorship in one form or another, and the educational system becomes increasingly integrated into the national security apparatus, turning students into technically skilled and politically eviscerated adults. And, eagerly or reluctantly, these adults tolerate governmental secrecy (often more helpful in concealing incompetence than in protecting information), and security clearances (as useful in isolating the patriotic non-conformist as in preserving legitimate secrets) along with mail covers, "security risk" files, and the other appurtenances of domestic spying and informing.

A collateral cost, less obvious but no less lethal to humane existence, is in the moral degeneracy and schizophrenia that often goes with the garrison state. Citizens—even those who are trained and educated to know better—applaud or acquiesce in assertions that are empirically absurd and logically inconsistent. We learn not only to be discreet in what we say and write, lest we be thought naive, soft on enemy-ism, or actually an agent or lackey of the rival regime and its perfidious ideology, but to give our assent to the intellectual rape of those who dare to resist. We use the climate of national security conformity to gain acceptance, to aggrandize ourselves, and to settle old scores; just as "partisan" groups under enemy occupation often justify vilification and murder on the grounds of collaboration with the enemy, citizens at all levels invoke national security to isolate, weaken, or destroy those whom they fear or dislike for rather different reasons. Worse yet, we come to acquiesce in duplicity, assassination, bullying, and mass murder as legitimate instruments of national security. In sum, we encourage in our children and accept in our contemporaries an erosion of morality, integrity, and intellectual autonomy. It should be little wonder that our students and our children become more egocentric, hedonistic, cynical, and dishonest, lose hope in their futures and trust in their societies, and cop out on drugs and alcohol.

Before leaving this itemization of the costs of preparedness for war, let me note three more immediate, politically salient, and self-amplifying costs. One of these is the stifling of political creativity at home and amongst our allies. Because it is considered naive if not unpatriotic to come up with ideas that might help ameliorate the rivalry, make it less costly and dangerous, or enhance the security of both one's own and the adversary nation, we put a premium on fatalism. A standard refrain from our political elites and their all-too-pliable allies is "what else can we do? we have no choice! the arms race is imposed on us by our enemies!" Yet any effort to take our destiny out of the hands of the adversary and restore some degree of control over our national fate is often dismissed, ridiculed, and condemned.

This psychological deterioration is, quite naturally, part of a larger and more menacing process: the incremental re-distribution of economic power, ideological legitimacy, and political clout away from the thoughtful, competent, and independent-minded people, and toward the super-patriots, the atavistic cheerleaders, the bloodthirsty, the profiteers, and those who get an emotional high out of psychological mobilization and hard-nosed crisis management. This not only makes for a less humane and dignified society, but for a far less competent national security policy. When we turn power over to the primitives, we need not be astonished to get primitive policies. The competents are replaced by the claque, and those capable of subtlety and differentiation give way to the Manicheans, dividing the world into those who are with us and those who are against us.

Then there are the destructive and self-amplifying consequences abroad. Those who would prefer non-alignment will frequently be pushed into the camp of our rival, and those who might serve as honest brokers are insulted into indifference. Clearly, the more militarized a major power's policies become, the less good-will and support it will get from allies and neutrals;

even when the U.S. or the USSR have their way in the short run, the seeds of secession become more firmly planted.

But the real damage is to the *rival* society, and the greatest cost is in the policy behaviour that one's own policies generate. The process should be self-evident, given the frequency of its occurrence over the past century or so, and given our awareness of the relationship between domestic power distribution and the main outlines of a major power's foreign policy. That is, when one of the rivals begins to increase its military preparedness, there will typically be two fairly short run consequences. First, there will be a small change in the distribution of power at home toward the more hawkish elements, given the resources and legitimacy that are allocated to those elements. Second, the rival will, in fairly short order, respond in kind, if it has not already anticipated the first's build-up and begun its own. This will in turn have similar effects of a modest degree within *its* domestic power configuration, and if the reactive process between the rivals continues for several years, the domestic consequences tend to become less trivial. Before too long, most of the self-correcting mechanisms in both societies will become too frail to resist the reciprocal dynamics between and within them; in their place will appear a variety of self-amplifying social and psychological mechanisms, and a bona fide arms race has begun.

There is, of course, a third class of phenomena at work in rivalries that are accompanied by an arms race, and that is the appearance of an increasingly bellicose foreign policy. This bellicosity is stimulated by the lethal interaction between one side's continuing arms build up and the hawkishness of the other's political elites; merely anticipating or countering the other's build-up is not sufficient. One must confront, challenge, counter, and deter the rival on all fronts; the alleged "lesson of Munich," learned and over-learned centuries ago, remains in good odour in all too many centres today, despite its fit to a very small fraction of modern international disputes.

Let me conclude this section, then, by suggesting that the costs of military preparedness are far higher than we often recognize, even if the preparedness program does *not* culminate in war. Many of these costs are less than obvious, and some of the bills come due long after those who incurred them have departed, leaving it to the next generation to make the payments. And when we compare these costs to the benefits that actually accrue one must wonder at the frequency with which nations enter into this Faustian bargain. While one can readily think of several alternative strategies by which a nation's security might be preserved, ranging from a more sophisticated diplomacy, through more effective supra-national institutions, to such unilateral measures as non-violent civilian defense, our knowledge base is far too modest to tell us which strategies are most likely to be effective under a given set of circumstances. While the evidence *against* the standard strategy of military buildup (with or without alliance building) is relatively compelling, the evidence *for* the various alternatives barely exists.

## AN ARMS MANAGEMENT TYPOLOGY

All of this suggests, then, that arms control and arms reduction must be taken far more seriously than they have to date. Let me, thus, lay out a typology—in the abstract—of arms control and reduction measures, and then turn to a few of the specifics. In the light of historical experience as well as logical possibilities it is useful to classify the types of disarmament along two particular dimensions. One such dimension is the *degree* of arms reduction, and the other may be called the *reciprocity* dimension. The first refers to the quantitative and qualitative extent of a nation's military reductions and the second refers to the extent to which its reductions are matched, or in some fashion, reciprocated by other nations.

## DEGREE

The "degree of disarmament" continuum is not, in fact, limited to disarmament measures in the literal sense. In accord with diplomatic custom and scholarly usage, we include arms *control* as well as a number of intermediate restraints that fall well short of *reduction*. Beginning at the upper end of the degree dimension is total or complete disarmament, involving the elimination of all military capability beyond that defined (by the disarming nation itself, or by those nations imposing the measures) as necessary for the maintenance of domestic order. That minimal level may include local and national police, border guards, or perhaps even a modest paramilitary force for anti-riot types of duty, depending on the treaty provisions, the requirements imposed by other nations, or the unilateral decision of the disarming nation itself. Complete disarmament has been proposed frequently, but it has never been achieved by formal negotiations among the major powers. It has, however, been imposed on defeated nations by victorious ones at the close of war, but seldom with lasting effect. As commitments shift according to the vagaries of international alignments, the victors either acquiesce in gradual rearmament, as after World War I, or even encourage it, as did the United States and the Soviet Union a few years after World War II.

At the opposite and lowest end of the degree continuum are *arms control* measures. Reference here is to provisions which may not call for reduction or prohibition of *any* weapons, yet which have the effect of inhibiting a nation's full development of a given weapon category. Thus, arms control measures do not directly prohibit the *production* or *possession* of that weapon type, but rather seek to work indirectly by limitations or prohibitions on the *testing, deployment* or *use* of it. Leaving out the latter (once weapons are made and deployed, any commitment not to *use* them is unlikely to survive even the mildest temptation after hostilities begin), we note that limits or prohibitions on testing may well prevent, retard, or diminish the quality of the weapon's production. Or, for a variety of political, military, or technological reasons, it may be desired to permit production (and therefore possession) but to restrict or ban their deployment within a given geographical region. One of the rare successes in negotiating a reciprocal ban on testing was the 5 August 1963 Treaty of Moscow which prohibited the signatories from experimental detonations of nuclear weapons in outer space, in the atmosphere, or under water; another is the deployment prohibition in the Antarctic, South Pacific, and Latin American zones.

Arms control also may be applied to certain less obvious measures having no effect at all on the quantity or quality of a nation's armed forces. Normally, they deal with *information about* military capability rather than the capability itself, and generally require more information than is available through normal military intelligence channels. In the past, much emphasis of this sort was on publishing military budgets, war college curricula, manning and organization tables, results of weapon experiments, inventories, and war plans; often observers were invited to attend maneuvers or to verify published information. As the advance of military technology enhanced the offense at the expense of the defense, however, surprise attack became an increasingly serious concern for the defenders of the status quo. As a consequence, much of the information exchanged (or proposed for exchange) in earlier days has become a potential aid to the aggressor and the types of information exchange proposed in the post–1945 era are intended to redress that imbalance and to aid the defender, or more accurately the *retaliator* since strategic defense has become nearly impossible. For example, it has been proposed that information regarding the location of land-based or sea-borne retaliatory weapons be kept secret and that the potential adversary commit himself not to seek out such information. In a similar vein, but tending toward *more* information, observation posts and limited aerial inspection within each nation have been discussed as a means of improving the early-warning system of its neighbours.

Closely related to such techniques for reducing the advantage of the attacker are those intended for crisis control. Thus in 1963 the Soviet Union and the United States installed a direct communication line between their two capitals, so that prompt and reliable information might be sought and transmitted during crises; the objective here was to mitigate the ever-increasing probability of accidental war due to erroneous reading of intelligence reports or radar and sonar displays. As in prior periods, the intent is to reduce the incentive to attack by reducing the fear of being attacked, and the objective remains one of preserving the relative military status quo.

A final form of arms control (liberally defined) is neutralization. In such a case, the neutralized nation or region is not necessarily prohibited from acquiring or maintaining armed forces, but is, however prohibited from joining a military alliance. Generally, it is an area either outside the sphere of influence of two potential enemy coalitions, or an area in which they overlap; hence such an arrangement usually requires formal or tacit negotiation between major powers. Though its enforcement may be assigned to an international organization or an *ad hoc* multinational commission, its continuance depends on the major powers' willingness to merely deny the region to the other rather than acquire it for themselves.

In the middle of the continuum are those measures known as *partial disarmament*, and reductions of such a partial nature may cover (a) incomplete reductions in *all* weapon categories or (b) complete reductions in *some* categories, or some combination of the two. In the former case, the tendency has been to seek across-the-board cuts or limits based on a budgetary or a manpower ceiling, the idea being that adherence to such a ceiling will compel nations to keep their armaments down accordingly. Normally the plan is to permit each nation to allocate its military resources, within the budgetary restriction, to whichever weapon types it sees fit. The monetary maximum for any given year or period may, in turn, be based on average expenditures during a prior period, on the highest expenditure during a given prior period, or on some ratios among the signatories so as to preserve their relative power positions vis-à-vis one another. If a mobilized manpower ceiling is contemplated, similar baselines or else a percentage of each nation's total of male, or male in a given age bracket, may be used. Normally a manpower ceiling prescribes numerical and age limits not only upon active duty personnel, but on reserves of different categories, and it will also set minimum periods of active duty in order to prevent the rapid training of many reserves by high turnover in a relatively small active force.

A final version of the across-the-board but partial measure is that based on real or hypothetical war-making units. A German periodical in 1909 proposed, for example, that each nation be allotted one unit for each 700 in its population, and that 10 army men or 50 tons of ship be thought of as one unit. Thus, under this scheme the 63 million Germans would have been entitled to 90,000 units and the 45 million British to 64,300, to be allocated among ships and men as the decision-makers of each thought best.

When the second type of partial reduction—complete prohibitions in a few categories—is attempted, the prospective signatories are left free to arm fully in the non-prescribed categories; such partial provisions are also referred to as *qualitative* disarmament. This type may be negotiated, imposed, or unilaterally undertaken in order to avoid the expenditure for more elaborate or costly weapons, eliminate the more inhuman ones if war occurs, make the soldier's burden lighter in weight, strengthen the defense vis-à-vis the offense in order to make aggression less attractive, or compensate for the asymmetries arising out of the different geographical or technological security needs of particular nations. All of the above considerations have been explicitly noted either in formal proposals or in actual agreements. Qualitative measures might embrace the prohibition, elimination, or ceiling upon: mobile artillery, rifles above a certain caliber, bullets under a certain weight, railroads within a certain distance of a border, ships above a certain length or tonnage, ships capable of submerging, armor plates of a given thickness or hardness, aircraft capable of carrying bombs, chemical weapons, nuclear weapons on board space satellites, delivery vehicles of given range, and so forth; they may also embrace certain classes of trained personnel. The incentives may not be completely pacifistic, and the results may actually be to increase a nation's overall military capability, but these partial measures clearly belong under the rubric of disarmament.

## RECIPROCITY

Turning now to the second major dimension—that of reciprocity—we come to the unilateral *versus* multilateral question: is a given nation disarming unilaterally and unconditionally, or is it receiving (or expecting) reciprocal behaviour from one or more others as a condition of its own limitations or reductions? There are many possible positions on this reciprocity dimension, five of which will serve to explore and define the continuum. At one end is a nation's elimination of its armaments and demobilization of its military personnel without any *quid pro quo* at all. Such a *unilateral* move might be prompted by the decision-makers' conviction that: (1) the maintenance, threat or use of armed force is morally wrong; (2) the domestic economy cannot afford them; (3) public opinion strongly favours such a move; (4) war is extremely unlikely in the relevant future; (5) their diplomacy does not require the threat of force behind it; (6) alternative sources of influence, such as wealth, skill or prestige are more effective; (7) other relevant nations are, or have finished, unilaterally disarming; (8) others will probably follow their example; (9) others will not exploit a disarming or disarmed nation; (10) third parties will intervene to prevent any attempted diplomatic exploitation; (11) others will defend them in case of attack; or (12) alternative responses to invasion, such as non-violent resistance or non-cooperation, will be more effective than military resistance, etc. Though not exhaustive of the possible reasons and combinations thereof which might prompt a nation's leaders to eliminate its war-making or war-threatening capacity, this list suggests the possible attractions of unilateral disarmament, even in a largely ungoverned world. When and if the political and military efficacy of global organization increases, such incentives would tend to be magnified.

At the opposite end of the reciprocity continuum would be the disarmament agreement which is embodied in a bilateral or multilateral treaty, following *formal negotiations*. In such a situation, every reduction undertaken by one nation is conditional upon the reductions accepted by others. The primary objective here is to assure the preservation (if possible, the improvement) of one's relative military power position vis-à-vis the other signatories, both during and at the end of the disarmament process. Normally, such negotiations involve nations of approximate military parity which are already in a partially conflictful relationship with one another, and though some or all of the unilateral incentives may be motivating the negotiators, the inevitable lack of trust between some of the parties creates serious domestic and international inhibitions to success. Thus, the propensity to compromise is generally low, the bargaining is hard, and the treaty (if ever concluded) tends to be full of detailed procedures, contingencies, and exceptions.

Somewhere between the pure unilateral and the pure reciprocal type of disarmament is *imposed* disarmament. Though it is usually the consequence of negotiation, it is negotiation between nations of extremely disparate power, however impermanent that disparity may be. And though it may be nearly unilateral in its effects, the dominant bargainer normally accepts certain limited restrictions on its own armed forces. The extreme form of imposed disarmament is that accepted by the defeated nation following a war whose conclusion is close to that of unconditional surrender, such as the Axis powers after World War II. In its milder version, it is a form of demilitarization that is demanded by one or more major powers and acquiesced in by minor ones.

At an intermediate point between the unilateral and the imposed form is a semi-voluntary process, undertaken on the premise that failure to do so voluntarily might require the nation to disarm later under duress. This usually occurs in minor powers which are clearly within a major power's sphere of influence. At the other intermediate position is the tacitly negotiated arrangement in which the political realities make it mutually evident that the nations are over-armed for their security purposes. As the perceived need for armed forces diminishes, one nation may express that perception by some minor reductions, and others may respond in kind, thus setting in motion a reciprocal process of apparently voluntary disarmament. However, if one party levels off at a certain state of preparedness, or reverses the process and begins to re-arm, the others are likely to follow suit.

## THE NEGOTIATING PROCESS

Of the five degrees of reciprocity outlined above, the one which is most frequently attempted, most frequently unsuccessful, and yet most relevant to the search for international stability and peace, is that of the formally negotiated, highly reciprocal agreement; hence this article's emphasis on it at the expense of the other forms. Thus, before turning to certain other considerations in, and obstacles to, negotiated disarmament, let us examine the effects of the forum or setting within which these negotiations might take place. Two dimensions are most relevant here: (a) which nations participate, and (b) under whose auspices?

Since reference here is not to an imposed arrangement, it is understood that at least two of the negotiating nations are not only powerful enough to resist dictation by one another, but they are not sufficiently in agreement to dictate to third parties. Consequently, the locale and composition of the negotiations is itself a subject for bargaining. The party whose position is most likely to be politically attractive to third parties, or who wants to bring extra pressure to bear on the negotiating partner will tend to advocate a larger number of participants and may urge that the sessions be held at the seat of, or under the auspices of, the relevant international organization such as the League of Nations or the United Nations. Preference for smaller, isolated sessions on the other hand, may reflect either a nation's unwillingness to bargain seriously or a conviction that the technicalities and sensitivities of disarmament require private negotiation among the major powers only. During the post-World War II period, the Soviet Union and many of the non-aligned nations have favoured the large and open conference, while the United States and its allies have tended to prefer private negotiations among a small number of major powers. As a consequence, both approaches have been used, but with equally limited success.

Despite the advantages of quiet and privacy, the larger forum is generally to be preferred. First, when the key nations *are* ready to parley in earnest, their representatives can easily meet in private. Second, the sharp bi-lateral cleavages become blurred by the involvement of third and other parties, with the key protagonists under pressure to satisfy their demands. Third, while some of these pressures will be purely nationalistic ones, many will create new incentives for compromise on the part of the major protagonists. Fourth, relations between the representative and his home government become more complicated by the injection of unexpected people and he may be given more bargaining latitude. Finally, even if one side is more interested in propaganda than diplomacy, the other side has an opportunity for face-to-face education of those third parties who might otherwise be easily misled at a distance.

A final point in regard to the negotiation of disarmament concerns the composition and latitude of the separate delegations. Generally speaking, if they arrive with rigid instructions and are required to clear all departures from them with the Foreign Office or Defense Ministry, the prospects for success will not be good. Equally unsatisfactory, a negotiator may be sent under quite flexible conditions only to discover that the bargains he has struck will not be honoured by his government, due to his lack of effective support at home. In this same vein, a government can easily paralyze negotiations by sending delegates who may have considerable bargaining freedom, but whose personal interests and associates are opposed to a treaty. At the first Hague Conference, for example, the United States was represented by Admiral Mahan, the British by Admiral Fisher, Germany by Colonel von Schwarzhoff, and so on; such men could not be expected to bargain away the basis of their careers and prestige, and they were quite adept at discovering and articulating technical and tactical reasons for rejecting the Czar's proposals. It is one thing to have military experts on hand and quite another to give them a dominant role in the negotiations. More recently, the difficulty has been compounded by assigning engineers and physical scientists to the delegations (or to the groups responsible for instructing the delegations) and the careers and prestige of these men are often dependent upon the very weapon programs whose termination the delegates are allegedly trying to negotiate.

Studies of almost all conferences and negotiations have been made by historians, political scientists and lawyers. Perhaps the two most useful general analyses of the several inter-war negotiations are Madariaga (1926) and Tate (1942). Among those concentrating on the post–World War II efforts are Bechhoefer (1961), Jensen (1962), Spanier and Nogee (1962), and Jacobson and Stein (1966).

## DIRECTION AND PHASING

Up to this juncture we have made two simplifying assumptions. One is that there is no essential difference between reducing armament levels *down* to some specified level and permitting increases *up* to such a level. The fact that in one case a nation begins with more than the agreed capability and must therefore come down to it, and that in the other case the nation begins with less than the ceiling and is free to go up to it, must obviously have some important implications. The other simplification is that the *rate* at which a nation moves up or down to a given threshold in a given weapon category need not be a source of concern, and that the nature of the limit or prohibition is of major if not sole concern. It is equally evident that phasing can be profoundly important to both the disarmament process and its outcome.

Examining the matter of *direction* first, experience and logic both point to the advantage of negotiating or deciding upon a ceiling or prohibition *before* it is breached, rather than after. First, for every weapon developed and produced, national decision-makers have had to invest a certain amount of money, national prestige, and their own personal reputations. Thus, these weapons have a high symbolic as well as security value and they will not be given up without a high price. Second, the technicians who developed the weapons, the manufacturers and labourers who produced them, and the military personnel who maintain them have profited financially and psychologically in the process; they are not only interested in continuing such profits, but they are likely to be more influential politically after than before performing these roles. Third, there is less certainty that the potential adversary is *reducing* his weapons than that he is *not adding* to them, due to the inspection problem, creating serious risks in the security realm. Fourth, the decision-makers will be uncertain how many of a given weapon type the others have and will therefore be reluctant to engage in reductions that possibly increase the others' numerical advantage.

Conversely, negotiations are likely to be more successful when material and psychic investments are low, the anti-reduction lobby has not yet been created or strengthened, the military risks are lower, and the inspection requirements are minimal. To put it another way, it is less difficult *not* to arm than to *dis*arm.

Closely related to the direction of arms limitation is its *phasing*, or the relative speed with which all or certain classes of weapons are to be limited, reduced, or eliminated. The critical nature of this problem is manifested when we recall that no two nations have precisely the same security requirements, even if neither is interested in aggression. From the first

Hague Conference of 1898 through the pre–World War II negotiations, for example, Britain's heavy reliance on sea power posed certain difficulties quite distinct from those facing France, Germany, Russia, and other land-oriented powers. Likewise, in the Soviet-American negotiations of the post-1945 period, the discrepancies in the two powers' needs and capabilities made successful bargaining especially difficult. There is not only the hoary problem of quantitatively equating battalions and battleships, tanks and submarines, bombers and missiles, but the fact that even successful equating of them can be dangerous to one party or another. Thus, if one side is superior in long-range strategic forces and the other in localized conventional forces, due to differing location, technology, demography, and military doctrine, it may feel justified in demanding the elimination of all or most of the other's forces before proceeding to any reduction of its own. Or one may require overseas bases while the other does not, making negotiation about bases nearly impossible.

But even if these were not such complicating qualitative differences, the phasing problem would pose awkward obstacles to negotiated disarmament. On the one hand is the necessity to reduce personnel, budgetary, or weapon levels fast enough to: (a) make it clear that there is a disarmament process under way; (b) escape from the instability of a heavily armed world; and (c) take advantage of and perpetuate the temporary period of mutual confidence that would probably accompany the signing and ratification of the treaty or convention. On the other are the fears of reducing one's capabilities before: (a) there is assurance that others are doing likewise; (b) there is evidence that the other has given up its "aggressive" designs; and (c) alternate modes of national protection have been developed. Further complicating the timing and phasing problem is the likelihood that some signatories, seeking revision of the global distribution of influence, will have developed and prepared to use non-military or other indirect techniques of waging international conflict; the status quo nations may, therefore, insist on a very gradual and prolonged disarmament schedule. Finally, all parties will have some fear that whatever inspection and control agencies are created will be unduly influenced or dominated by the others.

It is probably safe to say, on the basis of the few available analyses of disarmament negotiations, that the issue of phasing has been as much an historical obstacle to success as has the question of which weapons should be reduced or limited to what levels.

## INSPECTION AND VERIFICATION

Given the likelihood that disarmament negotiations will generally take place, if at all, within an atmosphere of moderate to high distrust and fear, it is reasonable to expect suspicion regarding compliance of whatever agreements might be reached. To weaken one's major source of security without some assurance that the others are doing likewise is so unattractive a prospect that inspection is generally considered an essential adjunct of arms reduction or limitation.

Such inspection may be carried out by other signatories, by *ad hoc* international commissions, or by international organizations, and the objects of such inspection may be budgets, war plans, training facilities, weapon installations, factories, transport junctions, or entire regions, depending upon the activities proscribed by the agreement. Just as in the reduction schedule itself, the problem of phasing in inspection is often a major source of failure; how much inspection is necessary and safe at which stages of reduction? In order of increasing intrusiveness, inspection may focus upon: the destruction or dismantling process to insure that the reduction schedule is being followed; test or production facilities to inhibit or prevent the acquisition of a weapon type; or upon present inventories (or a sample thereof) to insure that a given ceiling has not been exceeded. Often the negotiations reveal a marked difference in attitude toward the rate at which inspection should be introduced, and its intensiveness or extensiveness, once established. The dilemma is dramatized when we consider that a nation may refuse to consider any reductions or limitations until it knows the size and quality of the other's inventories, while inspection for such purposes would be the most wide-ranging, onerous, and costly. Yet the demand for even a modest form of pre-reduction surveillance before any arms reduction, may well be interpreted by another nation as motivated by espionage intentions only. These basic difficulties can be mitigated if the negotiations and early reductions occur in an environment of moderate trust, permitting each side to tolerate more, and demand less, inspection. Or, high inspection requirements can be mitigated by remote surveillance techniques, made increasingly possible by such advanced technology as intercontinental radar and orbiting camera satellites, or modern computer-based analysis of full production, inventory, and cost records.

## ENFORCEMENT AND PROTECTION

Whether a disarmament agreement provides for on-site or remote, human or machine, or adversary or international inspection, one problem always remains: how to respond to suspected or verified evasions?

At one extreme is the emphasis on unilateral abrogation and at the other is the demand for punishment by some international or supranational agency. Neither seems feasible. In all past, present, and future processes of arms reduction or limitation, many evasions can be expected; some will be intentional, some will be accidental, and many more will merely be suspicions of an evasion. If the purpose of inspection is to generate mutual confidence, responses must be graduated and appropriate. Thus, suspected violations should produce increased inspection, not a renewed arms race or premature punishment; only as evasions become patently intentional and serious, would extreme sanctions be relevant. When such a situation develops, of course, the signatories are at a critical turning point, the outcome of which will depend on the intentions and fears of the respective decision-makers, the distance already travelled toward fulfillment of the agreement, and the strength of the international institutions established in conjunction with the arms arrangements.

Considerations of enforcement, of course, go to the very heart of the disarmament problem. Recalling the earlier discussion of the incentives affecting a nation's armament policy, we note that the major source of national security has been and largely remains that of military capability relative to potential enemies. If the decision is to limit or reduce such capability, it is usually on the assumption of reciprocal measures by other nations. But even if reciprocal reductions were to carry most of the world's nations down to complete disarmament levels, without any upset by violation—and this has so far never occurred—there would still remain the problem not only of inspection and enforcement in a disarming world, but that of conflict control and protection in a disarming and a disarmed world. Put another way, nations require supranational agencies both to help in carrying through any disarmament process and to protect them at the end of the process. Incompatibilities among nations might well be as serious and dangerous *after* disarmament as during it, and conflicts all along the way are inevitable. Without supranational institutions, no disarmament process of any significance is likely to be completed, and without them in a world of already disarmed nations, the rearmament process would be nearly inevitable.

Thus, as and when nations disarm, they need to arrange, in a cautious and gradual manner, both the diminution of their own capabilities and the accretion of the international organization's capabilities. These shifts of relative capability must, of course, embrace both the military and the political realm, requiring the gradual build-up of supranational peace-keeping facilities. Implicit in such shifts is an inevitable modification, however slow and imperceptible, in the structure and the culture of the international system, and though all the specifics need not be negotiated in advance, the major powers and many of the minor ones must be quite aware of the transition which they are setting in motion. Therefore, there must be agreement on the rules by which the rules will be made and modified, even though the concrete future is only dimly perceived.

There may be less radical paths to disarmament, but they are unlikely to be irreversible ones. Historically, nothing approximating global disarmament has been successfully negotiated, and the more restricted attempts have tended to be short-lived. With no alternative means of self-protection and conflict resolution, the nations have always returned to armament, regardless of their peaceful intentions.

## CONCLUSION

In concluding these remarks, let me depart from the reasonable rule that it is not only bad manners, but politically risky, for a foreigner to come on a visit and proceed to offer "free advice." But the Indian intellectuals I have met on this journey have seemed so open-minded, and secure enough to suggest how my own nation might clean up *its* act, that it seems worth the risk. Furthermore, there is so much at stake and the situation is so precarious, that such niceties had best be dispensed with. So far, I have spoken largely in terms of the rest of the world, but the applicability of my comments to the Indian sub-continent is sufficiently evident.

As I see it, your country has two major responsibilities, one regional and one global. As to the former, it is imperative to take a hard and close look at your conflict with Pakistan, try to identify the dynamics of this relationship, and press the Centre for a shift to a more prudent and less provocative stance vis-à-vis your neighbour to the northwest. Without claiming an intimate familiarity with the Indo-Pakistan interaction sequence in recent years, one can certainly imagine a good many initiatives available to your government that might lead to a more businesslike relationship, without seriously jeopardizing your vital security interests.

At the global level, my hope is that the tradition of Mahatma Gandhi and Jawaharlal Nehru will be continued and amplified in the months and years ahead. The five-nation peace initiative is off to a promising start, but it must be pursued with a vigour and consistency virtually unknown in modern diplomacy. As already suggested, to wait for the super powers to move decisively away from their reciprocal madness on their own is to acquiesce in ultimate catastrophe. There must be pressure on Moscow and Washington, and on their allies in Europe and Asia, relentless but patient, vigorous but tactful, and creative but pragmatic. We all inhabit the same global village, and their behaviour is a menace to all of us. And in moving toward more exemplary foreign policies themselves, India and the other non-aligned nations will be in a stronger position to influence the superpowers and their allies. The hour is late, but with your efforts, we may yet be able to steer humanity back to a reasonable pursuit of peace with freedom, and security with prosperity.

# CHAPTER FOUR

■

# Negotiation by Proxy: A Proposal

ALTHOUGH IT REMAINS to be demonstrated empirically, the general impression among students of diplomatic history and international relations is that the fruitfulness of inter-nation negotiation as a conflict-resolving technique has tended to diminish as political participation of the masses has increased. If this proposition is essentially correct, it behooves us—given the increasing costs of diplomatic failure—to look for an explanation in the relationship between the negotiators and the national societies from which they come.

The negotiator or diplomat is unlikely to get much in the way of either reward or punishment from his opposite number across the bargaining table, but his own society can grant or withhold a great many of the perquisites and values which he may desire. And because there will almost always be, in any large national society, some group or faction which thinks it can benefit from *failure* in negotiations and a continuation of the unmitigated conflict, the negotiator is always vulnerable to attack from such quarters if he is successful. That is, in order to be successful (assuming approximate power equality between the two nations), the negotiator for nation A must "give away" something in the way of concessions to his opposite number from nation B. As a consequence, the "no peace" (or "peace on our terms only") faction in nation A will easily be able to accuse the negotiator—or the political party or administration which he represents—of having "sold out" or "surrendered." Is there any conceivable exit from

This chapter originally appeared in *Journal of Conflict Resolution*, vol. 9, no. 4 (Dec. 1965), pp. 538-541. Reprinted by permission of Sage Publications, Inc.

This memorandum was originally written in 1962, but several readers felt it was based on too pessimistic an interpretation of modern diplomacy. Hence it was filed away, only to be resurrected by the unhappy events of the period since then. Though one of the original critics (Inis L. Claude) would still quarrel with the diagnosis, and a recent reader (Bruce Russett) is uncertain about the prescription, the consensus is that its publication might be heuristically useful.

such a dilemma? To put it another way, is there any means by which we might partially depoliticize (in the domestic sense) diplomatic negotiations? Several analogous situations come to mind, and from them we might conceivably draw some useful suggestions.

One technique, already well-established in international relations, is the use of the mediator. In this case a more or less disinterested third party participates in the bargaining sessions or else acts as a go-between, meeting with each of the nation's representatives independently. In either event, some group of nationals representing their own government is bargaining with another group of nationals representing the other side. Thus, despite the theoretically improved probability of the success of the mediator, historical evidence suggests that this technique has been only slightly more successful than that of face-to-face confrontation. Is there a way to move the negotiators further from the pressures and considerations which inhibit their search for "businesslike" solutions?

One alternative comes to mind which might be worthy of further analysis. Let there be established, in a large number of countries, a new type of law firm, whose primary purpose is the representation of nations which are or might become involved in a particular dispute. These firms would be, in a sense, professional bargainers "for hire" to national governments. Once a government had selected a particular firm (preferably from a "disinterested" nation) to represent it in a particular round of negotiation, the following procedure might be applied.

In a very private and quiet meeting, the responsible political officials of the nation would provide their hired bargainers (or mercenaries) with this information:

(1) The most desirable outcome that could be imagined, from their point of view.

(2) The *minimum* price, in the form of concessions, which they are willing to pay for any particular concession from the other side.

(3) The *expected* price necessary in order to get such a concession.

(4) The *maximum* price they would pay to get that concession.

(5) The least desirable outcome, short of no agreement at all.

In addition to providing the bargaining firm with one's minimal, optimal, and maximal outcome preferences, certain other rules need to be articulated. Among the more important are the fee scales. If we accept the argument that one of the main inhibitors to successful negotiation between diplomats is the balance of incentives and disincentives, we can appreciate the importance of the monetary fees involved here. The important thing is to provide the bargainers with a very high incentive to negotiate a *successful* agreement, and at the same time to provide almost as high an incentive for striking a very hard bargain.

One way to meet these two needs is to stipulate that a very minimal fee will be paid if a formal agreement has *not* been reached in a specific period of time; this minimal fee might be more or less equivalent to the cost involved for the law firm in preparing for the negotiations, plus a nominal overhead charge. Under such conditions, firms that are not successful in negotiating agreements will be able to remain in business, but will never get rich! On the other hand, if an agreement *is* reached, let the firm be paid something on the order of three to six times their basic cost of preparation. And on top of this, the national representatives and their lawyers would negotiate a fairly detailed set of "contingency fees." Under such an arrangement, the firm would be given an additional increment depending on the number and extent of the concessions which they end up making in exchange for the desired concessions from the other nation's firm. Such a contractual arrangement would generate a very high incentive both to conclude an agreement and to strike the hardest possible bargain; it is, of course, essential that the bargaining firm have no incentive to "give anything away."

Of course this scheme could be sabotaged by fee-splitting or side payments; one firm could make a great many concessions to the other and collect its relatively modest fee, but supplement that with a prearranged share of the very large fee collected by the other firm, which had struck a highly successful bargain from its client's point of view. This kind of collusion would, however, be inhibited by the same factor which impinges on all professionals: the realization that one such episode would destroy the firm's reputation. Moreover, if the negotiation-by-proxy arrangement were to be part of an overall modification of conflict management techniques, including compulsory arbitration and compulsory adjudication, the incentives for honest bargaining would be increased. That is, unless one side's firm felt its position to be extremely weak, it would prefer to break off the negotiations and trust to third-party intervention than to submit to the equivalent of bribery and collusion.

Though this set of procedures may sound highly unorthodox, one should bear in mind that it is not basically different from certain activities in which law firms are already involved. First of all, in a great many potential litigations, the adversaries empower their attorneys to try to negotiate an "out of court settlement." Secondly, in some union contract negotiations— in the United States at least—both labor and management engage law firms to bargin with each other. In these cases the actual adversaries do not necessarily encounter one another in a face-to-face situation; rather, each side is represented by a group of professional, disinterested experts. Not only do such arrangements reduce the intrusion of inhibiting and extraneous considerations like ideology, personal antipathy, and (occasionally) downright incompetence, but they also—and this is the main point—permit the bargaining to take place between parties which stand to *gain*, rather than *lose*, from a successfully negotiated agreement.

Now it may be argued that the foreign ministry officials who instruct and bargain with their lawyers are, despite the attempted deception, still engaged in concession-making; therefore they would still be vulnerable to, and inhibited by, domestic criticism. Certainly there is no way around the fact that elected or appointed policy-makers must always, one way or another, be the ones to decide what the appropriate *quid pro quo* should be. But if these decisions were made in professional privacy and were more or less irrevocable during the bargaining period, many of those extraneous and irrelevant factors which regularly debilitate the normal diplomatic process could be reduced or eliminated.

It might also be charged that this would represent a serious departure from democratic procedures, and in a limited and literal sense this is correct. On the other hand, it is still up to the elected government to make the crucial policy decisions and to ascertain the acceptable payoffs; the next election can never be too far from their minds. The lawyers merely carry out instructions, albeit complicated and contingent instructions. As a matter of fact, by being compelled to spell out for these lawyers its bargaining rules and preferences, any government would be much more likely to reflect the national interest than under present conditions, where "seat-of-the-pants" hunches and pressure-group tactics lead frequently to highly irrational bargaining positions. Furthermore, there always remains the opportunity for rejection during the ratification process.

At least two alternative ratification arrangements come to mind. In one case the national governments might stipulate that, once the formal agreement is reached by their attorneys, it would still have to be approved and ratified by their own appropriate legislative and administrative processes. This procedure would most likely be the one insisted upon while the practice was being tested. But if it did turn out to be a successful approach to the postulated dilemma in negotiation, it is quite possible that governments and electorates would be willing, in a sense, to give their bargaining firms the "power of attorney." In such an event, the agreement reached would become binding merely on the countersignature of the foreign ministers or heads of state, signifying that the attorneys had faithfully adhered to the rules and stipulations.

Needless to say, there are a great many difficulties, small and large, which need to be thought through before a procedure such as that outlined above could ever be adopted by national governments. But as government has become increasingly susceptible to the caprices of public opinion and partisan efforts to exploit such opinion, diplomacy seems to have become less and less successful. The major powers thus find it nearly impossible to negotiate either on important political conflicts or on arrangements for the gradual reduction of national military capabilities. While this dismal record continues, the likelihood of nuclear war will probably increase. Given such an unpleasant prospect, a somewhat off-beat method of negotiation may warrant more serious attention than it would in less dangerous times.

# CHAPTER FIVE

■

# Negotiations, Initiatives, and Arms Reduction

## 1. GLIMMERS OF HOPE

Despite the sorry state of East-West relationships, with policies of detente in a shambles, and the virtual cessation of Soviet-American negotiations on arms reduction and other matters, there remain two faint glimmers of hope that reason and responsibility have not totally disappeared from contemporary world politics. One of these is the recent increase in concern among the major powers' allies on both sides, and a consequent tendency toward greater initiatives emanating from European capitals. It may even be that it takes a sequence of events as ominous as the Euro-missile crisis to remind the European elites that they need not be merely accomplices— and victims—of Soviet and American stupidity, but that they have both the responsibility and the possibility of bringing Moscow and Washington to their senses.

The second is that the super-powers—even as they continue to over-arm, to threaten, and to demonstrate "resolve"—appear to be inching toward a new approach to the arms race dilemma. The more traditional approach, going back to the 1920s, has been upon the slow negotiation of infrequent, but fairly comprehensive treaties, intended to set upper limits for the signatories in one or a few weapon categories. Seldom have actual *reductions* been sought, but even the establishment of agreed ceilings has been of only a temporary sort, soon to be eroded by inadvertent or conscious violations, or by advances and shifts in weapons technology. And despite the salutary results of the ABM and SALT I negotiations, the vertical and horizontal proliferation of strategic (and even "conventional") weapons has continued apace since World War II. More weapons of an increasingly provocative and destabilizing nature are in the hands of more nations than

This chapter originally appeared in *Bulletin of Peace Proposals*, vol. 15, no. 4 (1984), pp. 317–320. Reprinted by permission of International Peace Research Institute, Oslo.

ever before, and never have the objective and subjective conditions for turning away from major power war been less promising.

Might there be a more effective approach to arms limitation and arms reduction? Must we continue, like Sisyphus, to struggle manfully up the slippery slope, hoping that each heroic effort will finally bring us success, only to discover that we are further than ever from the plateau of arms stabilization? Before suggesting an alternative, let me indicate why the search for periodic, large, dramatic, one-shot agreements has proven so inadequate.

## 2. WHY HIGH-STAKES NEGOTIATION OFTEN FAILS

Without getting into the "origins of the cold war" swamp, let us recognize that nearly forty years of intense East-West rivalry not only produces distrust and hostility between the protagonists, along with an inexorable growth in the arsenals of war, but also some menacing changes *within* the contending societies as well. At each choice point, certain self-amplifying processes are strengthened. That is, when we choose to develop or deploy a new weapon system, we strengthen the position of those who supported it and weaken the position of those who opposed it. Each allocation of resources to the military adds to the economic clout of those who advocated it, and detracts from those who resisted it. And each decision to "hang tough" enhances the domestic credibility of the hard-liners and diminishes that of the more prudent and moderate elements. Further, with each such choice, the cumulative influence of the "hawks" increases, while that of the "owls" and the "doves" decreases.

Periodically, of course, a marginal consensus emerges that confrontational policies and arms build-ups may not be working, and this awareness typically leads to experimentation with less bellicose behavior. But given the increasingly dominant position of the hard-line factions in the rival power, as well as the endemic suspiciousness that has inevitably developed, such "experiments" are not likely to work. When concessions are offered, they are not promptly reciprocated, and when positive initiatives are attempted, they are often rebuffed. And by the time that the rival government finally chooses to respond in kind, it is too late. Once again, the hawks have demonstrated that "there is only one way to deal with those people," and the voices of reason are soon silenced or ignored.

Admittedly, we sometimes see a groundswell of opinion in favor of less belligerent policies, but it rarely endures. Whether it be motivated by a recognition of the dangers to national security, an awareness of the economic consequences of a continuing arms race, mere weariness, or even a resurgence of pacifism, two factors usually stem that tide with relative ease. One is the tendency of the rival to be quite unhelpful—even to the point of *increasing* its provocative behavior—thus discrediting the nascent "peace movement." The other is the domestic counter-attack mounted by those who, for material, psychological, or institutional reasons prefer the continuation or resumption of more militaristic policies.

In addition to these vested interests—as well as those who are naive enough to believe in the arms race as an acceptable basis for national security—there is another obstacle to success. I refer here to the psychological syndrome that inevitably goes with negotiations over very high stakes. First, there is the anxiety that we might "give something away" that could turn out to be vitally damaging to the nation's security. Hence, we are likely to agonize over every detail of substance or procedure, looking for some hidden danger, and call in all sorts of specialists and technicians to double check. This not only takes a lot of time, but it creates great opportunities for different agencies and offices to obstruct or scuttle a given move. Second, considering the breadth and magnitude of the possible bans and limitations, excessive and time-consuming attention will be given to the possibility of second- and third-order implications for future strategic developments. Third, with so much at stake, the natural suspicion of the other side's motives and honesty is further exaggerated, providing a field-day for the devotees of "worst case analysis."

Fourth, the longer and more acrimonious the discussions within and between the delegations, the greater the opportunity for frustration, suspicion, and hostility to fester. Fifth, the combination of technical, strategic, and emotional complexities tends to make the chief negotiators *even more* cautious than they normally might be. Finally, given the significance of the putative agreement and the cumulative clout of the domestic opposition to meaningful arms control, the negotiators will constantly be looking over their shoulders to be sure that they are not politically vulnerable back home to charges of being "soft." Given these dynamics, it is not surprising that so many can labor so long, and accomplish so little.

## 3. WHY LOW-STAKES NEGOTIATION MIGHT SUCCEED

If this diagnosis is essentially correct, we need a strategy that recognizes the powerful forces—political, economic, and psychological—which stand in the way of major breakthroughs in arms negotiations or other security-related efforts. The domestic resistance and technical difficulties must be overcome in a more pragmatic and piece-meal fashion, and the opponents' skepticism must be ameliorated in an equally gradual manner. All of this points, then, to the more *incremental* and fluid strategy in pursuit of arms control and arms reduction that seems to be developing.

If we look at the ways in which nations handle the equally complex incompatibilities of interest while nevertheless pursuing certain shared objectives in other realms, we may find an instructive example. In trade, investment, immigration, technology transfer, and even in many areas of diplomacy, we ordinarily find a pattern quite different than that employed in the high politics security sector. The negotiation process is more continuous, the agreements pursued are more limited, the results are more short-range, and the ebb-flow more fluctuating.

This emphasis on fluid, incremental, and low stakes bargaining offers certain advantages that might be applicable to arms negotiation. By working in the context of a continuous process, there is greater opportunity for short-run feedback in which small errors can be rectified, minor misperceptions modified, temporary violations alleviated, and momentary stalemates side-stepped. Further, the incremental process permits rolling readjustments and frequent multiple trade-offs within the domestic bargaining context. As modest gains are registered, the resistance of some agencies and interest groups might be softened, and the credibility of others enhanced. And as the costs and dangers of current policies are haltingly and erratically reduced, one might expect modest shifts in the distribution of domestic opinion as well as in the distribution of influence.

## 4. SOME USEFUL PRE-CONDITIONS

For such a process to really take hold, and for the resistance of the hawks and the confidence of the doves to reverse direction, three additional activities would be highly desirable. One is to address and try to ameliorate the material and symbolic costs that would be incurred by those in each society who have stood to gain by the arms race and the accompanying hardline policies. Not only economic conversion and job-retraining, but a range of other adaptive moves would be necessary to bring more groups into the pro-arms control coalition. And as these elements—in both the Western and Soviet camps—gain confidence and credibility while the forces of resistance begin to compromise, come around, or drop out, the ability to withstand temporary reverses would be enhanced.

A second set of efforts would be in the direction of economic, cultural, and diplomatic reinforcement of these incremental processes. As minor limitations and reductions of arms levels begin to emerge, East-West collaboration in these other sectors might become more feasible, and thus strengthen the overall tendencies toward detente. Some would contend that such confidence-building measures must *precede* any progress in arms control, but this seems much more necessary if we continue to strive for dramatic big breakthroughs than if we shift to the more incremental, process-oriented mode. Under the latter strategy, it would be less critical which sectors we concentrate upon first; continuous exploration, probing, and horsetrading could proceed whenever the incentives are strong enough and the obstacles—domestic and foreign—sufficiently surmountable.

A third critical emphasis would be that of an increasing role for the United Nations system, particularly the Secretariat. I see this as three-pronged. One is the need for a gradual shift away from sole reliance upon national means of verification and monitoring of the various limitations and restrictions that have been negotiated. Another would see the UN playing a more active role in the mediation of the disputes that must inevitably arise in such a complex, delicate and dangerous process as moving to some sort of durable arms control regime. The third prong here is that of an increasingly active role for the Office of the Secretary-General in preventive diplomacy and the institution of confidence-building measures.

While the so-called "conference diplomacy" of the Assembly and the Council continues, with little effect, it is desirable that the Secretariat staff initiate a process of what might be called "coalition diplomacy." In this vein, past emphasis on the passive availability of the Secretary-General (when requested by governments) would shift to a more active and vigorous intervention into nascent or ongoing disputes and difficulties. If handled in a skillful, tactful, and competent fashion, such a new set of initiatives might be found less obtrusive and more welcome than has been traditionally assumed.

## 5. A FEW POSSIBLE INITIATIVES

If, as suggested, we may expect greater activity on the part of the superpowers' allies (and perhaps even on the part of the nonaligned governments) and some shift toward more modest, pragmatic, and flexible negotiating strategies on the part of the Americans and the Soviets, what might be done to get things moving? Are there some plausible initiatives that might help to improve the climate and thus increase the attractiveness—and the likelihood of success—of such low-stakes negotiations? Given my conviction that the only really effective confidence-building measure is arms reduction itself, where might we look to attempt a new beginning? In as much as land-based counter-force missiles, both in Europe and America, are the major source of anxiety and the dominant source of no-confidence in the intentions of the rivals, these highly provocative and de-stabilizing weapons ought to get our highest priority. Would it be too much to expect one or both of the superpowers to recognize this fact, grasp that these weapon systems are a serious threat to their own security as well as their rival's, and put a halt to further deployment and "modernization" of land-based nuclear delivery vehicles? Would it be too much to expect the political leadership in these over-militarized societies to act responsibly on behalf of their own citizens as well as the rest of the human race?

It probably *is* asking too much, given the extent to which the US and the USSR have been morally and intellectually corrupted by their arms rivalry, but if there are any elements left in these countries who have both the power and the intelligence, they will move heaven and earth to halt, and then reverse, the deployment of vulnerable and accurate ballistic missiles anywhere. Having decided, and acted for national and global survival by putting a stop to further deployment—with or without reciprocity—their next step would be to begin an incremental phasing out of existing land-based systems. I do not argue here that sea-based or air-launched nuclear systems are the benefactors of humanity, but their existence is a less immediate threat to the human race, and can be dealt with when—and if—we see some signs of progress in reducing the number of essentially first-strike systems.

## 6. CONCLUSION

There are of course, several other ways of breaking into the arms-tension spiral, and we ought to be willing to accept and encourage any reasonable initiative from either side that holds any promise for a reversal of this deadly process. But it seems absolutely essential that we forget about the "go-for-broke" negotiations and start a process of unilateral initiatives, piece meal offers, tacit concessions, and flexible coordination between the major powers and their allies, while attending carefully to the domestic processes by which we might break the stranglehold of those who have edged us closer and closer to the nuclear abyss.

# PART TWO

———————— ■ ————————

# Beyond Policy Prescription

The previous five chapters focus on the problem of contemporary international war and suggest some unorthodox but largely prescientific responses to that problem. Although I recognize the urgency of thinking through the war problem even as the peace research effort gathers momentum, there is nevertheless the sense that "good thinking," creativity, honesty and intellectual rigor will probably not suffice. As I like to remind my students, good ideas are "a dime a dozen" in the policy sector and in the discipline as a whole. But to (a) convert these good ideas into discomfirmable form so that we can put them to the historical-empirical test, and (b) actually carry out the research test—that is the real challenge. Before that, however, we need to think through a number of essential questions, and in this part we look at several such questions—institutional and scientific—that seem relevant to the acquisition and the application of the relevant knowledge.

Chapter 6 offers a brief overview of the relationship between the research sector and the policy process and of the role of epistemology in bridging those two activities. Chapter 7 carries this line of reasoning a step further and explores the centrality of the education and research enterprise to the solution of a broader range of social problems. In Chapter 8 is a summary of my congressional testimony on the desirability—and the dangers—of establishing what has since come into being as the U.S. Institute of Peace, and in Chapter 9 is an illustrative list of research problems and research strategies that might be usefully addressed by such an institute and other peace research groups.

# CHAPTER SIX

■

# Conflict Research, Political Action, and Epistemology

AS ONE READS THROUGH THE ESSAYS in this volume, two rather contradictory thoughts occur. The first is that political science has come a long way in a relatively short time, with a steady increase both in the number of competent and creative researchers and in the amount of existential and correlational knowledge that they are generating. The second thought is as discouraging as the first is encouraging: the likelihood that this expanding body of knowledge will be applied to the amelioration or solution of serious political problems, especially problems of political violence, remains painfully low. This pessimism is, of course, partly a response to the fact that many of these problems are so deep-seated that knowledge alone will not suffice. It also is due partly to the fact political elites are seldom competent to understand and evaluate, let alone apply, social science findings.

In addition to these two considerations, there is a third: the relative failure of the researchers themselves to comprehend fully the knowledge-action relationship. It is to that set of considerations that this brief concluding essay is addressed. In my view, there is a continuous and intimate feedback loop that connects the researcher, the general public, the political elite, and the counterelite (by whom I mean those with roughly the same expertise and concerns as members of the elite, but who are not now in positions of high political influence). Until that loop is more fully examined and more clearly understood, our research findings will continue to have marginal consequences at most. There are, of course, several points at which we might break into this feedback loop, but given the fact that the acquisition and codification of knowledge must necessarily precede its application, let us begin there.

Before doing so, however, let me try to dispel one of the more recurrent and destructive myths surrounding applied social science, particularly with

---

Reprinted from *Handbook of Political Conflict: Theory and Research*, Ted R. Gurr, ed., 1980, pp. 490–499. Copyright © 1980. Reprinted by permission of The Free Press.

respect to political violence. This is the suggestion that conflict and peace researchers are either knaves or fools, inasmuch as they seek to provide the knowledge by which political elites and "the establishment" in general may placate and perhaps subjugate those who might otherwise resort to violence as a means of redressing injustice. Whereas it is indeed possible that such knowledge can be (and has been) so exploited, the problem is not inherent in the findings of these researchers. Rather it lies partly in the failure to get these findings to those who may be disadvantaged by asymmetries in knowledge; hence the importance of getting our findings to the counter-elites who most often speak and act on behalf of the disadvantaged.

But a corollary of this is that the counter-elites of the world had better turn away from what is often a Luddite mentality. As long as the reformers and the radicals hold to the view—as they seem to do in many parts of the world these days—that applied social science is inherently reactionary, if not pure sham, no amount of high quality research findings will be of use to the victims of exploitation and/or incompetence. Peace researchers of a scientific bent need not be, and usually are not, devoted to law and order at the expense of social justice, or to system maintenance in place of system transformation. Our aim is not to *eliminate* conflict, but to decrease the likelihood that it will be violent and reactionary and to increase the chances that it will have constructive and creative outcomes.

## THE ACQUISITION AND CODIFICATION
## OF KNOWLEDGE

Turning to some of the more interesting problems that arise in the acquisition and codification of knowledge that might later be applied, I find it difficult to side-step the most obvious issue of all: Does knowledge matter, and do ideas play any role in the modification or perpetuation of the properties of the social system and its behavioral regularities? In my view, these mental phenomena have been and always will be as important to the understanding of social systems as are more tangible phenomena such as resources, wealth, power, and institutions. The behavior of individuals and collectivities is a consequence, among other things, of the perceptions, predictions, and preferences that are brought to and accompany that behavior. Such behavior helps either to perpetuate or to modify existing social conditions. This is not to accept, of course, any simple-minded and extreme form of philosophical idealism. To the contrary, every social condition and human event is itself the result of a complex and still barely understood interaction among three acts of phenomena: voluntaristic, deterministic, and stochastic. Further, the voluntaristic component is itself a consequence of both deterministic and stochastic processes as well as of prior voluntaristic acts. Although so abstract a statement provides little in the way of knowledge, analyses that run afoul of its epistemological implications are bound to be scientifically flawed.

A second and closely related issue is not whether ideas affect the behavior of elites, counter-elites, and the public, but whether that effect in turn makes a science of social phenomena impossible. That is, the Karls Mannheim and Marx are quite correct in urging that each individual's ideas are indeed influenced by the time, place, role, and status of the individual. But their overly enthusiastic disciples are quite incorrect insofar as they urge that our ideas are *fully determined* by such immediate contextual factors. Clearly, the genetic heritage, social background, and specific experiences of each of us—and all of these *precede* our ideas of the moment—cannot be neglected in any explanation of a given individual's perceptions, predictions, and preferences. The implication is important in that it makes possible—and certain epistemological schools of the past and present notwithstanding, does not render impossible—the generation of fairly objective scientific knowledge about social events and conditions. Rather, the essential purpose of scientific method is to make our biases and predispositions quite visible, and our procedures thoroughly public and reproducible.

Of course, the scientific style does not guarantee the generation of socially useful knowledge; it is necessary, but not sufficient. To produce high quality knowledge that can be applied to the resolution of political conflict, several other criteria must be satisfied, and it is to some of these that we now turn.

Perhaps the most crucial criterion for socially useful knowledge is this: we must have reproducible observations, measurements, and records of the phenomena (past or unfolding) we wish to describe or explain, as well as of the phenomena that are introduced in the search for explanation. This, in turn, requires the invention and use of explicit, operational, and public procedures such that our observations are highly reproducible from one person to the next and from one observation to the next. In the language of science, we must utilize *reliable indicators* of the presence, absence, strength, direction, and so on, of whatever phenomena we invoke in our efforts at description and explanation. A second criterion is that our indicators be valid as well as reliable. By validity we mean the extent to which our indicators provide an accurate representation of the phenomena that we hope and claim to measure. This criterion is more difficult to satisfy because, unlike reliability—which can be tested by comparing independently reproduced observations—there is no direct and absolutely convincing test of the validity of a measure. Rather, through a variety of well-known strategies, we test and improve the validity of our indicators, knowing that they must always be regarded as approximations. More to the point here, neither the reliability nor the validity problem can be solved in the absence of conceptual clarity, and it thus behooves us to attend to that particular issue here.

One precondition of conceptual clarity is the obvious need for verbal precision; less obvious is the need to distinguish between the phenomenon that we seek to explain and those phenomena that we invoke in attempting that explanation. Both of these points will be, I trust, illustrated in the definitional overview that follows. Three concepts that are essential to peace research are science, knowledge, and theory, yet all are still used in a confusing and inconsistent variety of ways. By science, we mean nothing more than a body of procedures (and their underlying assumptions) that have so far proven superior to other sets of procedures in the acquisition, codification, and evaluation of knowledge. Thus the scientific enterprise is quite content-free and in principle need never foreordain the outcome of an investigation that adheres to its spirit and letter.

Whereas the basic assumption of science—that physical, biological, and social phenomena all manifest certain lawlike regularities, only some of which are now understood—is certainly a meta-theoretical one, and clearly conveys certain ontological as well as epistemological premises, it nevertheless remains essentially atheoretical. In other words, the "radical critique" of social science, while making some telling points along the way, must be rejected when it alleges that the scientific method *inherently* contains a conservative theoretical/ideological bias. Although many practitioners of social science proceed from conservative theoretical premises, these premises are not inherent in the basic methodology itself, but rather arise from the psychology and the social environment of the researchers and perhaps from their particular applications of scientific method. The epistemology of the scientific method, because it recognizes our ultimate reliance upon inter-subjective agreement among scholarly specialists, contains more opportunity and incentive for self-correcting procedures than any of the rival episte-mologies. To paraphrase Shakespeare, the fault lies, dear critic, not in our epistemology but in ourselves.

Related to this view of science is the need to drop certain invidious adjectives that continue to plague our enterprise. No one would suggest that the problems, models, and research strategies of the social sciences are identical to those of the physical and biological sciences, but it is equally misleading to exaggerate the differences. Hence reference to the "natural sciences" is to suggest that they are inherently superior in content and method and to ignore the interdependence of physical, biological, and social phenomena. Not only are the social sciences not unnatural; they are also, to take another pejorative label, not inexact. Any familiarity with the biological sciences indicates that in many realms of research, the social scientists' phenomena are indeed quite "natural" and our procedures of observation, measurement, and analysis equally or more exact, precise, and operational.

If the adjectives associated with the word "science" are misleading and confusing, those associated with "theory" are downright disastrous. Let me deal with some examples by first defining theory—at least in the scientific sense of the word—as a body of codified knowledge. To satisfy that definition, we need to have a series of logically consistent propositions, all of which are stated operationally and thus are susceptible to empirical or logical disconfirmation. Further, most of them should have been empirically tested and found largely consonant with the referent social phenomena that they allegedly describe. In addition, since the purpose of a theory is to explain or account for some regularity in an empirical phenomenon (including its direction and rate of change), that regularity and variation therein must first have been established. To devote untold time and energy to the construction of "theories," the distributions of whose outcome variable may have nothing in common with reality, might be a healthy intellectual exercise but is hardly a direct contribution to knowledge.

It follows that such distinctions as empirical versus speculative theory or positive versus normative theory are not particularly helpful. Any scientific theory is, of course, a mix of empirical evidence, disciplined speculation, and tight logic, and to speak of "speculative theory" is to speak, at best, of a model or a set of hypotheses or hunches. Speculation is that with which we begin, and we have no theory until our speculation has been systematized, operationalized, and largely confirmed vis-à-vis the empirical evidence. In sum, any scientific theory *must* be empirical. Further, a theory must be "positive" as the economists usually term it, and to speak of normative theory seems singularly unfortunate. To accept the positive-normative distinction means that we invoke high procedural standards when dealing with the world as it is or has been, but throw these standards to the winds when we come to the world as it should be or might be. To put it another way, normative theory is a contradiction in terms, and we might do better as policy-oriented scientists if we kept in mind that *theories provide the knowledge base from which we can try to move toward certain normatively preferred outcomes.* The more solid our theories, the more accurate will be our contingent forecasts, and such accuracy is essential both to the social usefulness of our research and to its credibility to those who make, shape, or challenge public policy.

By *contingent* forecast I mean only to emphasize that social scientists should insist that their forecasts are conditional upon certain preconditions and that unless those specified preconditions are satisfied, "all bets are off." As a matter of credibility, one ought to specify which behaviors by which actors, occurring in which context, will lead to which outcomes with which probabilities. And as a matter of usefulness to counter-elites and elites, we must similarly be able to identify which actions they would need to propose or to take in order to achieve or avoid a given outcome, and with which probability. To continue this digression a step further, it is worth noting that the basis for such a contingent forecast may range from sheer hunches, through observed correlation patterns from the past (or from highly analogous settings), to theories. The latter are, of course, the preferred basis for contingent forecasts, inasmuch as they not only take account of changes in correlation patterns over time, but also include some explanation as to why the specified outcomes might be expected.

Turning specifically to the need for conceptual clarity in our models and theories, I want to restate that a scientific theory is composed of logically consistent propositions so formulated as to be empirically or logically disconfirmable. Yet so many of the models (not to mention putative theories) in the social sciences run afoul of this requirement. One recurrent problem is the tendency to confuse a taxonomy and a model or theory. While a good taxonomy is necessary to the extent that it identifies the variables and classes thereof that will be used on the outcome or the explanatory side of a model, it is far from sufficient. Until we explicitly postulate the direction and strength of the empirical (as distinct from definitional or logical) associations between and among our variables, we do not have a model, and until most of those postulated associations have been empirically vindicated, we do not have a theory. Thus one way to recognize that we have something less than a model is to look for—and fail to find—explicitly hypothesized empirical associations between and among the variables. Were we to invoke this simple test more often, we would be less gullible, confused, and confusing. Similarly, we cannot claim to have a theory unless we have a model, outcomes predicted by it, and an explanation for those outcomes.

Empirical propositions, whether hypothesized or demonstrated, must meet standards of conceptual clarity. They must be articulated in ways that differentiate a given outcome from its putative causes and consequences and from the motivations of the actor. It is one thing to hypothesize the causes or consequences of a given set of behaviors, but quite another to embed both the act and its associated phenomena in the same variable. One of the more glaring examples is found in the so-called pattern variables of Parsons (1951), which classify behavior not by the action actually taken, but by its "meaning" for the social system and its alleged purposes and/or consequences: pattern maintenance, integration, goal attainment, and adaptation. Whether a given act has a given consequence, not to mention whether that consequence was intended, should be a matter of empirical observation, rather than a priori assertion (Singer 1980). Nor, one might add, does it help to use categories whose mutual exclusiveness and logical exhaustiveness are dubious. Whereas the need to differentiate between an event on the one hand and its cause, purpose, or consequence on the other may seem self-evident, one detects in the social sciences today a remarkable willingness to describe events in terms of their "deep structure" and "meaning" for those involved or for the system in which they occur. Such premature "explanation" is no more likely to produce powerful theories than the mere piling up of unrelated observed correlations.

## THE APPLICATION OF KNOWLEDGE

The problems diagnosed above represent but a fraction of the difficulties that stand in the way of a systematically developing body of knowledge regarding political violence. Nonetheless they provide a partial explanation for our lack of progress. Let us turn next to some of the problems associated with the *application* of conflict research findings. The first problem is that of goal selection by political actors, the second is what affects the realization of these goals. A widely shared notion among social scientists and social practitioners, many of whom differ sharply in other respects, is that the selection of goals (or preferred outcomes) is a purely normative, and hence subjective, matter. That easy and familiar assumption needs to be challenged on two counts. One is that humans are not really as divergent as is claimed when it comes to preferred outcomes. If we look far enough ahead in time, and use sufficiently general values, we find rather broad agreement among people of quite disparate nations, classes, ideologies, and personalities. For the global system and its regional, national, and other subsystems, most people would like to see high levels of physical security, material well-being, freedom from coercion, opportunity for self-actualization—and a relatively equal distribution of these four individual values (Singer 1971).

Even if we get more specific and more immediate, I suspect that the convergence would remain rather high. The more difficult problem comes only when we recognize the extent to which we differ on the *means* to these ends. And although normative considerations enter into one's choice of social instruments and procedures, these preferences are more dependent than we often appreciate on one's theoretical biases, knowledge about social dynamics, and the epistemological criteria invoked in evaluating social arguments. In other words—and this is the second count—we probably support, acquiesce in, or oppose social policies to a considerable degree according to the credibility of the contingent forecasts upon which they rest.

To the extent that this assertion is correct, it follows that our task is not just one of discovering which conditions and events are most and least conducive to nonviolent conflict resolution in which types of setting. To bring these discoveries to bear on the political process, it is essential that those whom we seek to reach are sufficiently sophisticated to distinguish between reproducible evidence and mere authoritative assertion, to take the extreme ends of the knowledge-belief continuum. Thus it behooves us to attend as much to the education of our audiences as we do to the solidity of our research; credibility depends as much on the recipient's cognitive competence as on the sender's skill and style. From this it follows that we dare not play the game of political persuasion in the traditional ways. If we do—and thus rely on the rhetorical tricks that reactionaries, radicals, and reformers have all used over the centuries—we will not only perpetuate the appalling mix of cynicism and gullibility that have marked the erratic and often disappointing road to a decent social order, we will also lose most of the political arguments, given the preferences of the epistemologically naive for simple solutions and less complex scenarios. Thus, in addition to the positive need for epistemological education in the schools, the media, and the corridors of power, there is a negative warning. No matter how urgent the specific issue may seem, we should refrain from the sort of simplistic rhetorical argument that short-sighted activists have used with fatal frequency since time immemorial. Their use will achieve little more than the recontamination of social communication channels.

Closely related to this issue is the issue of audience selection. All too often, we find incremental reformers concentrating on the political elites, and radical revolutionaries concentrating on the urban or rural masses. Assuming that most of us who do research on the causes of violence and the conditions of nonviolent conflict resolution are radical incrementalists (that is, we see the need for radical changes in the structure and culture of the social order, but find compelling the moral and empirical arguments for an incremental strategy), I would urge greater attention to the counter-elites. This is because the elites seldom have the incentive, the vision, or the competence (recall Weber's felicitous allusion to "a trained incapacity") to reconsider their assumptions, their goals, or their criteria of evidence, whereas the masses seem likely to continue in their cycles of alienation and activism until serious reform in political debate as well as in political action has taken root. The counter-elites, on the other hand, may well have that combination of concern and competence that could make them considerably more responsive to reproducible evidence and close reasoning in the pursuit of incremental, but radical, reform. This is not to suggest that we ignore the others, but that, as a matter of pragmatism and tactics, we address our evidence and our associated epistemological premises primarily to those who are most free to consider major system changes and most able to evaluate complex contingent forecasts.

In addition to these rather long-range considerations, let me suggest one possible payoff from our research in the short run. I refer to the construction and testing of "early warning indicators" that might serve two purposes of a pragmatic sort. First, even though we may be some distance from reasonably solid explanatory theories in our respective fields, there can be some valuable spinoff in the form of findings that show under which conditions or in the train of which events certain types of conflicts turn ugly and violent. If, for example, we discover (as we have in ongoing research of the Correlates of War project) that 75 percent of the 225 major-power confrontations occurring since 1816 ended in war under conditions of military parity and rapidly escalating expenditures, whereas the overall frequency of such escalation was only 13 percent, we can suggest two policy implications. One is that under these conditions it is particularly crucial to avoid confrontations and the other is that if history is any guide any effort to move from parity to superiority is a highly dangerous enterprise. Such knowledge in the hands of opponents and critics of contemporary security policies in the United States and the Soviet Union might enhance the credibility of their warnings.

The second purpose of such indicators is to call attention to the flimsy base of knowledge upon which such decisions often rest and to emphasize the importance of bringing more knowledge—even of a purely correlational sort—to bear on the policy process. In a recent anthology (Singer and Wallace 1979) one finds nine papers that utilize quantitative indicators to postdict the escalation of a variety of intra- and international conflicts. Some of the work in this area even demonstrates the direction and rate of change over time in the accuracy of certain indicators of warning and/or assurance. Thus there may well be some "redeeming social value" in data-based conflict research, even though in most areas we have yet to construct explanatory models which are decisively confirmed.

## CONCLUSION

In this brief essay I have chosen not to lay out yet another blueprint for achieving a just and peaceful social order. Too many such plans have already been put forth, and the knowledge base on which they rest is much too thin. What we do know about effective conflict resolution and social change is much less than we need to know, and basic research must remain our highest priority. Rather I have chosen to assume that as our research goes forward and cumulative theory-building leads to a growing body of applicable knowledge, we will be in a better position—morally and intellectually—to propose and advocate specific political, economic, and social reforms.

As we move toward a more solid basis for understanding and reducing political violence, it will be essential that we help to prepare the mental climate in which our arguments, rival hypotheses, and contending predictive models can be intelligently and honestly evaluated and acted upon. This will require a degree of across-the-board educational work that few of us have yet appreciated. But if the reorientations suggested in the second section of this essay are to lay the groundwork for the systematic application of our research findings, those elaborated in the first section must first be acted upon. If our own epistemological house is in a state of disarray, there is little likelihood that the requisite knowledge will ever be acquired and codified, much less applied.

# CHAPTER SEVEN

———————— ■ ————————

# Social Science and
# Social Problems

AS WE EDGE CLOSER TO THE twenty-first century, we remain face to face with an issue that has bedeviled us for several centuries: the alleged conflict between the scientist and the humanist. For many humanists, it looks like a losing battle, with the physical artifacts and social consequences of science and technology moving inexorably toward ultimate conquest. In this Orwellian anti-utopia, we will all be fully "programmed"; what little choice we have will be multiple choice on an IBM card, and individuals will be converted into ID numbers in a computer's memory unit.

And for many technocrats, the question of victory or defeat remains open, but victory—if it comes—would mean a great increase in efficiency, early choice (or assignment) of career lines, and an effective mix of reward and punishment meted out by behavioral scientists cum political elites. The issue, of course, is not merely an aesthetic one; it becomes increasingly infused with political ideology. Some contemporary sociologists of a Marxist persuasion, for example, see industrial technology as leading inescapably to oppression and exploitation of the many by the few, with social science as the willing handmaiden to the emerging Leviathan.

The issue, thus drawn, is as ancient as it is unfortunate. From the Luddites of the early industrial revolution, smashing the mechanical looms of Manchester and Liverpool, to the university students of the past decade striking against computerized course registration, some have feared and some have cheered each technological and/or scientific advance. In contemplating what seemed to be the oppressive implications of science run-rampant on the opening of the Crystal Palace exhibition in the 1860s, Dostoevsky has his underground man sneer at the proposition that the laws of nature apply to human behavior, and then suggest that "we better kick over all that rationalism at one blow, scatter it to the winds, just to

Published by permission of Transaction Publishers, from *Society*, vol. 16, no. 5 (July/Aug. 1979), pp. 49–56. Copyright © 1979 by Transaction Publishers.

send those logarithms to the devil and to let us live once more according to our own foolish will."

## KNOWLEDGE AND ACTION

As might be surmised, the serious social scientist would have trouble with this dichotomy. The choices are considerably greater than suggested by these conventional stereotypes, and it would be tragic were this *not* the case. It is true enough that we can no longer afford the ignorance that lies behind the mindless application of every new discovery in the physical, biological, and the social sciences. But neither can we afford the equally mindless *resistance* to the application of new knowledge. Twentieth-century social science has been marked by many failures, along with some impressive gains, but our most costly one has been the failure to think through the relationship between knowledge and action.

This failure cannot, of course, be blamed solely on the social science community here or abroad. First, there are those ill-educated opinion makers in government, business, and the media whose social influence is matched only by their scholarly ignorance. Accepting and perpetuating the convenient stereotype of social science as the endless construction of new typologies and unpronounceable vocabularies, those who control our social institutions, shape our schools, and manage our media have done much to keep us in a state of thralldom. These elites have, to be sure, good reasons for keeping their constituents eternally ignorant about social phenomena, even if the reasons are seldom articulated. From the shaman and witch doctor of yore to the corporation lawyer, television commentator, and university president of today, their power and prestige rest all too heavily on the inability of their subjects and clients to identify a problem, classify it with comparable other ones, recognize the full range of possible responses, and predict which option is most likely to produce the desired outcome. Also at fault here are the physical and biological scientists—and the engineers who apply their research findings—following as they do a hoary double standard. Science, they usually suggest, is something done in laboratories by "real" scientists examining the intricacies of the material world. Not only are social phenomena inherently more complex, they would have us believe, but since they cannot be brought into the laboratory and subjected to controlled experiments, they just cannot be studied scientifically. Why else do these people speak condescendingly of the "so-called social sciences," and why do we perpetuate the idiotic distinction between the "natural" sciences and the social (unnatural?) sciences, or equally misleading, between the "hard" or "exact" sciences and the "soft" or "inexact" sciences?

Recognizing the sources of our ignorance is, of course, no assurance that they will be readily overcome. After all, the mythology and mystification are deeply ingrained in both the leaders and the led, the perpetrators and the victims of this ignorance. Those of us who teach, conduct research, or write about social phenomena will also have to mend our ways. And the purpose of this article is to examine a few of the things that might be done, in and out of the social sciences, to remedy this sorry state of affairs.

## SEMANTICS AND SOCIAL SCIENCE

While scholars tend to be notoriously tolerant, if not cavalier in regard to semantics, I would begin with that particular problem. It may be fashionable to not care "what they call it" as long as they "define their terms," but the consequence of that rule is that every article and lecture would have to be accompanied by a very large special-purpose dictionary. Let me begin, then, with certain concepts that are central to an understanding of the social science enterprise and whose misuse helps to perpetuate our ignorance: science, knowledge, theory, and rationality.

It would probably be better if we were to drop the noun "science" and rely more heavily on the modifier "scientific," used to describe the ways in which we go about the acquisition and codification of knowledge. In a nutshell, scientific research is that which uses explicit assumptions, reproducible procedures, reliable techniques of observation and measurement, and mathematical or statistical reasoning to interpret the resulting observations. Whether we seek knowledge about individual behavior, collective decision making, or global politics, doing so in a scientific way requires that we satisfy all of these criteria.

One problem with this definition is that when we talk of reproducible procedures, observation and measurement, and statistical reasoning, the idea of an experiment usually comes to mind, and correctly so. But as noted earlier, most of us think of experimental procedures as occurring only in the laboratory, and this is quite *incorrect*. Consider the amount of knowledge that has been acquired and codified by archeologists, astronomers, ethologists, geologists, and zoologists, for example, even though little of their research is conducted inside a laboratory. The same is true of psychologists, sociologists, economists, and political scientists, even though the idea of bringing scientific methods to bear on their concerns is a much more recent one. The important distinction between scientific and non-scientific (or more precisely, pre-scientific) work is not *where* it is done, but *how* it is done.

It follows from the above that it would be inaccurate to describe as scientific any research merely because it happens to be conducted in a laboratory, or it includes numbers, is polysyllabic, is conducted by one with a Ph.D., or even appears in a scholarly journal. Unless the basic methodological requirements are met, it may be scholarly, but it just is not scientific.

## KNOWLEDGE: COMMUNICATED INFORMATION

The objective of scientific research is to produce knowledge, and this term, too, can give us a bit of confusion. Knowledge, in the scientific sense, is information that—because of the way in which it is generated—can be checked out and more or less confirmed by many other researchers. I hedge and say "more or less" in view of the fact that, in any given problem area, there will often be two or more bodies of information that are thought of as knowledge, even though they are incompatible with one another. The point is that scientists are almost always working at the boundary between relatively hard knowledge and intelligent speculation, with their theories serving both as a bridge between and a canopy embracing the two. As different researchers move out into the more speculative realm, they discover regularities, and from these they normally try to infer some explanatory or "causal" principle. But since there are usually several different theoretical models guiding our research, we are often examining different explanatory phenomena, even though we may be trying to explain the same class of outcomes. Naturally enough, the more committed the researcher is to his/her favorite model, the more readily he/she will believe the early results and classify them as knowledge.

In other words, knowledge is not inherent in the universe but, roughly speaking, "in the eye of the beholder." It is, then, a coherent body of belief that is shared by many (but not all) specialists in a given field of inquiry. Further, it is a body of belief whose credibility should rest primarily (but given the universal frailties of the human mind, this is not always so) on the fact that it can be represented with verbal, numeric, graphic, or electronic symbols, and therefore communicated to others. Until information and ideas have been successfully communicated, they do not constitute scientific knowledge. Thus, when a scholar with a certain gleam in his eye claims to know something, but cannot communicate it, the rest of us rightly treat it as something less than knowledge; perhaps "revealed wisdom" is the apt phrase. This emphasis on communicability is not so much for the purpose of passing the knowledge on to posterity or across the oceans as it is to permit its confirmation, or as one school of thought would insist, its dis-confirmation. Usually, thanks to the norms of the scientific community, each of the more credible bodies of knowledge is put to the test over and over, leading in due course to its general acceptance or rejection.

## FEW SOCIAL SCIENCE THEORIES

This leads us to the third troublesome concept: that of theory. As I mentioned earlier, theories serve to bridge the *well* known and the *unknown*, with the *allegedly* known located at the boundary between the two. Thus, if a given area of investigation in a given discipline is fortunate enough to have a fairly solid theory, scientists will attempt to square the new findings and explanations with the existing theory, expanding, contracting, or otherwise modifying it to do so. The trouble is that scientists as well as laymen use the word in a dazzling variety of ways, meaning anything from a wild hunch, to a precise hypothesis, to a complex typology, to a well-confirmed body of knowledge. From my point of view, only the latter use is appropriate, and hunches, hypotheses, and typologies, not to mention forecasts, hopes, or moral convictions, are best so labelled. To summarize, then, we use theory here to mean a body of propositions that: offer a credible explanation of the outcome phenomena, are logically compatible with one another, are essentially consistent with other relevant knowledge, are stated in testable language, and—most of which have been successfully tested. Using these criteria, it is clear that social scientists have produced, so far, precious few theories, despite audacious or careless claims to the contrary. Whether our speculation takes the form of a long-winded tome, an elegant series of mathematical equations, or an ingenious computer program, it remains less than a theory until its essential propositions have passed a rigorous sequence of empirical and logical tests. Here, clearly, there is a pressing need for "truth in packaging."

## RATIONALITY

Finally, no discussion of social science and social practice is adequate these days without a brief reference to rationality. Because some laymen use it to cover anything of which they approve, and others decry it to reaffirm their individualistic abhorrence of science, it remains a matter of some confusion. To begin with, there is the trivial and not very helpful definition often found in economics and in game theory: rationality consists of nothing more than selecting the outcome that one most prefers. This is not helpful because social and personal *outcomes* are seldom selected; rather, *strategies* of behavior are selected in the hope that they will *lead to* the preferred outcomes. Thus, a more useful approach is to begin by distinguishing between rational on the one hand, and functional (or adaptive) on the other.

The word "rational" should, it seems to me, only be applied to the decision process: Has all relevant knowledge and information been considered and carefully evaluated? A highly rational individual or group makes its decisions in this way, trying to predict which behaviors are most likely to result in which outcomes. But rational selection of strategies, while it almost always improves performance, does not guarantee that the most functional or adaptive outcome will be achieved. Not only is the knowledge base insufficient to give us very high batting averages, and not only can others in the system, on learning of or guessing our preferences and our strategies, behave in a contrary way, confounding our predictions. In addition, the social psychological factors in decision making—especially when it is collective—tend to be stronger than the commitment to rational decision rules, and as a result, all sorts of irrational (anti-rational) and nonrational (extra-rational, such as interoffice conflict over power or money) factors mess up the process.

To put it another way, we not only need more knowledge to get more rational behavior in social decision making, but we also need people who have access to that knowledge, and know how to evaluate, assimilate, and apply it. Needless to say, few such skills are found in the products of our liberal arts colleges and law schools; thus, even if we were to achieve major advances in our knowledge of economic or political or sociological phenomena, that would only be part of the game. Unless social scientists are as good at their teaching as they are at their research, the chances of their research findings leading to any improvement in the human condition will remain all too small.

## DIVIDED DISCIPLINES

By now, it should be clear that I think that the social sciences *could* have had a major impact, for good or for evil, in our search for a dignified existence, but that the impact to date has been negligible. Let me return to the future possibilities later in this article, but a brief overview of the structure and culture of the social science establishment—present and predicted—would seem to be in order first. What are some of the dominant characteristics of the way in which we go about our research, our teaching, and our social action? What changes are underway or likely? How desirable are they? As most of my readers know, there is a professional field known as "the sociology of science" and some of these questions are regularly dealt with by those professionals. But since the sociology of science—like the history of science field—has produced, in my view, precious little hard knowledge and only an occasional insight, it seems appropriate for a practitioner to step back and take a clinical and impressionistic look at his guild. As a matter of fact, if all of us were asked to do so from time to time, we could probably become more sensitive to the sins of omission and commission that continue to mar our research and teaching, and thus increase the likelihood of gradually liberating humanity from oppression as well as incompetence.

There are, of course, all too many factors at work—within, between, and outside the social science establishment—that inhibit our drive for integrated and cumulative knowledge, but one of the most critical is that of the division into separate disciplines. To be sure, as the size and number of universities grew in the U.S. and in Europe, particularly after World War II, it made considerable sense to depart from the earlier organizational patterns. That is, one found all the social sciences in a single department at most American colleges and universities for a good many years, and often they included philosophy, religion, and history faculties as well.

Now, the differences among the professors in such "integrated" departments were not merely those of subject matter. Given such additional differences as the age and legitimacy of the discipline and the peculiarities of each such department of social sciences (or, quite justifiably in those days, social studies), there were also bound to be interesting if not dramatic differences of intellectual style. Alongside of such substantive differences as that between political science and economics (and there is now a movement toward reintegrating them as political economy), one found differences as to levels of analysis such as micro-level individual psychology vs. the macro-level, collective emphasis of the others.

There were also differences of epistemology: ideas as to how knowledge is generated, how it is evaluated, and different criteria as to what constitutes knowledge. Even today, it is a rare social science department that has more than a handful of members committed to social science in any literal sense of the term; perhaps half the sociologists, anthropologists, and political scientists in the world today should be, by intellectual style and epistemology, in departments of either philosophy or history.

In addition to providing an intellectually friendly context for teachers and researchers of relatively similar orientations, this trend toward decentralization permitted a greater variety of approaches to the study of social phenomena. When, for example, Mannheim and Marx are the fashion in anthropology, or structuralism dominates sociology, or political science has generally embraced an antiinstitutional approach, separateness permits the other disciplines to go their separate ways. Given the faddishness and cyclical nature of these preferences, and the relative absence of scientific justification for them, this is not a negligible advantage. It is bad enough that revisionism and counter-revisionism appear and reappear with appalling regularity in one or another discipline, but if *all* of them followed the *same* couturier-like schedule, each generation of students would be short-changed regardless of their course selections, and even less cumulative research would occur.

## COSTS OF PAROCHIALISM

On the other hand, the disciplinary division is not without its costs. Most serious is the extent to which these barriers encourage a theoretical and methodological parochialism that has stunted our collective growth. At the risk of a slight overstatement, we find widespread ignorance of one another's fields. The macro-social disciplines remain woefully unaware of the psychologists' discoveries, and as a result we find putative theories (especially in economics and political science) that are utterly inconsistent with the knowledge that psychologists have generated over the past half century or so. At the same time, there is precious little in the way of an integrated scientific theory in psychology, partly because psychologists remain equally naive about political, social, and economic phenomena.

Now, some have urged that ignorance or even incorrect assumptions as to how individuals and/or groups behave in certain situations is not a serious problem. Economists, for example, are fond of saying that assumptions need not be true as long as they are useful, and that as long as their models do a good job of predicting, we need not fault either the models or the assumptions on which they rest. But this overlooks two problems. First, most of the models do an adequate job predicting for only a limited temporal and spatial domain. Thus, very few economists were able to predict the simultaneous occurrence of both inflation *and* unemployment that the U.S. has experienced in the 1970s, and it may be that their assumptions about "economic man"—not to mention their notorious lack of interest in long-term retrospective studies—are at fault.

Second, despite the folklore to the contrary, *prediction* is neither the major purpose nor acid test of a theory; the goal of all basic scientific research is *explanation*. A strong explanatory theory will—because it is better able to account for and explain the effects of changing conditions—provide a more solid base for predicting than one that rests on observed covariations and postdictions alone. And since by definition it is built around fairly hard knowledge as to how individual and collective decision makers respond to changing stimuli, it permits us to trace, and hence explain, the entire causal process from background conditions to observed and predicted outcomes. The alternative, adequate as a short-run expedient, is to "black box" the human perceptions, thought processes, and behaviors that serve to link background conditions and stimulus events to the observed outcomes, in order to get on with the testing of alternative predictive and postdictive models. But, once we have narrowed these contending models (and if they are not explanatory in a fairly complete sense, we had best not call them theories) down to one or two that are relatively consonant with the observed "referent" world, we must return to the individual and group psychology of the decision processes. Often, familiarity with the theories, models, and findings of psychology and group dynamics is all that is necessary, but usually that knowledge only helps to *clarify* the explanatory options rather than to definitely select from among them. Were those two disciplines further along, we macro-social scientists would often be able to "plug" their micro-social theories directly into our models, or better still, build them in from the beginning.

This, then, is a major liability of the often impermeable boundaries between and among the disciplines. While no one expects each of us to fully master the work of all the other social sciences, we should be much more familiar with their concepts and findings than we are, and a breaching of the interdisciplinary barriers would be an important step in that direction.

## INTERDISCIPLINARY FOCUS

Several partial remedies come to mind. Perhaps the place to begin is with undergraduate education, which seems to become more and more specialized and parochial, especially when jobs are scarce and students are encouraged to get career-oriented training rather than a broad education in college. Ironically, by encouraging very career-oriented programs for their undergraduate and graduate students, scientists and humanists alike not only contribute to parochialism. They also jeopardize their *own* career prospects, while aiding only those who teach in schools of business, law, engineering, medicine, etc. Were we to emphasize the importance of a broad and rigorous education to a fuller and more effective personal as well as professional life—and actually *offer* such an education—the decline in enrollments might be reversed. Why should students study sociology or political science when the jobs are in social work and in law? Similarly, why should midcareer people return to college or graduate school, if the major justification for school is preparation for a job they already have?

Were we to look not only at the 18–21 age cohort (of which only about one-third begin college) but at all adults, and then construct (some would say reconstruct) a solid, broad, and rigorous curriculum, there might well be a reversal of the declining enrollment syndrome.

In addition to encouraging a more integrated social science program for all those majoring in any one of them, we might also build more of our courses around a given set of theoretical and/or policy *problems*, rather than around a catalog of the given discipline's body of knowledge (often more putative than real) and theories (most of which really are something less). This would give our courses more focus, and reduce the student's sense of being adrift in a welter of concepts and abstract schemata. More important to the issue before us, it would encourage teacher and student alike to range beyond the disciplinary boundary in the search for solutions. The *problem* might well be located within a single discipline (juvenile delinquency, racial discrimination, or war come to mind), but the factors that *account* for these outcomes are certainly not going to be found in the literature of any one discipline. Of course, this solution has its risks, and when consciousness-raising and relevance are the order of the day, we can end up with courses that are frivolous, if not downright mischievous.

At the graduate level, the need for an interdisciplinary (or transdisciplinary) focus is even greater, since it is here that the next generation of professional social scientists is being educated. Ignorance of, indifference to, and even contempt for our sister disciplines are all too common in the M.A. and Ph.D. programs, partially because those teaching at a given moment have themselves been reared in a relatively parochial culture. Several suggestions come to mind in addition to more of a problem-oriented focus. First, since almost every department includes a few people with strong interest and some competence in one or more of the other social sciences, we might offer first-year graduate students a seminar on, for example, "The Related Disciplines and World Politics." (I introduced such a course at Michigan in 1964 and taught it for several years, but it was discontinued because of declining student interest and its marginal importance for professional placement.) A second possibility is to increase the number and variety of "cognate" courses in the graduate program. Typically, the Ph.D. student will take only two or three seminars in another department, and will be discouraged from exploring additional courses, not to mention additional departments. By cutting back on what I take to be a surfeit of highly specialized courses and seminars in the same subject area (my department offers six different graduate courses on foreign policy alone, most of which are partially and inevitably redundant), there would be more time for the work suggested above.

Another option is to bring back a practice that has been largely abandoned of late: seeing that faculty and graduate students of several departments are given greater opportunity for professional interaction. Partly, this can be achieved by making our seminars less parochial, with the above-mentioned focus on problems rather than on disciplines, making them more useful and attractive to students from neighboring departments. Then there is the possibility of locating social science faculties in the same building; at Michigan, for example, political science is in the same building with English and history, while anthropology, sociology, economics, and psychology are each housed separately. Equally important is the interdisciplinary colloquium, so popular in the 1950s and 1960s, and now virtually unknown. For graduate students to hear and participate in these would be an opportunity to broaden perspectives and learn more of the concepts, findings, and methods of their sister disciplines. Finally, another way of breaking out of today's parochialism would be for one or more of the foundations to support postdoctoral fellowships in related disciplines. Having been the victim of an extremely limited doctoral curriculum in the late 1940s and early 1950s, I was one of about 30 young scholars "salvaged" by a Ford-financed year, in my case, at Harvard's Department of Social Relations in 1957–58. Parenthetically, that marvelously interdisciplinary department is now all but defunct.

While most of the preceding discussion is addressed to the divisions that separate the disciplines, a brief reference to those divisions that "bind" them might also be in order. What I mean by this phrase is that the efficacy of the social science community has been inhibited not only by the divisions that separate the disciplines but also by those that unite them. Space does not permit any extended treatment of them here, but we should note in passing the mixed effects of such alleged issues as qualitative vs. quantitative methods, theorizing vs. experimenting, deductive vs. inductive research strategies, and institutional vs. behavioral approaches, not to mention the ubiquitous facts vs. values issue, to which we will, however, return in the concluding pages.

## PROFESSIONAL SCHOOLS AS AN ALTERNATIVE

If the standard social science departments at the leading universities suffer from as many liabilities as suggested here, and are thus not performing as well as they might on either the research or teaching side, it is not surprising that alternatives have been explored. And while it may seem unconventional to include schools of education and library science as well as schools of social work, law, and public administration under the same rubric, all of these are engaged in the effort to prepare people for careers in applied social science. That is, their students are, in principle, expected to learn enough to then go out and solve social problems that range from educating our youngsters, managing our libraries, aiding our disadvantaged, and settling our conflicts, to carrying out within a broad discretionary range the general policies decided upon by our legislatures. Do these enterprises show much prospect of turning out well-rounded, intellectually rigorous, and methodologically competent professionals? Despite their generally high prestige and their continued growth, my conclusion is clearly in the negative.

Taking schools of social work, education, and the burgeoning field of library science, let me tempt the wrath of my colleagues and suggest what is wrong with this popular solution. While they usually begin with a healthy commitment to interdisciplinary social science training, the professional guild mentality usually takes over before too many years, making for an increasingly lethal case of tunnel vision for both faculty and student. Even worse, what begins as an interdisciplinary culture often becomes a *non-disciplinary* one, in the sense that professional school faculty and students are physically and intellectually isolated from the mainstream; and they develop their own organization within the university, create their own professional societies, and inexorably begin to publish their own scholarly journals. They increasingly lose touch with the research community in the relevant social sciences, and pick up research findings or methodological innovations years later and often in watered down or emasculated form. And, as if to guarantee intellectual isolation and cultural lag, they end up offering their own inadequate versions of courses that are better (if not magnificently) taught in the substantive departments. While this may seem an overly harsh summary, and no reproducible evidence is adduced, it reflects many conversations with students and graduates of these programs as well as some familiarity with their course outlines, textbooks, and scholarly journals. If professional schools of social work, education, or library science *are* the answer to disciplinary barriers, the cure has to be viewed as worse than the disease.

## LAWYERS AND SOCIAL SCIENCE

Somewhat similar is the situation of law schools in the U.S., and to a lesser extent, in Europe. To be sure, this professional training is not even intended to be a response to the interdisciplinary problem, nor can it be viewed as an exercise in applied science. It is, rather, a straightforward effort to train people in a technical field for filling technical positions, allegedly the same as in medicine or engineering. But whereas the latter two build their training program to a considerable extent on the knowledge generated by the biological and physical sciences respectively, very few law curricula include courses that rest on social science knowledge, not to mention social science methods. When a law school adds a part time economist, political scientist, or psychologist to its faculty, it is often seen as a concession to some silly vogue, to be temporarily and embarrassingly endured. The "true professional" needs no such frills in his/her education.

The good news that many of today's law graduates never practice law is overshadowed by the bad news that lawyers are still the most numerous professional group in most legislative bodies, including the U.S. Congress, and staff many of the top positions in the federal bureaucracy. That is, the American polity is largely run and managed by people whose only exposure to the social sciences may have been introductory psychology, intermediate economics, and a senior seminar on the presidency. Thus, when a law-trained functionary refers to the evidence in support of a policy he advocates, it is useful to remember that the difference between evidence in the legal and the scientific sense is far from negligible.

## TRAINING FOR RESEARCH

Turning to graduate schools or programs of public policy or public administration, generalization is more difficult, partially because they are less homogeneous than the professional schools which, after all, have to satisfy accreditation boards of their respective guilds. It is also more difficult because the development is largely a recent one, and their curricula are still in a state of flux. But the omens are hardly encouraging, if one examines the course outlines, converses with their faculty and students, or reads their fast-multiplying journals. While they do tend to be interdisciplinary, with economic models and methods as well as some sociology included alongside of political science, they seem quite like these three disciplines in their disdain for the findings of the social psychologists.

Equally serious, in my view, is the basic premise behind the creation of these schools and programs in the first place: that the preparation for policy roles in government should be quite different from preparation for a research or teaching role. I would agree that it should be radically different from that given to the lawyers who end up in government, but it should not deviate fundamentally from that found in the better social science M.A. and Ph.D. programs now being offered. That is, we need not expect policymakers to *do* a great deal of research, but unless they learn how it *should* be done, they will be in no position to either initiate research grants to universities and think tanks, or to evaluate the results that come in. Further, how can we expect social science research results to be applied to public policy decisions if the policymakers do not know—and are therefore hostile to—what social science is about? As difficult as it is to achieve constructive communication between the researcher and the legally trained functionary, the problem vis-à-vis a traditionally trained, pre-scientific, product of these programs in the U.S. and Western Europe is even greater. At first blush, some of the newer programs look quite scientific in orientation, but learning about econometric models of the business firm and perhaps applying them to the foreign ministry of China is not likely to produce reliable forecasts of that nation's diplomacy. And picking up some linear programming skills, but learning nothing about the measurement of social conditions, hardly leads to high-quality "evaluation research" (which is the trendy name for estimating the effects of an innovative welfare program, for example). In sum, these efforts to overcome disciplinary barriers may well produce people who are successful in their career advancement, but we had better not count on them for rational problem solving or social solutions that are adaptive and functional for their communities.

## KNOWLEDGE, PRACTICE, AND ETHICS

Throughout this discussion, I have implied that our concern with social science research and teaching is not "merely academic." Let me now spell out the connection more explicitly, indicating the ways in which our knowledge—and lack thereof—can affect the human condition. Prediction is, of course, the "name of the game," in several senses. First, those who make policy decisions are essentially engaged in predictions, usually of a contingent nature. That is, they (in principle) lay out a set of policy options, try to predict the consequences of each, and then select that action which they believe will produce the most desirable—or avoid the least desirable— outcome. Second, they try to predict which sectors of the public—interest groups, legislative factions, other executive agencies, etc.—will support, oppose, facilitate, or sabotage which policy alternative if selected. And in the foreign or military policy realm, they also try to predict how other governments and *their* domestic groupings might respond to each of the policies, if selected. Third, individuals who are involved in the decision process will also try to predict the extent to which their personal support, neutrality, or opposition vis-à-vis each of the options might affect their own careers, future credibility and clout, etc.

It should, however, come as no surprise to be reminded that the accuracy of these contingent forecasts has not been particularly high, in any part of the world. Moreover, most of the social science evidence to date suggests that virtually all social phenomena—from child rearing to the arms race— are becoming more complex and interdependent. It also suggests that domestic and foreign policy prediction has become less accurate in the post-World War II period. The connection seems not only obvious, but because the consequences of erroneous forecasts tend to be more destructive and widespread than in the past, ominous as well. There may have been a time when societies could afford to muddle through, but it is probably long past. Not only are the implications of a high error rate more devastating in the physical, economic, and social sense, but in addition, more and more people are refusing to put up with the consequences of policy decisions of which they are the intended or unintended victims.

It will, of course, be argued that I badly miss the mark here, and that poor policy and its deleterious effects are not the result of substantive ignorance or methodological naiveté. Rather, it can be argued, it is the result of an all-too-sophisticated and/or callous indifference on the part of the ruling elites. While no social scientist would suggest that these ethical failings can be dismissed, many would remind us of two points. First, ignorance of the consequences of public policy choices creates an opportunity for all sorts of chicanery, and second, high error rates in policy forecasting can lead to disasters even when elite motivation *is* perfectly wholesome.

Let me expand on these. In the public and private debate and discussion that precedes, accompanies, and follows most policy decisions, there are two major sources of disagreement. One concerns the *desirability* of alternative outcomes, and typically we find a variety of oft-conflicting goals and objectives being pursued, and not always explicitly. The other concerns the *likelihood* of arriving at certain outcomes, with a variety of viewpoints as to how best achieve one or another of the objectives being pursued.

Furthermore, the less evidence available on which to base the contending predictions, or the less competent the decision makers are in assessing that evidence, the more room there is for the play of irrational and extra-rational arguments. If, for example, there is little credible evidence available in support of two contending predictions as to how best achieve an agreed objective, participants in the governmental process will come down on the side of those with the most charisma or clout. This is especially likely when there is a strong consensus, in and out of government, for that particular strategy.

## RESEARCH AND THE VIETNAM WAR

One of the more dramatic examples can be drawn from the Vietnam War. Leaving aside for the moment those whose objective was the creation of an American colony in Southeast Asia, most of the argument was over the best way to prevent a "Communist takeover" or to "preserve the freedom of the Vietnamese people." Behind the debate over military escalation, bombing, mining of harbors, and the like was the assumption that a victory for the Vietcong-Hanoi forces would lead to Communist control over all of Indochina, with Laos and Cambodia falling like dominoes. This would, in turn, culminate in a permanent stranglehold on the region by agents of international communism, be they of the Moscow or Peking variety. Had high-quality research findings on the outcome of civil wars in underdeveloped regions over the past 75 years or so been available, these predictions could have been more effectively challenged. That is, some opponents of U.S. policy predicted that the regimes themselves would continue to change regardless of which side won the next round militarily. They argued that it probably would not matter whether the left-wing or right-wing autocrats ended up on top, because neither could govern effectively for long without some role for those on the other side. Further, many critics predicted that whatever the political complexion and similarities of the regimes, they would resume the pursuit of their respective interests the way sovereign states always have, including the resort to war. Finally, many urged that neither the Soviets nor the Chinese could control the domestic or foreign policies of these nations.

At this writing, it seems that these critics were much more accurate in their forecasts than were the establishment spokesmen, but the cost of demonstrating this has already been astronomical to all parties, with the second- and third-order effects still ahead of us. The conventional wisdom and bureaucratic momentum, with plenty of amplification from the media, rode roughshod over these critics, who could argue only from speculation or from morality. The fact that the government spokesmen had no hard evidence either did not matter; the burden of proof in U.S. foreign policy since World War II has consistently fallen on those who did not accept the standard Cold War assumptions and predictions. Had there been available during the 1945–1975 period a respectable body of social science research findings in the area of international conflict, along with officials who knew how to evaluate and apply those findings, the world might be a safer, more prosperous, and more humane place than it is today.

Returning to the point that we may be more often the victims of greed and ambition than incompetence, and that social science knowledge helps little in the face of individual or collective avarice, I would return to one of my opening comments: political elites and (usually) counter-elites tend to prefer ignorance on the part of the led. The less the general public knows about social phenomena and what policies lead to what outcomes, the more easily it can be manipulated. Again, that manipulation *can* occur over the opposition of the outs, but more often it occurs with their tacit if not overt connivance. In U.S. foreign policy, for example, bipartisanship has been little more than a smokescreen for a "conspiracy of silence." During those decades in which today's disasters were gathering momentum, it was nearly impossible to find any public discussion of the arms race, environmental pollution, the depletion of energy sources, or inflation. Politicians of both major parties concentrated on all sorts of short-run questions and nonissues, ignoring the rather discernable trends, and the media played their accustomed and comfortable "show business" role. And now that these issues have finally become newsworthy, one can hardly suggest that the elites or the counter-elites are addressing them in a systematic and precise, not to mention scientific, fashion.

## TAKING SOCIAL SCIENCE SERIOUSLY

While the same unfortunate policies and decision processes could obtain even if the relevant social science knowledge and decisional expertise were available, at least the odds might be improved. There is no *guarantee* that major advances in the social sciences will improve the human condition, but it is virtually certain that no improvement can come *without* those advances. Thus, it behooves America and the world to begin taking social science seriously. But that is unlikely until more social scientists themselves take it seriously, and begin treating their profession as a public trust rather than a personal playground. This is, of course, not to suggest that we work on the problems assigned to us by the regime, in a way specified by the regime. Rather, we should ourselves determine which problems seem most important, most challenging, or both, and set to work, recognizing that the traditional distinction between basic and applied research has always been exaggerated. In the social sciences especially, almost all research is *applicable* research, and if our research and our teaching become more imaginative and more thorough, that applicability could redound to the advantage of almost all of us. Clashes of interest there will always be, but with a small dose of altruism and a massive dose of scientific competence, we might just make the world safe for such clashes and conflicts.

## BUILDING A CUMULATIVE SCIENCE

Since our theme in this symposium is on the future of the social sciences, and most of this essay has dealt with their history, let me shift briefly from the retrospective to the prospective focus. To use my earlier phrase, here is a dramatic illustration of the *contingent forecast:* If social scientists continue as they have in the past half century, the prospects are foreseeably grim. We and our work will by and large be ignored in coping with the big issues of our times, and most of us will be called on, as in the past, to do the dirty work: improve the performance of combat crews, sell office seekers to a cynical yet gullible citizenry, draft testimonials to the wisdom of those in power, or most pathetically of all, crank out consciousness-raising polemics against the establishment without the foggiest idea of how things got this way or how they might be remedied.

If, conversely, we pull up our socks, and stop playing around as we oscillate between despair and euphoria, and begin the hard task of building and utilizing a cumulative science of human affairs, the picture need not be grim. The current drift of humanity is hardly an encouraging one, and if the social scientists of the world do not take a hand in it, we could easily stumble into the last, final, catastrophe.

# CHAPTER EIGHT

■

# Campaign for a U.S. Peace Academy

ON SEVERAL OCCASIONS SINCE the American Revolution, thoughtful observers have called for the establishment, in one form or another, of a national peace academy. The first was President Washington himself, and the most recent is a coalition of concerned members of the House of Representatives. But like most innovative proposals, this time the idea was initiated by an outside group—the National Peace Academy Campaign—that reflected a variety of professional backgrounds as well as a range of political orientations. And as in any such campaign, the initiators sought to elicit support from whomever might be helpful in one role or another, whether to lend prestige, expertise, or mere numbers to the effort. As chairman of the Peace Research Committee of the International Political Science Association as well as former president of the Peace Science Society, I was one of the all-too-likely candidates. When first approached, my reaction was relatively skeptical, and since the issues that exercised me might be similar to those entertained by others, let me briefly raise several of them here.

While any increase in the number and strength of pro-peace institutions in the United States is inherently worthwhile, it is not difficult to think of the mischief that *could* ensue from the establishment of a peace academy. Like many sound principles, there is always the danger of distortion in practice. One possible danger is that the academy could, if established, turn out to be more of a propaganda and/or consciousness-raising institution than is desirable. In this vein, three equally unattractive directions are possible:

• An overly nationalistic, America-is-always-right orientation, such that it could become essentially an instrument of U.S. foreign policy (every nation has too many such institutions already);

Reprinted by permission of the *Bulletin of Atomic Scientists* (March 1979), pp. 84–86. Copyright © 1979 by the Educational Foundation for Nuclear Science, 6042 S. Kimbark Ave., Chicago, IL 60637, U.S.A.

• A dogmatic "Third World" orientation, in which the teaching, research, and public education activities take on a blend of vulgar Marxism and Third World propaganda; or

• The academy could become little more than a sermonizing agency, exhorting individuals, interest groups, and governments to "be good" and earnestly to pursue peaceful and conciliatory policies (surely we have enough of these as well).

My concern, then, is that such an academy could turn out to be a propaganda agency rather than a research, teaching, and public education agency. This is not to deny the importance of finally having, somewhere in the government, one agency whose mission is peace and whose message is clear. Certainly the Arms Control and Disarmament Agency has not fulfilled that role. Despite occasional moments of glory, it has served largely as "the poor man's Pentagon." We definitely need one agency that speaks for conflict resolution and conciliation, but that voice must reflect scientific knowledge, rather than conventional wisdom or a body of folklore.

This leads, in turn, to some of the assumptions from which the academy campaign proceeds, perhaps best articulated in the preamble to a resolution introduced in the 95th Congress by Rep. Helen Meyner of New Jersey, which calls for such an academy. Most of these assumptions are so reasonable that nothing need be said in this brief commentary, but two of them require cautionary comment.

The *first* of these states that the techniques of conflict resolution are teachable and usable. While no peace researcher or social scientist is likely to quarrel with the proposition, many of us *would* quarrel with the implication behind it: that there exists a well-founded body of techniques whose efficacy rests upon solid research and has been demonstrated in practice. In my judgment, there are many valuable ideas, insights, and anecdotes, coupled with a limited number of generalizations whose accuracy has been demonstrated by social scientists from various disciplines.

But the unanswered questions far exceed those that have only been partially answered; for many of the more plausible generalizations about techniques of conflict resolution, we often have equally persuasive reasons for believing the opposite generalization. For example, all of us can cite reasons why "broadening the agenda" can facilitate the resolution of a serious conflict; but we can also tell why, in certain cases, the desired outcome is more likely to result from *narrowing* the agenda, and dealing with the issues one at a time. Problems of this type are not only interesting, important, and controversial; they are also researchable, but such research has barely begun.

The *second* problematic assumption is that "the scarcity of highly trained and experienced negotiators" largely explains why more conflicts are not resolved by mediation and conciliation. But one reason for this scarcity is that we have only a marginal idea of what to teach them and how to train them. If the knowledge existed, we could readily find people to impart it to those technicians and specialists who would, in turn, apply that knowledge to specific, difficult cases. But we know much less than we should about the factors and processes that make some conflicts escalate to violence and others remain at a mild level of verbal disagreement. Thus, I would conclude that a lot more first-rate research is still required.

These comments lead to a consideration of the missions of a national peace academy, and their relative priority. In the current proposal, one finds the following missions: teaching of conflict resolution techniques; collecting data; forwarding public education; and coordinating research. The implication, however, is that no research would actually be conducted at or by the academy, and this could be quite unsatisfactory.

As already emphasized, our existing knowledge base is very limited, and the few empirically confirmed propositions have not been integrated into a coherent theoretical whole. Thus some scholars believe that war is more likely when the international system is highly bipolarized and when military-industrial capabilities are concentrated in the hands of one or two superpowers, and others believe that such bipolarization and concentration help to *reduce* the incidence of war. Careful research on the past century by competent social scientists so far supports *both* theoretical models, and much more work is required before this typically complex relationship is unraveled. Similarly, many behavioral scientists would advocate removing negotiators as far as possible from domestic political pressures, in order to increase their flexibility, while others suggest that negotiating flexibility rests largely upon maximum contact with political realities. To my knowledge, no systematic research on this important issue has been carried out and reported.

If ignorance of the consequences of our actions is a major obstacle to a less warlike world, and the requisite knowledge could indeed be generated by competent and creative researchers using systematic and reproducible procedures, the next question is "where?" Of course, much too much remains to be done for any single institution to conduct all of the necessary research. The resolution introduced by Rep. Meyner thus sensibly calls for the proposed academy to coordinate research that would ostensibly be conducted at universities and perhaps at private "think tanks." But I would urge that the proposed peace academy itself also conduct peace and conflict research.

My reasons are several. One is implicit in the above discussion: so much remains to be done that any increase in the number of high quality research centers is inherently desirable. But three additional considerations are relevant.

• Perhaps the most salient is the connection between teaching and research. Bluntly stated, those who are actually involved in the search for knowledge are—all else being equal—far better at teaching than those who are not. Unless a scholar is personally immersed in solving the problems of discovery, verification, and integration of findings, he or she will normally have a rather superficial understanding of the processes by which knowledge is acquired and codified. This is not surprising, and it is borne out day after day in the teaching that we see in primary and secondary schools, in the professional schools of social work, education, and librarianship, in our liberal arts colleges, and even in our universities.

While the fraction of teachers who are also doing research is progressively higher as we proceed from primary school to the university, the number is painfully low even at that higher level; perhaps 10 percent of the typical university faculty conducts 90 percent of its research. Similarly, the more its faculty engages in peace and conflict research, the better will be the teaching offered by the proposed academy.

• This leads in turn to a second important consideration: that of the academy's policy role. While other scholars and many practitioners would not put it as strongly, I suspect that a central factor in the error rate of most diplomatic and military decision-makers is ignorance, though not of the recent and contemporary *facts* of international affairs. One could, for example, seldom find practitioners whose grasp of historical events equalled that of a George Kennan or a Henry Kissinger, and some lesser-known policy-makers here and abroad with an equally impressive command of the facts.

I refer, rather, to ignorance of: (a) how facts fit together, and (b) how to evaluate rival hypotheses about that fit. Very few of all those who influence, make, and implement policies that affect war and peace have even the foggiest view of either. To be sure, they have all sorts of hunches as to which types of diplomatic behavior produce certain conditions, and strong views as to how to deal with different types of nations, but these are almost always anecdotal and impressionistic.

Thus, when confronted with a choice among several policy options, the typical decision-maker has little basis for predicting the likely results of choosing one or another of the available options. If we escalate when the other side backs down, and only discover after the outbreak of war that such a response led to war under similar conditions on 20 out of 25 prior occasions, many people will have died out of ignorance.

Equally dangerous is the inability of policy-makers to evaluate conflicting evidence. Knowing little about probability distributions and statistical inference, not to mention scaling and measurement of social phenomena, they can be all too gullible. During the Vietnam War for example, operations researchers (who often knew little about war or diplomacy) produced statistical analyses of body counts, pacified villages, and bombing sorties, usually emphasizing the success of U.S. policies there. But if the lawyers and other poorly trained officials had known something about scientific method, they might have been less impressed with all that computer printout.

To the extent that scientific research becomes one of the missions of the academy, its graduates will go on to policy positions having learned more about what *is* known as well as how to evaluate what is *allegedly* known. Such training could appreciably reduce the error rate in future international conflicts and thus the likelihood of stumbling into war. Equally important to the discussion at hand, the faculty members could move back and forth between research that is essentially knowledge-producing and work that is largely knowledge-applying. Those in the latter role could be available as consultants or seconded to other government agencies, negotiating teams, foreign governments, and international organizations. They would not give direct advice but would use their expertise to clarify for the responsible decision-makers the likely consequences of alternative options.

• Yet a third reason for including research among the academy's responsibilities is that of faculty recruitment. In general, the most knowledgeable and competent behavioral and social scientists carry a fairly steady research program along with their teaching. To induce these scholars to leave highly attractive university or other positions, the academy would almost certainly have to offer excellent opportunities for them to continue doing research, even if in a slightly different area.

Many other interesting problems and possibilities exist in connection with the establishment of a peace academy, and many have been treated in a series of small meetings, a variety of written and telephone exchanges, and a large conference at Emory University in March, 1978. I have only singled out here a few of the more interesting ones, and I hope that these comments will stimulate wider awareness of and interest in the peace academy proposal. Those who have waged this political and educational campaign have not only put forth a potentially valuable idea, but have also given all scientists (physical, biological, and social) who are concerned with the war-peace question a fine opportunity to re-examine the complex relationship between knowledge and action. Our cliches are all too common, and some of them could turn out to be fatal.

# CHAPTER NINE

——— ■ ———

# A Manhattan Project for
# War Prevention Research

I. Introductory Assumptions

    A. Major power war is not inevitable, but neither is peace; historical evidence and intuitive analysis suggest a probability of about 0.3 for war between U.S. and USSR in the next two decades.

    B. Such other global problems as lack of economic development, poverty, ignorance, famine, disease, mental illness, crime, racial oppression, etc., are unlikely to be solved or even ameliorated as long as war—and preparation for it—remains as likely and legitimate as it is now. Major progress on war prevention is essential to major progress on other problems.

    C. Political elites seldom "want" war, but:
        1. they often benefit politically from preparation for war.
        2. they often cannot predict the likely consequences of policy moves and thus often select the less appropriate policy.
        3. they often make policy choices on the basis of such extra-rational considerations as factional, bureaucratic, and individual interests because their/our knowledge base is too limited, and the inferences from it are not credible enough.

    D. Hard knowledge and reproducible evidence could/would:
        1. reduce the potency of the extra-rational (as well as ir-rational) considerations.
        2. increase the likelihood of correctly predicting the consequences of policy moves, and
        3. therefore be taken *fairly* seriously in due course.

    E. The truly desirable amount of knowledge base will "never" be acquired and codified—no less acted upon—but:

1. a number of relatively consistent generalizations are now in the literature (see Singer, "Accounting for International War: The State of the Discipline," *Journal of Peace Research*, Vol. 18, no. 1 (1981): 1–18).
2. even when data-based knowledge from the international system is inconsistent, weak or unavailable, certain generalizations from inter-group and inter-personal research may be nearly as relevant and useful.
3. certain principles are sufficiently "self-evident" that we may use them in our models, analyses, and predictions with relative confidence, despite the absence of systematic research.

F. War prevention is not the same thing as capitulation or appeasement, nor is it identical to the elimination of competition, rivalry, and conflict.

II. Illustrative Policy Problems of War Prevention

A. National Level and System Level Queries
   1. Which behaviors create structural and cultural conditions in the system that make war more likely five or ten years later?
   2. Which behaviors generate predictions and perceptions in the adversary that make intelligent crisis management more difficult two, five, or ten years later?
   3. Which behaviors generate political processes in the adversary's society that strengthen the hawkish elements and weaken the more prudent factions?
   4. Under which systemic or regional conditions is it essential to avoid confrontation or crisis, given that war is most likely then?
   5. Given the apparent fluctuations in inter-nation tension during long rivalry, are war prevention efforts more likely to be successful during the high-tension, low-tension, up-side or down-side periods? Which decisional structures are most efficacious or most dangerous at which phases of the process? Is secrecy more essential to war prevention at certain phases?
   6. Under which conditions, and vis-à-vis which types of adversary, are different behaviors most destabilizing? When to use threats, promises, rewards, punishments? When to increase military preparedness, when decrease, and when is it essential not to change?
   7. If the adversary is suffering losses of influence elsewhere in the system and/or if his regime is facing dissension/strong opposition at home or in satellite nations, is it more prudent to press him hard, or to ease up?
   8. When relative capabilities vis-à-vis the adversary are declining (or increasing or are stable) in the region or globally, is it more prudent to be aggressive or conciliatory or merely passive?

9. If one of the rivals has, and expects to continue, a steady and clear superiority in weapons technology, is it more prudent to *offer* concessions on the matter of arms control and reduction, to *demand* concessions, or to avoid negotiation?
10. Are there certain optimum levels of hostility, fear, etc. that rival regimes should strive to maintain at home? Can these levels get too low, too high? Which tension-generating and tension-reducing tactics are most effective, most reversible, etc.?
11. When formal negotiations have been agreed to, are the chances of overall agreement enhanced by a broad agenda or a narrow one? Is it better to deal with one problem at a time?
12. During periods of rivalry, is it safer to keep certain ideological or personality types out of power? If so, which types? How can they be identified and isolated politically?
13. During long rivalries is it safer to form countervailing alliances, coalitions, trade blocs, etc., or to perpetuate a more polycentric and/or flexible system structure?

B. Individual, Cultural, and Intra-Societal Level Queries
1. To what extent does the education process in most nations make for greater or lesser war proneness? Would more knowledge of social science methods and greater epistemological sophistication reduce the error rate in decision making, would the news media become more competent, and would the general public become less gullible?
2. How effective could cultural exchange, language training, and awareness of others' histories be in making a population less xenophobic and chauvinistic?
3. Does the childhood socialization of boys, in home, school, youth organizations, etc., perpetuate primitive notions of masculinity, courage and intrepidity, and are such notions a major contributor to war?
4. Do regimes that differ economically and politically "produce" citizens who systematically differ in their epistemological criteria, moral preferences and priorities, and problem solving competence?
5. To what extent does ethnic, religious, and linguistic discrimination in society increase the likelihood that the victims (and children of the victims) of such discrimination will gravitate toward careers (such as strategic analysis) that especially affect their nations' war-proneness.
6. Does discrimination lead to an exaggerated need to demonstrate excessive patriotism, or alternatively, create a sub-conscious desire to see the society suffer or be destroyed?
7. Would widespread knowledge of the consequences of nuclear or conventional war affect the tendency of the public or opinion

makers to support policies of potentially provocative weapon systems and military strategies? In which direction?

8. Would solid research and dissemination of the results re: economic conversion and the feasibility of phasing out military production and service help increase public support for more prudent and pragmatic security policies?

9. To what extent do the classification and treatment of disease, mental illness, and crime correlate with a nation's security policies and/or war-proneness?

III. Research Strategy Options for the Next Phase (not mutually exclusive)

A. Begin with the relatively solid data-based work that has been done, focussing on efforts to solve the "genuine puzzles" and on anomalies emerging from that work.

B. Begin with a literature review to ascertain:
   1. which explanatory models are taken most seriously by the scientific community.
   2. which models are most well-specified and/or empirically substantiated.
   3. which variables show strong post-dictive power—even if not embedded in well-specified explanatory models—and might thus be used for indicators of early warning and assurance.

C. Prepare tentative estimates as to which variables of promise:
   1. have been operationalized and validated sufficiently to command reasonable confidence.
   2. have been measured across a sufficient range of cases, years, nations, etc., but which still require some additional data-generation.
   3. show short-run variation and are not so slow-changing as to be only marginal in their political relevance.
   4. show relatively high manipulability; e.g., respond rather rapidly (weeks or months) to national behavior and discussion.

D. Side-step, largely or entirely, the improvement of existing theoretical models or the formulation and testing of new ones, and focus instead on the construction and validation of indicators of early warning and timely assurance (see Singer and Wallace, *To Augur Well: Early Warning Indicators in World Politics*, 1979).

E. Some division of labor, among the above strategies and/or others.

IV. Some Logistic and Organizational Suggestions

A. Establishment of a World Intelligence and Early Warning Center (see proposal in *Journal of Conflict Resolution* (1957) I/1 by Quincy

Wright, and the Snyder, Hermann, and Lasswell report on "Global Monitoring for Policy Intelligence and Appraisal," 1975).

B. Establishment of Information Exchange Center for Research in War Prevention.

C. Organization of Periodic "Data Confrontation" workshops.

D. Institutionalization of educational and research coordination between Soviet and American scholars.

E. Establishment of "permanent" Centers for War/Peace Research at one or more major universities with strong track records in rigorous and systematic work.

# PART THREE

■

# The Research Outlook
# and Options

*Whereas the previous four chapters considered some of the factors that
make basic research essential and looked at the intellectual-institutional
interface between policy and research, little was said about research strategies: the ways in which we might go about our research into the causes of
war, organize our ideas, measure the important variables, and so forth. In
this part, we do exactly that.*

*Chapter 10, as will be evident, was written in response to an invitation
to take on directly the arguments made by the more traditional scholars as
those of us working from a behavioral science orientation appeared on the
scene. Despite the attempt at satire, the argument itself is deadly serious
and unhappily as relevant today as in 1968. Chapter 11 is, in my view,
equally important inasmuch as most of us have little experience with the
quantification of social concepts, and without that sort of operational measurement, we cannot expect to articulate and test alternate explanations of
war or any other human activities. In Chapter 12, we challenge the proposition that real scientific research can only occur in a laboratory experiment. Chapter 13 is a somewhat facetious overview of those practices that
occur all too frequently and thus serve to inhibit the cumulative acquisition
and codification of social science knowledge.*

CHAPTER TEN

———————■———————

# The Incompleat Theorist:
# Insight Without Evidence

AS I WEIGHED THE PROS AND CONS of taking up the editors' challenging invitation to contribute to this volume, an unkind thought kept returning to me. Could it be, I wondered, that all of us are a part of some unconscious conspiracy such that we keep writing about what research in our field *should* or should *not* be, in order to avoid getting down to the hard work of doing it? Do we "hard science" advocates really *prefer* to theorize about theory and philosophize about method, and do the literati take advantage of this flaw in our characters to fling down the gauntlet from time to time? I wondered, further, if there was anything else to say. Wouldn't the publication of solid research findings constitute a more compelling demonstration than yet another hortatory essay? Wrestling with my conscience, and winning all too easily, I banished these subversive considerations to their rightful place in the subconscious, and reassured by the editors that it was merely a matter of adapting one or two of my earlier sermons on "the importance of being scientific,"[1] my thoughts turned into more constructive channels.

## I. SOME DELICATE DECISIONS

What strategy to follow? How could I engage my friends and colleagues—however errant in their ways—without seeming to attack them personally? Could I urge that they have sinned egregiously and then face them at the next professional meeting, or their fellow-sinners before classes tomorrow morning? Worse yet, how could I publicly differ with my behavioral science allies without giving "aid and comfort to the enemy"? One option would be to gracefully overlook the minor flaws in Professor Kaplan's excellent

From Klaus Knorr and James N. Rosenau (eds.), *Contending Approaches to International Politics*. Princeton, N.J.: Princeton University Press, 1969. Copyright © 1969 by Princeton University Press. Reprinted with permission of Princeton University Press.

paper and join in the American counter-attack against Professor Bull. Another would be to dismiss our errant colleague's position as beyond salvation and go on to an intimate discussion of some of the finer points raised by my fellow Midwesterner, strictly *entre nous*. Or, I could follow a recent ploy and turn to my own musings after a perfunctory nod of recognition that someone else was indeed in the room.[2]

Other options also come to mind, but the reader can already appreciate the delicacy of my role. On the grounds that we have seen altogether too many flanking movements in the friendly war between the intuitionists and the scientists, and too few direct engagements,[3] I decided to respond explicitly to Bull's opening barrage here. Whereas Kaplan does this in a more general fashion, my intention is to take up the charges specifically, *ad seriatim*. It also turns out that Professor Kaplan and I can defer our tête-à-tête for another occasion, inasmuch as Professor Levy's paper assures that he will not be ignored in this particular volume.

In Professor Bull's inventory of the scientific school's deadly sins, seven allegedly discrete propositions emerge, but despite claims to rigor and precision (p. 36) we quickly discover that at least one traditionalist is quite indifferent to the requirement that categories be conceptually comparable, logically exhaustive, and mutually exclusive. Rather than try to impose a degree of order on the scattershot arraignment, let me show how uncompulsive we behavioral science types can be, and skip about just as casually as the most discursive intuitionist.

After responding to these arguments with epistemological counter arguments and some anecdotal illustrations, I will try to formulate a position which may hopefully command not only the assent of the reader but of the prosecutor himself. In the process, I hope to demonstrate that the war between rigor and imagination in international politics is not only over, but that it was to some extent a "phony war" all along—a war which, despite its similarity to that which most other disciplines have been through, need not have been fought but for the recalcitrance of some and the exuberance of others.[4]

## II. ALLEGATIONS AND REJOINDERS

Let me turn, therefore, in a spirit of conciliation—if not ennui—to the all-too-familiar propositions by which it will once again be proven that the bee will never fly, the weather will never be predicted, the atom will never be smashed, and human nature (whatever that is) will never change. In his present incarnation, the agnostic intends to demonstrate (p. 26) that "the scientific approach has contributed and is likely to contribute little to the theory of international relations, and in so far as it is intended to encroach upon and ultimately displace the classical approach, it is positively harmful."

Before dealing with these charges, however, it is important to identify the perpetrators of these various crimes, or at least those who are included in my defense. By avoiding either the pejorative label of "scientism" or the misleading one of "behaviorism,"[5] Professor Bull helps us to avoid a good number of irrelevancies. Without going into all the definitional labyrinths, it should be emphasized that no scientific theory of international politics is possible if it only embraces *behavioral* phenomena; as the traditionalists have long appreciated, due attention must be paid to *institutional* phenomena, by which I mean structure, culture, and relationships. Moreover, no matter what our views on "reductionism," most adherents of the scientific school understand the need to study the behavior of ministries, governments, and nations (for example) as well as that of single individuals. Accepting, then, his label of "scientific" (or, to avoid being repetitive, the "behavioral science," "social science," or "modern" approach) it is necessary to note—as does our critic—the diversity within this school. Most relevant is the distinction between those who have merely borrowed the concepts and vernacular of the behavioral sciences and those who have gone the crucial extra step, and borrowed their research strategies and methods as well. Unfortunately, most of the criticisms leveled by Bull are directed toward the former, and show little familiarity with the work of the latter.

## The Puritan Intellect

The first fantasy one encounters in this morose recitation is the assertion that the scientific approach is so intellectually puritanical that it eschews the use of wisdom, insight, intuition, and judgment. Nonsense! If this were true, we would not only never write a word, but we would never address a class, consult for a government agency, cast a ballot, or even get up in the morning. The scientific view is that, while we can never be satisifed until the proposition in doubt (for example) has indeed been verified,[6] we need hardly decline into cerebral immobility while waiting for the final word. The important difference is that the prescientific chap equates "Eureka!" with divine revelation, while the more rigorous type permits himself that moment of pleasure for basking in the warmth of private discovery, and then gets on with the job of publicly visible, explicit, reproducible authentication.

Our classicist also urges that most of the important moral, as well as theoretical, questions "cannot by their very nature be given any sort of objective answer" (p. 26). While I concur with his aside that the conversations of science and of ethics are always inconclusive[7] (a somewhat milder charge), that is no reason to stop where we are, barely beyond the edge of superstition. On matters moral, scholar and layman alike have been emasculated by the folklore which sees the world of values and the world of facts as deeply and forever separate and distinct. At a certain level of generality, almost all men can find ethical consensus, but as we move toward the specific, we inevitably begin to part company. However, much of the division turns out to be not so much a matter of preference as it is one of prediction.

Very few western diplomats in 1939, for instance, *preferred* Nazi expansion in Central Europe, but most of them *predicted* that the Munich agreement would avoid it. And while few American leaders *preferred* a continuation of the war in Vietnam, many *predicted* in 1965 that rapid military escalation would terminate it. These were errors in prediction—which a more solid research base might have helped us avoid—more than disagreements over ends. To be more general, very few of those court astrologers who have urged the doctrine of "*Si vis pacem, para bellum*" on their leaders have actually preferred war; they merely predicted poorly in almost every case. In other words, even though there will inevitably be differences among men as to their preferred ultimate outcomes, or ends, the bulk of our disagreements turn on the different consequences which we expect (or predict) from the means we advocate and select. My view here is that, as our knowledge base expands and is increasingly integrated in the theoretical sense, the better our predictions will be, and therefore, the fewer policy disagreements we will have. That is, more and more value conflicts will be translatable into the more tractable form of predictive conflicts, thus bridging the gap between fact and value, and liberating our predictions from our preferences.

I certainly do not mean to argue that whenever men, individually or collectively, find themselves pursuing incompatible ends, it is always due to a failure in their knowledge. All too often we do actually want the same object (one type of scarcity) or a different set of environmental conditions (another type of scarcity). But even in those cases, greater knowledge might lead to the calculation that compromise in the short run is less costly than victory in the middle or long run. And in situations which do not now permit the translation of conflicts into predictions, and hence into compromise and cooperation, greater knowledge would help us to so modify the structure and culture of diplomacy that the payoff matrix would indeed be more conducive to mutually advantageous resolution of international conflict. If nations behave as they do largely because it's a dog-eat-dog Hobbesian environment, why not investigate those system changes which might make it a safer one for vigorous—but informed—pursuit of the national interests? Even the highway safety people are beginning to understand that the structure (roads, exits, and embankments) and culture (norms and expectations) may have as much to do with vehicle fatalities as the skill or aggressiveness of individual drivers.

To sum up this first point, then, I defer to no one in my condemnation of a curriculum which embraces "systems theory, game theory, simulation, or content analysis" at the expense of any "contact with the subject" or "any feeling either for the play of international politics or for the moral dilemmas to which it gives rise," (p. 27) but utterly reject the notion that a scientific approach requires us to choose between the two. Our mission in both teaching and research is nothing more than an effective amalgamation of insight with evidence, and of substance with technique. When one of the most eminent of our traditionalists describes his method as the art of "mustering all the evidence that history, personal experience, introspection, common sense and . . . logical reasoning" make available, it is difficult to quarrel.[8] But, it must be added that history, experience, introspection, common sense, and logic do not in themselves generate *evidence*, but ideas which must then be examined in the light of evidence.

## If This Be Plagiarism

The second and closely related allegation is that the scientific approach only succeeds in casting any light upon substantive matters when it steps "beyond the bounds of that approach" and employs the classical method (p. 28). As suggested above, classical concepts and historical insights are very much *within* (and not beyond) the bounds of the scientific spirit. We cannot confirm or disconfirm a proposition until it has been formulated, and the first draft of any such formulation almost invariably finds its expression in the classical mode. A great deal of careful empiricism,[9] and a considerable amount of conceptual integration of such facts have been done by observant, experienced, sophisticated scholars from Thucydides through Carr, Wolfers, Claude, and Morgenthau. While these scholars have actually "pinned down" very little in the way of verified generalizations, they have brought shreds of partial evidence together, have developed conceptual schemes of some elegance and clarity, and have raised an impressive array of important questions. No responsible scientist would throw away that fund of wisdom and insist on beginning all over again, *tabula rasa*.

Let me try to illustrate the continuity of the prescientific and the scientific approaches by brief reference to a study of my own. In close collaboration with a diplomatic historian, I have begun a systematic inquiry into those events and conditions which most frequently coincided with the outbreak of interstate war during the period 1815-1945. Beginning with a survey of the traditional literature, we gradually assembled a number of propositions which seem to be: (a) widely accepted by historians and political scientists; (b) quite plausible on their face; and (c) generally borne out by the illustrations which their proponents have selected. By converting the traditional insights into operational language and gathering data on all relevant cases, we have already begun to find evidence which supports certain propositions, casts serious doubt on others, and leads to the revision of still others. We have found, for example, that of the 247 cases in which an alliance partner had a wartime opportunity to fulfill a prewar commitment, the defense pact commitment (fight alongside the ally) was fulfilled 33 percent of the time, the partner remained neutral 65 percent of the time, and opposed the partner only 2 percent of the time; the neutrality pact partners did indeed remain neutral 93 percent of the time, never actually aided the partner, and fought against him only 7 percent of the time. While defense, neutrality, and entente pact commitments may not be ironclad, the general performance level is certainly above that suggested by the "scrap of paper" or "pie crust" arguments. In this same study, we found that the 82 nations which qualified as members of the international system between the Congress of Vienna and the onset of World War II entered into a total of 112 formal alliance commitments of a defense, neutrality, or entente nature, and 86 of these were accounted for by the major powers.[10]

To do this type of analysis, or to make any quantitative generalization (even if "merely descriptive") about the international system, it is mandatory to first describe the population about which one is generalizing. It turned out that (to the best of our knowledge) such an obvious but frustrating task had never been undertaken, and in carrying out that prior assignment, we found that the system had 23 qualified states in 1817, rose to 42 in 1859 and remained close to that figure until World War I, and then remained in the low 60s during the interwar period. Further, by devising a preliminary measure of diplomatic importance or "status," we were able to trace the rise and fall of each system member over nearly a century and a half; particularly evident were the constant high scores of France and Britain, the strong upward climbs of Japan and the United States, and the sharp drops sustained by nations which were defeated in war.[11]

In subsequent studies, moving from the descriptive to the correlational side, we have found a number of strong and not always expected patterns regarding the relationship between alliances and war. For example, the greater the level of alliance involvement throughout the system, the more war the system experiences, but this holds true only for the twentieth century. In the nineteenth century, alliance aggregation shows a strong *negative* correlation with the onset of war, suggesting that a key element (the alliance) in the balance of power doctrine may well have been useful up to the turn of the century, but has perhaps been a source of disaster since.[12]

I think that even this small sample of only one project's results should suffice for the nonce to illustrate the value of combining the traditional and the scientific approaches. There are, of course, a few people who will look at the results of this and similar research and tell us that they "knew it all along." My retort is of two kinds. First, and rhetorically, if the traditionalists knew this, that, or the other thing all along, how come so many of them "knew" exactly the opposite at the same time?[13] More seriously, such a response to data-based findings reveals an alarming insensitivity to the crucial distinction between subjective belief and verifiable knowledge.[14] Again, we are not likely to do much interesting research unless we have, and act upon, our hunches and insights, but we will never build much of a theory, no matter how high and wide we stack our *beliefs.* Conversely, a few strategically selected empirical studies can produce the evidence necessary to complete an existing theoretical edifice. It is also essential to remember that we make as many important discoveries by the incremental accumulation of modest, limited studies, many of which may seem trivial by themselves, as we do by attacking the big questions directly and all at once. Unfortunately, very few scholars make even a single great discovery in their lifetimes, regardless of discipline, but all competent research *contributes,* directly or indirectly, to those great discoveries.

### The Triumph of Trivia

The third deadly sin is that our work has been, and will continue to be, restricted to peripheral and to insignificant subjects. This weakness is due, we are given to understand, not to the traditional neglect of scientific method, but to the "characteristics inherent in the subject matter." (p. 30). Among those factors which make our prospects "very bleak indeed" are: the unmanageable number of variables of which any generalization must take account; the difficulty of controlled experiment; the transitory and elusive nature of our material; and the extent to which our research affects the empirical world, such that "even our most innocent ideas contribute to their own verification and falsification."[15]

As to the large number of variables, three points are worth noting. First, modern analytical tools permit us to work with as many independent and intervening variables as we care to when seeking to account for the frequency of any particular type of outcome. Second, we can always reduce this number by combining those variables which *seem* to be conceptually similar, and more to the point, we can then ascertain—via such techniques as factor analysis—the extent to which they actually are highly similar; if a dozen variables all show an extremely high covariation, we can either drop eleven of them for the moment or use them all to create a single combined variable.[16] Third, and most important, we often start out with a large number of variables because our theory is relatively weak, but once the data are in on a sufficiently large number of cases, we can proceed to analyze them in a search for correlational patterns or causal linkages. Beginning with fairly standard bivariate techniques, we can ascertain: whether there is any statistical relationship between the observed outcome and each alleged predictor, such that it could not have occurred by sheer chance; whether that relationship is linear or more complicated; and most important, which predictor (independent variable) accounts for most of the variance, and is therefore most potent in influencing the observed result. Somewhat more complex are those techniques which permit us to combine a number of independent and intervening variables in a wide variety of ways in order to determine which ones in which pattern or sequence covary most strongly with the observed outcome, and therefore constitute the most powerful determinants.[17]

As to the difficulty of controlled experiments in the "real" (or, more accurately, referent) world, Bull will find a number of advocates of the scientific approach in agreement with him. While he falls back on his "scientifically imperfect" *intuition* (p. 20), several of the latter fall back on *simulations* of the referent world, using students or government officials in place of nations or blocs or ministries. Elsewhere I have spelled out my disagreements with the man-machine—as distinct from the all-machine— simulation study;[18] suffice it to say here that there are many ways to skin this particular cat, and that the natural experiment and the *ex post facto* experiment can often get as controlled as one might desire. [See Chapter 12.]

Regarding the difficulty of catching and categorizing our material, the evidence is beginning to mount that it may not be all that elusive. Many of us in comparative, as well as international, politics have begun to enjoy some fair success in observing, measuring, and recording much of the phenomena which, according to the traditionalists, would always be beyond the scientific reach, available only to the practised eye and sophisticated antennae of scholarly wisdom.[19] If they could stop persuading themselves how "impossible" certain things are and how "intangible" the important variables are, and merely look at the literature, they would discover that the pessimism was probably unwarranted;[20] of course, it is one thing to think that one has developed a measure of certain national or global attributes, or relationships, or behavioral events, but quite another to demonstrate that the measure is not only reliable, but valid. A measure is described as *reliable* if it is used by different observers at the same time, or the same observer at different times, and it always produces essentially the same score when applied to the same state of affairs; among familiar measures whose reliability is well demonstrated are the Dow-Jones stock market index, the United States Department of Commerce cost-of-living index, the gross national product of many industrial societies, and the periodic Gallup survey on how well the United States' President is "doing his job." To achieve that sort of acceptance and the opportunity to demonstrate its continuing reliability, a measure must embody a theoretical concept which seems important and do it in a fashion which is not only operational but persuasive. In the next several years, we may well find a few measures around which such a consensus has developed.

But reliability is far and away the simpler of the two demands one must make of a quantitative index; more difficult to satisfy and to evaluate is the demand of validity. An indicator is *valid* to the extent that it actually does measure the phenomena it is alleged to measure. There is, for example, the recent controversy over whether certain "intelligence tests" used in the United States really measure intelligence as it is generally defined and conceptualized in psychology or whether it measures achievement, or social class, or parent's educational level. The same challenges can be addressed to Galtung's measure of social position, Hart's measure of technological advancement, the Rummel and Tanter measures of foreign conflict, or the Singer and Small measures of lateral mobility, alliance aggregation, bipolarity, diplomatic status, or magnitude of war. The trouble with validity is that we never really pin it down in any final fashion.[21] A measure may seem intuitively reasonable (and we therefore say it has "face validity"), or it may predict consistently to another variable in accord with our theory, or it may covary consistently with an "independent" measure of the same concept. None of these is really conclusive evidence of a measure's validity, but all help to make it a useful and widely accepted indicator; whereas reliability is strictly a methodological attribute, validity falls precisely at the juncture of theory and method. [See Chapter 11.]

### The Model Is Not for Marrying

Turning to the fourth of our intellectual vices, I find some possible grounds for convergence, as well as collision, with our critic. Here we are reminded of all the things that can be—and in our field, often are—wrong with models. On the convergence side, let me readily admit that many of those we find are indeed lacking in internal rigor and consistency, often constitute little more than an intellectual exercise, and do occasionally bootleg some invisible assumptions. But lots of people do lots of things badly, especially when they are just learning, but many do these same things well; should historians be forbidden to think and should lawyers be forbidden to write merely because some performances are on the inadequate side? Granting the flaws which are all too often present, would he have us believe that knowledge comes to those who insist on gazing only at the "real" world through the conventional and culture-bound lenses passed on to us by either the ancients or by the practitioners of the moment? Did the early disciples have the clearest picture of Christianity? Does the boy with his finger in the dike best comprehend hydraulics?

Models, paradigms, and conceptual schemes are merely intellectual tools by which we order and codify that which would otherwise remain a buzzing welter. Some bring us clarity and others only add to our confusion, but no matter what we call them, each of us uses abstractions to give meaning— or the illusion of meaning—to that which our senses detect. Furthermore, as generations of philosophers (East and West) have reminded us, we can never describe the "real" world; all we can do is record and exchange symbolic representations of it. Those symbols may be verbal, numerical, pictorial, and even photographic, but they remain only *representations* of reality. Even though we must (and do) strive for the truest representation, we can never be certain that we have found it. Thus, it is as legitimate to ask whether our models are useful as it is to ask if they are true; the physical and biological sciences, for example, advanced rather nicely with tentative models that were more useful than true. In sum, I concur that our models leave much to be desired, and that they would probably be more useful were they designed to be more representational, but insist that the promising path here is to build them around concepts that are more operational, rather than more familiar, and to discard them when more accurate or more useful ones come along.

### By Gauge or by Guess

Our fifth alleged flaw is the "fetish for measurement" (p. 33), and it is worth noting at the outset that Professor Bull had to shift his sights away from Kaplan (who can hardly be accused of being a compulsive quantifier) and select Deutsch and Russett as his culprits; perhaps there is a greater diversity of style and strategy in the scientific camp than he has recognized.[22] We are arraigned here on three subsidiary counts. First, we tend to "ignore relevant differences between the phenomena that are being counted." This is partly an empirical question and partly an epistemological one; in due course the various measurement efforts will show us where we have erred in lumping the unlumpable. But it seems to me that this undue preoccupation, yea obsession, with the unique, the discrete, the non-comparable, is what has largely kept history from developing into a cumulative discipline, and has led to so much frivolous debate between the quantifiers and the anti-quantifiers in sociology, psychology, economics, and political science. The fact is that no two events, conditions, or relationships are ever exactly alike; they must always differ in *some* regard, even if it is only in time-space location. The question is whether they are sufficiently similar to permit comparison and combination for the theoretical purposes at hand. To borrow a metaphor of which the anti-quantifiers are quite fond, there is absolutely nothing wrong with adding apples and oranges if fruit is the subject at hand! And if we want to generalize at a more restricted level, we had better distinguish not only between apples and oranges, but between McIntosh and Golden Delicious as well. If we cannot combine and aggregate, with due attention to the matter of relevant differences, we cannot make empirical generalizations; and in the absence of such generalizations, we may generate a great deal of speculation, but blessed little theory.

The second allegation here is that we attach more significance to a quantitative indicator or a statistical regularity than it deserves. This, too, is primarily an empirical question, and if we can discover that a common enemy unifies a nation only under certain limited conditions, that the percentage of national product going to foreign trade decreases rather than increases as productivity rises, that domestic conditions correlate with a nation's foreign policy only under special conditions, that estimates of relative military power become distorted as diplomatic tension rises, or that nations are more war-prone when their status is falling rather than rising, we must conclude that the quantifying exercises were useful.[23] Once more, there is something to the charge, and, as suggested above, we must be careful not to equate reliability and plausibility with validity in our measures. Likewise, because we can engage in a wider variety of statistical analyses with interval scales than with ordinal ones, which give nothing more than a rank ordering, there is some temptation to develop such measures even when the situation does not justify the degree of precision implied in an interval scale.

A final point here is Bull's willingness to take seriously only those quantitative results which "confirm some intuitive impression" (p. 35). Here again is the old faith in the folklore and conventional wisdom of a particular time and place. When rigorous methods produce results which are intuitively reasonable, we should not only find this reassuring, but should be careful to avoid pointing out that we "knew it all along." As I suggested above, it would be most instructive to go through our scholarly literature and see how often we have known one thing all along in one section or chapter and something quite different in the following section or chapter. The fact is, we seldom even know what we know, because our assertions are usually made in regard to a small and highly selective sample of cases and in an extremely limited context.

## No Monopoly on Precision

The sixth item in Bull's "propositional inventory" is his allegation that the practitioners of the classical approach are as likely to be precise, coherent, and orderly as are members of the scientific school. He reminds us that in the past many classicists (especially the international lawyers) have indeed shown real conceptual rigor, and that the self-styled scientists have often failed in this regard. The claim is all too true, but beside the point. First, the ratio of high-to-low verbal and conceptual precision in the literature of the two schools would certainly not be flattering to those on the classicist side. When social scientists do historical work, we set up our coding rules and then examine *all* the cases which qualify; there is much less of a tendency to ransack history in search of those isolated cases which satisfy one's theoretical or rhetorical requirements of the moment. We need only glance through both sets of literature for tentative but striking evidence of this difference. Closely related, and perhaps an inevitable corollary of this difference, is the fact that when most traditionalists do a serious historical analysis, it takes the form of a case study, whereas the scientist knows that: (a) one can never describe all the variables relevant to a given case, and (b) that what happened only once before is not much of a guide to what will happen in the future. Thus, we tend to select a *few* variables on (please note) intuitive grounds or on the basis of prior research findings, and then examine their interrelationship over *many* historical cases.

Second, and in addition to specific procedures, the scientific researcher usually has an intellectual style that substantially increases the probability of better performance in this regard. Even when we deal with a variable that need not be operationalized in the study at hand, we tend to ask how it *could* be so refined and clarified. Once in the habit of thinking operationally, it is difficult to settle for constructs and propositions that are not—or could not be translated into—"machine readable" form. As the traditionally trained scholar moves further in this direction, and looks at propositions as interesting problems to be investigated or hypotheses to be tested—rather than as the revealed truth—the gap will begin to close. But vague and fuzzy notions cannot be put to the test, and whatever respect for precision there is in the classical tradition will have to be resurrected and mobilized.

## The Rootless Wanderers

Our seventh deadly sin is that we have often cut ourselves off from history and philosophy, with certain dire consequences, among which is the loss of some basis for stringent self-criticism. I take the charge to mean that it is from those two intellectual *disciplines*—rather than the phenomena they study—that the severance has occurred. I would hope so on two grounds. First, if we in the scientific school *have* neglected the political and diplomatic past, or such philosophical concerns as ethics, the "big picture," and the long view, then we are indeed in trouble. The fact is, unhappily, that the charge of our being ahistorical is far from unfounded, and an appreciable fraction of the modernists do indeed restrict themselves to the study of only the most recent past or the most trivial problems, and largely for the reason implied in Bull's earlier point: because the data are more available or the cases are more amenable to our methods. But this criticism applies equally to the more traditional scholars. For reasons too complex to explore here, almost all training in political science (with perhaps the exception of political philosophy) is weak in historical depth and extremely restricted in its time frame, particularly in England and America.

As to our philosophical rootlessness, the picture seems to be more mixed, with the modernists quite alert to the epistemological concerns of philosophy but often indifferent to its normative concerns. For example, the traditionalists seem much more willing than the modernists to speak out on matters of public policy, with the latter often hiding behind the argument that our knowledge is still much too inadequate, or that we should not use our status as "experts" to exercise more political influence than other citizens. These counsels of perfection and of misguided egalitarianism are, to me at least, a source of embarrassment if not dismay. Of course, American political science (as a professional discipline) has been "hung up" on these issues for many decades. My generation, for example, was largely taught that political commitment implied emotional involvement, and that such involvement destroyed scholarly objectivity. The argument only holds water if there are no mechanisms for avoiding the pitfalls of political involvement, and if our field remains one in which most issues of importance *are* merely matters of opinion and belief. The whole point of scientific method is to permit us to investigate whatever problems interest and excite us, while largely eliminating the possibility that we will come out where we *want* to come out.[24]

The more ethical position, it seems to me, is to recognize that individual responsibility cannot be put on the shelf until we are absolutely certain of our political perceptions and predictions. First, most social events will always retain an element of the probabilistic, and since we are—as citizens or consultants—usually called on for judgments about a single case, rather than the large number of cases around which science is built, certainty is something we will rarely experience. In the meantime, of course, the thing to do is advance our data and theory base so that we *can* be more knowledgeable on matters of public policy. Second, if we withhold expression of our judgments until our science is more fully developed, we run a fairly high risk that so many errors in judgment will have been made that the situations we face then will be even less tractable than those of the present, or—and it is not impossible—we will already have stumbled into Armageddon.[25]

As to the modernist's concern that we might "exploit" our status and prestige (itself a dubious quality) by speaking out publicly and identifiably, and therefore put the layman at a disadvantage in influencing the policy process, the anxiety is neither logical nor historically justified. On matters of bridge design, the hazards of smoking, auto safety, construction of the

SST, or real estate zoning, the specialist in international politics is no more powerful than most of his fellow citizens, with decisions inevitably made on the basis of some mix of political pressure and expertise. As retarded as our discipline may be, we have as great a right and responsibility to take public stands in our area of special competence as the engineer, medical researcher, lobbyist, sales manager, planner, or land speculator have in theirs. In my view, knowledge is meant to energize, not paralyze.

Thus, I would part company with Professor Bull when he suggests earlier in his paper that most moral questions are "by their very nature" not open to any objective answer, but wholeheartedly concur with his warning on the dangers of remaining "as remote from the substance of international politics as the inmates of a Victorian nunnery were from the study of sex" (p. 26).

Returning to the original charge, my other reason for hoping that he refers not to the substance, but the style, of history and philosophy is that we probably have little more to learn from them in terms of method or concept. At the risk of alienating some of my favorite colleagues, I would say that these disciplines have gone almost as far as they can go in adding to social science knowledge in any appreciable way. True, the historian can continue to pile up facts and do his case studies, but only as he borrows from the social sciences can he produce hard evidence or compelling interpretations of the past; one reason that we must heed Bull's implied advice and move into historical research is that otherwise our understanding of the past will remain in the hands of the literati, responding to one revisionist or counter-revisionist interpretation after another, as the consensus ebbs and flows. Of course, some historians are beginning to shift to the scientific mode now,[26] but while encouraging that trend, it is up to the social scientists to meet them half-way, chronologically as well as methodologically. As to the philosophers, their discipline is too broad and diverse to permit any sweeping statements, ranging as it does from theology to philosophy of science, but logic, deduction, speculation and introspection can only carry us so far. Thus, while new formulations in philosophy (and mathematics) can be expected, the odds are that the scientist himself will continue to be his own best philosopher and theorist, as long as he looks up from his data matrix and statistical significance tables periodically, and asks "what does it all mean?"

So much for Professor Bull's critique for the moment; while his attack, as he courageously admits, was more shotgun than rifle, he did bring down some worthy targets, and if a few already dead horses are somewhat more riddled than before, the ammunition was certainly expended with style and flair. Let me try now to summarize my position on the general issues, adding the hope that this volume may represent the last round in what has been considerably less than a "great debate."

## III. CONCLUSION

My thesis should now be quite clear, but in the unlikely event that my touch has been too light or my rhetoric too subtle, let me reiterate it here in the baldest terms. All kinds of men contemplate and think about all kinds of problems. Some are intrigued with physical problems, ranging from biology to celestial mechanics; some are more preoccupied with social phenomena, from child development to world politics; and some are intrigued with that elusive interface at which the physical and the social domains appear to meet, whether in psychophysiology or human ecology. When men first began to think about any of these problems, they had little to go on. There was not much in the way of recorded experiences, philosophical schemes, tools of observation, or techniques of measurement. Over the centuries, however, some knowledge began to accumulate; witch doctors, court astrologers, and theologians all contributed—even in their errors— to the growth in understanding of the world around us. Philosophical schemes and cosmologies, inclined planes and brass instruments, psycho-analysis and mathematical statistics all tended to further the increase in knowledge. In some fields of inquiry, progress was quite rapid. In others, due to social taboos as well as the inherent complexity of the phenomena, things did not move quite as well. Thus, long after Lavoisier had demonstrated the fallaciousness of the phlogiston theory, and the systematic observations of Galileo and Brahe had discredited the Ptolemaic conception of astronomy, students of social phenomena—relying on authority rather than evidence— continued to accept notions that were equally inaccurate.

Where do we stand now? In some of the social sciences, progress has been steady and impressive; in others, it has been more halting. It would seem that those disciplines which are most advanced are precisely those in which imagination and insight have been combined with—not divorced from—rigor and precision. In each of these, one finds that the early work, no matter how creative, remained largely speculative, with several theoretical schemes—often equally plausible—contending for position. Until systematic observation, operationally derived evidence, and replicable analytical pro-cedures were introduced, skillful rhetoric and academic gamesmanship often carried the day. Thus, in sociology, Comte and Spencer played a key role in the transition from speculation to measurement; Hume and Smith come to mind as those who represent the convergence of theoretical insight and systematic quantification in economics; and in psychology, one might select Wundt and Titchener as the scholars who bridged the gap between the preoperational and the operational. At the other pole, such social science disciplines as anthropology and psychiatry remain largely impressionistic— but far from nonempirical—in their evidence, and thus unimpressive in their theory.

We in political science stand very much at the threshold. In certain subfields, operational measurement and the quantitative evidence which result are more or less taken for granted now; opinion surveys, voting studies, and roll-call analyses are, except in the intellectual backwaters, seen as necessary—but not sufficient—ingredients in the growth of political theory. But in international politics, there are still those few who raise the same old spectres, rattle the same old skeletons, and flog the same old horses. They sometimes tell us that Thucydides or Machiavelli or Mahan knew all there was to know and at other times they tell us that the subject matter is intrinsically unknowable. Perhaps the best answer to both assertions is to "look at the record"; a decade ago there was little published scientific research beyond the pioneering work of Quincy Wright's *Study of War* and Lewis Richardson's scattered articles.[27] Five years ago, a handful of us were getting underway and perhaps a dozen or so data-based papers had appeared. In mid-1967, I find (as mentioned in an earlier footnote) in the English language journals almost 100 articles that bring hard evidence to bear on theoretically significant questions, and more than a dozen books.[28] Whether the traditionalists will find these persuasive—or as Bull recognizes, whether they will even read them—is uncertain. The quality is clearly uneven, the theoretical relevance is mixed, the methodological sophistication ranges from naïve to fantastic, the policy payoffs seem to differ enormously, and the craftsmanship runs from slovenly to compulsive, but the work is already beginning to add up.

The war is clearly over. Many traditionally trained scholars are beginning to tool up, via self-education, consultation with colleagues, and the still-too-few summer institutes and post-doctoral programs. While a handful of political science departments in the United States are still sitting complacently by, most have begun to move in our direction, recruiting (or, given the serious shortage, trying to recruit) scientifically oriented teacher-scholars in international and comparative as well as national politics. While Professor Marshall (see Note 2) may feel that he is "sitting through an extraordinarily long overture," if he would glance up from the yellowing pages of his libretto he would discover not only that we are well into the first act, but that some of his best friends are on stage or waiting in the wings.[29] To push his metaphor a bit further, he may be paying too much attention to the now familiar "systems chorus," and not enough to the more operational *recitativo*. If he—and perhaps Professors Bull and Vital with him—were to listen closely, they would discover that, while the diction may be on the exotic side, the content is really quite familiar; and during the next few years, as the self-conscious amateurishness of the cast gives way to increasing confidence, the content will become more familiar still. He will need a new libretto, of course, and perhaps a week of the "total immersion" treatment (no offense to Berlitz here!) but in no time he will not only be following the *recitativo*, but even humming along with the arias.

My point, then, is that there is no longer much doubt that we can make the study of international politics (or better still, world politics) into a scientific discipline worthy of the name. But it requires the devotees of both warring camps to come together in collaboration if not in sublime unity. We on the scientific side have little ground for exultation. Whatever progress we have already made is due in large measure to the wisdom, insight, and creativity of those from whom we have learned. What is more, the war would not be over if the traditionalists had waited for us to meet them half way. It is a tribute to the classical tradition, in which many of us were of course reared, that its heritage is rich and strong enough to permit the sort of growth and development which now is well along. All that remains is for those in the scientific camp to shift from the digital to the analog computer and recognize that every serious scholar's work is on the same continuum. If we modernists can master the substantive, normative, and judgmental end of it as well as the traditionalists are mastering the concepts and methods at our end, convergence will be complete, and the "war" will not have been in vain.

## ACKNOWLEDGMENTS

I am indebted to Karl W. Deutsch for his comments on an earlier draft of this paper.

—————— ■ ——————

# CHAPTER ELEVEN

# Variables, Indicators, and Data: The Measurement Problem in Macro-political Research

ONE OF THE MORE DEBILITATING digressions in the evolution of the scientific enterprise is the controversy over the relative importance of models and data. Time and again, in every discipline from archaeology to zoology, the issue has reappeared with sufficient force to engage scholarly attention and to generate reams of rhetoric. In the social sciences, as in the biological and physical sciences, we have expended considerable energies on the data versus model (some would say "theory") emphasis, usually to the detriment of scientific advancement.

Worse yet, in the universities and institutes of the scholarly world, students are often reinforced in such a way that they enter into their scientific careers committed to pursuing one or the other activity, rather than both. Some are so persuaded of the primacy of modeling and theorizing that they disdain empirical work, neither reading that of others nor sufficiently mastering the techniques of data acquisition and data analysis to conduct empirical work themselves. And others become so enamored of the concrete, referent world and so suspicious of abstractions and of speculation that they neither read about nor engage in those particular activities. While these are extreme cases, they have been all too visible in most of the social sciences since their inception.

The way this dichotomy is put makes it clear that I consider it as unnecessary as it is dysfunctional, and the hope here is to articulate an intelligently balanced and integrated view. Certainly there are times in the development of a discipline when we have gone so far toward one or the other of these extremes that the cumulative processes of science are seriously jeopardized. Then, of course, it is time to shift our emphasis, attention,

This chapter originally appeared in *Social Science History*, vol. 6, no. 2 (Spring 1982), pp. 181–217. Copyright © 1982 Social Science History Association. Reprinted by permission.

and resources in order to redress the imbalance. To put it cybernetically, we have no objections to fluctuations around a relatively stable "steady state," but when these perturbations are of appreciable duration and magnitude, they may end up requiring corrective feedback that is too extreme, lasts too long, and costs too dearly.

## The Data-Model Connection

One way to reduce the frequency and magnitude of these radical swings in scientific activity is to recognize the critical—and early—role that data play in mediating the continuous interaction between theoretical hunches and empirically testable models. On the basis of all sorts of things, from current folklore and idle fantasy to the hard evidence produced by prior investigations, the researcher formulates speculative schemes that might help to explain the phenomena of interest. But as these schemes take on coherence and plausibility, the social scientist begins to translate them into operational models that can be put to the test and checked out against the "real," referent world. This translation, in turn, rests heavily upon the strategies that will be used to generate the data that represent empirical reality. To put it another way, the concepts that go into the model have to be converted into operational indicators, so called because they make explicit the operations or procedures by which the phenomena of the referent world are expressed in sets of scientifically useful data.

The wide range of processes by which we make this conversion or translation from intellectual construct to machine-readable data set is quite broad, and will be described later. But they rest heavily on what might be thought of as instrumentation: The development of techniques and procedures by which we can observe phenomena that are not visible to the naked eye. The same, of course, has been equally true of the physical and biological sciences; as Clark (1971: 109) noted in his biography of Einstein, "pure" science has always relied on measurement techniques in order to move forward. If we recall Kepler's need for Tycho Brahe's systematic observations and measurements, or Hershel's reliance on a more sensitive thermometer, or Michelson and Morley, whose mercury float and mirrors permitted them to demonstrate that "ether flow" had no effect on the movement of light rays, we find further grounds for concurring with Maxwell's statement that he was "happy in the knowledge of a good instrument maker." We know more about the physical and biological world today, Clark reminds us, "not because we have more imagination, but because we have better instruments." In the social sciences, where many of our explanatory concepts refer to symbolic behavior, intrapersonal processes, and other equally intangible phenomena, we need to be even more creative and diligent in our instrumentation.

All of this is to emphasize that the scientific enterprise—be it carried out in the laboratory, the field setting, or in the reconstruction of history (Singer, 1977)—is equally dependent upon the big picture and the precise technique, creative explanation and meticulous description, uninhibited speculation and disciplined measurement. We cannot construct and test models in the scientific sense of the word without data, and we cannot efficiently generate or acquire data without close attention to the models that we now have, and to the theories we hope they will become (Deutsch, 1966, 1969).

### Toward a Clarification of Terms

While laymen and dictionaries may accept the proposition that *data* is merely the plural of *datum*, the scientific definition should be somewhat more stringent. That is, any item of factual or existential truth may well be a datum: the Treaty of Versailles took effect in January 1920; the Japanese fleet was victorious in the Battle of Tsushima Straits; there are 154 sovereign states in the world today, and so forth. But a number of such existential statements would not constitute data until we had very clear and explicit coding rules by which we defined the effective date of treaties (relatively simple), victory in naval battles (less simple), and national sovereignty (even less simple). Without such criteria for coding and classifying, we cannot generate a set of data, and therefore cannot make a scientifically useful descriptive statement about some population of treaties, naval battles, or sovereign states.

Second, and closely related, is the matter of quantification. In each of these three examples, we can decide which cases are included or excluded without invoking any quantitative criteria; purely qualitative criteria will often suffice. While an appreciation of this truth often leads to the statement that one need not quantify to do scientific research, such reasoning is flawed. Even though we can assign each particular case, condition, or event to a given category without necessarily quantifying, the moment that we generalize about the set of cases, we must enumerate how many fall into each category. Thus, even if quantification is not essential—and often it is essential—for identifying a datum, it is always essential for describing the data set into which it falls.

While discussing matters definitional, let us also deal with two labels that are sometimes applied to macro-social data sets. One of these is "aggregate data" which, if taken literally, would apply to sets of data that describe groupings or populations without describing the individuals or small units that constitute the aggregation. These are summed or averaged scores for the aggregation, but not the scores for its individual components, leaving us in the dark as to how the characteristics are distributed within the aggregated population. But since scientists can (in the aggregate!) be as imprecise in their terminology as journalists, public officials, and laymen, we often see the label applied to any data set other than the tabulation of election results or opinion surveys. However, since most of these data sets only have the aggregated results of the election or survey, and nothing on the specific individuals were involved, it is unsettling to see them set apart and labeled as something distinctly different from aggregate data! There are, of course, important differences between these and other data sets, but rarely does the aggregated/disaggregated dimension capture it. In practice, then, all too many of us use the label to describe a residual category, a nondifferentiated melange. Some lump everything that is not based on the observation of individual human traits or behaviors into the aggregate data category, while still others use it to include quantitative data produced by governmental or commercial organizations for their policy purposes, rather than by social scientists for research purposes.

Another label—more recently coined but equally imprecise—is that of "process produced" data, by which is usually meant the latter-mentioned type of aggregate data. Since all data sets, by definition, are produced by some sort of intellectual and social process, it is not particularly useful to include corporate earning reports or governmental estimates of unemployment, but to exclude election votes or public opinion distributions. In the paragraphs that follow, we suggest a typology that rests on rather different dimensions, leading, we trust to a more precise and useful set of categories.

## A Proposed Typology of Data

Having rejected some of the more misleading labels and definitions, we should propose some alternatives, and we do this in the context of a proposed typology of social science data. As we see it, a useful typology must deal with at least three dimensions along which the many types of data might be differentiated. The first dimension embraces the type of variable that we hope to describe via our data set, or to put it another way, the concept that is represented by our data. The second is the level of aggregation at which the data-making observations are conducted. And the third is the procedure by which the observation is conducted and the data thereby generated.

To clarify these rather abstract statements, let us reiterate that any effort to describe or explain a social process must begin with a number of concepts (Kerlinger, 1973: 28–29). But those are only mental constructs. We can imagine them but we can seldom see, touch, or hold them; few of the variables with which we speak and think can be directly measured or scaled or categorized. Normally, these conditions or events cannot be directly observed because they are too intangible, or because they occurred so long ago or far away as to be out of sight, or are too spread out in time or in space, or comprise too many components to be observed simultaneously. Thus, we often have no choice but to observe carefully those conditions and events that *are* accessible to our direct senses, and then infer from them the value or state of the unobserved phenomenon. In other words, what we do observe is the indicator (or proxy, or representation) of what we would like to observe, and the values or magnitudes manifested in our data serve as indirect indicators of the fluctuating values of the concepts. To put it another way, we think and theorize in terms of concepts, and our data serve as convenient surrogates that represent them and can be subjected to statistical analysis.

Turning, then, to our first dimension—the types of variable that the data set is supposed to represent—we can identify three such types: the attributes of social entities, the relationships between and among entities, and the behaviors that these entities manifest vis-à-vis one another. By *attribute* we mean some property or characteristic of any social entity ranging from a single individual to the global system, and from a loose and transitory band of hunters or coalition of pressure groups, to a formal and meticulously organized corporation or national government. More specifically, any social entity may be described in terms of its physical, structural, or cultural attributes. By physical attributes, we mean the size of a person or group, the age profile of a nation or political party, the racial composition of a province or a professional association, the geography of a continent, the fertility of a nation's soil, the productivity of an industry, the range of a navy's guns, and so forth. While some of these physical attributes may be due to the structural or cultural attributes (or the behavior) of certain groups, the distinction between cause and consequence must always be kept in mind. All too often, a physical attribute such as steel output, for example, is treated as a structural or cultural attribute because it is to a great extent affected by the structure and culture of the nation.

As to structural attributes, we have in mind the institutional and organizational arrangements and patterns by which sociologists, economists, and political scientists might describe a given social entity. Such concepts as social stratification, oligopoly, or bicameralism might be obvious examples; the first two are fairly informal and unofficial attributes of a system, whereas the latter would be formally institutionalized in legal documents. And while many structural attributes of an entity or system are inferred from the relationships and links between and among its component entities or subsystems, this hardly justifies the open-ended use of "structure" that we find in today's social science literature. Some use the word to embrace any set of social relationships among entities; others can mean statistical relationships among variables, recurrent historical patterns, and just about anything else for which no other word comes to mind.

Cultural attributes can also cause confusion inasmuch as the word culture has been used to describe virtually every attribute of a social entity, from its beliefs to its behaviors and from its pottery to its agricultural practices. We use it here in the more restricted sense of the distribution of perceptions, preferences, and predictions held by the people who comprise the entity; that is, beliefs about what is or was, what should be, and what will be (Singer, 1968).

With these three sets of attribute dimensions, any social entity can be described, compared with itself across different points in time, and compared with any other entities. To borrow from Gordon Allport's insightful distinction (1955), they permit us to deal with our social entities in terms of both their being and becoming, but not their behaving, to which we will attend after a look at the class of variables that falls between attributes and behavior: that of *relationships* among entities.

Unfortunately, the concept of relationship also has a multitude of meanings, of which only two concern us here. Our sense is that of comparison: The relationship between the USSR and the United States in nuclear capabilities is that, for example, the Soviets have about 2500 strategic delivery vehicles versus 2000 for the United States, but only 7000 deliverable warheads versus 9200. When we are merely making a comparison between or among entities along a given attribute dimension, we will not speak of a relationship but of a *comparison*. The second, more complex meaning—and the one that we will use here—is that of connections, links, bonds, and associations between and among entities. How interdependent, durable, cooperative, open, and so on is or was the relationship between or among some specified population of entities, groups, nations, and the like?

The final class of variables, after the attributes of entities and the relationships among them, is that of *behavior*, which we can use in its most literal form. What is a given entity doing, in the verbal or motor sense of the word? For example, is an individual speaking, a group of individuals negotiating, a pair of nations trading, an alliance of nations fighting a war? Note that we do not use behavior to include either changes in the attributes of an entity or in the internal conditions that might account for its behavior. That is, the brain cells may behave and interact when an individual expresses a thought, or individuals may converse prior to a group's acting, or bureaus may interact before an international organization condemns a member, and so forth. But this refers, in each case, to the behavior of a component, and not to the behavior of the entity itself.

We stress all of these distinctions not only because the vocabulary of social science is often imprecise, but because conceptual and semantic precision are essential to valid indicator construction and systematic data generation. When we turn to the connections among concepts, their indicators, and the data sets that emerge from the application of these indicators, it will be clear that semantic idiosyncrasies can lead to considerable mischief and confusion.

So much then, for the first dimension in our typology of data: the type of social phenomenon (attribute, relationship, or behavior) involved. The second dimension revolves around what is often called the level of analysis, or more accurately, the level of aggregation. In the above discussion, we have alluded occasionally to the distinction between a social entity and its component units or sub-entities, and we have inevitably spoken of entities that may range in size and complexity from the single individual up through the global system. Let us now address these distinctions in a more explicit and systematic manner, since they are as central to the validity of our index construction and data acquisition as are the distinctions between and among one's classes of variables (Singer, 1961; Moul, 1973).

For most social science disciplines, this great variety of social entities can be arranged along a vertical axis, with the individual human being at the lower end and the global system at the upper. In between, and working upward, one thinks of primary groups, such as the family, the face-to-face work group, and the friendship clique. At the next level are such secondary groups as the extended family; bureaus of municipal, provincial, or national governments; offices of commercial firms, departments of universities, labor unions, and so forth. At a fourth level are the governments, firms, universities, and labor unions themselves. Next, might be such territorial and subnational entities as provinces or regions, and then nations themselves, followed by international or supranational coalitions, alliances, or formal organizations at the continental or global level. The specific grouping and the specific level of social aggregation is not particularly important for our purposes here, and one's choice of grouping and level will reflect the theoretical question at hand. But, as already intimated, after choosing one's outcome variable and the explanatory variables whose predictive or postdictive power is to be examined, one must be extremely precise in going about the construction of the indicators and the acquisition of the data. To put it in more formal language, the validity of the inferences we make in linking our indicators to our variables will rest heavily upon the appropriateness of the aggregation levels at which each is found, as well as upon the reasoning that lies behind the types of variables (attribute, relationship, or behavior) themselves.

With these preliminary (but by no means trivial) matters of epistemology and terminology behind us, we now turn to our primary assignment: the role of variables, indicators, and data in macro-political research.

## DATA ARE MADE, NOT BORN

While there are exceptions to the proposition that "data are made, not born," we will ignore them for the moment, on the grounds that the social sciences have paid an exorbitant price by assuming that the only available data are "born data." As McClelland (1972: 36) reminds us, too much social science research has rested on data sets that have been "requisitioned" from some other source. To advance further, he suggests that we will have to go after more difficult data: "needed bodies of facts will have to be quarried by hand out of hard rock." While the metaphor may be overly stark, it emphasizes that we must sift through vast and messy bodies of disparate facts in order to produce neat and tidy data sets. Perhaps the panning of gold—in which the few cherished flakes and nuggets are separated from the abundant gravel and sand in the river bed—might be an equally appropriate metaphor.

Either way, the point is that we cannot expect the macro-social sciences to advance if we rely primarily upon "requisitioned" data that are readily at hand. To the extent that we do follow that strategy—and thus acquiesce in the popular myth that social science is not "really" a science because most of its concepts are not readily measured or already found in quantitative form—we perpetuate our backward condition. We turn, therefore, to the procedures and reasoning that are followed in the making or generating of macro-political data. Following that, we can briefly identify some of the sources in which we find our data more nearly ready-made.

## The Validity of Indicators

In any discussion of indicators and their validity, we often use words like "proxy" and "surrogate," and thus call attention to the fact that our data are not identical either to our conceptual variables or to "real world" phenomena, but are rather detectable traces of the latter and representations of the former. We utilize our data—via our indicators—to infer the presence and strength of our variable in a given real world, empirical setting. To emphasize the point further, try to imagine directly observing such attributes as the nationalism of an individual, the rationality of a decision unit, the centralization of a political party, the cohesiveness of an alliance, or the power of an international organization. Similarly, how might we directly observe the existence of the strength of relationships such as a marriage between individuals, the hostility between ethnic groups, or the economic interdependence among nations?

Even behavior and interaction—the most visible and audible of our three classes of social phenomena—are seldom directly observable, at least in a scientifically useful sense. That is, we may see or hear reports of a revolution or a diplomatic visit or the making of a trade agreement, and we may witness some part of the event or episode. But even here, we or our informants only see or hear a small fraction of the behaviors and interaction sequences. And, as noted earlier, if these events occurred before we came on the scene, or across a wide area of space or span of time or behind closed doors, we can only piece together certain bits of information and then *infer* the occurrence of certain behaviors (Webb et al., 1966).

The purpose of an indicator, then, is to help us generate a data set from whose magnitudes and values we can validly infer the values of the actual phenomena that interest us. While we suggested earlier that our data provide the observed values from which we infer the values and magnitudes of our unobserved variables, this can occasionally be an overstatement. If, for example, our variable is "severity of war," a perfectly reasonable indicator might be the number of fatalities "caused" by the war, and that should be observable. But a moment's reflection reminds us that, even if we could reliably discriminate between those fatalities that were caused by the war and those that were merely associated with it in time and space, the former number would itself not be directly observable. Rather we would first have to infer it from all sorts of reports and records, and then make the second inference from that number to the conceptual variable called severity.

Similarly, in the electoral behavior field, if our variable is that of voters' attitudes toward the political parties in a campaign, we usually offer the voters the stimulus of a questionnaire, and from their oral responses we infer their opinions about certain attributes of the parties. From those inferred opinions, we go on to infer a general attitude toward the parties, and on occasion we even go to a third inference as to whether they will vote, and if so, for which party. In the social sciences, such examples of our reliance on inferential leaps are numerous, and their frequency—as well as their often heroic proportions—should make us attentive to ways in which we might ascertain the validity of our indicators.

By validity, we mean the extent to which our indicators bridge the gap between the referent world and the observed variable that is purported to represent the referent world: the extent to which they actually measure what we claim to measure (Kerlinger, 1973: 457). While most scientists agree that the validity of an indicator is never fully demonstrated, there are four basic tests that help us to estimate how close we have come. First, there is "face validity," by which we mean that most other specialists agree that the indicator seems to get at the concept it allegedly represents. In more refined terms, face validity rests on the plausibility of the reasoning behind the indicator: Why should we expect it to tap the concept we have in mind? A somewhat pretentious label for that reasoning is the "auxiliary theory" (Blalock, 1968), but since it would be naive to expect, and costly to construct, a genuine theory to buttress every indicator we use, we prefer to stay with reasoning or rationale.

In addition to this intuitive criterion of face validity, there are three empirical tests that may be involved. The most direct is that of carrying out the operations called for by the indicator and then examining the scores that result. To the extent that they coincide with what we and other specialists expected, the indicator's alleged validity is further enhanced. Next, we can ascertain how strongly the indicator at hand correlates with a well-established alternative indicator of the same phenomenon (Campbell and Fiske, 1959). Suppose, for example, one were using the number and rank of officerships in universal intergovernmental organizations (IGOs) as an indicator of a nation's "diplomatic importance," but wanted to go back to 1820, a century prior to the League of Nations. One solution might be to use instead the number and rank of diplomatic missions sent to each nation's capital by all the other nations in the system (Small and Singer, 1973). If we found a high correlation between the IGO and the diplomatic scores for most of the nation-years since 1920, we would have greater confidence in the validity of the IGO officership indicator, given the fact that the diplomatic mission indicator not only seems reasonable, but produces scores that also seem reasonable.

But this test also has its weaknesses, one of which is the danger of spurious inference. To take another example, just because there happens to be a strong and positive correlation between total population and other indicators of national power—and there usually is (Russett et al., 1964; Rummel, 1972)—one would not argue that population is a valid indicator of the concept. Not only are there many cases in which the correlation is weak, but there are even quite a few nations whose "power score" for certain periods will be *negatively* correlated with their population size.

Examples of this pattern include nineteenth- and early twentieth-century China and India, and modern Israel.

A third empirical test of an indicator's validity is its "criterion validity" (Kerlinger, 1973: 459), or its performance in the context of a well-supported theoretical model. If the variable that it allegedly taps is, according to the model, supposed to rise or fall in a certain correspondence with another variable (the validity of whose indicator is generally accepted), and it indeed rises and falls as it should, many would consider it quite valid. But given how few solid theories there are in political science (or economics or sociology) this could be a very unsatisfactory test. The chances of the suspect indicator being invalid are certainly no less than the chances of the "theory" itself being wrong. And, of course, the accepted indicators with which the new one is supposed to covary could, themselves, turn out to be less than valid reflectors of the variable they allegedly tap.

## The Reliability of Indicators

While social scientists must, of necessity, devote a great deal of attention to the validity of their indicators, and even more to the analysis of the data generated via these indicators, we often tend toward the cavalier when it comes to the quality of the information upon which these more interesting activities must ultimately rest. The problem of "data quality control" (Naroll, 1962) is all too often relegated directly to our data collection assistants and indirectly to the historians, archivists, clerks, biographers, and journalists who generated and assembled the raw material from which we begin. This quality problem can be viewed as two subproblems: the reliability of the indicators that convert the facts into data, and the accuracy (and completeness) of the facts to which the indicator's operations are applied.

As to reliability, we mean the extent to which we come up with the same scores when the same procedures are applied by the same coders to the same factual materials over and over, or by different coders at the same or differing times. The former is known as test-retest reliability and the latter as intercoder reliability. Both are primarily a function of the clarity, explicitness, and precision of the coding rules; the less the ambiguity in these rules, the higher will be the reliability of the indicator and the higher the probability that our coders are detecting, selecting, classifying, and recording the facts as intended by those who developed the indicator. To put it another way, the coding rules describe the operations by which the raw recorded traces of empirical reality are converted into scientifically useful data.

Perhaps the most typical procedures for such conversion are those known, somewhat misleadingly, as "content analysis" (Pool, 1959; Berelson, 1952; Holsti, 1969; and North et al., 1963). We say misleading because it is not an analysis procedure at all, but one for generating data. In any event, the procedure is designed to sift through a tremendous body of written materials in order to identify certain patterns that would otherwise remain lost. Without imaginative and rigorous procedures, the empirical "gold" that we seek would remain obscured by all the associated verbiage that is not relevant to the patterns we seek, but within which the rare items are embedded.

The same basic principles are followed when we code and classify events and conditions that unfold in the natural world, or that have already been more impressionistically recorded by historians or on-the-spot observers in years gone by. In any utilization of the content analysis approach, the same principles apply: We articulate our concepts, operationalize them, set up our coding rules, and count the frequency with which indicators of variables appear. The major drawback of this method, especially when applied to large amounts of material, is that it takes a long time. Electronic computers are now used for tabulating and sorting the results via such programs as the General Inquirer (Stone et al., 1966), but the basic assignment of words, phrases, and themes to a given category must still be done by the human eye, mind, and hand. It may be, however, that we will soon have electronic optical scanners, which, when programmed with the coding rules, will be able to "read" thousands of pages very quickly and count—when found in the specified context—the frequencies of the words and phrases that interest us in a particular study.

If, for example, we suspected that a government had gradually become more willing to negotiate an arms reduction agreement without insisting on on-site inspection, but had never explicitly expressed that shift, a careful coding of its articulations might reveal a declining frequency of references to such inspection. Of course, if a decline were found, it could reflect mere carelessness, an effort to engage in tacit bargaining, or perhaps even an attempt to bypass certain domestic elements that might oppose the policy shift, were it made explicit. The need for careful inference always remains.

Alternatively, a subtle and gradual shift in mood could be unwittingly communicated if a political group's statements revealed, via content analysis, a changing ratio of hostile and friendly adverbs and adjectives when dealing with certain other groups. Even more subtle, albeit intended, could be a regime's effort to deemphasize the dangers of radioactive fallout in its domestic press, as a stratagem for preparing its citizens for a resumption of nuclear weapons tests in the atmosphere (Singer, 1963).

The point is that we can use such data-generating procedures to magnify certain information and ignore other information, and to detect certain obscure "signals" that might otherwise be lost in a sea of "noise." And the principle is the same whether we code historical narratives in order to detect certain classes of events (Merritt, 1966), newspapers to detect changing reliance on certain political strategies, or legislative debates to detect shifting political values (Namenworth and Lasswell, 1970). The procedures and rationale are dealt with more fully in the specialized literature, but enough has been said here to make clear the need for a well-conceived research design and a carefully constructed set of rules by which the coders will detect, classify, and record only what is intended by the researcher.

If designed and executed carefully, the content analysis procedure can generate highly reliable data, and thus reduce our reliance on impressionistic or highly selective interpretation of a wide variety of written (and pictorial or graphic) materials. And, as already suggested, the reasoning and procedures are virtually identical, whether we are sifting through official statements in search of certain symbolic themes, through newspaper reports in search of certain economic traces, or through historians' monographs in search of certain behavioral patterns.

### The Accuracy of Data Sources

While the political scientist can—through competence, resourcefulness, and diligence—eventually solve most problems connected with indicator reliability, the accuracy of the source materials to which our indicators are applied often lies beyond our control. In those cases, we can only eschew perfection, and adapt to the unpleasant realities in a thoughtful, creative, and frank fashion (Morgenstern, 1963). Let us illustrate the problem by reference to certain types of data sources and suggest a few of the strategies for dealing with them.

There would seem to be three basic types of error in the factual materials with which we work, and each calls for a slightly different response. The most serious is the *systematic* distortion of the facts, due either to some fundamental but unintended flaw in the original procedures for observation and reportage, or to the desire of the compilers or editors to mislead the potential user. In the former category might be a set of putatively complete trade figures, but with transshipped products omitted, or military personnel figures that exclude national police or border guards without so indicating.

More likely to be intentional would be an official chronology of major power conflicts, in which all the other nations' allies are also included, but not those of the compiler nation, or military budgets in which the compiler includes supplementary appropriations for the other governments but not for his own. These possibilities of systematic distortion, intended or not, remind us of the importance of familiarity with the historical context, the relevant literature, alternative sources, the bookkeeping practices employed, and statistical techniques by which to compare various sets of distributions. Needless to say, the researcher's failure to discern systematic bias in the data sources will produce badly distorted data, and thus highly dubious findings.

The second problem is that of *random* errors, often resulting from carelessness, naiveté, and incompetence at the origin or in the reportage, or in typographical and transcribing errors, or even in efforts to correct for systematic error. Normally referred to in the aggregate as "measurement error," these random inaccuracies often cancel one another out and may even have no discernible effect on the results that emerge from subsequent analyses of the data. More likely, however, there will be some effect, and if the errors are in the sources of the outcome variable data, we will merely get a poorer fit between our theoretical model and the observed regularities.

But if the errors lie in data sources on the predictor side, the effect could be somewhat more serious. Random error in the values of these "independent" variables will result in attenuation biases in their coefficients, and the greater this random error, the more nearly will their coefficients approach zero.

A third type of error in the sources to which we turn for data is that of *incomplete* compilations, either because the original observations were incomplete, or because some of them were lost or eliminated later on when the compilations were being made. An illustrative example is that of some class of government expenditure or activity, with certain nations in certain historical periods consistently falling into the "missing" category. Often we cannot tell whether that class of activity just did not occur, or whether it occurred but was not recorded. Another frequent example is the tendency of regimes that are bureaucratically underdeveloped to publish, or report to an international body, figures that are so obviously wide of the mark that they are omitted from any compilation that is undertaken.

Missing facts and estimates need not, however, necessarily lead to the "missing data problem"; there are several strategies for estimating the value of those points that are missing. The simplest is merely to make an "informal estimate," and while this method may well produce an accurate estimate, it rests on something less than a perfectly reproducible algorithm. Equally simple is the arithmetic interpolation or extrapolation, but the virtue of its reproducibility is offset by its neglect of all information other than the trend line along which it is presumed to fall. Slightly more complicated, when working with a cross-temporal series, is to calculate the interpolated or extrapolated entries via simple statistical regression if the trend is linear, and polynomial or logarithmic regression if the trend is more complex. And if there is no clearly visible overall trend, but a fairly high degree of autocorrelation, autoregression models can be used (Nelson, 1973). Somewhat more complex, but quite justifiable, is to take another series for which we have a relatively complete set of entries, and with which the incomplete series is highly correlated (positively or negatively), and then use statistical regression procedures to solve for the missing entries.

Other strategies can also be developed for making the estimates as accurate as possible, but regardless of the technique used, we must check its reliability by comparing the results with the values of a well-established data series that might be expected to correlate highly with the one at hand. Also important, if we make extensive use of missing data estimation techniques, is our need to test the sensitivity of the data analysis results to the estimates used. This is readily accomplished by running the analyses with, and then without, the estimated cases, and if there is a discernible difference in the results, it is clear that the missing data estimates need to be reexamined, even if only to identify the systematic bias in the error source. This is not, however, to say that the estimates must be discarded. Since data points that are unavailable usually have more of a systematic bias than those that *are* available, they really could be deviant in their values and thus should be expected to exercise a clear impact on one's analytic results.

If, despite the three types of inaccuracy (random, systematic, or missing) in a set of raw data, we decide that we have no choice but to use the set nevertheless and then go ahead with one or more of the remedial procedures outlined above, two additional steps may be considered. One is to correct the obtained/estimated values to a lower level of measurement: from ratio to interval, from interval to ordinal, and in extremis, from ordinal to nominal. In principle, if the inaccuracies are not too severe, this procedure will generally discard the more erroneous information, but preserve that which is essentially correct.

Similarly, if we are working with time series, we can smooth out the trend line by the use of the moving average. This procedure treats each individual observation as unjustifiably precise in appearance, and hedges by combining it with one or two of the readings just before and just after, using the average of those three or five readings. Needless to say, the moving average solution, while eliminating misplaced precision and giving us a smoother set of values with smaller and fewer perturbations, leads inevitably to a marked increase in the autocorrelation coefficient. As a result, if one were interested in the interobservation differences—such as in arms race analyses or in evaluations of the short-term effects of a policy change—these smoothing procedures would be highly inappropriate.

Before leaving this matter of factual accuracy, there is the unavoidable issue of the so-called confidence interval, and I approach it with some trepidation. Those who have done a fair amount of indicator construction and data generation are often asked to attach some numerical value to the accuracy of the data generated from one or another data source. One possible response might be to provide as honest an estimate as we can, indicating what fraction of the data points fall within each of several error ranges. This would require three distinct calculations. First, how far off could each point in each series possibly be? Second, how probable is that extreme error, and how probable are the descending error ranges as we approach perfect accuracy? And, third, for a given data set, made up of several series, what fraction of the points falls into each of those probable error and/or confidence intervals? If we could intelligently make the first two estimates, it would be a simple matter to combine them into a single index of accuracy, such as the "standard error" of an observation, or perhaps even a Gini-like index. But experience suggests that steps one and two would not only be very time-consuming, but also could result in a misleadingly precise representation of a highly subjective and impressionistic process.

A more modest indicator of the data generator's confidence—adapted from the weapons technology community—might also be worth examining. When a large salvo of missiles is fired, accuracy is expressed in terms of "circular error, probable," indicating the radius of a circle within which half of the missiles could be expected to fall. In the same vein, we could ask how many standard deviations out from the mean of the distribution curve we would have to go to capture half of the points in the series. If either of these methods has been used in the macro-social sciences, we have not encountered it.

A final point regarding the accuracy of our data, or the factual materials from which they are generated, concerns the uses to which the data will be put. We noted earlier that a data set based upon moving averages, interpolations, and other smoothing procedures will suppress or eliminate the temporal fluctuations that could be critical to certain types of investigation. The point is that every data set that rests upon multiple sources will require certain internal adjustments, even if only to achieve comparability across actors and observation points on a given dimension. While this should cause no concern to the social scientist, it could make many data sets quite useless to the historian. But since the latter usually focus on a limited number of actors or years—while introducing an impressive number of variables and thus ending up with a poor N/V ratio (Deutsch et al., 1965)—they are unlikely to turn to a large data matrix when they need only a few of its cells. They are also wise in not doing so.

Thus, every data set must be examined closely, along with the coding rules by which it was generated, prior to its use in systematic analysis. This is not, however, to agree with the assertion that one must only generate one's data after formulating the research design. A given data set can—and should—be utilized for an appreciable array of investigations reflecting a diversity of theoretical orientations, and the idea of tailor-made data for each theoretical problem and orientation is errant nonsense. Not only would (and does) such practice make for gross inefficiency in the social sciences, but it also drastically impedes cumulativeness, since each study could end up resting upon a slightly different data base, making comparison and synthesis highly questionable (Leng and Singer, 1970). Moreover, it would lend support to the suspicion—already accepted by many of our critics—that we carefully select our data and tailor our indicators in order to assure the statistical results that accord with our "theories."

## DATA GENERATION VIA
## INDICATOR CONSTRUCTION

In the previous section, we have examined the criteria that need to be approximated—if not fully satisfied—in the construction of indicators, and the way in which they are used to generate the data that represent the changing values or magnitudes of a variable. Bearing both activities in mind, let us shift now from these general considerations to a number of specific data generation problems. The plan here is to illustrate the wide range of data sources and data-making procedures in the context of our three types of variables: attributes, relationships, and behaviors.

## Indicators of Attributes

We illustrate first with attributes, not only because they are the most familiar and usually require less in the way of heroic inferences than do indicators of relationships and behaviors, but also because—paradoxically—constructing indicators of attributes can lead to more problems of conceptual slippage than with those of relationships and behaviors.

To illustrate, suppose that a key attribute in a planned investigation is the "diplomatic importance" of nations, to which we alluded earlier. How might we go about measuring such an attribute in a reliable fashion, and what sort of indicator would be valid for a wide variety of nation types across perhaps a century and a half? The most obvious indicator would probably be one that rests upon the verbal behavior of diplomats, calling for them to rank today's nations in response to certain questionnaire items. But if we wanted to go back in time more than a few years, contemporary diplomats would not be very helpful; in that case, we might turn to the expert judgments of diplomatic historians of the periods and regions of interest.

Leaving aside the cost in time and money for such an opinion survey, it would suffer from the familiar flaws of all intuitive judgments, no matter how carefully stimulated, recorded, and combined. Within the population of respondents, there would be a wide range of criteria as to how the nations' diplomatic importance should be evaluated, with some thinking largely in terms of military or industrial capability, others relying on protocol or conference participation or diplomatic visits, and still others trying to recall which nations most regularly "had their own way" in the various regions and periods. Even if provided with explicit criteria, our respondents would be inclined to reinterpret or modify them between start and finish, either unconsciously or because of their belief that we should not use the same ones for such varying nations or periods. Further, since our historians will normally be truly expert in rather narrow bands of time and space, they will bring highly detailed knowledge to bear only within the intersection of those bands, and considerably less to bear in evaluating or scaling nations in other regions and periods. Yet another source of inconsistency might be the moment at which the interview or questionnaire was used: Has a recently encountered article or document left the strong impression that Austria-Hungary was overrated by the other powers in the 1890s, for example? Would an earlier or later interview produce a different estimate? In sum, threats to consistency across judges and across time, and hence to reliability would, along with the logistical problems, be disabling, even if the researcher's instrument were carefully designed to maximize the validity of the responses.

Wisely rejecting expert opinion as a basis for estimating the diplomatic importance of nations, the researcher might turn to a less expensive and more reliable method: content analysis of a carefully drawn sample of books or monographs on the relevant time-space intersections. With a good library, explicit criteria as to what is meant by the concept of diplomatic importance, precise instructions as to which passages to read and how to classify certain types of statements, and well-trained and thorough coders, this could be a highly satisfactory procedure for generating diplomatic importance scores. The major advantage here is that we secure the more stable judgments of our experts without the trouble and expense of interviewing live subjects, merely by going through their writings and systematically recording all of their statements regarding the diplomatic importance of the nations with which they were dealing in each study. If we are trying to generate data reflecting a concept that is widely used and whose definition—however pre-operational—is widely shared, the content analysis strategy is surely preferable to that of questionnaires or interviews. But if major time-space domains have been ignored in the literature, or if the concept at hand is neither widely used nor consistently defined, content analysis of scholarly works will not suffice.

A closely related research option might be to content analyze, not the writings of scholars, but the writings of those whose role it is to observe and comment on foreign affairs as they unfold: journalists, columnists, and editors. There are and have been newspapers with good coverage of foreign affairs in every region of the world, and there are copies of these papers going back many decades, if not centuries. Moreover, given the shared perceptions and the inevitable symbiotic relationship between the elite press and the political elites, it is reasonable to infer that the press (especially on the editorial page) will provide, over the long run, a fair expression of the elite consensus in each nation regarding the relative diplomatic importance of most of the nations in the international system.

Yet another possibility might be to code the diplomatic communications among the world's foreign ministries or between the ministries and their embassies and legations, but at least two factors would argue against this source of data. One is that evaluative statements regarding the relative importance of other nations seem to be relatively rare in these communications. The other is that newspaper files are considerably more available and accessible than the diplomatic archives, if the written trace is our preferred vehicle.

But as the previous section reminds us, there may be alternative vehicles for getting at our concept, and if they look as if they might be less costly and time consuming—as well as equally strong on the validity and reliability dimensions—they may be preferable. That we (Small and Singer, 1973) so thought when faced with the need to measure diplomatic importance is clear from the fact we indeed selected the bureaucratic-behavioral trace of diplomatic missions. The "auxiliary theory" or line of reasoning is quite simple. For reasons of economy, tradition, personnel limits, and so forth—as well as for policy reasons—the typical government over the last 150 years has established diplomatic missions in only about 45 percent of the world's capital cities, with 55 percent of them ignored. This produces, in effect, an ongoing plebiscite in which all the nations are continuously "voting with their missions" as to which of the others are more or less important to them. While some of the individual decisions may be quixotic, the net effect when all these decisions are aggregated year after year provides us with a collective judgment on the part of those who decide where their nations' primary interests lay.

Although the face validity of this attribute indicator (reflecting both the reasoning behind it and the rankings that it produces), and its correlational validity vis-à-vis the international organization officerships mentioned earlier are reassuring, it is too soon to tell whether its role in a well-founded theory will further enhance our confidence in it. While awaiting that particular test of validity, a reasonable researcher would certainly go ahead and use it, but with the prudence that should accompany the use of any less-than-proven instrument, along with the knowledge that it may well contribute to the very growth of theory that will permit its most demanding tests.

Despite the apparent indirectness of the above indicator, the number of inferential steps from conceptual variable to indicator to data can be even greater. Let us illustrate this via an attribute of the international system's structure, using an indicator that reflects *distribution of national attributes*, rather than a directly observable attribute of the system per se. In the classical literature, we often find the proposition that peace is preserved by maintaining approximate parity among the major powers, and by avoiding conditions of preponderance. The closer the distribution of capabilities is to perfect equality, the less the likelihood of war, and the closer that distribution is to pure monopoly, the greater the likelihood of war. To test that very plausible proposition, one would first have to develop an indicator of major power capabilities, and then develop an indicator of the extent to which they are concentrated in the hands of a small number of powers. A multidimensional indicator now in use (Singer, Bremer, and Stuckey, 1972) and whose validity seems quite adequate, is based upon: population (total and urban); industrial activity (energy consumed and steel produced); and military preparedness (armed forces size and expenditures). First, we have to acquire—requisition would surely underestimate the difficulty— the raw facts for each nation in each year on each of the six dimensions, using national government statistics, summaries prepared by international organizations, commercial yearbooks, scholarly monographs, and (in extremis) unpublished archival materials.

Once these raw facts have been transformed into comparable data series, we convert the absolute values into each nation's percentage share of the total. Thus, if there are five major powers in the system in a given year, and each holds precisely 20 percent of the overall capabilities, the distribution is equal, and the concentration score is therefore zero. Conversely, if one or two of them hold the lion's share, making for something akin to monopoly or duopoly, we would get a very high concentration score. Of course, the pattern usually lies between these extremes, and in any case we calculate the indicator's value using the (Ray and Singer, 1973) formula:

$$\text{CON} = \sqrt{\frac{(\Sigma \ S_i^2) - \dfrac{1}{N}}{1 - \dfrac{1}{N}}}$$

Thus, to indicate the magnitude of this particular system attribute at a given moment, we begin with data on each nation's capability attributes, combine and weight them according to one or another theoretically persuasive formula (or perhaps even treat them as equally important), convert those absolute scores into percentage shares of the aggregation's total, and finally convert those shares into a single indicator summarizing the inequality of the distribution for that month or year. This is hardly an observation of a systemic attribute, but that is increasingly true as we move toward more realistic indicators of theoretically sophisticated concepts. Nor is there anything wrong with using such indicators, as long as the line of reasoning is very explicit and the cross-level inferences are empirically and logically justified; illustrative of such indicators of distribution are: Alker and Russett (1964); Cutright (1967); Duncan and Duncan (1955); Greenberg (1956); Hall and Tiedeman (1967); and Lieberson (1969).

One may also get at certain structural properties of a complex system by using dyadic relationship or bondedness data. Macro-political investigations rest quite often on notions of cleavage or fragmentation (Rae and Taylor, 1970), segregation (Bell, 1954), or polarization in the system at hand (Wallace, 1973; Bueno de Mesquita, 1975), either as an outcome to be explained or as an explanatory variable that might help account for the variation in some theoretically interesting outcome. In that case, we would first requisition, gather, or generate the data reflecting the presence and magnitude of a certain class of bond or link between each pair of entities that comprise the system at the time of each observation. This could be a relationship as constant and given as geographical distance, or one that reflects a consciously chosen and often changing bond, such as alliance commitments or commercial exchanges.

Here, the data would be entered into an actor-by-actor matrix in which every component entity is given both a row and a column. In the cell marking the intersection between A's row and N's column, the bondedness data are entered for every pair that is bonded on that dimension; for those pairs that have no such bond, a zero is entered. Once these data are entered into our computer files, we use one of a number of matrix (Guttman, 1968; Lingoes, 1973) or data reduction routines (Harmon, 1976) to ascertain the number of discernible clusters or poles, the depth of cleavage between clusters, the strength of the bondedness within them, and so forth. Further, depending on the theoretical question at hand, one may compare the configurations at successive times to measure the direction and rate of change in them, or compare those reflecting two or more different types of bondedness (such as economic interdependence or political alignment) in order to tap the extent to which the different configurations reinforce or counteract one another.

## Indicators of Relationships

As already suggested, the word "relationship" in social science can have a multitude of meanings, and two of the possible meanings concern us here. One reflects the similarity of two entities along a given atttribute or property dimension: the relationships between entities A and B in terms of their relative size, power, wealth, organizational complexity, cultural homogeneity, and the like. Strictly speaking, we should use such words as comparability or similarity in this connection, reserving "relationship" for links and associations that bond or relate them to one another. Let us do so here, and explore some of the ways in which macro-political relationships might be ascertained and measured.

While it is true that some attribute or property variables rest upon the relationship among the component units of the entity (and we return to that issue shortly), most of them tend to be more directly observable, or else inferable from data that are observable. But when we try to describe relationships, we are dealing not only with "the two-body problem," but with that most intangible of phenomena, a bond or link or association. Even addressing something as elusive as a cultural *attribute* (an organization's morale or a political party's credibility), there is some directly observable trace from which reasonable inferences may be drawn, but almost all inter-entity bonds are beyond direct observation. Unlike the bonds that connect physical or biological entities, those that connect social entities are largely symbolic and intangible.

Illustrative examples are contracts between commercial firms, treaties between nations, multilateral agreements linking international organizations to member governments, and so forth. In these cases, there is at least the written document that describes the bond. But equally important to the student of comparative or international politics are those bonds and links that do not rest upon tangible documents but upon inherited or arranged understandings, or even upon historical concatenations that were never intended. For example, two nations may be found in the same grouping or cluster based on the fact that their diplomatic missions are in virtually the same capitals, or on their tendency to belong to the same international organizations. On the other hand, their membership in a given alliance cluster would not only be the result of more conscious choice, but would also be a condition of which its elites could hardly be unaware.

The above-mentioned relationships would normally be inferred from the close scanning of a bondedness matrix, in which every entity is listed in both a column and a row of the type of matrix described earlier, with the presence, absence, or strength of the bond connecting each pair shown in the cell marking the intersection of one's column with the other's row. Once the raw data reflecting these bonds had been acquired or generated, and entered into the matrix, we could use one of the several computerized decomposition algorithms to ascertain which entities clustered together on that type of bond at that particular moment.

Yet another type of data that can be used for inferring relationships is that of interaction. While, as suggested earlier, there is often a failure to discriminate between these two classes of variable, conceptual precision in our data making—and thus our theory building—requires it to be made. By relationship, of course, we mean the sorts of bonds and associations referred to above, and by interaction, we mean behaviors that are directed toward, and responsive to, one another. While a relationship may affect interaction patterns (partners in a coalition government, for example, are likely to vote with the government on a confidence measure) and interactions may affect relationships (courtship leading to marriage, negotiation leading to a formal agreement, trade leading to a common market), they are clearly not the same phenomenon. Further, we may predict interaction patterns from a relationship (exchanging military plans on the basis of a defense pact) and a relationship from observed interaction (membership in opposing coalitions on the basis of conflictual behaviors). And, of course, we may infer the existence of a relationship from observed interactions (a most-favored nation agreement from the mutual reduction of tariff levels). Bearing these distinctions in mind, we turn to our third type of indicator: that reflecting behavior and/or interaction.

## Indicators of Behavior and Interaction

We suggested earlier that these phenomena are generally more visible than attributes or relationships, but this does not mean that it is necessarily easier to observe and measure them in the scientific sense. One reason for the difficulty in observation is that behavioral events occur rapidly, and if the observer is not on the scene at the precise moment, the action will be missed. And if they happen to occur very slowly, one would require a sequence of observers to relieve one another (Alger, 1966). Also problematical are behavior and interactions that occur across so wide a swath of space that they are beyond our capacity to see, or otherwise sense. Thus, despite their tangibility (unless carried out in secrecy), interactions require us to develop particularly ingenious indicators and sensitive strategies for picking up their traces.

The traces that are left by the behaviors and interaction of political entities can be sought in a variety of places. For nations vis-à-vis other nations, these might be the memoirs of, or (if our interest is in relatively recent events) interviews with the participants or close observers; diplomatic archives; foreign ministry chronologies; official records of international organizations; newspaper accounts; and the standard narrative monographs by historians working from these other sources. For legislative bodies, government ministries, political parties, or interest groups, the sources will not be that different: memoirs, interviews, newspaper accounts, official documents, and so forth.

Again, however, knowing where to look for the traces (or recollections) left by behavioral phenomena is only part of the game. Once the raw material has been located—if at all—the problem remains of converting what is essentially an undifferentiated welter of facts and impressions into scientifically usable data sets. In addition to the issues discussed under basic procedures for the generation and extraction of data, there are two particular problems.

First, there is the conceptual distinction between behavior and interaction, and while it is seldom noted, our failure to do so can lead to some foolish interpretations. The most dramatic example would be that of conflict escalation, in which there is a strong tendency for the observer to assume that all belligerent moves by one party are directed toward, or are in response to, the self-evident opponent or adversary. Just as nations in an arms race may well be arming vis-à-vis third and fourth parties (Moll, 1974)—not to mention vis-à-vis a variety of domestic actors—all political actors attend to several others simultaneously. Thus, rather than make an easy inference from the separate behaviors of an "obviously" interacting pair, it is essential that we begin by coding each party's behaviors separately, and only then ascertain the degree to which they constitute interaction. The existence of an obvious relationship is insufficient evidence, as is the mere temporal or geographical proximity of their separate behavior sequences. Usually, it is necessary to examine one facet or another of the respective decision processes prior to concluding that the behavior patterns constitute a literal interaction process.

The second problem with behavioral and interactional data sets is that we are never certain that the full population of events has been identified. Those who have tried to generalize about behavioral regularities only to discover that their generalizations rested upon an incomplete and highly skewed set of cases can appreciate this problem, but there seldom is any ironclad procedure for assuring a complete universe. When we deal with such behaviors as legislative roll-call votes or the cases before a court during a given session, the danger of missing any of the events is very low. But if our concern is with behavior that occurs in a less fully institutionalized environment, the probability of missing some of the cases can be all too high. This is particularly true if the researcher is only interested in a subset of the population, such as only those inter-nation disputes in which military force was mobilized or deployed. In such a situation, how do we know whether the chroniclers, journalists, or historians might have omitted some or most of those qualifying cases because "nothing important" came to them? The standard solution here, when secondary materials are the only data source available, is to code several of them, written from different perspectives in time as well as place and culture.

## CONCLUSION: SOME MODEST PROPOSALS

Of all the skills that go into the growth of social science knowledge, the least developed is that of data generation. While data generation and index construction—like model building and data analysis—are not sufficient in themselves, they are absolutely necessary to the scientific enterprise. Yet the college and graduate school curricula seldom include courses on the subject, journal articles on it are extremely rare, there seem to be fewer than ten texts on the subject in English, and worst of all, most of the scores of texts on social science methods provide only a superficial glance at the problems and strategies associated with the generation of data. Further, whereas the philosophers of science have turned out reams on the ways in which to *interpret* observed patterns, they have virtually ignored the processes by which the observations themselves might be carried out and recorded.

We might speculate as to the sources of this unfortunate asymmetry. Do we consider the acquisition of data so simple and obvious a task that "anyone" can do it? Or do we assume that it is best left to the historians? Or if the past holds no key to knowledge about the future, that journalists and bureaucrats and librarians can do the job for us? Perhaps we are all "closet theorists," persuaded that logic, elegance, and imagination are all we need to understand social phenomena? Or, to invoke a football metaphor, with the quarterback basking in the limelight, why become a guard? The possibilities are nearly endless, but far from reassuring.

Several solutions, in addition to those implied above, come to mind, and an article on political research methods is surely the appropriate place to suggest a few of them. Despite a plethora of discouraging tendencies in the macro-social sciences today—ranging from such gimmickry as "evaluation research" and "futurology," to increasing faith in pure cerebration, to perpetuation of the dubious fact-values dichotomy—there are several encouraging ones. Among these is the increasing interaction between social scientists and historians, reflected in the establishment of the Social Science History Association. The central objective, as we understand it, is to help social scientists become more longitudinal and historians to become more scientific. In our view, this convergence holds considerable promise for both sets of disciplines, and perhaps even for an ultimately integrated science of human behavior. More particularly, political scientists, economists, and sociologists can profit by taking a more retrospective view of the phenomena that engage them, and can become more familiar with a greater diversity of cases from which to generalize. But most germane here is a third possibility: that we will learn from historians how to get at and then evaluate the incredibly rich variety of traces left to us by earlier generations. The interaction will, we hope, also lead them to think nomothetically, both in the formulation of explanations and in the gathering of facts. Just as the social scientist needs to be more attentive to the intricacies of single episodes and the hidden secrets of half-forgotten artifacts, historians can become sensitive to the need for comparability in their facts and generality in their explanations.

Another possibility, also institutional, might be the establishment of a journal or annual (preferably multilingual) devoted to data generation and index construction in cross-national and international politics. Such a journal could help to educate those who are unfamiliar with the methods and results in this sector, and help the more avant garde to expand their repertoires. And it could signal the discipline's recognition that models without empirical evidence may be good fun, but incomplete science. Perhaps most importantly, it could create incentives, rewards, and legitimacy for those who might otherwise continue in the comfortable ways of waiting for the other fellow's data set, or of theorizing without data entirely. Another possibility, involving the foundations, comes to mind. Rather than continue to invest largely in research that is neither reproducible nor cumulative, perhaps one or two of these quasi-public institutions might be persuaded to establish a few centers whose primary task might be the generation, maintenance, and diffusion of data sets of potentially wide applicability. Such units as the International Relations Archive of the Inter-University Consortium for Political and Social Research have intermittently considered and even entered into such activities, but none has yet done so in a vigorous and sustained fashion because of the financial constraints, the difficulty of deciding which data sets would most be worth producing, and the absence of strong demand. Despite these constraints, and the lack of strong institutional support, we have nevertheless turned out a number of data collections, ranging widely in both substantive focus and scientific quality; among these are: Banks (1971), Banks and Textor (1963), Morrison et al. (1972), Russett et al. (1964), and Singer and Small (1972), and Taylor and Hudson (1972); an excellent critique of several of them is Gurr (1974).

Finally, those of us who teach and do research in the macro-social sciences stand in need of some modest reforms. First, we can set a better example by increasing the inductive element in our own research mix, and by investing in the generation of more ambitious data sets. Second, when we write up our results, we can describe and justify our data-making procedures, eschewing the tendency to treat those activities as somehow too trivial to mention. Third, as teachers, we can break away from the stereotyping behavior that has kept us so data-poor: the early classification of our students, especially at the graduate level, as either "brilliant and creative theorists" or "competent, but plodding empiricists." This sort of practice discourages our most capable people from taking on the important and challenging work in indicator construction and data generation. Worse yet, it virtually assures the perpetuation of our peculiar two-culture problem, and makes it quite unlikely that we will begin to turn out what the discipline and the world need most: the complete social scientist.

## ACKNOWLEDGMENTS

The author is especially indebted to Michael Champion for his assistance, to Ted Gurr for his constructive criticisms, and to the National Science Foundation for supporting the basic research from which many of these lessons were learned.

———————— ■ ————————

# CHAPTER TWELVE

# The Historical Experiment
# as a Research Strategy
# in the Study of World Politics

## INTRODUCTION

As one looks back on the important developments in political science over the past two decades, there is much to be applauded. While it may be premature to say that we have come "of age" as a scientific discipline, the field is clearly in better shape today than it was in the early 1950s. One indicator is the ratio between mere speculation and observed empirical regularities reported in our journal articles. Another is the decline in the percentage (if not in absolute numbers) of our colleagues who insist that political phenomena are just not amenable to scientific examination. A third might be the dramatic increase in the number of political scientists who have been exposed to training in the techniques and rationale of data making and data analysis. The list could be extended, but we need not do so here.

On the other hand, a stance of comfortable complacency would be very premature. Not only have we fared badly in coming to grips with the knowledge-action relationship in the abstract, but we have by and large done a poor job of shaping the policies of our respective national, provincial, and local governments. Since others as well as myself[1] have dealt—if not definitively—with these issues before, let me eschew further discussion of the knowledge *application* question for the moment, and go on to matters of basic research. Of the more serious flaws to date, two stand out particularly. One is the lack of balance between a concern for cumulativeness on the one hand and the need for innovation on the other.[2] My impression is that students of *national* politics (at least those who work in the vineyard of empirical regularities) have been more than conscientious in staying with one set of problems, such as the relationship between political attitudes

Reprinted from *Social Science History*, vol. 2, no. 1, 1977, pp. 1–22. Reprinted by permission.

and voting behavior. But students of *inter*-national politics have, conversely, tended to move all too quickly from one problem to another, long before cumulative evidence has been generated and before our findings are integrated into coherent wholes.

A second weakness, as I see it, is our general failure to appreciate the full relevance of the experimental mode to our research strategies. This observation is meant in two senses. First, when we do longitudinal studies, we often fail to conceive of them in experimental terms. Second, and perhaps more important, macro-social scientists tend to focus heavily upon contemporary phenomena, and thus overlook the great scientific potential of longitudinal analyses conducted in the experimental mode. This *should* be a matter of some surprise, when we consider the extent to which our data analysis techniques rest upon, and flow out of, the experimental metaphor. From the pioneering work of Pearson and Fisher, up through Stouffer, Blalock, and Campbell and Stanley,[3] a strong preoccupation of our best methodologists has been with experimental (or quasi-experimental) design in one version or another. Yet, with few exceptions,[4] we have tended to view experimentation in rather narrow terms, and to think of it as a research activity that should be confined to the laboratory.[5]

In the pages that follow, I should like to offer a somewhat broader view of the experimental mode, and suggest that we have barely begun to exploit its possibilities in the investigation of political phenomena. Although my illustrations will draw heavily from the study of international politics in general, and the war-peace question in particular, my hope is that the possibilities that are illuminated here will find relevance in other sectors of the social sciences as well.[6]

## THREE TYPES OF EXPERIMENT

When the concept of experiments comes up, most of us—scientists as well as laymen—tend to think of laboratories. In them, we expect to find all sorts of instruments by which one observes and measures the phenomena associated with the predictor or outcome variables. These might include, for example, a bubble chamber or spectroscope for the physical scientist, a microscope or centrifuge for the biological scientist, and a moving picture camera or GSR console for the social scientist.

The laboratory is, of course, associated with scientific research because it facilitates the conduct of "controlled" experiments, in which one can: (a) manipulate many of the factors that might affect the outcome; (b) isolate the effects of one factor at a time; and (c) run the same experiment over and over to ascertain the consistency of a given set of results.[7] As I hope to demonstrate in a later section, there are serious obstacles to a clean experiment even in the laboratory. But first let us take note of the fact that two *other* types of experiment can also be envisaged.

The second type occurs, not in the laboratory, but out in the "field," or in "nature." Here, the investigator need not—and often cannot—generate all the events and conditions of interest. Rather, he or she first observes and records the normal sequence or concatenation of events, and then either waits for or instigates some intervening event in order to ascertain its effect on the previously observed pattern of outcomes.[8] The astronomer, for example, waits for a number of planets to arrange themselves in a given configuration, and then tries to measure the effect of that configuration on the orbit of an Nth planet. Or the medical researcher divides a number of patients into two groups whose members are more or less identical on the relevant background characteristics. He or she then subjects each group to a different treatment (or perhaps to a placebo "treatment") and waits to see whether one treatment "produces" more cures or ameliorations than the other.

Similarly, the sociologist might identify twelve cities that are closely matched along the most relevant dimensions and then anticipate (or arrange) that the appropriate agencies will divide them into three groups, using a new job referral policy A in four of them, another policy B in another four, and retaining the old policy in the others. A year later, the unemployment scores can be compared to ascertain which of the three policies "leads to" the lowest unemployment figure. While such field experiments do not offer the same opportunities for control as do those conducted in the laboratory, we can appreciate that a modicum of control is nevertheless achieved. Equally important, in the field, one often makes up in realism what one loses in control, or, to put it in more formal language, the threats to the experiment's internal validity may be more than compensated for by the improvement in its external validity.[9]

So far, then, we have considered the well-known laboratory experiment and the by-no-means-unknown field experiment. Let us now turn to the third type, or historical experiment. Some will object to the pairing of these two words, and this is quite understandable. Treating events or conditions which have already transpired, in which no intervention—obtrusive or otherwise[10]—is possible, does not seem consonant with our traditional ideas of experimentation, or perhaps even with "quasi-experimentation," to use Donald T. Campbell's term.

To sum up this section, one might prefer the conventional definition of experiment, but as Jean Laponce[11] reminds us, the more restricted interpretation is "fraught with dangers," and could lead us to focus "too exclusively on the laboratory." The more narrow definition, he adds, "is ill-adjusted to the variety of data and conditions to which the social scientist can apply experimental techniques." The balance of this paper should, however, not only indicate that the historical experiment is a perfectly legitimate mode of research, but that it actually offers certain advantages vis-à-vis those experiments that are carried out in the laboratory or in the field.

## KEY PROBLEMS IN SCIENTIFIC EXPERIMENTATION

Having committed myself to demonstrating the proposition that the experimental mode is as applicable to history as to the laboratory or the field, I must first determine how best to make that demonstration. One promising point of departure is to identify some of the major preoccupations and key problems of the scientific experimentalist, and then to compare the opportunities and constraints offered by each of the three experimental settings. Let me, thus, attempt that in a rather general sense in this section, and then go on to *the* central issue—that of control—in the subsequent section.

### Observation and Measurement

While systematic observation is highly interdependent with data analysis and theoretical inference, one can separate out these activities for the sake of expositional clarity. Once one's model or hypothesis is reasonably well formulated, the next major step is the acquisition or generation of one's data. And, unless another researcher or some problem-oriented "consumer" has generated the necessary data, one must set about the establishment of procedures for systematic observation and measurement.

In the laboratory, this task *can* be as simple as defining a "known material" and then weighing out the specified amount of it or measuring its spatial dimensions. But, with increasing frequency, the physical or biographical experimenter must wrestle with more complex procedures. For example, without the elaborate device known as a bubble chamber, the high energy physicist would be unable to observe and photograph the path of ionizing particles. Similarly, without the diffusion of a silver nitrate solution that blackens on contact with organic matter, the medical researcher would be unable to trace those proteins whose presence may indicate the symptoms of certain forms of schizophrenia.

For the social scientist working in the laboratory, the range of observational techniques can likewise be from the simple to the complex, and from the direct to the indirect. A simple and direct technique would be the identification of each experimental subject by sex, height, weight, and hair color, but if one required indicators of a less tangible phenomena, the technique would be less direct. In experimental games, we can classify the subject's response to a variety of electoral ballots[12] or to a combined stimulus of payoff matrix and opponent's moves via a simple behavioral coding scheme.[13] More elusive, but fairly operational, might be the use of trained observer-coders who infer the motivation behind a wide variety of acts emitted by the subjects[14] and whose performance can be checked in part by tests of inter-coder reliability.

Shifting now from laboratory to field, the experimentalists' problems again have a great deal in common, regardless of discipline. The astronomer can now ascertain the size or infer the orbital pattern of a given planet with high-powered telescopes. And the meteorologist's observation techniques can range from the simple reading of barometric pressure to the complex interpretation of radar traces left by a passing storm. Similarly, the medical scientist will work with such easily measured factors as vital lung capacity or blood pressure, and such elusive ones as level of anxiety or family medical history. And, once more, the social scientist can conduct field experiments in which the observation and measurement problems may range from the highly operational to the ambiguous, and from the obvious to the improbable. For example, we can code and scale children's behavior[15] or scale the differential campaign appeals directed to different members of the electorate,[16] or measure the degree of centralization in the decisional process of two different government agencies as part of an inquiry into problem-solving efficiency.

Even at the international level, a field experiment might require the measurement of, let us say, the voting consensus of a given United Nations bloc before an expected crisis or series of weapons tests, in order to ascertain the "effect" of those events on the subsequent voting pattern. To take another example, one might scale the threat perception levels in one nation's diplomatic articulations prior to, and then following, a major election in an adversary nation. To go a step further in emphasizing the extent to which one can satisfy the requirements of reliability and validity in the measurement of historical phenomena that are germane to comparative and international politics, let me note that many events and conditions do indeed leave traces and records. And, with a modicum of ingenuity, political scientists have already observed and measured—long years after the fact— many critical types of events and conditions. Among these are alliance configurations, diplomatic rankings, polarization and fractionalization of various systems, the frequency and magnitude of wars and insurrections, the shifting capabilities of nations, and so forth.[17] And, as some of these labels suggest, one need not be restricted to simple and direct measures such as a nation's territorial size, population, or even the reconstruction of its national income. One may also get at more complex, derived measures whose reliability and validity will turn out to be every bit as high as those generated in the laboratory or field.[18] The point, then, is that the observation and measurement problems and opportunities are essentially the same for all the sciences, and are so regardless of the setting within which the experiment is carried out.

## Ascertaining Covariation

Although it is now a truism to note that correlation is not equivalent to causation, few scientists would object to the proposition that the establishment of covariation—while not *sufficient*—is indeed *necessary* to the search for causation. Given the central role of covariation, then, it behooves us to examine the ways in which it may be ascertained in the three different research settings: laboratory, field, and historical—and the three—physical, biological, and social—sciences.

This discussion can be briefer than that concerning observation and measurement because the similarities are even more evident as we move from one setting to the next. That is, once we have satisfied certain minimal conditions of reliability and validity in our indicators, and have gone on to generate the data sets for predictor and outcome variables, the statistical problems begin to look very much alike.

For example, there is the universal problem of adopting the analytic technique that is appropriate to the fineness of our measurement scales. If our data are measured on a nominal scale only, we have little choice but to analyze them via contingency tables, using such coefficients of association as the chi-square, Yule's Q, tau-beta, phi, and so forth. If we can do better than mere nominal classification of our data, and rank the observations on some sort of ordinal scale, we may then utilize such rank-order coefficients as Spearman's rho, the Kolmogorov-Smirnov and Mann-Whitney tests, or one of Kendall's several measures of rank covariation between (or across) ordinally-scaled data sets. And as we improve the precision of our indicators and utilize data that are measured on interval or ratio scales, we can go to more refined coefficients of association and covariation. One of the most widely used is Pearson's product moment correlation (r), and beyond that is a panoply of statistical regression techniques, most of which permit a modicum of prudently inferred causality.[19]

The measures of covariation that we use will depend more on the quality of the data with which we work, and on where we stand on the road from exploration to discovery to confirmation of associations than upon the milieu within which the investigation takes place. One can, for example, think of no good reason for avoiding the path analysis technique when involved in an historical experiment, or a simple contingency table analysis when in the biological laboratory.

## Inferring Causality

As we move from the data making and data analysis phases of a scientific investigation to the problem of interpreting the results, the apparent differences among laboratory, field, and historical experiments take on greater magnitude. Thus, even if the arguments of the preceding two sub-sections seem quite reasonable, some will urge that, in *this* sub-section, we find the inescapable gulf between "real" science and social science, especially that version of the latter that does not occur in the controlled environment of the laboratory.

In the methodological literature, one increasingly encounters the concepts of internal and external *validity* when examining a research design.[20] Essentially, the validity issue can be translated into the question: to what extent does the research design permit us to infer "causality" or some approximation thereof? To be more precise, the issue is not one of the validity of the *design* (or of the experiment), but of the *inferences* we seek to draw from the results of the investigation.[21]

The labels are slightly unfortunate in another sense as well, because internal validity is seen as germane to the study itself, whereas *external* validity refers to the generalizability of the study's findings to some larger population of unobserved cases. While agreeing that (a) the design must reflect both concerns, and (b) they are interdependent, and the researcher must therefore often accept trade-offs between the two, I would nevertheless prefer a sharper semantic and conceptual distinction. In any event, let us attend mainly to the first of these considerations at this juncture.

In *any* research setting, the central issue is that of experimental *control*: The arrangement of the investigation such that any inferences we draw will not turn out to be ill-founded or spurious. Or to put it another way, adequate controls permit us to conclude that the specified predictor (independent) variables were indeed the ones that produced the variation in the outcome variable, and that such variation cannot be attributed to other events or conditions. The virtues of the laboratory, versus the field or history, in the social sciences, may be summarized briefly. One is the ease with which we control the environment within which our subjects are observed. *In principle*, only those external incentives and constraints which we want are present in the laboratory, whereas such control is very difficult to achieve in the natural or historical setting. Second, we can (again, in principle) control and manipulate the specific social stimuli to which our subjects are exposed. Whether those stimuli are generated by the experimenter, a stooge, or other subjects, our control over them is thought to be quite effective. Third, we can control the information which reaches our subject to a degree not found in the field. Fourth, and in some social scientists' eyes the most important, is the reproducibility of the experimental setting. The operations may be repeated as often as necessary—and with successive groups of subjects—at modest cost in time or effort. Conversely, one must wait days, months, or years and still not find the "same" set of conditions again in the natural world.

On the other hand, *all* the problems of experimental control are not easily solved by using the social science laboratory setting. One of the more serious is that of a behavioral baseline. That is, if we want to ascertain the effects of certain experimental stimuli on the behavior of individuals or groups, there is little value in using some artificial baseline to represent the "before" regularities. Yet it is well known that we often get rather different behavior patterns in the laboratory than those that really occur in nature or in the field. Sometimes we try to get around this artifact by relying on the subjects' self-reports as to their actual, pre-stimulus, behavior patterns. But this is often just as unreliable as the laboratory-generated behavior, and the experimenter is thus left uncertain as to what the actual pre-stimulus patterns might have been.

Other disadvantages of the laboratory experiment also come to mind as possible threats to effective control, and these range across all eight items listed by Campbell and Stanley[22] in their treatment of experiments and quasi-experiments, which I take to mean field experiments.[23] Rather than go into further detail on the disadvantages of the laboratory or field setting, however, let me move now to the ways in which one might solve some of the control problems in conducting historical experiments, noting similarities and differences vis-à-vis the other two settings as the discussion unfolds. Before doing so, however, a modest epistemological digression is in order.

So far, we have acquiesced in the implicit assumption that "causality" exists in the physical, biological, and social worlds, and that in due course we will identify the causes of all these phenomena that interest us. As I see it, this view contains two possible flaws.

First, a great many phenomena occur as the "result" of several alternative processes; thus a given outcome pattern could arise out of two or more causal sequences. In some cases, we will find that a single variable, if present in sufficient strength, will largely determine the outcome. In others, the specified outcome may require the presence of two or three variables, whose additive strength exceeds the critical threshold. In more complex cases, the outcome is dependent, not upon the total *sum* of the magnitudes of our necessary and sufficient conditions, but upon their *interactions*. That is, the potency of certain variables—no matter how great their magnitude—will be negligible until combined with some catalytic variable.

Second, "causality" usually implies a deterministic process, in which the outcome is *not* a result of random or stochastic elements. This may be true of such trivial outcomes as the descent of a cannon ball in a perfect vacuum, but not of the more interesting and humanly important outcomes that occur in the referent world. All social events may be thought of as the outcome of a concatenation of some deterministic, some stochastic, and some voluntaristic elements; and, of course, the so-called voluntaristic elements are themselves the consequence of both deterministic and stochastic elements. In that vein, even though we recognize that our "unexplained variance," error terms, or residuals, are indeed partly a function of our limited knowledge, we also recognize that there will always be *some* fraction of the observed variance that cannot be attributed to a specific causal element.

Thus, in place of the notion of "causality," my preference is for the related notion of "explanation." In using that concept, we explicitly come to terms with the fact that knowledge results from the interactions between the observer and the referent phenomena. Further, it recognizes that the adequacy of an explanation, in the final analysis, rests on the inter-subjective agreement of the relevant specialists in that research sector. In sum, we design our investigations and go about observation, analysis, and interpretation in such a way that we not only satisfy the more or less objective canons of scientific method, but satisfy the skepticism of our more competent and critical colleagues. In the balance of this paper, then, our focus will be more on the devices by which we can enhance the explanatory powers of our models, and less upon the search for that chimera known as "causality."[24]

## ESTABLISHING CONTROLS IN
## THE HISTORICAL EXPERIMENT

Shifting now from the concept of experimental controls in the abstract, let us examine some of the specific devices by which such controls may be established in the macro-social sciences. These are of three basic types. The first is the comparative case study, in which we actually find in the referent world two or more situations which appear to be similar in certain of their key variables, and whose *dissimilarity* in other variables is the object of investigation.[25] The second device is that of post hoc statistical manipulation, whereby we systematically isolate the effects of one variable or group of variables at a time. The third is simulation of either the all-human, all-machine, or mixed human-machine combination, in which we seek to replay or recreate the historical processes under investigation. Let us examine these devices, comparing their assets and liabilities for the historical experiment as well as vis-à-vis the other two experimental modes.

## The Comparative Case Study

The moment that one goes beyond the telling of a single narrative or the interpretation of a single case, one is into the "nomothetic" mode, and is thus laying the groundwork for cumulative knowledge. Although most historians remain within the "ideographic" mode, and seldom attend—in any explicit fashion—to matters of comparison and accumulation, social scientists increasingly invade their empirical domain, using a rather different intellectual style.[26]

One element in that style is the self-conscious search for two or more historical cases, on the basis of which a systematic comparative analysis might be constructed. There are four basic options in making that search. First, one might try to identify *all* the cases that satisfy the inclusion criteria and that fall within the specified spatial-temporal domain. Second, one might identify that population (or universe) of cases, but only examine a sample drawn from the population. Third, one might bypass the very costly and frustrating task of identifying the population, and merely draw a "sample" whose relationship to the population remains unspecified. And fourth, one may search out a finite number of cases (two or more) whose characteristics are such that they permit the sort of comparison desired. In this section, let us focus on the fourth option, as it is the simplest device for approximating (if not establishing) certain minimal controls.[27]

Here, we explicitly look for those few cases that are identical or similar in *some* specified characteristics, and different in others. If, for example, we wanted to test the proposition that communist regimes make for longer life expectancy of their citizens than capitalist ones, we would look for two or more nations whose *other* cultural and structural characteristics are fairly similar, but whose political regimes are of the two crude types mentioned above. Then, if satisfied that the relevant genetic, environmental, and social conditions were reasonably similar, any difference between the two sets of (allegedly reliable) life expectancy figures *could* be attributed to the regime differences. This would be a primitive, but by no means useless, device for establishing a degree of experimental control. That is, it permits an approximate isolation of certain variables so that they can be held constant while the "experimental" variable is, in effect, manipulated to ascertain its effect upon the outcome variable.

To take another illustration, suppose that we seek to differentiate between those few international conflicts that ended in war during a given time period, and those many that did *not* end in war. We might well begin the inquiry by measuring the relative military-industrial capabilities of the protagonists, and then isolating all those cases in which the difference between their scores is 10 percent or less. This rests on the reasonable assumption that if a greater discrepancy in their relative strengths obtains, the weaker party will tend to make sufficient concessions to avoid a military confrontation; the weaker lack the *strength* to fight, and the stronger lack the *incentive* to fight. Having now divided our cases into those of "approximate parity" and "clear disparity," the next step is to subdivide further the former cases according to their *dissimilarity* on one or more other variables.

One reasonable candidate might be the polarization of the interstate system at the onset of the crisis. Then, we ask whether—controlling for relative capabilities as the parameter variable—those crises that occur in periods of high polarization show a significantly higher frequency of ending up in war than those that occur in periods of medium or low polarization. (The relevant assumption here is that nations will have fewer cross-pressures working on them when the system is polarized, with most of the other nations readily identifiable as friend or foe.)[28] Even though all of the events and conditions have unfolded prior to the analysis, and even though we know the outcome of each crisis, we do *not* know what the statistical distribution will be until the analysis has been conducted. In several senses, then, we have conducted a controlled experiment, albeit a rather simple one, and it seems appropriate to answer a partial "yes" to Beer's rhetorical question as to whether the comparative case study might be regarded as "the social scientists' equivalent of the natural scientists' laboratory."[29]

### Statistical Manipulation and Sequential Analyses

In one of the more suggestive papers to come out of the comparative politics literature, Arend Lijphart asserts that "the statistical method can be regarded, therefore, as an approximation of the experimental method."[30] He then goes on to quote Ernest Nagel to the effect that "every branch of inquiry aiming at reliable general laws concerning empirical subject matter must employ a procedure that, if it is not strictly controlled experimentation, has the essential logical functions of experiment in inquiry."[31] This is essentially the point of view I hope to reflect here in examining a second type of device for achieving or approximating the controls essential to an historical, post hoc, experiment. While the comparative case study (with a low N) usually rests upon nominal or ordinal differentiations and can be analyzed via contingency table analyses, we now rely upon interval or ratio scales, and on concomitantly more elaborate data analysis techniques, but the difference goes beyond matters of measurement and analysis.

Here, we usually turn to the construction of abstract models that reflect our theoretical hunches and/or prior research findings, and then go on to test them for "goodness of fit" vis-à-vis the observed referent world. Those models may, in turn, reflect a variety of methodological orientations as well as substantive foci. At one extreme, one might use product-moment correlations in order to ascertain which of several alternative predictors are most strongly associated with the variations in our outcome variable. At the other, we might postulate a complex model in path analysis form and then use the relative strengths of the path coefficients to ascertain which version of the model best fits the observed historical phenomena. Perhaps most typical, however, is the multiple regression approach, in which we statistically "isolate" the effects of each predictor variable (and groups of them) in our model, one at a time.

It should be noted, however, that as we shift to these more elaborate analytical tools, we often move away from the orientation that characterizes a creative experimental strategy. Let me illustrate with an imaginary example whose detail is not excessive, given the importance of this point to my overall argument.[32] In the columns below are the magnitudes of war and of three hypothetical predictor variables for twenty observation periods, and below them are some of the statistical characteristics of those four distributions:

| | Amount of War | Stratification | Polarity | Concentration |
|---|---|---|---|---|
| | 5 | 14 | 1 | 10 |
| | 98 | 3 | 87 | 3 |
| | 76 | 90 | 5 | 19 |
| | 14 | 4 | 20 | 4 |
| | 29 | 11 | 3 | 7 |
| | 87 | 13 | 7 | 88 |
| | 93 | 22 | 89 | 11 |
| | 64 | 81 | 4 | 2 |
| | 85 | 19 | 1 | 90 |
| | 2 | 2 | 3 | 9 |
| | 7 | 7 | 12 | 3 |
| | 95 | 5 | 92 | 12 |
| | 81 | 86 | 14 | 2 |
| | 86 | 13 | 2 | 97 |
| | 91 | 10 | 88 | 1 |
| | 94 | 87 | 26 | 5 |
| | 1 | 28 | 47 | 16 |
| | 40 | 7 | 13 | 10 |
| | 16 | 42 | 18 | 27 |
| | 90 | 23 | 4 | 79 |
| min | 1 | 2 | 1 | 1 |
| max | 98 | 90 | 92 | 97 |
| mean | 57.7 | 28.4 | 26.8 | 24.8 |
| s.d. | 38.05 | 31.10 | 33.70 | 33.44 |

Under the traditional mode, one would begin—or unfortunately, also end—by examining the product-moment correlation matrix:

| | War | Stratification | Polarity | Concentration |
|---|---|---|---|---|
| War | 1.00 | | | |
| Stratification | .25 | 1.00 | | |
| Polarity | .39 | -.24 | 1.00 | |
| Concentration | .34 | -.17 | - .36 | 1.00 |

It turns out that all of the predictors show a *positive*, but weak association with war, and equally weak, but *negative* associations with each other. From this, the orthodox inference would be that all three predictors rise and fall with war over time, but that their impact on war is far from impressive.

Suppose, however, that one then reverted to the simpler mode, and examined these associations via a set of $2 \times 2$ contingency tables, as follows:

| Stratification | War Hi | War Lo |
|---|---|---|
| Hi | 4 | 0 |
| Lo | 8 | 8 |

| Polarity | War Hi | War Lo |
|---|---|---|
| Hi | 4 | 0 |
| Lo | 8 | 8 |

| Concentration | War Hi | War Lo |
|---|---|---|
| Hi | 4 | 0 |
| Lo | 8 | 8 |

When we examine this type of display, we tend to ask fewer questions about mere covariation and begin to pose more experimental questions. For example: which conditions *have* to be present (i.e., are necessary) for war levels to be high and which have to be present for those levels to remain low? Or, can a high or low level on one or more of the predictors "guarantee" high or low magnitudes of war? That is, is any one, or combination of them, sufficient by itself?

As the tables show, the frequency distributions in our imaginary case are identical, and the chi-square value of 3.33 is significant at the .07 level for all of them. Experimentally speaking, then, if we had hypothesized that it is *necessary* for stratification or polarity or concentration to be high in order for war levels to be high, we would have been wrong. That is, for eight of the twenty observation periods, we get high war levels with low levels of these three predictor variables. Conversely, if we had hypothesized that it was *sufficient* for any one of them to be high for war to be high, we would have been quite right. That is, each is high in only four of the twenty periods, and in each of those periods, war is also high, and war is never low when any one of the predictors is high. To put it another way, despite the rather weak correlations, we nevertheless find that four of our hypotheses were correct (when any predictor is high, war will be high), and none was incorrect (war is never low when any of the predictors is high). In addition, in sixteen of the twenty periods in which any of the predictors was low, there is no clear pattern, since half of these were high war periods and half were low on war. In sum, despite the crudeness of our dichotomous indicators and the simplicity of the analysis, the contingency table clarifies the relationship and thus illuminates a facet of the experimental problem that might have gone unnoticed in the search for mere correlation.

Returning to statistical analysis once more, the important point is not only that we exercise whatever isolation and control we can in a particular investigation. What *really* makes the difference in the longer run is whether we can design a *sequence* of experiments such that we may eventually differentiate between those conditions that play an important role in shaping a set of outcomes and those that merely *appear* to do so. The reasoning is nicely articulated in John Platt's "Strong Inference" article which warns against the mere accumulation of correlational findings.[33] The essential idea is to move systematically from analysis to analysis, always trying to design the next one such that the strongest possible inferences about the "causal" process can be made. In his language, we try to move as quickly as possible toward "the critical experiment," by which he means the one that permits us to reject all but one remaining alternative explanation. This requires us, of course, to think in more cumulative long run terms, rather than in terms of a series of disconnected and quite discrete experiments. The concept of meta-experiment seems to convey the essential point as we expand our horizon from a single investigation to a series of clearly connected investigations that add up to a coherent research strategy.

### Simulation

In addition to the comparative case study strategy and the use of statistical, post hoc manipulations, there is a third way in which a fair degree of experimental control can be achieved: the simulation. As indicated in the beginning of this section, simulations may be differentiated along several dimensions, one of which is the relative role of humans and machines in generating data. At one end of that continuum is the simulation in which humans are assigned roles as officials, ministries, nations, etc., and are permitted to act out those "roles" in a free and unstructured environment. In the middle are simulations in which these roles are acted out in a more structured and preprogrammed environment, with some of the more important outcomes generated by the interaction of the players' decisions and the programmed computer routines. Those routines may, in turn, reflect the hunches and suspicions of the researcher or may actually rest upon referent world findings; ordinarily, it is a mix of the two.[34]

Toward the other end of the continuum is the all-machine simulation, in which no role players are used at all, and the magnitude and variation of *every* input is fully controlled by the researcher. Even if we choose to inject one or more stochastic elements into the simulation, we know their magnitude and place in the simulation, and can modify them at will.[35]

At first blush, the use of human players seems attractive, as they offer a diversity, richness, and realism that is not easily generated by the computer. And in terms of generalizability, these are assets that are not to be ignored.

Furthermore, if the players happen to be actual policymakers (rather than students, for example), one could argue that we not only get realistic behavioral inputs and outputs from them, but can even approximate a laboratory experiment. While these considerations are by no means negligible, the loss of effective control is a serious one. First, when a foreign ministry official moves from his natural setting into a laboratory-type setting, the new environment is likely to have a systematic but unknown effect on his behavior. Second, in the laboratory, he knows that the consequences of his decisions will be of minor importance, whereas in his official role, they could be earthshaking. Third, a key element in the behavior of bureaucrats is the realization that they must live with and work with their colleagues tomorrow, next week, and next year. This constraint is seldom present in the laboratory or simulation setting. Thus, if our objective is to isolate, observe, and measure the effects of each stimulus that might be accounting for the variation in our outcome variable, the use of human players is not an attractive option.

On the other hand, as we noted above, such control is easily achieved in the all-machine simulation. One can work with inputs (and outputs) that range in veridicality from the purely speculative to the thoroughly grounded. Whether the input be a set of facts, a number of correlations, or a coherent sub-model, its closeness to reality is itself a matter of considerable controllability.

Another important virtue of the computer simulation is that it permits an exciting approximation to the *replication* of experiments. One of the key differences between the ideographic and nomothetic styles is that devotees of the former are inclined to tell us that contingent or speculative history is a waste of time, or worse. There is, we are told, no point in asking "what if—" questions, since what has happened is already in the past. One (admittedly extreme) implication of this view is that what *did* happen is what *had* to happen, and that nothing else *could* have happened. Such an over-determined view has ominous consequences in that it not only stifles creative speculation about the past, but would also prohibit a form of computer simulation that holds a great deal of promise.

That form might be thought of as "re-playing history" to achieve some of the greatest virtues of a controlled experiment. Without going into much detail, let me summarize the possibilities of reconstructing—and thus replicating—the conditions and events out of the past. As indicated above, one may use this strategy even in the absence of much existential and correlational knowledge, with testing for the internal consistency of one's models as the major objective.[36] But mathematical and logical manipulation is only one of the pay-offs in computer simulations.

If such simulations are preceded by an adequate (if undefined) number of comparative and longitudinal historical studies, we then are provided with the basic experimental ingredients: (a) a sufficient data base; (b) a fairly clear picture of the statistical regularities and relationships among our variables; (c) some idea as to where in time these relationships change in direction or magnitude; and (d) a fair sense of which predictor variables are most powerful in accounting for the variance in our observed outcomes.

With such an empirical and conceptual base, we can then go on to the "reconstruction of history" to which we alluded earlier. One strategy is to set all of the initial conditions of the referent system as of the beginning of the historical process, and then put the simulation in motion. Then, as each change in the predictor variables occurs in the simulation (which is, we hope, matching the actual observed events from the past), their combined effects should lead to the predicted fluctuations in the outcome variable. These events should, in turn, impinge on the predictors if we utilize a feedback model, and move the system into its next temporal cycle.

Depending on the solidity of our model and our data, the computer output should match rather closely the historical realities that have already been recorded. But if we examine a fairly long time span (such as the century and a half of the Correlates of War project), that goodness of fit will not last for the entire run. Conversely, we can expect the effects of the variables that shape the direction and magnitude of our outcomes to shift over time. Their relative potency may change, the sequence in which they interact with each other may change, and the pattern of that interaction is likely to change.

Now some scholars will urge that this very inconstancy of the relationships among predictors, and between them and our outcomes, is what makes social science impossible. If the causal sequence changes from epoch to epoch or case to case, it is argued, how can we discover or articulate behavioral generalizations or speak of law-like regularities? Admittedly, this is one of the harsh realities that makes social science in general, and experimentations in particular, often more difficult than in the physical and biological fields. But the problem is far from insoluble, and the computer simulation offers a promising route.

In the straight longitudinal study, relying on statistical manipulation as the major control device, it is difficult (and very time-consuming) to identify the inflection points at which variables and relations among them undergo change. But in the simulation, we can accomplish five things. First, as we watch the historical "events" unfold, we can quickly spot these inflection points. Secondly, having done so, we can—on the basis of our prior empirical findings— estimate what those changes were. Third, we can then modify our model and its parameters accordingly, via a simple set of program instructions. Fourth, we can re-run the longer historical period to ascertain whether these changes were of the correct type and injected at the appropriate juncture. Fifth, if not, we continue to experiment until the print-out once again fits the historical realities.

In sum, then, the all-machine simulation—if based on sufficient empirical and theoretical work—gives us a remarkably close parallel to the laboratory experiment. With it, we can try out a wide variety of ideas, run them and re-run them against historical reality, and eventually emerge with a fairly good fit between the simulation and the reality. In other words, we can isolate and control for the effects of all sorts of possible stimuli, constantly improving our model until it finally plays out the historical drama. It may not be as rich in detail as that found in the historians' narratives, and it may be more numerical than our more verbal colleagues might prefer, but it can, in principle, be very close to the "real thing."

## CONCLUSION

For too long, we in the macro-social sciences have labored under the handicap of a severe inferiority complex. That sense of inferiority is, I would submit, far from justified. But, like our colleagues in the physical and biological sciences, as well as our non-scientific brethren, we have accepted all too readily a number of dubious myths.

One of these is the notion that social phenomena are too complex to ever be comprehended by the human mind, whereas physical and biological phenomena are not. Another is that social phenomena are nearly impossible to observe, partially because they are largely symbolic and intangible, and partially because they occur across too broad a spatial and temporal domain. A third is that even if we could observe these phenomena, they are too subtle and fast-moving to permit operational measurement. A fourth is that most social phenomena cannot be put into the laboratory, and since science is only done in the laboratory, there can be no social science. While these epistemological myths are overstated here for emphasis, their milder versions pervade much of the scholarly literature, not to mention the belief systems of most of the world's cultures. As I have tried to indicate in the paper at hand, none of them is well-founded. There are difficulties, to be sure, but this is true of every area of investigation.

Further, we could readily find many of the so-called "natural" scientists who would also dispute these myths. The galaxies are complex, yet astronomers continue to expand our understanding of their dynamics. Elementary particles are hardly visible to the naked eye, yet physicists continue to observe them and trace their behavior. Impulses in the central nervous system move at incredible speed, yet biochemists continue to improve their grasp of the way in which that system operates. And, tornadoes or cold fronts can hardly be brought into the laboratory, yet meteorologists measure their characteristics and are increasingly able to predict their effects. To put it bluntly, the distinctions among the sciences are severely over-drawn, and we need to recognize the great potentialities of scientific method for the understanding of human phenomena.

Of course, our inferiority complex arises not only out of naive beliefs as to what is possible: they also arise out of the very real fact that we have, to date, not done nearly as well as the physical and biological sciences. In some crude way, one might estimate that we are where the physical sciences were about 200 years ago, and where the biological sciences were 50 years ago. Our models are primitive, our procedures are inadequate, and our research strategies are often incoherent. But this is, I suspect, less a function of the innate inaccessibility of social phenomena to scientific inquiry, and more a result of our beliefs to that effect.

Furthermore, these myths and beliefs are not, in turn, natural to the human condition. Humanity has been governed for thousands of years by elites who have a vested interest in perpetuating our ignorance. Because ignorance about social phenomena helps to keep us in a state of thralldom, these elites—and counter-elites—have created, sanctioned, or enforced a combination of taboos and constraints that account for a large part of our contemporary ignorance.

While it is incumbent on all human beings to resist and reject these taboos and constraints, scientists have an additional obligation. Those in the physical and biological sectors should learn enough to recognize that their work is inherently no different from ours, and they should stop acting like magicians engaged in occult and esoteric activities that only the initiated can comprehend. But, most important, we in the historical and social sciences must set ourselves free from those epistemological—as well as ideological—fetters that keep us in a state of perceived inferiority and inhibit our efforts to "crack" some of the most important problems facing humanity. Fuller utilization of the experimental mode may not guarantee our success, but it should make our recurrent failures of the past a bit less likely in the future.

# CHAPTER THIRTEEN

■

# Cumulativeness in the
# Social Sciences:
# Some Counter-Prescriptions

IN EVERY SOCIAL SCIENCE, there tends to be a recurrent and cyclical preoccupation with the lack of cumulativeness. Some attribute this to the familiar "absence of theory," and lay it at the door-step of "barefooted empiricism." Others might see the culprit lurking in the conceptual morass that often passes for theory, and would suggest that grand schemata that *are* not—and usually *cannot*—be tested will hardly make for greater cumulativeness.

There seems to be more than a germ of truth in both of these suspicions, but let me suggest a third possible source of our disappointment. I refer to certain norms and practices found among *both* the theorizers and the empiricists: those folkways that we pick up in college and graduate school, and are seldom able to shake in the post-doctoral years. On the assumption that an awareness of them and their implications may lead to their gradual extinction, I itemize here a few of what may be our less attractive foibles. While some of them may be peculiar to the field of world politics, most seem to be found all across the discipline.

## A—Terminology

1. If our discipline is concerned with global politics, be sure to call it "international relations;" then all will know that we're interested only in the *relations* among *nations*, and not the attributes, relationships, and interactions of all sorts of entities.
2. As long as you precede your efforts with the phrase, "it doesn't matter what we call it, provided we define our terms," feel free to ignore all conventional definitions.

---

This chapter originally appeared in *Political Science* (Winter 1975), pp. 19-21. Reprinted by permission of the American Political Science Association.

3. Any time you happen across an isolated fact or a welter of verbiage, be sure to label it "data."
4. If we already have a well-accepted word for a generally understood concept, be sure to coin a new one; don't be transparent when you can be prismatic or refractory.
5. When you're not sure which dimensions of a phenomenon you're trying to describe, refer to the "nature of _____ ."
6. If you're referring to any observed or hypothesized regularity, call it "structure."
7. If you have trouble differentiating among hunches, suppositions, convictions, preferences, and findings, just call them "theories."
8. If you're using the word "relationship," don't let on whether you mean: covariation of variables, similarity between entities, bonds and links between entities, etc.
9. When using the word "paradigm," don't let on whether you mean: model, research strategy, a set of axioms, epistemological criteria, etc.
10. When using the word "parameter," don't let on whether you refer to: the isomorphism between the sample and the population, a constant, a slowly changing variable, a non-measured variable, a boundary condition, etc.
11. If you're unable to articulate an idea clearly, begin to crank out a large number of examples; we'll eventually figure out what you're driving at.
12. Whenever you refer to physics, chemistry, or biology, call them the natural (or exact) sciences; then it'll be clear that we're in an un-natural or in-exact science.

## B—Taxonomy and Typology

1. As you shift from one research problem to another, be sure to change your taxonomy in subtle and unreported ways; this reduces the probability of integrating the results.
2. When discussing roles, relationships or interactions, avoid identifying the social entities that play these roles or experience these relationships and interactions; otherwise, you'll be taken for a stodgy "institutionalist."
3. When constructing a typology, don't use categories that are mutually exclusive, logically exhaustive, or rest on explicit dimensions.
4. When focusing on conflictful interactions, be sure to say that you're dealing with "the conflict system," and when focusing on bargaining in conflict, say that you're dealing with "the exchange system."
5. If you're concerned with the impact of unemployment on national foreign policies, emphasize that you're examining "the economic system," and if unemployment happens to fall unevenly among different ethnic groups, note that this requires study of "the cultural system;" the more "systems" you examine, the less you'll worry about putting your findings together.
6. When one or two attributes of a system show change over time, insist that "it's a completely new system."

7. If the folklore has it that the mitrailleuse or satellite surveillance or public diplomacy have affected the course of world politics, insist that these have led to different and successive systems.

## C—Epistemology

1. If you disagree with a colleague's epistemology, tell him how they "do it in physics."
2. If it is suggested that certain attributes of a social system can be described by observing the distribution of certain attributes among its sub-systems, mutter something about "the ecological fallacy" or perhaps "the ecological fallacy in reverse."
3. If a given piece of work doesn't spell out—in mathematical form of course—all the possible relationships among variables that might obtain, observe laconically that "barefooted empiricism remains far from dead."
4. If a colleague's work strikes you as too deductive, remind him of the importance of all those chemists in their labs, and if too inductive, quote Einstein or Bohr.
5. If a colleague's work shows a strong preoccupation with reproducibility and precision, alert others to his or her "indifference to theory."
6. If, after years of urging that insight and intuition have no place in science, you discover the limits of hyper-positivism, announce that science is a failure.
7. If a colleague is not persuaded by the logic and evidence you adduce, invoke a carefully selected metaphor from everyday life; any discontinuities between child-rearing and strategic deterrence, or between driving a car and running a foreign office, will be graciously overlooked.

## D—Research Strategy

1. When undertaking a new investigation, don't bother to read prior studies in that area; until you came along, no one did it right.
2. If your methodological repertoire is limited, emphasize that you only employ those methods "appropriate" to the specific inquiry at hand.
3. When you're stymied on the measurement of one of your critical variables, put that project aside and write another essay on what Thucydides *really* meant.
4. When another's study explicitly focuses on the interaction effects of predictor variables A and B, quickly note his or her "indifference" to variable C.
5. When beginning a new set of investigations, don't be misled by the plausibility of alternative models; pick one that you like and get on with the derivation of "nontrivial deductions."
6. If your model has no recognizable similarities to the referent world, remind your critics that models are supposed to be "useful, not truthful."
7. When a colleague strays into other disciplines for new concepts or models, alert others immediately to these dilettantish tendencies.

8. If you find a colleague working on a given class of problems for several years, point out his or her "lack of breadth."

9. When drawing analogies from inter-personal to inter-national relationships, never go to the findings of psychologists; their experimental evidence might be inconsistent with your argument.

10. If another project has invested considerable effort in identifying a population of nations, IGO's, or other actors, be sure to either ignore their listing or quibble about that South Pacific island that was omitted.

11. When our critics point out the absence of cumulative knowledge about world politics, press the button that says, "after all, we're an infant discipline."

12. If several people, at the same institution or not, are unoriginal enough to be working on the same problem (such as the causes of war problem), be sure to observe that they are mere replicas of one another. And if they're working within a common paradigm, ask what ever happened to creativity?

## E—Reportage and Communication

1. When publishing more than one paper on a given problem, don't indicate where it falls in your sequence of reports, or whether it represents an extension, refinement, or revision of earlier reports; a little mystery is good for your scholarly reputation.

2. Since it's too much trouble to revise a manuscript to incorporate the comments and suggestions you solicited from others, just tack on the necessary footnotes; the tightness of your reasoning is less critical than the illusion of exhaustive scholarship.

3. If your paper is on the casual side, don't worry about identifying sections and subsections in it; merely insert a numeral—preferably Roman—on every fifth page.

4. In writing up a nice and tight empirical study, don't waste time putting it into a larger context; get right down to the matter at hand.

5. Be sure that the title of your article or book promises considerably more than is delivered.

6. If you've picked up a good idea or insight from someone else's work, be sure to write it up as something brand new and creative.

7. If you're a panel discussant, paraphrase all of the authors' caveats and self-criticisms, being sure to imply that they were oblivious to such problems.

8. Never specify or reiterate the spatial-temporal domain to which you hope to generalize; all propositions are universal.

9. Avoid the rigid tendency of making your opening and closing paragraphs consistent with each other, and in any event, don't let either of them be consistent with the actual operations you carried out.

10. Be sure that the major query of a study is carefully camouflaged, and that the outcome variable remains shrouded in mystery; otherwise, another researcher might be able to refute your findings.

11. Rather than spell out the case for the validity of your indicators, allude to your "auxiliary theory" (citing Blalock, of course), and get on to the important matters.

12. When your student turns in a paper that is incoherent, disorganized, grammatically improper, and replete with errors of spelling and punctuation, ignore such trivial weaknesses and assure him/her that we're scientists, not literary critics.

13. To use your time efficiently, never consider undertaking the construction of a data set, but follow others' work closely, and as soon as you hear of a potentially useful set, request it from the drone who put it together; that kind of scut-work is inappropriate for creative scientists.

14. If, with the support of a public or private funding agency, you generate a useful and high quality data set, refuse it to others until you've milked it dry; you can always say that the set is not yet complete or clean.

15. If someone proposes the creation of a new journal, or a section in an existing journal, devoted to data-making and index construction, cite Conant to the effect that empiricism is not science, but is merely a poor substitute for good theory.

16. If someone suggests a different way of printing and distributing journals, remind them that we've always done it this way.

17. If you've read a colleague's paper and can't figure out what the hell he did or why, be sure to praise its "heuristic value."

## F—Ideology and Policy

1. When a colleague's work is addressed to some minor social inconvenience, such as war, hasten to note his or her indifference to poverty or injustice.

2. If a colleague's empirical findings are inconsistent with your ideological premises, point out that "it is no accident" that his or her research is supported by the _____ , or that his nation is the richest (or poorest) in the world, or that he is not a she, an underdog, an African, or un-tenured.

3. When a colleague uses the same coding categories to describe both Soviet and American diplomatic actions, tell others that *you* don't worry about his patriotism, but. . . .

4. When you're challenged as to the accuracy of your facts on the Chinese ABM, tell the critics "if you knew what I know, and had a Q clearance, you'd believe me."

5. If a taxpayer asks whether your research will lead to an improvement in U.S. policy, remind him that you're a scientist, not a politician.

6. If the question of policy implications should arise, put on your other (citizen's) hat and note that social scientists are no different from barbers.

7. When you're trying to account for the difference between the infantry's and the cavalry's share of the defense budget, invest a minimum of 12 man years, and when you're trying to account for the differences

between crises that end up in war and those that do not, write a learned essay over the Easter holidays.

8. When examining the ratio between Yale and Harvard men in the Navy Supply Corps, break out your entire methodological armamentarium, but in examining the ratio of military to civilian fatalities, rely heavily on an exegesis of the "just war" doctrine; that's what "normative theory" is for.

9. If, after extolling the virtues of "value-free" science for years, you discover that ethical considerations might just be relevant, denounce scientific method as a hoax perpetrated by the establishment in order to preserve the status quo; allusions to the Karls (Marx and Mannheim) should wrap up the argument.

## G—The Clincher

Finally, if by some remote chance, we begin to gather scientific momentum, and there is a real danger that cumulativeness and codification might get out of hand, allude to Kuhn and call for a new paradigm.

# PART FOUR

■

# The Research Program
# and Some Results

This part of the book is where "it all comes together"—or begins to come together, in two senses of the word "begin." In one sense, no matter how much research of excellent quality and addressed to the most relevant policy questions is completed and published, the probability of human survival will be largely unaffected unless those results find their way into the policy process. That set of questions has been considered in Part Two. The other sense of "begin" is also intimated in earlier parts of the book, but needs reiteration here. From one point of view, scientific peace research has made great gains: Virtually unknown when we initiated the Correlates of War project in the early 1960s, there is today a fair body of correlational knowledge, several excellent journals, increasing legitimacy, and even some occasional impact on policy. But there have been many reverses, and as these lines are written it would be naive to say that "the movement" is vigorous and expanding rapidly; the foundations—epistemological, technical, normative, and pedagogical—are clearly in place, but the essential growth rate remains to be realized.

Be that as it may, I want the reader to get a sense of the sorts of studies that emerge out of the interplay of such considerations in the context of our peace research program. Although each of these investigations clearly has implications for the policy process, those implications may be lost on the elites and counter-elites whose roles are central to the policy process in many societies. This might be a consequence of their ignorance, insensitivity, or indifference—and these remain monumental obstacles to the formulation and execution of foreign policies that are prudent and humane—but it may also be a function of the abstractness of the inquiry or the researcher's indifference to the policy dimension. Not all of us engaged in systematic scientific research give serious attention to the utilization of our results, and furthermore, there will be, of necessity, many preliminary studies that need to be successfully completed as part of the groundwork out of which the more applicable research may emerge. Nor will all of my colleagues share my conception of the most powerful way to design and carry out a research program of cumulative and integratable inquiries such that we will better be able to appreciate, for example, which policies are most likely to produce which consequences under which set of conditions, or when it is more or less prudent to follow a given set of policies and strategies.

In Chapter 14, we examine the extent to which fluctuations in the amount of alliance aggregation as well as bipolarization of the system predict fluctuations in the incidence of international war. This was not only the first set of analyses conducted by the Correlates of War project, but it was also in the first publication ever to be devoted solely to database research in international politics: Quantitative International Politics (New York: Free Press, 1968). As such, it is considerably more attentive to the then unfamiliar procedures of data analysis and date manipulation than would be necessary or appropriate today. In Chapter 15 we shift from the role of commitments to that of capabilities and examine a question of considerable relevance to past and to present, even as the Soviet-American armed rivalry seems to be winding down. To what extent do military superiority and high military allocations enhance major power security? The findings are an interesting mix of the expected and the unexpected, worth pondering as the Western powers hesitate before an extraordinary window of historical opportunity.

The next two papers address questions of a more general sort. In Chapter 16, we take a statistically rigorous look at a significant and not purely philosophical question. Are there any clear trends, up or down, in the incidence of international war, and to what extent are there discernible cycles in these recurrent episodes of human slaughter? Then, in Chapter 17, I attempt to integrate and account for the apparently inconsistent results that emerge out of several prior investigations into the relationship between system structure and the distribution of war across two quite different centuries.

CHAPTER FOURTEEN

■

# Alliance Aggregation and the Onset of War, 1815–1945[1]

## J. David Singer and Melvin Small

### A FRAMEWORK FOR INQUIRY

In any search for the "causes" of international war, there are at least four possible levels of analysis at which we might focus our attention: the individual, the sub-national interest group, the nation, and the international system. Furthermore, each of these four possible classes of empirical referent may be examined in terms of its *structural* attributes or in terms of its *behavior*. That is, the individual, the interest group, the nation, or the system is an object of analysis which reveals relatively *static* properties such as size, composition, organization, power, or capacity for change, and relatively *dynamic* properties such as activity level, aggressiveness, cooperativeness, responsiveness, initiative, or communicativeness. In addition to these two sets of attributes, an individual or a social organization will reveal *relationship* attributes vis-à-vis other actors at the same or other levels of organizational complexity. Nations, for example, may be geographically near or distant, more or less interdependent economically, politically hostile or friendly, ethnically or industrially similar, and so forth. In sum, we may look for the causes of war in structure, behavior, or relationship at—or across— many levels of social organization. Combining these three classes of variables with the four suggested levels of analysis, we can postulate at least twelve different classes of information one might examine in any systematic search for those factors most often associated with war.

Of course, the moment these twelve categories are filled in with illustrative variables, it becomes evident that the structural-behavioral-relational trichotomization is not always clear-cut; one might argue, for example, that an individual personality attribute, such as rigidity, or a national one, such

This chapter originally appeared in *Quantitative International Politics: Insights and Evidence,* J. David Singer, ed. (New York: Free Press, 1968), pp. 247–288. Reprinted by permission.

as autocracy, is more a behavioral than a structural property. At the least, we must recognize that we may have to infer one set of attributes from the observation of another set.

Regardless of the level of organization (or class of variable) at which we look, we must make at least two epistemological assumptions: (1) that explanatory variables will be found in more than one place, the exact number being a function of one's theoretical predilections; and (2) that the interaction of two or more such classes of variables will have more explanatory power than the mere correlation of any single class of variable with our dependent variable: the incidence of war. Which particular levels or classes one gives priority to is likewise a matter of individual judgment, with two considerations deserving attention in that selection. First, there is the question of parsimony, and this should lead to a preference for variables that are at the more general rather than the more idiosyncratic end of the continuum. Second, certain classes of possible predictors to events such as war seem to get considerable attention in the scholarly literature, at the expense of others of intuitively equal significance. On the basis of these considerations, and with the intention of turning later to other possible predictors (and combinations thereof) we focus here on one cluster of *structural* variables at the *systemic* level of analysis: alliance aggregation.

## ALLIANCE AGGREGATION AS
## A PREDICTOR TO WAR

Without going into the quagmire of terminological and normative dispute which has characterized much of the theoretical literature on the balance of power, we can nevertheless note that its defense or justification clearly rests on the assumption that the stability of the international system can be maintained without reliance on superordinate political institutions.[2] In the words of Kaplan (1957), it postulates a system which is "sub-system dominant"; that is, one in which most authority is found at the national actor, or sub-systemic level, rather than at the supranational or systemic level. The same notion is conveyed by the international lawyers' distinction between a system in which most of the authority lines are horizontal and one in which they tend to be vertical in direction (Falk, 1959).

In the absence of significant legal or political institutions at the supranational level, the preservation of relative stability and the survival of the nations are seen as depending upon the presence or absence of one or more of the following phenomena, depending in turn upon the theoretical predilections or national outlook of the observer: For the nations themselves, the phenomena are their restraint and limit of ambition, their similarity of values, their approximate parity, the absence of permanent friendships and hostilities, or their willingness to coalesce against a challenger. For the system, these conditions might be the absence of alliances, the presence of a minimum number of alliance coalitions, the approximate parity of the coalitions, the fluidity and impermanence of these coalitions, or a high level of normative consensus. That some of these requirements are vague and that others are inconsistent seems not to discourage those who consider supranational institutions as unnecessary. In one fashion or another, they would rely upon what might be characterized as the diplomatic equivalent of Adam Smith's "invisible hand," a mechanism whereby the individual pursuit of individual interests redounds to the advantage and stability of the community as a whole.

Central to this notion is the understanding that the invisible or unseen hand will function only to the extent that all nations are free to deal and interact with all others as their national interests dictate. Thus, it is assumed that every dyadic relationship will be a mixture of the cooperative and the conflictful, with political, economic, ideological, and other issues all producing different interest configurations for each possible pair of nations. The net effect, it is believed, is such a welter of cross-cutting ties and such a shifting of friendships and hostilities that no single set of interests can create a self-aggravating and self-reinforcing division or cleavage among the nations; A and B may well have competitive economic interests in the Middle East, but harmonious strategic interests in the Caribbean, while B and C's political interests may coincide in regard to West Africa and clash in an international organization setting.

It follows from this sort of a model that anything which restrains or inhibits free or vigorous pursuit of the separate national interests will limit the efficacy of the stabilizing mechanism. And among those arrangements seen as most likely to so inhibit that pursuit are formal alliances. Nations in the same alliance are less free to compete with their allies in such spheres of incompatibility, and less free to cooperate with outsiders in areas of overlapping interests.[3] Just how *much* freedom to pursue normal interests is lost by an allied nation is, of course, most difficult to measure. Although some approximation of the degree of inhibition—or loss of interaction opportunity—can be gleaned from the text and associated documents of a given alliance treaty, a fuller appreciation would require a laborious examination of the treaty's context, and the motivations, relative power, and performance of the signatory nations. Despite the obvious simplifications, however, a differentiation based on the documents themselves is not without some merit, and we will therefore distinguish all the alliances examined as to whether they are military, neutrality, or entente commitments; the specific coding rules are outlined in a later section.

Be that as it may, if each alliance commitment reduces, to *some* degree, the normal interaction opportunities available to the total system, and the loss of such interaction opportunities is supposed to inhibit the efficacy of the balance-of-power mechanism, we should find that as the system's interaction opportunities diminish, war will increase in frequency, magnitude, or severity. Moreover, if the alliance configurations show less and less partial overlap, and they instead increasingly reinforce a tendency toward a very few (but large-sized) coalitions, the system's loss of interaction opportunities becomes even more severe. Carried to its extreme condition, this tendency culminates in a completely bipolarized system, with interaction opportunities reduced (theoretically, at least) to one; each nation would then have only friends or foes, and few relationships in between these two extremes. On the other hand, if there are no alliances in the system at all, these interaction opportunities will be equal to the total number of pairs or dyads possible with a given total number of nations in the system; this would be equal to $N(N - 1)/2$.

There are, of course, several other lines of reasoning by which one might be led to predict that alliance commitments will negatively affect the stability of the international system, but they are largely variations on the present theme and several have been presented elsewhere (Deutsch and Singer, 1964). Thus, rather than dwell any longer here on the plausible reasons why alliance aggregation *should* correlate with the onset of war, it might be more useful to ascertain the extent to which it does. In order to put this proposition to the historical test, however, a number of preliminary steps are essential. These are the following:

1. Articulate the hypothesis in the various forms it might reasonably take.
2. Delineate the empirical world in time and space from which the evidence will be gathered.
3. Describe the procedures by which the chaotic welter of historical fact is converted into data.
4. Present the raw data which emerge from the above operations.

Once those steps have been completed, we can move on to:

5. Ascertain the strength and direction of any correlations which would tend to confirm or disconfirm the various hypotheses.
6. Interpret the results of this search for correlations.

In the sections which follow, the above procedures will be described in appropriate detail.

## THE BASIC HYPOTHESES

Having articulated the reasons for examining the relationship between alliance aggregation and war, we can now spell out in more detail the hypotheses to be tested. In the next section, we can then move on to a specification of the procedures by which the key variables were converted from their widely scattered verbal state to collated and codified numerical form.

The hypotheses may be thought of as falling into two general classes, both of which belong to the systemic level of analysis. The first concerns alliance aggregation and the consequent loss of interaction opportunities in general; that is, it ignores the specific nature of the alliance configurations which are produced, and looks merely at the system's aggregate loss of such normal opportunities. The second of these is as concerned with the specific configurations as it is with the aggregate loss of normal dyadic interaction, and focuses on the extent to which the alliance commitments produce a bipolarized system. Bipolarization may thus be thought of as a special case of alliance aggregation.

## Alliance Aggregation and the Magnitude or Severity of War

Looking first at the matter of general alliance configurations, and the extent to which they reduce normal interaction opportunities, we may articulate the first basic hypothesis: *The greater the number of alliance commitments in the system, the more war the system will experience.* The second hypothesis pays more attention to specific alliance configurations, and thus reads: *The closer to pure bipolarity the system is, the more war it will experience.*

In order to put these propositions to the test, we must first identify the empirical world within which the postulated relationships are to be sought. Let us describe and justify the world which we have selected, but a preliminary indication of the basic procedure might best precede that. Basically, the method to be employed is a trend analysis. After developing several different measures of alliance aggregation and several measures of the onset of war, we will examine the extent to which the two sets of variables rise and fall together over time.

As to the empirical domain in which the longitudinal data will be compared, the problem is to examine a span of time which is not restricted to the all-too-recent, and therefore most salient, period upon which much theorizing in international relations seems to be based. On the other hand, if we go too far back we may well find ourselves examining international environments of such disparity that generalizations embracing them become foolish and irrelevant. For the contemporary scholar, there does seem to be a chronological cutting point which provides a sufficiently extensive empirical world while nevertheless permitting a reasonable degree of comparability. We refer to the period opening with what we normally recognize as the beginning of the modern international system (the Congress of Vienna) and closing with the Japanese surrender in Tokyo Bay. Despite the many changes in the pattern and process of international relations during that 130-year period, we find a remarkable constancy. The national state was the dominant actor and the most relevant form of social organization; world politics were dominated by a handful of European powers; the Napoleonic reliance upon the citizen's army endured, with all of its implications for public involvement in diplomacy; the concept of state sovereignty remained relatively unchallenged; and while technological innovation went on apace, the period postdates the smoothbore and predates the nuclear-missile combination. In sum, it seems reasonable to conclude that this period provides an appropriate mixture of stability and transition from which generalization would be legitimate. As to whether such generalization might be extended beyond 1945 and into the present, we would be skeptical, but this is, of course, an empirical question, and one to which we will return in our conclusion.

Stated in the preceding rather general form, the hypotheses immediately raise a number of important conceptual and methodological problems. In addition to the procedures for operationalizing "number of alliance commitments" or "closer to pure bipolarity" (the independent variables) and "more war" (the dependent variable)—and these will be articulated in the next section—there are three relevant concerns of substance: (1) the time lag between the presence of a given number or percentage of alliance commitments and its effect in the form of international war; (2) the differentiation between separate regions of the world, especially between the "central" and the "peripheral" portions of the system; and (3) the differentiation between distinctive time periods in our 130 years, especially that between the nineteenth and twentieth centuries.

Let us look first at the matter of time lag. If, indeed, there is any relationship between the loss of interaction opportunities and war, that relationship must take a certain amount of time to make itself felt; the system certainly cannot be expected to respond immediately to a specific increase or decrease in interaction opportunities. Not only do we not find in the literature any compelling reason for assuming a given response time, but that response time might well differ for, let us say, different decades.[4] Consequently, each year's interaction opportunity measures have been correlated with the war indices for not only the following year $(Y + 1)$, but for the following three $(Y + 3)$ and five years $(Y + 5)$ as well; for example, if a given alliance aggregation index for 1851 is relatively high, we want to know whether its effect is felt by 1852, by 1854, or 1856. That is, our dependent variables for 1851 will reflect the amount of war which began in 1852, the amount which began between the beginning of 1852 and the end of 1854, and the amount which began between the beginning of 1852 and the end of 1856.

Two points of clarification are in order here. First, note that we are distinguishing between the amount of war which *began* in the specified time period, regardless of how long it endured, and the amount of war which the system experienced during that period. Second, we are looking at the amount of war which began at any time *within* three time periods of increasing length: within one, three, or five years, not during 1852, or 1854, or 1856 alone. Thus all forms of the basic hypothesis will be tested under three different chronological conditions.

Beyond the refinement of the hypothesis in order to account for varying time lags, we should also refine it to permit its testing within several different time- and space-bound worlds. That is, if we recognize the extent to which theorizing about diplomatic history has been dominated by European-centered scholars and practitioners from the Western world, it seems prudent to wonder whether a given relationship might be found in one region but not in another. Combining that awareness with a recognition that it was not until relatively recent times that the international system could be treated as a more or less single and interdependent one, it makes perfect sense to look for a point in time at which the non-European nations "joined" that central system. The most reasonable such point seems to be that which closed out World War I and marked the birth of the League of Nations; this organization, while its pretensions to universality were never fulfilled, quite explicitly included many non-European members and concerned itself with all continents. Thus, while treating the post-1920 system as a single one, we look upon the pre-1920 epoch as having both a central, Europe-oriented system and a peripheral one. Consequently, all sets of correlations will be examined in two systemic contexts. The first will be called the *total system* and will include all "independent" nations which existed during any part of the entire 130-year period. The second context will be one in which we "shuck off" the peripheral nations prior to 1920, in order to eliminate the statistical "noise" generated by the less important and least active nations. This we will call the *central system*, and its composition is the same as the total system's for the final 25 years, but smaller for the first 105 years.

Further, we do not restrict attributed membership in the central system to European nations only, nor do all European nations fall into the central category for the pre-League period. In order to qualify for inclusion in the central system during that earlier period, a nation must either be located in Europe or deeply involved in relatively durable relationships with European nations. Given the difficulty of operationalizing this latter phenomenon and given the high degree of consensus among historians, we have adhered closely to that consensus.[5] To be more specific, we have *excluded* a number of European nations from our pre-League central system in line with the following criteria. Outside of Prussia and Austria, the German states are excluded because their 1815 treaty of confederation sharply restricts their diplomatic independence; for example, they are prohibited, formally and effectively, from alliances which might be directed at other members of the confederation. As for the Italian states other than Sardinia, they, too, enjoy few of the perquisites of real independence prior to their unification in 1860. Modena, Parma, Tuscany, and the Two Sicilies are closely linked by dynastic ties to Austria and turn out to be little more than satellites of Vienna. As to the Papal States, the French and Austrian guarantees effectively preclude them from any significant degree of normal diplomatic interplay.[6]

Turning to the considerations which led us to *include* several non-European nations in (and exclude others from) the pre-League central system, only a few political entities even qualify (by population and recognition criteria) as independent nations at all (if we forget Latin America for the moment) and almost none of these are regularly involved in Continental diplomacy or with the Continental powers abroad. In Asia and Africa, for example, only China, Japan, Persia, Siam, Ethiopia, Korea, and Morocco meet the population and diplomatic recognition requirements between 1815 and 1920.[7] They are, of course, considerably more independent than the subordinate German and Italian states, and they do occasionally interact with the European powers (for example, Persia in the 1850's and Siam in the 1880's), but they remain largely unrelated to the wars and treaties of Continental diplomacy. China and Japan, however, are brought into our central system in 1895 as a consequence of the Sino-Japanese War. As to Western Hemisphere nations, the same considerations apply. Aside from the United States after the Spanish-American War, the Americas are even less involved in Continental affairs than the Asian and African nations. Between 1815 and our cutoff date of 1920 there are no alliance ties with a European power and there are only two international wars involving Europe in Latin America: that between France and Mexico in 1862–1867 and that involving Spain with Bolivia, Chile, and Peru in 1865–1866. And there are no cases of Latin American nations engaging in European wars.[8]

In sum, then, we treat the post-1920 international system as a relatively interdependent one, but divide the pre-League system into two parts: the central and the peripheral. The search for correlations between alliance aggregation and war is thus conducted in two somewhat different empirical worlds so that we may, in one, ignore those political entities which qualify as independent nations, but which may hardly be thought of as active participants in international politics. For the pre-League period, then, the following nations are treated as members of the *central system*, as of the year indicated; it should be noted that Sardinia, Prussia, and Serbia become, respectively, Italy in 1860, Germany in 1871, and Yugoslavia in 1919, and that Austria and Hungary are treated as a single nation until 1918. Those in the left-hand column are members throughout the entire period.

| | |
|---|---|
| Austria-Hungary | Greece—1828 |
| Denmark | Belgium—1830 |
| England | Serbia—1878 |
| France | Romania—1878 |
| Holland | China—1895 |
| Portugal | Japan—1895 |
| Prussia | United States—1899 |
| Russia | Norway—1905 |
| Sardinia | Bulgaria—1908 |
| Spain | Albania—1914 |
| Sweden | Czechoslovakia—1919 |
| Switzerland | Poland—1919 |
| Turkey | Finland—1919 |

The following nations are excluded from the pre-1920 central system and treated as members of the *peripheral system* only, between the dates shown. The earlier date marks its qualification as a sovereign nation and the latter, if any, marks either its disqualification (via federation for the seven German and the five Italian states or annexation for Morocco and Siam) or its entry into the central system (marked by an asterisk); needless to say, the precise date at which the population criterion was met cannot always be shown, and others might select a year or two later or earlier.

Baden, 1815–1870

Bavaria, 1815–1870

Hanover, 1838–1870

Hesse-Electoral, 1815–1866

Hesse-Grand Ducal, 1815–1867

Mecklenburg-Schwerin, 1843–1867

Saxony, 1815–1867

Württemberg, 1815–1870

Modena, 1842–1860

Papal States, 1815–1860

Parma, 1851–1860

Tuscany, 1815–1860

Two Sicilies, 1815–1861

Morocco, 1847–1911

Korea, 1888–1905

Ethiopia, 1898

Persia, 1855

United States, 1815–1899*

China, 1860–1895*

Japan, 1860–1895*

Brazil, 1826

Colombia, 1831

Mexico, 1831

Peru, 1837

Chile, 1839

Argentina, 1841

Venezuela, 1841

Bolivia, 1848

Guatemala, 1849

Ecuador, 1854

Haiti, 1859

Salvador, 1875

Uruguay, 1882

Santo Domingo, 1887

Siam, 1887

Paraguay, 1896

Honduras, 1899

Nicaragua, 1900

Turning to the post-1920 setting, in which we drop the distinction between central and peripheral systems, we find the following additional (not previously listed) nation members and their dates of qualification for entry into the total system:

Estonia, 1920

Latvia, 1920

Lithuania, 1920

Hungary, 1920

Luxembourg, 1920

Liberia, 1920

South Africa, 1920

Australia, 1920

New Zealand, 1920

Canada, 1920

Afghanistan, 1920

Nepal, 1920

Mongolia, 1921

Costa Rica, 1920

Panama, 1920

Ireland, 1921

Saudi Arabia, 1927

Iraq, 1932

Yemen, 1934

Cuba, 1934

Egypt, 1936

In addition to these spatial differentiations, a case can be made for an explicit chronological differentiation. Contemporary theoreticians are, all other things being approximately equal, more likely to argue from recent than from remote diplomatic events. Therefore, they may well be basing their postulated correlation between alliance aggregation and war on twentieth century diplomatic history while tending to forget the nineteenth. To ascertain whether or not this has been the case, we have explicitly divided our 130 year epoch from Vienna to Tokyo Bay into two distinct periods, with the turn of the century marking the break. As to selecting this cutoff point rather than one closer to the midpoint, a number of considerations seemed relevant. First of all, there seemed to be an appreciable qualitative difference between World War I and the wars that preceded it. And bearing in mind the fact that time lags of up to five years are used, we must of necessity use a cutoff year no later than 1908. Secondly, the period *prior* to World War I is markedly different from that preceding most other wars, in that it produced a sharp and clear confrontation between the Central Powers and the Allies, and this bipolarization was well under way by 1902. To be sure, some of the alliances contracted before 1899 (Triple and Dual alliances) transcend both periods, but in order to evaluate their effects, we would have had to go back to 1879. Had we chosen this date, we would have eliminated from the nineteenth-century pattern those several interesting, though ephemeral, configurations of the 1879 to 1899 period which had little relationship to the post-1900 world. Moreover, only after 1900 does the rate of alliance activity show that marked increase which culminates in the grouping of France, England, Russia, and Japan into several interlocking alliances and ententes which by 1908 had resolved itself into the pre–World War I bipolarization.

Finally, there appears to be a marked difference in the amount and rate of diplomatic and military activity between the nineteenth and twentieth centuries, so that while 1899 does not represent an exact chronological midpoint, it is probable that the 85 years prior to 1900 represent an approximate equivalent of the 45 post-century years in terms of "diplomatic time."

To summarize this part of the discussion, then, our hypothesis will actually be put to the test in eighteen different forms, in order to differentiate among: (1) three different time lags, for (2) six different time-space systems. In matrix form, we would want to show the correlation between our several alliance indices and wars beginning for each of the spatial-temporal cells in the chart below:

|  |  | Time Lags or Spans | | |
| --- | --- | --- | --- | --- |
| Period | System | $Y + 1$ | $Y + 3$ | $Y + 5$ |
| 1815–1945 | Central only |  |  |  |
| 1815–1945 | Total |  |  |  |
| 1815–1899 | Central only |  |  |  |
| 1815–1899 | Total |  |  |  |
| 1900–1945 | Central only |  |  |  |
| 1900–1945 | Total |  |  |  |

## Alliance Aggregation and the Frequency of War

Up to this point we have been discussing a relationship which, however interesting, may possibly not be getting at the basic theoretical proposition. That is, we have been assuming that any positive relationship existing between aggregate alliance commitments and war would be revealed in the correlation between our various alliance indices in a given year and certain indices of the *magnitude* or *severity* of war in certain years immediately following. It could be argued that the existence of a statistically significant correlation between interaction opportunity losses and the severity or magnitude of war is really, by indirection, a *disconfirmation* of the hypothesis. The reasoning might be that not only do magnitude or severity seldom covary with frequency, but that they are more likely to vary inversely. A glance at figures for sickness, auto or industrial accidents, or battle casualties for example, would show that the *least* serious events occur most frequently, and that in their most disastrous form these phenomena occur much less often. As a matter of fact, this is precisely what Richardson (1960) found in his *Statistics of Deadly Quarrels*. Classifying deaths on the basis of a $\log_{10}$ scale, he found that in 282 cases of mass violence between 1820 and 1945, deaths were distributed as follows:

$$3 \pm \tfrac{1}{2} - 188 \qquad 6 \pm \tfrac{1}{2} - 5$$
$$4 \pm \tfrac{1}{2} - 63 \qquad 7 \pm \tfrac{1}{2} - 2$$
$$5 \pm \tfrac{1}{2} - 24$$

Likewise, if we look at his observed frequency of ninety-one wars classified by the number of participants, a similar distribution holds:

$$2-42 \qquad 7-3$$
$$3-24 \qquad 8-2$$
$$4-\ 8 \qquad 9-1$$
$$5-\ 7 \qquad 10-0$$
$$6-\ 3 \qquad 20-1$$

Our own results reveal the same pattern, even though our more stringent criteria for war produced a much smaller number of cases. Whether the seriousness of war is measured in terms of number of participants, duration, or battle-connected military deaths, the same inverse correlation between frequency and seriousness is found, as shown in Table 1.[9]

Given this rather critical observation, it certainly behooves us to pay as much attention to the correlations between interaction opportunity and the *frequency* of war as to those between such phenomena and the *magnitude* or *severity* of war. This we shall do in the sections which follow.

TABLE 1. *Frequency Distribution of all International Wars, 1815–1945, by Size, Duration, Magnitude, and Severity (N = 41)*

| | No. of Participants | | Months Duration | | Magnitude in Nation-Months | | Severity: Battle Deaths in Thous. | |
|---|---|---|---|---|---|---|---|---|
| | Range | Freq. | Range | Freq. | Range | Freq. | Range | Freq. |
| High | 21–26 | 1 | 61–84 | 2 | 750+ | 1 | 10,000+ | 1 |
| Med.-High | 16–20 | 0 | 46–60 | 4 | 151–750 | 3 | 1001–10,000 | 1 |
| Medium | 11–15 | 1 | 31–45 | 1 | 31–150 | 8 | 101–1000 | 7 |
| Med.-Low | 6–10 | 2 | 16–30 | 5 | 5–30 | 25 | 11–100 | 13 |
| Low | 1–5 | 37 | 0.5–15 | 29 | 1–5 | 4 | 1–10 | 19 |

## OPERATIONALIZING THE VARIABLES

In order to put any hypothesis to the empirical test, of course, one must at the very least demonstrate a correlation between the independent and dependent variables. Though a positive correlation between alliance aggregation and war, high enough not to have occurred by sheer chance, cannot be interpreted as a demonstration of any causal connection, the search for such a correlation is a necessary first step. That the presence or absence of covariation between alliances and war is not a mere artifact requires considerable subsequent analysis, but the first order of business, and that which concerns us here, is whether the hypothesized correlations are indeed borne out by the historical evidence.

This enterprise, in turn, cannot be launched until the constructs have been operationalized—until the researcher has converted the ambiguous verbal labels into variables whose shifting presence or absence or strength can be repeatedly observed and recorded. That is, we must devise explicit and visible procedures by which the welter of events and conditions may be coded, sorted, and classified in so reliable a fashion that other scholars will, in applying the identical coding procedures to the same body of information, come up with almost exactly the same data. Whether these highly reliable procedures do, however, produce data which index the qualitative variables we seek is another matter. Whereas the relative *reliability* of our measures is easily established, their *validity* always remains a matter of some dispute. Recognizing, then, that the search for operational (or machine-readable) variables may well lead to the observation of phenomena quite remote from those about which we seek to generalize, let us turn to the procedures used here.

### Magnitude and Severity of War: The Dependent Variables

Before examining the frequency and distribution of our *independent* variables, we had better know what it is they are supposed to be predicting to. In the overall project of which this study is a small part, war is one of the major dependent variables; the object is to ascertain which structural, relational, and behavioral phenomena at which levels of social organization most strongly correlate with war. War, however, means many things to many people, and as a consequence, some definition and operationalization are essential; a full and detailed treatment of the problem is presented elsewhere (Singer and Small, 1972), but a brief recapitulation is clearly in order here.

First of all, there are many deadly quarrels (to borrow Richardson's quaint phrase) which are not normally thought of as war: riots, murders, assassinations, pogroms, executions, duels, punitive expeditions, retaliatory strikes, and so on. Even when the deadly quarrel endures and involves nations, many ambiguities remain. How many nations must be involved, for how long, and with how many men or arms? And what is a nation? Secondly, even if we agree upon the meaning of war, there are several different classes of war, each having different relevance to the search for meaningful generalization about the international system.

In order to handle these ambiguities and inconsistencies, a two-step coding procedure was used. First, adapting from the schema found in A Study of War (Wright, 1942, App. 20) four classes of war were differentiated: international, imperial, colonial, and civil. The criterion here is strictly one of the political-legal status of the participants. Thus, an *international* war is one in which at least one participant on each side is an independent and sovereign member of the international system, with a population exceeding 500,000 and enjoying diplomatic recognition from our two legitimizers, Britain and France. If only *one* side includes one or more independent system members, then the war is classified as imperial or colonial, depending on the political status of the adversaries, as follows. When the dominant (and usually there is only one) adversary is a more or less independent political entity, but *not* a qualified system member by our criteria, the war is classified as *imperial*; examples might be Serbia before 1878, Persia before 1855, or a Pathan tribe. When the dominant adversary is an entity which not only fails to qualify as a system member but which is also an ethnically different people formerly or presently under the suzerainty of the system member(s) against which it is fighting, the war is seen as *colonial*; examples of such wars might be the Russo-Polish ones of 1831 and 1863 or the Spanish-Cuban of 1868–1878. Wars of this latter category would generally fall, in contemporary parlance, under the rubric of wars of national independence. Finally, a *civil* (or internal) war is one between a system member's government and such sub-national factions as are able to engage in armed resistance, insurgency, or revolution. Of course, any war may *become* an international war by the intervention of one or more independent members of the international system, and the classification of a war may therefore change between its onset and its termination.[10]

However, not all international wars are of equal interest to us here, nor is reliable information on all of them available. Thus, we exclude those wars in which the best estimate of total battle-connected deaths is less than 1,000.[11] Using these criteria of war type and casualty threshold, we find that there were forty-one international wars in the total international system between 1815 and 1945; if we ignore the pre-Versailles peripheral system, that number drops to twenty-four.

Having identified those international wars which interest the student of international relations as he examines the effects of alliance patterns, the next point to note is that these wars differ markedly in their duration, magnitude, and intensity. Thus, the correlation of alliance aggregation with mere war frequency would be of limited interest (if not downright misleading) and further gradation is clearly necessary. This gradation is achieved in the first instance by use of the nation-months-of-war measure, so that the simple *magnitude* of each war is the sum of the months which all nations individually experienced as participants in the war; other political entities, even though they participate in a qualifying war, do not contribute to that war's nation-months if they fail to meet the recognition and population criteria for system membership.

A second-order refinement is also necessary, on the recognition that a nineteenth or twentieth century British war-month holds rather different implications for the international system than, for example, a Bulgarian war-month. This differentiation could be recognized by introducing several different factors as modifiers. We might want to classify the nations by power, status, or size, and then weight their nation-months by the consequent absolute or relative score. But no such satisfactory index yet exists, especially when it must be applied not only to the early nineteenth century but to many non-European powers for which we have little accurate data at present. We have, therefore, resorted to the simple distinction between major and minor powers and calculated their wars and nation-months of war separately. Though the major-minor dichotomy may be too primitive for some theoretical purposes and not too readily operationalized, diplomatic historians have found it quite useful for centuries. Moreover, despite the invisibility of their criteria, they show near unanimity in the classification results.[12] Thus, our major powers and the dates during which they enjoyed that status are:

Austria-Hungary, 1815–1918
Prussia or Germany, 1815–1918, 1925–1945
Russia, 1815–1917, 1922–1945
France, 1815–1940
Britain, 1815–1945
Japan, 1895–1945
United States, 1899–1945
Italy, 1860–1943

A final point regarding our nation-months (magnitude) measure concerns the chronological placing of our forty-one wars. It should be reiterated here that our major concern must be not with the amount of war *going on* in the given year or years following each year's level of alliance aggregation in the system, but with the amount of war which *commenced* within that one-, three-, or five-year period. Our interest is in measures reflecting the *onset* of war. That most of the nation-months of World War II, for example, occurred during 1942 and 1943 is of much less interest in this study than the fact that they commenced in 1939.

In addition to nation-months as an index of the magnitude of war, at least one other factor seems to justify consideration. That factor we will call *severity* and it will be measured by the number of battle-connected deaths of military personnel sustained by all participants in any given war. As with the identification and classification of our wars, a full treatment of the problems encountered in locating, evaluating, and converting the casualty information into reliable data is provided in the aforementioned paper, and again only a brief summary is offered here. There have, of course, been several prior efforts to collect data on war casualties (Bodart, 1916; Dumas, 1923; Sorokin, 1937; Klingberg, 1945; Richardson, 1960; and Urlanis, 1960), but none provides a fully satisfactory compilation, even for the primitive statistical purposes encountered in this undertaking. All are partially guilty of employing either shifting or invisible criteria of classification, and as a consequence, several different sets of such figures were collected and then our own best estimates finally used. For each nation in each international war, we calculated (and estimated) two types of deaths: (1) military personnel who died, or were reported as permanently missing, as a consequence of malicious acts of the enemy; and (2) military personnel who died from accidents, wounds, disease, or exposure during the period of hostilities. Note that, in partial contradistinction to Richardson's criteria, we did *not* include: (1) civilians of participating nations who died as a result of enemy actions (and to have included this category in our World War II figures would not have changed appreciably the fact that almost half of all deaths in our forty-one wars were accounted for by this single holocaust); (2) such civilians who died from exposure or disease; (3) neutral civilians; and (4) those children who might have been born had there been no war. Battle-connected deaths of military personnel, thus, will provide our index of each war's severity.[13]

To summarize this section, then, our raw data are presented in Table 2. Note that *wars* are the items listed, and that in order to use these data for our purposes they must be transformed so as to show the magnitude and severity of all international wars which began in each of our 130 years. The results of that transformation as well as more detailed data and procedures are in a forthcoming statistical handbook.

## Alliance Aggregation: The Independent Variable

Shifting our attention now from the outcome, or dependent variable, to the predictor, or independent variable, what procedures might be used to operationalize and quantify the extent to which alliance commitments reduced the interaction opportunities available to the international system? The problem here is somewhat more complex than that confronted in regard to the magnitude and severity of war, since a modest inferential

TABLE 2. *International Wars by Duration, Magnitude, and Severity: 1815-1945*

| Name of War and Participants | Dates | International System | | | Each Nation | | National Dates (if different) |
|---|---|---|---|---|---|---|---|
| | | Duration (Months) | Nation Months | Battle Deaths (thousands) | Duration (Months) | Battle Deaths (thousands) | |
| 1. Franco-Spanish | 4/7/23–11/13/23 | 7 | 14 | 1 | | | |
| France | | | | | 7 | .4 | |
| Spain | | | | | 7 | .6 | |
| 2. Russo-Turkish | 4/26/28–9/14/29 | 16.5 | 33 | 130 | | | |
| Russia | | | | | 16.5 | 50 | |
| Turkey | | | | | 16.5 | 80 | |
| 3. Mexican | 5/12/46–2/12/48 | 21 | 42 | 17 | | | |
| Mexico* | | | | | 21 | 6 | |
| U.S.A.* | | | | | 21 | 11 | |
| 4. Austro-Sardinian | 3/24/48–8/9/48, 3/20/49–3/23/49 | 4.5 | 9 | 9 | | | |
| Austria | | | | | 4.5 | 5.6 | |
| Sardinia (incl. Ital. rebels) | | | | | 4.5 | 3.4 | |
| 5. Danish | 4/10/48–8/26/48, 3/25/49–7/10/49 | 8 | 16 | 6 | | | |
| Denmark | | | | | 8 | 3.5 | |
| Prussia | | | | | 8 | 2.5 | |
| 6. Roman | 4/30/49, 5/8/49–7/1/49 | 2 | 7 | 2.2 | | | |
| Austria | | | | | 2 | .1 | 5/8/49–7/1/49 |
| France | | | | | 1 | .5 | 4/30/49, 6/3/49– |
| Papal States* | | | | | 2 | 1.5 | [7/1/49 |
| Two Sicilies* | | | | | 2 | .1 | 5/8/49–7/1/49 |
| 7. La Plata | 7/19/51–2/3/52 | 6.5 | 13 | 1.3 | | | |
| Argentina* | | | | | 6.5 | .8 | |
| Brazil* | | | | | 6.5 | .5 | |
| 8. Crimean | 10/23/53–3/1/56 | 28 | 115.5 | 264.2 | | | |
| England | | | | | 23 | 22 | 3/31/54–3/1/56 |
| France | | | | | 23 | 95 | 3/31/54–3/1/56 |
| Russia | | | | | 28 | 100 | |
| Sardinia | | | | | 13.5 | 2.2 | 1/10/55–3/1/56 |
| Turkey | | | | | 28 | 45 | |
| 9. Persian | 10/25/56–3/14/57 | 4.5 | 9 | 2 | | | |
| England | | | | | 4.5 | .5 | |
| Persia* | | | | | 4.5 | 1.5 | |
| 10. Italian | 4/29/59–7/12/59 | 2.5 | 7 | 22.5 | | | |
| Austria | | | | | 2.5 | 12.5 | |
| France | | | | | 2 | 7.5 | 5/3/59–7/12/59 |
| Sardinia | | | | | 2.5 | 2.5 | |
| 11. Moroccan | 10/22/59–3/26/60 | 5 | 10 | 10 | | | |
| Morocco* | | | | | 5 | 6 | |
| Spain | | | | | 5 | 4 | |
| 12. Roman | 9/11/60 – 9/29/60 | .5 | 1 | 1 | | | |
| Italy | | | | | .5 | .3 | |
| Papal States* | | | | | .5 | .7 | |

*Indicates peripheral system nation.
ªNumber includes central system nation-months only in Austro-Prussian and Franco-Prussian Wars.
ᵇAll foreign losses insignificant in Boxer Rebellion.
ᶜVichy 11/30/40–1/31/41, 11/8/42–11/11/42.

TABLE 2.—continued

| Name of War and Participants | Dates | International System Duration (Months) | Nation Months | Battle Deaths (thousands) | Each Nation Duration (Months) | Battle Deaths (thousands) | National Dates (if different) |
|---|---|---|---|---|---|---|---|
| 13. Sicilian | 10/15/60–1/19/61 | 3 | 6 | 1 | | | |
| Italy | | | | | 3 | .6 | |
| Two Sicilies* | | | | | 3 | .4 | |
| 14. Mexican Expedition | 4/16/62–2/5/67 | 57.5 | 115 | 20 | | | |
| France | | | | | 57.5 | 8 | |
| Mexico* | | | | | 57.5 | 12 | |
| 15. Colombian | 11/22/63–12/6/63 | .5 | 1 | 1 | | | |
| Colombia* | | | | | .5 | .3 | |
| Ecuador* | | | | | .5 | .7 | |
| 16. Schleswig-Holstein | 2/1/64–4/25/64, 6/25/64–7/20/64 | 4 | 12 | 4.5 | | | |
| Austria | | | | | 4 | .5 | |
| Denmark | | | | | 4 | 3 | |
| Prussia | | | | | 4 | 1 | |
| 17. Spanish | 10/25/65–5/9/66 | 6.5 | 17 | 1 | | | |
| Chile* | | | | | 6.5 | .1 | |
| Peru* | | | | | 4 | .6 | 1/14/66–5/9/66 |
| Spain | | | | | 6.5 | .3 | |
| 18. Austro-Prussian | 6/15/66–7/26/66 | 1.5 | 15.5 | 36.1 | | | |
| Austria | | | 4.5[a] | | 1.5 | 20 | |
| Baden* | | | | | 1.5 | .1 | |
| Bavaria* | | | | | 1.5 | .5 | |
| Hanover* | | | | | .5 | .5 | 6/15/66–6/29/66 |
| Hesse-Electoral* | | | | | 1.5 | .1 | |
| Hesse-Grand Ducal* | | | | | 1.5 | .1 | |
| Italy | | | | | 1.5 | 4 | |
| Mecklenburg-Schwerin* | | | | | 1.5 | .1 | |
| Prussia | | | | | 1.5 | 10 | |
| Saxony* | | | | | 1.5 | .6 | |
| Württemberg* | | | | | 1.5 | .1 | |
| 19. Franco-Prussian | 7/19/70–2/26/71 | 7 | 26.5 | 187.5 | | | |
| | | | 14[a] | | | | |
| Baden* | | | | | 4 | 1 | 7/19/70–11/22/70 |
| Bavaria* | | | | | 4 | 5.5 | 7/19/70–11/15/70 |
| France | | | | | 7 | 140 | |
| Prussia | | | | | 7 | 40 | |
| Württemberg* | | | | | 4.5 | 1 | 7/19/70–11/25/70 |
| 20. Russo-Turkish | 4/12/77–1/3/78 | 8.5 | 17 | 285 | | | |
| Russia | | | | | 8.5 | 120 | |
| Turkey | | | | | 8.5 | 165 | |
| 21. Pacific | 2/14/79–12/11/83 | 58 | 170.5 | 14 | | | |
| Bolivia* | | | | | 58 | 1 | |
| Chile* | | | | | 58 | 3 | |
| Peru* | | | | | 54.5 | 10 | 4/5/79–10/20/83 |
| 22. Central American | 3/28/85–4/15/85 | .5 | 1 | 1 | | | |
| Guatemala* | | | | | .5 | .8 | |
| Salvador* | | | | | .5 | .2 | |
| 23. Sino-Japanese | 8/1/94–3/30/95 | 8 | 16 | 15 | | | |
| China* | | | | | 8 | 10 | |
| Japan* | | | | | 8 | 5 | |

TABLE 2.—*continued*

| Name of War and Participants | Dates | International System | | | Each Nation | | National Dates (if different) |
|---|---|---|---|---|---|---|---|
| | | Duration (Months) | Nation Months | Battle Deaths (thousands) | Duration (Months) | Battle Deaths (thousands) | |
| 24. Greco-Turkish | 2/15/97–5/19/97 | 3 | 6 | 2 | | | |
| Greece | | | | | 3 | 6 | |
| Turkey | | | | | 3 | 1.4 | |
| 25. Spanish-American | 4/2/98–8/12/98 | 4 | 8 | 10 | | | |
| Spain | | | | | 4 | 5 | |
| U.S.A.* | | | | | 4 | 5 | |
| 26. Boxer | 6/17/00–8/25/00 | 2 | 18 | 2 | | | |
| China | | | | | 2 | 1.5b | |
| Austria | | | | | 2 | | |
| England | | | | | 2 | | |
| France | | | | | 2 | | |
| Germany | | | | | 2 | | |
| Italy | | | | | 2 | | |
| Japan | | | | | 2 | | |
| Russia | | | | | 2 | | |
| U.S.A. | | | | | 2 | | |
| 27. Russo-Japanese | 2/8/04–9/15/05 | 19 | 38 | 130 | | | |
| Japan | | | | | 19 | 85 | |
| Russia | | | | | 19 | 45 | |
| 28. Central American | 5/27/06–7/20/06 | 2 | 6 | 1 | | | |
| Guatemala* | | | | | 2 | .4 | |
| Honduras* | | | | | 2 | .3 | |
| Salvador* | | | | | 2 | .3 | |
| 29. Central American | 2/19/07–4/23/07 | 2 | 6 | 1 | | | |
| Honduras* | | | | | 2 | .3 | |
| Nicaragua* | | | | | 2 | .4 | |
| Salvador* | | | | | 2 | .3 | |
| 30. Moroccan | 7/7/09–3/23/10 | 8.5 | 17 | 10 | | | |
| Morocco* | | | | | 8.5 | 8 | |
| Spain | | | | | 8.5 | 2 | |
| 31. Italo-Turkish | 9/29/11–10/18/12 | 12.5 | 25 | 20 | | | |
| Italy | | | | | 12.5 | 6 | |
| Turkey | | | | | 12.5 | 14 | |
| 32. 1st Balkan | 10/17/12–4/19/13 | 6 | 20 | 82 | | | |
| Bulgaria | | | | | 4 | 32 | }10/17/12–12/3/12, |
| Serbia (& Montenegro) | | | | | 4 | 15 | }2/3/13–4/19/13 |
| Greece | | | | | 6 | 5 | |
| Turkey | | | | | 6 | 30 | |
| 33. 2nd Balkan | 6/30/13–7/30/13 | 1 | 4 | 61 | | | |
| Bulgaria | | | | | 1 | 18 | |
| Greece | | | | | 1 | 2.5 | |
| Romania | | | | | .5 | 1.5 | 7/11/13–7/30/13 |
| Serbia | | | | | 1 | 18.5 | |
| Turkey | | | | | .5 | 20 | 7/15/13–7/30/13 |

TABLE 2.—*continued*

| Name of War and Participants | Dates | International System | | | Each Nation | | National Dates (if different) |
|---|---|---|---|---|---|---|---|
| | | Duration (Month) | Nation Months | Battle Deaths (thousands) | Duration (Months) | Battle Deaths (thousands) | |
| 34. World War I | 7/29/14–11/11/18 | 51.5 | 606.5 | 10,000 | | | |
| Austria | | | | | 51 | 1,200 | 7/29/14–11/3/18 |
| Belgium | | | | | 51 | 87.5 | 8/4/14–11/11/18 |
| Bulgaria | | | | | 35.5 | 14 | 10/12/15–9/29/18 |
| England | | | | | 51 | 908 | 8/5/14–11/11/18 |
| France | | | | | 51 | 1,350 | 8/3/14–11/11/18 |
| Germany | | | | | 51.5 | 1,800 | 8/1/14–11/11/18 |
| Greece | | | | | 16.5 | 5 | 6/29/17–11/11/18 |
| Italy | | | | | 41.5 | 650 | 5/23/15–11/11/18 |
| Japan | | | | | 50.5 | .3 | 8/23/14–11/11/18 |
| Portugal | | | | | 32.5 | 7 | 3/1/16–11/11/18 |
| Romania | | | | | 15.5 | 335 | 8/27/16–12/9/17 |
| Russia | | | | | 40 | 1,700 | 8/1/14–12/5/17 |
| Serbia | | | | | 51.5 | 48 | |
| Turkey | | | | | 48.5 | 325 | 10/28/14–11/11/18 |
| U.S.A. | | | | | 19 | 126 | 4/17/17–11/11/18 |
| 35. Greco-Turkish | 5/5/19–10/11/22 | 41 | 82 | 50 | | | |
| Greece | | | | | 41 | 30 | |
| Turkey | | | | | 41 | 20 | |
| 36. Chaco | 5/12/28–12/19/33, 1/8/34–6/12/35 | 84 | 168 | 130 | | | |
| Bolivia | | | | | 84 | 80 | |
| Paraguay | | | | | 84 | 50 | |
| 37. Sino-Japanese | 12/19/31–5/6/33 | 16.5 | 33 | 60 | | | |
| China | | | | | 16.5 | 50 | |
| Japan | | | | | 16.5 | 10 | |
| 38. Italo-Ethiopian | 10/3/35–5/9/36 | 7 | 14 | 20 | | | |
| Ethiopia | | | | | 7 | 16 | |
| Italy | | | | | 7 | 4 | |
| 39. Sino-Japanese | 7/7/37–12/7/41 | 53 | 106 | 1,000 | | | |
| China | | | | | 53 | 750 | |
| Japan | | | | | 53 | 250 | |
| 40. Russo-Finnish | 11/30/39–3/12/40 | 3.5 | 7 | 90 | | | |
| Finland | | | | | 3.5 | 40 | |
| Russia | | | | | 3.5 | 50 | |
| 41. World War II | 9/1/39–8/14/45 | 71.5 | 910 | 16,000 | | | |
| Australia | | | | | 71.5 | 23 | 9/3/39–8/14/45 |
| Belgium | | | | | .5 | 7.8 | 5/10/40–5/28/40 |
| Brazil | | | | | 10 | .1 | 7/6/44–5/7/45 |
| Bulgaria | | | | | 34.5 | 10 | 12/8/41–10/28/44 |
| Canada | | | | | 71 | 37.5 | 9/10/39–8/14/45 |
| China | | | | | 44 | 1,350 | 12/7/41–8/14/45 |
| England | | | | | 71.5 | 270 | 9/3/39–8/14/45 |
| Ethiopia | | | | | 5.5 | 5 | 1/24/41–7/3/41 |
| Finland | | | | | 39 | 42 | 6/25/41–9/19/44 |
| France | | | | | 19.5 | 210 | 9/3/39–6/22/40, 10/23/44–8/14/45° |

TABLE 2.—*continued*

| Name of War and Participants | Dates | International System | | | Each Nation | | National Dates (if different) |
|---|---|---|---|---|---|---|---|
| | | Duration (Months) | Nation Months | Battle Deaths (thousands) | Duration (Months) | Battle Deaths (thousands) | |
| Germany | | | | | 68 | 3,500 | 9/1/39–5/7/45 |
| Greece | | | | | 6 | 25 | 10/25/40–4/23/41 |
| Holland | | | | | .5 | 6.2 | 5/10/40–5/14/40 |
| Hungary | | | | | 43 | 40 | 6/27/41–1/20/45 |
| Italy | | | | | 57 | 77 | 6/10/40–9/2/43, |
| | | | | | | | 10/18/43–5/7/45 |
| Japan | | | | | 44 | 1,000 | 12/7/41–8/14/45 |
| Mexico | | | | | 3.5 | .1 | 5/1/45–8/14/45 |
| New Zealand | | | | | 71.5 | 10 | 9/3/39–8/14/45 |
| Norway | | | | | 2 | 1 | 4/9/40–6/9/40 |
| Poland | | | | | 1 | 320 | 9/1/39–9/27/39 |
| Romania | | | | | 39 | 300 | 6/22/41–9/13/44 |
| Russia | | | | | 47 | 7,500 | 6/22/41–5/7/45, |
| | | | | | | | 8/8/45–8/14/45 |
| South Africa | | | | | 71 | 6.8 | 9/6/39–8/14/45 |
| Thailand | | | | | 45 | .1 | 11/30/40–1/31/41, |
| | | | | | | | 1/25/42–8/14/45 |
| U.S.A. | | | | | 44 | 292 | 12/7/41–8/14/45 |
| Yugoslavia | | | | | .5 | 410 | 4/6/41–4/17/41 |

leap is required. Referring back to the rationale behind our general hypotheses, we argued there that the effect of each alliance of any type was to reduce the extent to which the pluralistic, self-regulating mechanism could operate effectively. And two different lines of reasoning were suggested, depending upon the intervening constructs selected. In one, we concentrated upon the loss of interaction opportunity due to aggregate alliance commitments of all nations in the system; this may be thought of as a simple subtractive procedure. In the other, we examined the loss of interaction opportunity due to the bipolarizing effect of these alliance commitments. To put it briefly, there should be a difference between the effects of a structure which reflects a crazy-quilt pattern of all sorts of overlapping alliance membership and one in which that membership approaches or reaches a state in which only a very few easily distinguishable coalitions emerge. There may, of course, be a close interdependence between these two conceptually distinct conditions, since it is perfectly plausible to assume that alliance-building is by and large an activity directed *against* other nations and other existing or anticipated alliances. If such is the case, then, the mere aggregation of alliance commitments may well move the system in the direction of some minimum number of coalitions and hence *toward* bipolarity. We will revert to this matter when we present our data, and will then have some evidence for the extent to which these two conditions covary.

Returning, then, to our operationalizing procedures, let us look first at the aggregate measure of interaction opportunity loss, in its various forms. Perhaps the most orderly procedure would be to begin with an overview of the large number of alliance ties that interest us in an analysis such as this. The typology is based upon: (1) the nature of the obligation or commitment undertaken toward one ally by another; and (2) the nature of the signatories in terms of whether they are major or minor powers.

As to the first dimension, three classes of alliance commitment are considered. Class I, which will be called a *defense pact*, commits each signatory to intervene with military force on behalf of the other(s). Class II, which is called here a *neutrality or non-aggression pact*, commits each to refrain from military intervention against any of the other signatories in the event that they become engaged in war. Class III, labeled *entente*, merely requires that the signatories consult with one another in the contingent eventuality. It should be noted here that these classifications are based upon the treaty text itself and not upon the way in which the alliance was adhered to in actual practice.[14]

Perhaps a brief justification of our reliance on written alliances in general and their texts in particular is in order. Admittedly, other phenomena would reveal more fully the friendship-hostility, close-distant, or dependent-independent dimensions of international relationships, but two considerations are relevant here. First, it seems perfectly reasonable to assume that the decision to undertake such an alliance commitment does indeed reflect and respond to many of these more specific, prior relationships. Moreover, one cannot argue that the commitments are undertaken in a frivolous manner, with little awareness of the implications or little intent to honor them. On the basis of our earlier analysis of such commitments, we found, for example, a significant positive correlation between alliance membership and war involvement on the side of the alliance partner. Second, there are some serious obstacles to getting at the more complex phenomena surrounding alliance formation. For example, much of this could be ascertained via content analysis of diplomatic communications, yet the availability of all, or a representative sample of, such documents is problematical; and that method is still a costly and time-consuming one. Moreover, other research groups are moving ahead on the "automation" of content analysis, and there is little point in duplicating that important pioneering venture at this juncture (Holsti, et al., 1964).

Turning to the second dimension, there is the matter of the signatories' power status. Here our interest is in whether a given alliance tie—and every multilateral alliance is treated, for analytical purposes, as if it were a number of separate bilateral ones—is between two major powers or between two minors, or between a major and a minor. Combining the two sets of dimensions, then, we see that nine types of bilateral alliance commitment are possible.[15]

As should be quite evident by now, it is no simple matter to identify all alliances of all relevant types for 130 years and ascertain their scope, membership, and duration. For a study of this type, based as it is on what aims to be the complete population of events rather than a sample thereof, this requirement is mandatory. Let us summarize, therefore, the coding rules which are developed in greater detail in the above-cited paper. First, only those alliance commitments embodied in a formal, written treaty, convention, or executive agreement were included, whether or not it was secret at the time. Among those which were excluded were (1) collective security agreements, such as the League Covenant and the United Nations Charter; (2) charters and constitutions of international organizations such as those of the Universal Postal Union, International Labour Organization, or the Danube River Commission; (3) treaties of guarantee to which all relevant powers registered their assent, such as the Belgian Neutrality Agreement of 1839, the Washington Conference Treaties of 1921–1922, and the Locarno Pacts of 1925; (4) agreements limited to general rules of behavior, such as the Kellogg-Briand Pact and the Geneva Conventions; (5) alliances which were consummated during, or less than three months before, a war in which any of the signatories participated, unless the alliance endured beyond the formal treaty of peace; (6) any alliances contracted during the two world wars, whether or not the signatories were belligerents; and (7) any alliance which did not include at least two members of our system.

In addition to these problems of ambiguity regarding inclusion or exclusion, there was the matter of chronological coverage. The effective inception date is almost always stipulated in the text or associated documents; if not, the date of ratification was used. In those few cases for which formal termination is not clear, we have relied upon a consensus of the historical monographs available. Finally, renewals were not counted as separate treaties unless the specific commitments were changed, as from entente to defensive alliance. The hundred and twelve alliances which met our criteria are shown in Table 3, along with the effective dates and the class of commitment undertaken by the signatories.

Once all of the relevant alliances were discovered, classified, and counted, it was a simple matter to complete the operationalization of our aggregate interaction opportunity indices. For each year, we merely converted the raw numbers of each type of alliance into a percentage figure, so that we ended up with a list of the five following independent variables:

1. Percentage of all nations having at least one alliance *of any class* with any type of nation, major or minor.
2. Percentage of all nations having at least one *defensive* pact with any type of nation.
3. Percentage of *major* powers having at least one alliance *of any class* with another major power.
4. Percentage of major powers having at least one *defensive* pact with another major.

TABLE 3. *Inter-Nation Alliances, 1815–1939, with Commitment Class and Dates*

| Members | Incept. | Termin. | Class | Members | Incept. | Termin. | Class |
|---|---|---|---|---|---|---|---|
| Austria<br>Baden*<br>Bavaria*<br>Hesse-Electoral*<br>Hesse-Grand Ducal*<br>Prussia<br>Saxony*<br>Württemberg*<br>Hanover*<br>Mecklenburg-<br>  Schwerin* | 6/1815–1848,<br>1850<br><br><br><br><br><br><br>1838**<br><br>1843** | 1866 | 1 | Austria<br>Parma* | 1851 | 1859 | 1 |
| | | | | France<br>Sardinia | 1/1859 | 1859 | 1 |
| | | | | Modena*<br>Parma*<br>Tuscany* | ?/1859 | 1860 | 1 |
| Austria<br>England<br>Prussia<br>Russia<br>France | 11/1815<br><br><br><br>11/1818 | 1823 | 1 | Ecuador*<br>Peru* | 1/1860 | 1861(?) | 1 |
| England<br>France<br>Russia | 7/1827 | 1830 | 3 | England<br>France<br>Spain | 10/1861 | 1862 | 3 |
| Russia<br>Turkey | 7/1833 | 1840 | 1 | Prussia<br>Russia | 2/1863 | 1864 | 1 |
| Austria<br>Prussia<br>Russia | 10/1833–1848,<br>1850 | 1854 | 3 | Colombia*<br>Ecuador* | 1/1864 | 1865(?) | 1 |
| England<br>France<br>Portugal<br>Spain | 4/1834–1840,<br>1841 | 1846 | 1 | Baden*<br>Prussia | 8/1866 | 1870 | 1 |
| | | | | Prussia<br>Wurtemberg* | 8/1866 | 1870 | 1 |
| Austria<br>England<br>Prussia<br>Russia<br>Turkey | 7/1840 | 1840 | 1 | Bavaria*<br>Prussia | 8/1866 | 1870 | 1 |
| | | | | Bolivia*<br>Peru* | 2/1873 | 1883 | 1 |
| England<br>Russia | 6/1844 | 1846<br>(1853?) | 3 | Austria<br>Germany<br>Russia | 10/1873 | 1878 | 3 |
| | | | | Austria<br>Russia | 1/1877 | 1878 | 2 |
| Austria<br>Modena* | 12/1847 | 1859 | 1 | England<br>Turkey | 6/1878 | 1880 | 1 |

Classes of alliance are: 1-Defense Pact; 2-Neutrality or Nonagression Pact; 3-Entente.
Inception dates show month and year, but termination dates cannot be ascertained with the same precision; where no consensus exists for that date, an alternate year (?) is also shown.
Comma between dates indicates temporary break in the alliance.
Brackets indicate that one or more bilateral alliances were merged in a new and larger grouping.

*Indicates that nation belongs to peripheral system only.

**Indicates that nation qualified for system membership *after* joining alliance, i.e. this date.

***Indicates that the same nations negotiated a new alliance of another class, effective this date.

TABLE 3.—*continued*

| Members | Incept. | Termin. | Class | Members | Incept. | Termin. | Class |
|---|---|---|---|---|---|---|---|
| Austria<br>Germany<br>Italy | 10/1879<br><br>5/1882 | 1914 | 1 | France<br>Spain | 10/1904 | 1914 | 3 |
| Austria<br>Germany<br>Russia | 6/1881 | 1887 | 2 | England<br>Spain | 5/1907 | 1914 | 3 |
| | | | | France<br>Japan | 6/1907 | 1914 | 3 |
| Austria<br>Serbia | 6/1881,<br>1889*** | 1889<br>1895 | 2<br>1 | Japan<br>Russia | 7/1907 | 1914 | 3 |
| Austria<br>Germany<br>Romania<br>Italy | 10/1883<br><br><br>5/1888 | 1914 | 1 | England<br>Russia | 8/1907 | 1914 | 3 |
| Germany<br>Russia | 6/1887 | 1890 | 2 | Japan<br>U.S.A. | 10/1908 | 1909 | 3 |
| Austria<br>England<br>Italy | 2/1887 | 1895<br>(1897?) | 3 | Italy<br>Russia | 10/1909 | 1914 | 3 |
| Austria<br>Italy<br>Spain | 5/1887 | 1895 | 2 | Bulgaria<br>Serbia | 3/1912 | 1913 | 1 |
| France<br>Russia | 8/1891,<br>1894*** | 1894<br>1914 | 3<br>1 | Bulgaria<br>Greece | 5/1912 | 1913 | 1 |
| China<br>Russia | 5/1896 | 1902(?) | 1 | Greece<br>Serbia | 6/1913 | 1914 | 1 |
| Japan<br>Russia | 6/1896 | 1903 | 3 | Czechoslov.<br>Yugoslavia | 8/1920 | 1933 | 1 |
| Austria<br>Russia | 5/1897 | 1908 | 3 | Czechoslov.<br>Romania | 4/1921 | 1933 | 1 |
| England<br>Portugal | 10/1899 | 1914 | 1 | Romania<br>Yugoslavia | 6/1921 | 1933 | 1 |
| France<br>Italy | 12/1900,<br>7/1902*** | 1902<br>1914 | 3<br>2 | Czechoslov.<br>Romania<br>Yugoslavia | 2/1933 | 1939 | 1 |
| England<br>Japan | 1/1902 | 1921 | 1 | Belgium<br>France | 9/1920 | 1936 | 1 |
| England<br>France | 4/1904 | 1914 | 3 | France<br>Poland | 2/1921 | 1939<br>(1934?) | 1 |
| | | | | Poland<br>Romania | 3/1921 | 1939 | 1 |

TABLE 3.—*continued*

| Members | Incept. | Termin. | Class | Members | Incept. | Termin. | Class |
|---|---|---|---|---|---|---|---|
| Afghanistan<br>Turkey | 3/1921 | 1939 | 1 | Persia<br>Russia | 10/1927 | 1939 | 2 |
| Persia<br>Turkey | 4/1926 | 1937 | 2 | Greece<br>Romania | 3/1928 | 1934 | 2 |
| Afghanistan<br>Persia | 11/1927 | 1937 | 2 | Greece<br>Turkey | 10/1930 | 1934 | 2 |
| Afghanistan<br>Iraq<br>Persia<br>Turkey | 9/1937 | 1939 | 2 | Romania<br>Turkey | 10/1933 | 1934 | 2 |
| Austria<br>Czechoslovakia | 12/1921 | 1927 | 2 | Turkey<br>Yugoslavia | 11/1933 | 1934 | 2 |
| Estonia<br>Latvia | 11/1923 | 1939 | 1 | Greece<br>Romania<br>Turkey<br>Yugoslavia | 2/1934 | 1939 | 1 |
| Czechoslovakia<br>France | 1/1924,<br>1925*** | 1924<br>1939 | 3<br>1 | Greece<br>Italy | 2/1928 | 1938 | 2 |
| Italy<br>Yugoslavia | 1/1924 | 1927 | 2 | Italy<br>Turkey | 5/1928 | 1938 | 2 |
| Czechoslovakia<br>Italy | 7/1924 | 1930 | 3 | Hungary<br>Turkey | 1/1929 | 1939 | 2 |
| Russia<br>Turkey | 12/1925 | 1939 | 2 | Bulgaria<br>Turkey | 3/1929 | 1938 | 2 |
| Germany<br>Russia | 4/1926 | 1936 | 2 | Bulgaria<br>Greece<br>Romania<br>Turkey<br>Yugoslavia | 7/1938 | 1939 | 2 |
| France<br>Romania | 6/1926 | 1939 | 2 | | | | |
| Afghanistan<br>Russia | 8/1926 | 1939 | 2 | France<br>Turkey | 2/1930 | 1939 | 2 |
| Lithuania<br>Russia | 9/1926 | 1939 | 2 | England<br>Iraq | 1932 | 1939 | 1 |
| Italy<br>Romania | 9/1926 | 1930 | 3 | Finland<br>Russia | 1/1932 | 1939 | 2 |
| Albania<br>Italy | 11/1926,<br>1927*** | 1927<br>1939 | 3<br>1 | Latvia<br>Russia | 2/1932 | 1939 | 2 |
| France<br>Yugoslavia | 1/1927 | 1939 | 2 | Estonia<br>Russia | 5/1932 | 1939 | 2 |
| Hungary<br>Italy | 4/1927 | 1939 | 2 | Poland<br>Russia | 7/1932 | 1939 | 2 |

TABLE 3.—*continued*

| Members | Incept. | Termin. | Class | Members | Incept. | Termin. | Class |
|---|---|---|---|---|---|---|---|
| France | 11/1932, | 1935 | 2 | Argentina | 12/1936 | 1939 | 3 |
| Russia | 1935*** | 1939 | 1 | Bolivia | | | |
| | | | | Brazil | | | |
| England | 6/1933 | 1936(?) | 3 | Chile | | | |
| France | | | | Colombia | | | |
| Germany | | | | Costa Rica | | | |
| Italy | | | | Cuba | | | |
| | | | | Dominican Republic | | | |
| Italy | 9/1933 | 1939 | 2 | Ecuador | | | |
| Russia | | | | Guatemala | | | |
| | | | | Haiti | | | |
| Argentina | 10/1933 | 1939 | 2 | Honduras | | | |
| Brazil | | | | Mexico | | | |
| Chile | | | | Nicaragua | | | |
| Mexico | | | | Panama | | | |
| Paraguay | | | | Paraguay | | | |
| Uruguay | | | | Peru | | | |
| Colombia | 4/1934 | | | Salvador | | | |
| Panama | 11/1936 | | | U.S.A. | | | |
| Finland | 2/1938 | | | Uruguay | | | |
| | | | | Venezuela | | | |
| Germany | 1/1934 | 1939 | 2 | | | | |
| Poland | | | | Italy | 3/1937 | 1939 | 2 |
| | | | | Yugoslavia | | | |
| Austria | 3/1934 | 1938 | 3 | | | | |
| Hungary | | | | Arabia | 4/1937 | 1939 | 1 |
| Italy | | | | Yemen | | | |
| Estonia | 8/1934 | 1939 | 3 | China | 8/1937 | 1939 | 2 |
| Latvia | | | | Russia | | | |
| Lithuania | | | | | | | |
| | | | | France | 12/1938 | 1939 | 3 |
| France | 4/1935 | 1938 | 3 | Germany | | | |
| Italy | | | | | | | |
| | | | | Portugal | 3/1939 | 1939 | 2 |
| Czechoslovakia | 5/1935 | 1939 | 1 | Spain | | | |
| Russia | | | | | | | |
| | | | | Germany | 5/1939 | 1939 | 1 |
| Mongolia | 3/1936 | 1939 | 1 | Italy | | | |
| Russia | | | | | | | |
| | | | | Denmark | 5/1939 | 1939 | 2 |
| Egypt | 10/1936 | 1939 | 1 | Germany | | | |
| England | | | | | | | |
| | | | | Estonia | 6/1939 | 1939 | 2 |
| Germany | 11/1936 | 1939 | 3 | Germany | | | |
| Japan | | | | | | | |
| Italy | 11/1937 | | | Germany | 6/1939 | 1939 | 2 |
| | | | | Latvia | | | |

5. Percentage of major powers having at least one alliance *of any class* with any *minor* power.

In addition to these five measures of aggregate interaction opportunity loss[16] we also sought a measure of the extent to which the various alliances created a degree of *bipolarity* in the system for each year. Here the procedure was a bit more complicated, and to balance off manageability with relevance, the computations were only made for *defensive* pacts among *major* powers. The first step was to calculate the maximum number of dyads that could be formed from among the population of major powers, using the formula $N(N - 1)/2$. Then we calculated the percentage of these which had been exhausted, via the following steps. All defensive pact links were counted, and the target(s), if any, of each identified; either a single nation or all members of a given alliance can be classified as targets. Next, we eliminated all linkages that were *no longer possible:* (1) those between members within each alliance; (2) those between members of opposing alliances; and (3) those between a target nation and all members of the alliance directed against that target nation. For any nation which was neither a target nor an alliance member, the maximum number of linkages still open was then counted, using the rule that it might contract an alliance with: other non-allied or non-target nations, plus either all members of the largest alliance, or all the non-allied target(s), whichever was the larger number. Once the number of feasible remaining defensive alliance links was ascertained, that number was divided by the original number that would have been possible in the absence of any such alliances, to give the percentage of major power defensive alliance ties exhausted.

One problem that confronted us was the occasional ambiguity regarding the target nation of a given alliance. That is, in 48 of our 130 years, there was sufficient disagreement among historians as to whether or not there is any target at all. In those cases, we computed an alternative bipolarity index. As in other places where professional consensus was used in place of a costly and complex operationalizing procedure, our authorities are identified in the basic descriptive article (Singer and Small, 1966b). In the tables, therefore, two sets of bipolarity indices and two sets of correlations are shown, and in the next section the intercorrelations between them are also shown. Let us illustrate (Figure 1) this procedure by reference to the alliance configuration of 1913; in that year, there were eight major powers, offering a maximum of twenty-eight possible linkages.

In the diagram, we see that twenty-one (or 75 percent) of those twenty-eight possible linkages were exhausted by alliances or by the logic of the targets as follows:

| By Alliance (5) | By Target (14) | |
|---|---|---|
| England-Japan | England-Italy | France-Germany |
| France-Russia | England-Germany | France-Austria |
| Austria-Germany | England-Austria | Russia-Italy |

FIGURE 1. *Major Power Alliance Configurations, 1913*

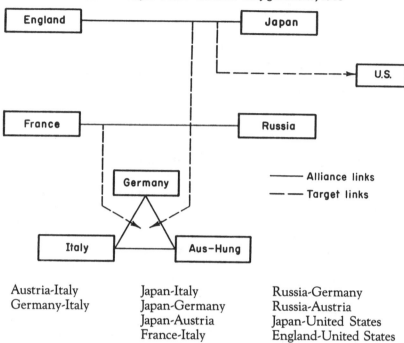

| Austria-Italy | Japan-Italy | Russia-Germany |
|---|---|---|
| Germany-Italy | Japan-Germany | Russia-Austria |
| | Japan-Austria | Japan-United States |
| | France-Italy | England-United States |

Two (2) more linkages are exhausted because if the United States allied with Germany, Austria-Hungary, and Italy, it obviously could no longer ally with France and Russia.

Before leaving this section, one more procedure needs to be described. Just as we ran correlations for three different time lags during which the onset of war could be measured, we felt that there was no *a priori* justification for assuming that our alliance data for a single year gave us the best independent variable. It could just as readily be argued that the system's alliance patterns are best reflected in their average magnitude over a longer period of time; for example, the duration of a given configuration might be as important as its magnitude. Therefore, three separate indices for each year and each independent variable were computed, showing that year's index, an average for that year plus the two preceding years, and an average for that year plus the four preceding years. Thus, for 1908 we have indicators on the independent variable side for 1908, the 1906–1908 average, and the 1904–1908 average. While all correlations have been run, only the three-year average is reported. (The remaining figures may be requested from the authors.)

These, then, represent our effort to convert the chaotic welter of historical facts or impressions on wars and alliances into relatively operational and machine-readable variables. The rigorous social scientist may well argue that intuition and apparent consensus among historians was permitted too large a role, while the diplomatic historian may hold that we have forced a large number of discrete events and unique relationships into too few Procrustean categories. Be that as it may, we have sought the most reasonable balance between reliability and validity, and urge others to examine and perhaps improve upon, the detailed coding procedures outlined in the two descriptive papers cited earlier.

## OBSERVED CORRELATIONS

With our operationalizing procedures out of the way, and our raw data's legitimacy more or less established, we can now turn to the many alternative correlations which were sought and/or found. Because of our uncertainty as to which represented the best measure and because of the low marginal cost of the additional measures, we developed and gathered data on a multiplicity of indices for both the dependent and the independent variables. Therefore, prior to an examination of the correlations between our independent and dependent variables, it might be helpful to look *within* each of these groups, summarize their intercorrelations, and ascertain the extent to which each of our seven independent variables and our five dependent ones seem to be measuring the same phenomena.

### Comparing the Dependent Variables

It will be recalled that we collected our data in such form as to permit the measurement of both the amount of war *underway* in any given year and the amount which *began* in any given year. In this study, however, concerned as we are with the extent to which alliance aggregation predicts to the *onset* of war, we will only present the data showing the number, magnitude, and severity of wars *beginning* in a given year. For a number of theoretical and methodological reasons, the underway data will be reserved for a separate and later paper.

The reader will also recall that the exploratory nature of the study demanded that we allow three different time lags during which a given alliance pattern's "effects" could be measured. That is, uncertain as to how long it took for the hypothesized consequences of alliances to be felt, we gathered data to show the effects within one year, within three years, and within five years following each year's alliance configuration. Thus, if we are looking, for example, at the alliance data for 1868, those various indices were all correlated with the data for wars which began in 1869, which began between January 1869 and December 1871, and those which began between January 1869 and December 1873. Once these data were in, however, it became clear that, if any alliance effects were to be found, they had largely made themselves felt within three years, especially in the twentieth century.[17] Thus, only the Y + 3 correlations will be shown in the Tables here.

TABLE 4. *Correlations Among Dependent Variables: The Onset of War within Three Years of each Year's Alliance Aggregations, 1815–1945*

| | Total System | | | | Central System | | | |
|---|---|---|---|---|---|---|---|---|
| | N-M War Begun–All | N-M War Begun–Majors | Battle Deaths–All | Battle Deaths–Majors | N-M War Begun–All | N-M War Begun–Majors | Battle Deaths–All | Battle Deaths–Majors |
| N-M War Begun—All | | | | | | | | |
| N-M War Begun—Majors | 95 | | | | 96 | | | |
| Battle Deaths—All | 97 | 96 | | | 98 | 97 | | |
| Battle Deaths—Majors | 97 | 97 | 99 | | 98 | 98 | 99 | |
| No. Wars Begun | 34 | 35 | 28 | 27 | 52 | 54 | 49 | 47 |

As Table 4 reveals, whether we look at the total international system or the central system alone, there is indeed an impressively high correlation among most of these dependent variable indicators.[18] It is patently evident that we were overly concerned. That is, whether we look at the total system or the central system, and whether we look at all nations or major ones only, the correlation coefficient between nation-months and battle deaths is only a shade less than one. (Unity, of course, would show that the indices were all measuring precisely the same thing.) The only low, but nevertheless still significant, correlations are between the magnitude and severity measures on one hand and the frequency ones on the other. Given the distributions described earlier, this was to be expected.

### Comparing the Independent Variables

Comparing the alliance aggregation figures to one another is a somewhat more complex matter than that involving the war data. Here, we have not only the standard spatial and chronological subsets, but the various combinations of signatory status and alliance class. Further, there is the distinction between aggregate commitments and those which generate our two alternative indices of bipolarity. In addition to these latter, which, as indicated earlier, are based solely on the polarization among the major powers, there are (1) all classes of alliance among all nations; (2) all classes of alliance among major powers; (3) defense pacts among all; (4) defense pacts among majors; and (5) all alliances between majors and minors. As noted earlier, we are not examining here the extent to which neutrality pacts and ententes "predict to" war, inasmuch as the count on these is somewhat misleading; that is, neutrality or entente commitments were counted only when no defense pact existed between the nations in any dyad. In other words, only the highest class of commitment between each pair was counted.

TABLE 5. *Correlations Among Independent Variables: Annual Alliance Aggregations, 1815–1939*

| | Total System | | | | | | Central System Only | | | | | |
|---|---|---|---|---|---|---|---|---|---|---|---|---|
| | % Nations in Alliance | % Nations in Defense Pact | % Majors in Alliance | % Majors in Defense Pact | % Majors Allied with Minors | Major Bilateral Defense Exhausted-a | % Nations in Alliance | % Nations in Defense Pact | % Majors in Alliance | % Majors in Defense Pact | % Majors Allied with Minors | Major Bilateral Defense Exhausted-a |
| % Nations in Defense Pact | 74 | | | | | | 80 | | | | | |
| % Majors in Alliance | 50 | 53 | | | | | 77 | 74 | | | | |
| % Majors in Defense Pact | 32 | 60 | 81 | | | | 58 | 83 | 81 | | | |
| % Majors Allied with Minors | 64 | 61 | 64 | 59 | | | 80 | 70 | 42 | 33 | | |
| Major Bilateral Defense Exhausted—a | 00 | –01 | 47 | 57 | 26 | | 54 | 53 | 47 | 57 | 51 | |
| Major Bilateral Defense Exhausted–b | 45 | 50 | 60 | 68 | 67 | 58 | 57 | 70 | 60 | 68 | 48 | 58 |

As Table 5 reveals, there exists a very impressive intercorrelation among these several alliance measures. In the central system, every indicator correlates strongly with every other, and in the total system, the only absence of correlation is that between the initial and the alternative bipolarity figures on the one hand, and the all-allied and all-in-defense-pact figures, on the other. This lack of significant correlation need not surprise us, given the fact that the bipolarity measures reflect major power cleavages only. Again, but to a considerably lesser extent than with war, we are tapping approximately the same structural phenomena.

Having digressed for the important purpose of ascertaining the extent to which our many different measures tend to tap the same phenomena, we may now move on to the primary concern of the study: the extent to which alliance aggregation in its various forms predicts to war.

## Total System, 1815–1945

In order to make more comprehensible the many pairs of correlations within our six different systemic settings, a brief recapitulation would seem to be in order. The correlations will be so presented in the separate tables as to identify: (1) the international system or portion thereof which is

TABLE 6. *Total System, 1815–1945: Correlations Between Alliance Indicators and Magnitude, Severity, and Frequency of War Beginning Within Three Years*

| | % of All in Any Alliance | % of All in Defense Pact | % of Majors in Any Alliance | % of Majors in Defense Pact | % of Majors with Minor | Bipolarity Initial | Bipolarity Alternate |
|---|---|---|---|---|---|---|---|
| Nation-Months War—All | *30* | −05 | 05 | 06 | 17 | 08 | 13 |
| Nation-Months War—Majors | *28* | −01 | 10 | 04 | 22 | 14 | 18 |
| Battle Deaths for All | *34* | −01 | 11 | 01 | 21 | 15 | 19 |
| Battle Deaths for Majors | *31* | −01 | 12 | 04 | 21 | 17 | 21 |
| Number of Wars | 07 | −01 | 06 | 04 | 18 | −03 | 01 |

under examination; (2) the time period for which it is being examined; (3) the specific independent variables being used; and (4) the specific dependent variables. As we indicated earlier, a great many more correlations were run than are reported here; among those not shown here are (1) eight of the nine $r$ values for each cross-correlation, with only the three-year average for alliance indices and the three-year lag for war indices correlated in the text and accompanying tables; (2) all neutrality pact and entente data, with only the defense pact and all alliance class categories shown in the text; and (3) all data dealing with war actually underway, with only the data on *onset* of war shown in the text. Contrary to some practice, we will include all $r$ values in each table, even those which are not equivalent to statistically significant levels; those which equal or exceed the .01 level requirement will be italicized. As to sequence, we begin with the total system for the entire 1815–1945 period, and then drop the peripheral nations and concentrate on the central system only for the same full period. Next we look at the total system in the nineteenth century, and then move on to the central system only for that eighty-five-year period. Finally, we examine the twentieth century total system and central system in that order.

Turning, then, to our first and most comprehensive empirical world—that of the total international system for the entire 1815–1945 period (shown in Table 6)—we find one set of consistently high correlations. That is, the grossest of the independent variables—percentage of *all* nations in at least one alliance of *any* class—shows significant correlations with all four of the magnitude and severity indicators, but not with the number of wars beginning within three years. On the major power side, however, no such findings emerge. As a matter of fact there are no other sufficiently high $r$

TABLE 7.  *Central System, 1815–1945: Correlations Between Alliance Indicators and Magnitude, Severity, and Frequency of War Beginning Within Three Years*

| | % of All in Any Alliance | % of All in Defense Pact | % of Majors in Any Alliance | % of Majors in Defense Pact | % of Majors with Minor | Bipolarity Initial | Bipolarity Alternate |
|---|---|---|---|---|---|---|---|
| Nation-Months War—All | *33* | 11 | 06 | −02 | *34* | 12 | 16 |
| Nation-Months War—Majors | *34* | 14 | 11 | 03 | *34* | 15 | 13 |
| Battle Deaths for All | *35* | 12 | 11 | 01 | *34* | 15 | 18 |
| Battle Deaths for Majors | *35* | 14 | 12 | 04 | *34* | 17 | 20 |
| Number of Wars | 19 | 07 | 05 | −03 | 28 | −07 | 16 |

values at all for this total system-entire period setting, although the major with minor correlation approaches that level.

## Central System, 1815–1945

Let us now take the first of several steps in the direction of increasingly restrictive empirical worlds, and shuck off all the peripheral system nations, leaving the central system only, but still for the entire time period. The picture is pretty much the same, as we see in Table 7; that is, the percentage of all nations in any class of alliance correlates strongly with all four magnitude (nation-months of war) and severity (battle deaths) indices. Again, defense pacts among all, or among majors only, do not show a high covariation; but in this more restrictive setting, the percentage of majors having at least one alliance of any kind with a minor power does predict significantly to all the war measures. Note that even the frequency measure correlates, albeit modestly, with the major-minor measure, but not with any of the other alliance indicators.

## Total System, 1815–1899

As suggested in a previous section, it seemed useful to inquire as to whether the relationship between alliance commitments and war might be stronger or weaker in different epochs; thus we have not only divided our total population into central and total systems, but have also divided it into nineteenth and twentieth century systems. Let us therefore shift from the full population (that is, total system, entire 130-year period) and examine the total system up through 1899 only. A brief glance at Table 8 indicates that this concentration upon the nineteenth-century total system exercises

TABLE 8. *Total System, 1815–1899: Correlations Between Alliance Indicators and Magnitude, Severity and Frequency of War Beginning Within Three Years*

|  | % of All in Any Alliance | % of All in Defense Pact | % of Majors in Any Alliance | % of Majors in Defense Pact | % of Majors with Minor | Bipolarity Initial | Bipolarity Alternate |
|---|---|---|---|---|---|---|---|
| Nation-Months War—All | −16 | −16 | −23 | −34 | −21 | −32 | −23 |
| Nation-Months War—Majors | −04 | 01 | −26 | −14 | −01 | −23 | −19 |
| Battle Deaths for All | −27 | −23 | −38 | −42 | −33 | −33 | −28 |
| Battle Deaths for Majors | −26 | −19 | −41 | −38 | −27 | −30 | −25 |
| Number of Wars | −00 | 01 | −10 | −05 | 05 | −21 | −12 |

a striking effect on our correlations. That is, we no longer find alliance aggregation in general predicting to war, and those *r*'s that are close to significant are all in the *negative* direction. And when we move over to include major powers only, their general alliance involvement does indeed show a strong—but negative—correlation with both the severity measures; the same holds for major-minor alliances vis-à-vis battle deaths for all. As to our initial bipolarity measure, we find relatively strong correlations vis-à-vis one of the magnitude measures and both of the severity measures.

Although the statistically alert reader may already anticipate what our *post*-1900 correlations will look like, it would be premature either to present them next or to offer an interpretation of the above rather consistent negative correlations. Rather, let us stay in the same nineteenth-century time frame, but again shuck off the nations of the peripheral system and look exclusively at the nineteenth century central, or European, state system.

## Central System, 1815–1899

Here, as Table 9 makes evident, the same nineteenth century pattern continues. That is, all of the strong correlations are in the negative direction, with the severity indices again most sensitive to alliance aggregation. Worth observing is that every one of the alliance indicators correlates strongly and inversely with all battle deaths and with major-power battle deaths arising from war beginning within three years of the alliance condition.

## Total System, 1900–1945

We can now look at some of the evidence that should have been anticipated once the nineteenth century data were contrasted to data for the entire period. That is, if alliances and war show some modest positive

TABLE 9.   *Central System, 1815-1899: Correlations between Alliance Indicators and Magnitude, Severity and Frequency of War Beginning Within Three Years*

| | % of All in Any Alliance | % of All in Defense Pact | % of Majors in Any Alliance | % of Majors in Defense Pact | % of Majors with Minor | Bipolarity Initial | Bipolarity Alternate |
|---|---|---|---|---|---|---|---|
| Nation-Months War—All | −19 | −14 | −15 | −08 | −16 | −19 | −14 |
| Nation-Months War—Majors | −20 | −14 | −19 | −09 | −13 | −17 | −16 |
| Battle Deaths for All | *−45* | *−45* | *−44* | *−45* | *−33* | *−34* | *−30* |
| Battle Deaths for Majors | *−46* | *−41* | *−48* | *−42* | *−30* | *−32* | *−28* |
| Number of Wars | −05 | −02 | −03 | 07 | −04 | −20 | −06 |

correlations for the entire 130 years and somewhat stronger, but *negative* correlations for the first 85 years, we may logically expect positive and somewhat stronger *r*'s for the twentieth century data. This indeed is what we find, despite the fact that our N of only 45 years raises the *r*-value requirement to a coincidental .45. Thus, the percentage of all nations in any class of alliance, as well as in defense pacts, correlates highly with all four magnitude and severity measures in every case but one (.43 with nation-months of war for all). Likewise, the major-minor figure predicts well to three of these four dependent variables. On the bipolarity side, however, none of the correlations are high enough to be interesting.

## Central System, 1900–1945

Turning to the last of our empirical worlds, the pattern is essentially the same for the central as for the total twentieth century system. Though defense pacts among all do not predict to war compellingly in this case, alliances in general among all do, as do major-minor alliances in three of the four cases. Again, the bipolarity correlations are all moderately in this direction, but as in the total system, they still fail to satisfy the .01 requirements.

## SUMMARY AND INTERPRETATION

Given the material with which we worked, the data-making operations, and the observed correlations between and among our many variables, what can we now say regarding the basic hypothesis? Do alliance aggregations in general, or bipolarity tendencies in particular, correlate in any meaningful

TABLE 10. *Total System, 1900–1945: Correlations Between Alliance Indicators and Magnitude, Severity, and Frequency of War Beginning Within Three Years*

| | % of All in Any Alliance | % of All in Defense Pact | % of Majors in Any Alliance | % of Majors in Defense Pact | % of Majors with Minor | Bipolarity Initial | Bipolarity Alternate |
|---|---|---|---|---|---|---|---|
| Nation-Months War—All | 53 | 43 | 24 | 05 | 43 | 15 | 28 |
| Nation-Months War—Majors | 46 | 48 | 35 | 16 | 47 | 24 | 36 |
| Battle Deaths for All | 56 | 48 | 29 | 08 | 46 | 19 | 31 |
| Battle Deaths for Majors | 51 | 48 | 31 | 13 | 45 | 23 | 36 |
| Number of Wars | 18 | 29 | 50 | 26 | 54 | 27 | 26 |

TABLE 11. *Central System, 1900–1945: Correlations Between Alliance Indicators and Magnitide, Severity, and Frequency of War Beginning Within Three Years*

| | % of All in Any Alliance. | % of All in Defense Pact | % of Majors in Any Alliance | % of Majors in Defense Pact | % of Majors with Minor | Bipolarity Initial | Bipolarity Alternate |
|---|---|---|---|---|---|---|---|
| Nation-Months War—All | 45 | 04 | 23 | 05 | 42 | 14 | 27 |
| Nation-Months War—Majors | 49 | 17 | 35 | 18 | 47 | 24 | 36 |
| Battle Deaths for All | 50 | 09 | 29 | 09 | 46 | 19 | 32 |
| Battle Deaths for Majors | 50 | 13 | 31 | 14 | 45 | 23 | 36 |
| Number of Wars | 25 | −02 | 24 | −05 | 40 | −05 | 02 |

way with the onset of international war in the nineteenth and twentieth centuries?

Assuming that our measures are as valid and reliable as claimed, the evidence seems to be relatively unambiguous. We say relatively because there are two quite distinct and incompatible patterns, but the incompatibility is easily resolved by dividing the entire historical epoch into two periods. That is, if we look at the twentieth century segment only, the hypothesis is rather strongly confirmed. (Taking the seven independent variable indicators and the four measures of war magnitude and war severity, for both the central and the total systems, we have fifty-six opportunities for a strong positive correlation to appear. Our results show such a correlation on seventeen of these occasions.) Looking first at the alliance aggregation measures, for both the central and the total systems, we find that the percentage of all nations in the system having at least one alliance with any other nation predicts to the amount of war on all eight of the possible occasions. And the percentage of major powers having at least one alliance with a minor does likewise on six of the eight possible occasions. Combining this powerful tendency with the fact that there are quite a few more correlations that are only slightly weaker and that not a single negative correlation appears, we may only conclude that the well-accepted hypothesis has indeed been borne out by our historical evidence.

Does the hypothesis do as well in an earlier epoch? Clearly not. To the contrary, on all eight of the possible occasions for a positive correlation to turn up between gross alliance aggregation and the magnitude or severity of war in the nineteenth century, the correlation was negative. And if the same matrix were constructed for defense pacts, seven of the eight turn out to be negative. Furthermore, if we look at all classes of alliance among major powers only for the nineteenth century, all eight correlations are again negative, four of them strongly so. Even if we focus on major-power defense pacts for both of these nineteenth century systems, five of the eight negative correlations meet our rather stringent threshold criteria. Finally, all eight of the war correlations with major-minor alliance percentages are negative, three at the .01 equivalent level. The observed relationship between alliance aggregation and the onset of war in the nineteenth century, then, is clearly a negative one, and shows a distribution which is diametrically opposed to, and almost as strong as, that found for the twentieth century.

To what extent is the alliance aggregation pattern repeated when we try to predict to war from *bipolarity*? In general, the same tendencies appear, but with somewhat lower coefficient values. That is, if we look at both the initial and the alternative indices of major-power bipolarization, and correlate them with our four magnitude and severity indices in both forms (central and total) of the twentieth century system, all sixteen $r$'s are positive, but only twelve of these are in significance ranges better than .1 (not .01). Any doubt as to the general tendency is dispelled, however, when we examine the nineteenth century total and central systems. As with alliance aggregation, every one of the $r$ values is negative, with eight of the sixteen meeting the .01-level requirement.

Given the extraordinarily low probability of such correlations occurring in such consistent form by sheer chance, we have no choice but to conclude that alliance aggregation and bipolarization do indeed have a meaningful relation to the onset of war. But it is important to note the theoretical implications of these relationships. It is certainly clear that formal alliance patterns do not exercise a uniform impact over time. To the contrary, both alliance aggregation and bipolarity covary strongly with the amount of war that follows within three years during the twentieth century, and correlate *inversely* to almost the same degree during the nineteenth century.

Regardless of the war-onset measure we use, the pattern is similar. Whether it is nation-months of war or battle-connected deaths, whether the data are for the total system or the central one only, and whether they reflect all members of the system or major powers only, when alliance aggregation or bipolarity in the nineteenth century increases, the amount of war experienced by the system goes down, and vice versa. And in the twentieth century, the greater the alliance aggregation or bipolarity in the system, the more war it experiences.

Now the cautious or skeptical reader may say that "it depends" upon what we mean by "amount of war," and ask whether the same picture emerges when we look at the sheer *number* of wars. As a matter of fact, it does, but not quite as impressively. That is, almost all of our independent variables correlate negatively with the number of wars beginning within the Y + 3 period during the nineteenth century, and positively during the twentieth century. And the five exceptions out of the fourteen opportunities are barely perceptible: we find $r$'s of .01, .05, and .07 for the nineteenth, and $-.02$ and $-.05$ for the twentieth. Moreover, if there were any concern that it is the sheer magnitude and severity of the two world wars that accounts for the twentieth century positive correlation, it should be noted that when the *number* of wars begun is used as the dependent variable, the $r$ values for percentage of all nations in alliances of any class are .18 and .25. For all major power alliances, these are .50 and .24, and for major-minor alliances, they are .54 and .40, for the total and central systems respectively.[19] In sum, whether we measure amount by number of wars, the nation-months involved, or battle deaths incurred, alliance aggregation and bipolarity predict strongly away from war in the nineteenth century and even more strongly toward it in the twentieth. One might say that those who generalize about the effects of alliance activity—and most postulate a destabilizing effect, especially in regard to bipolarity—have been so preoccupied with more recent history that they have neglected the patterns which obtained in an earlier, but by no means incomparable, period; one recent exception is Waltz (1964).

It is obvious that correlation and causality are rather different things, and that correlation at a high level is *necessary* to the establishment of a causal relationship, but not at all *sufficient*. Unless a logically tight and empirically correct linkage between the independent variables and the dependent ones can be presented, and competing explanations can be disconfirmed, we have established something less than causality. Thus, it seems appropriate to conclude on a cautious note, by indicating the sorts of substantive and methodological questions which remain.

For example, are we able to demonstrate a close empirical and chronological connection between specific alliances and specific wars? At this juncture, our data are not in the form which would permit a direct answer, but we do have some results of a tangential nature. That is, if we look at the frequency with which a given nation belongs to any alliance within three years prior to any war, and compare that figure to the frequency with which it participates in any war, we find that for all 82 of our nations over the 130 year period, the correlation is .60; and for the 67 central-system members, the figure is a very high .72. But this still doesn't establish a causal connection. Again, there is the simple, but not unreasonable, argument that national decision makers will tend to step up their alliance-building activities as they perceive the probability of war to be rising. This might well account for our twentieth century correlations, and we have, as yet, produced no evidence to contravene the hypothesis.

Beyond this, even though we have uncovered a compelling relationship between alliances and the onset of war, the magnitude of that relation still remains an empirical question, and it may well be that other factors will account for much more of the variance than these two sets of variables. As a matter of fact, if we use the statistical rule of thumb which permits us to say that the amount of variance accounted for by a given independent variable—the coefficient of determination—is approximately the square of the product-moment correlation, we see how limited the alliance effect may be. With the twentieth century (positive) correlations averaging out at .29 and the nineteenth century (negative) ones averaging out at .26, these alliance factors may be interpreted as accounting for somewhere between 8.4 and 6.8 percent of the variance.[20]

Furthermore, a number of qualifications and caveats regarding some of our independent variables come to mind. As to the five different alliance aggregation indices, we did indeed cover a wide range of possibilities, using all classes of alliance, as well as defense pacts alone, using all nations as well as major powers alone, using six different spatio-temporal forms of the international system, and using nine different lead and lag combinations, but the exploration nevertheless remains incomplete. Again, though we have gathered data on neutrality pacts and on ententes, data on these classes of alliance have not been processed for use here, and it may well be that their presence and absence might shed further light on the alliance-war relationship. Another possibility worth examining might be that of *changes* in alliance aggregation; that is, each year's increments or decrements vis-à-vis the previous year or years might reveal a discernible pattern that either strengthens or challenges the tendency discovered in this study. Likewise, an investigation into the *rates* of change might produce some valuable results. Finally, a closely related systemic property is that of the number of individual alliance changes and shifts made in a given year or more by all nations in the system. This measure we call lateral mobility, and some preliminary work on it is already underway.

Similar thoughts occur when our bipolarity measures are considered. First of all, the measure itself reflects the degree of cleavage among major powers only, and while one would intuitively expect the total system to partially parallel the major power sub-system, we have no hard evidence that it does. Moreover, the measure is by no means as compelling an indicator of bipolarization as it might be. Since embarking on this project we have discovered in the sociometry and graph theory literature some promising alternative operations by which such cleavage might be measured; some of these operations require that we first develop a better procedure for identifying alliance targets, while others do not.[21] In the same vein, it immediately occurs to us that bipolarity by itself may not be as interesting or compelling a predictor as when it is combined with one or more additional variables. For example, it might well pay to examine the joint effects of polarity and parity: is high bipolarity more likely to precede the onset of war when the two coalitions are approximately equal in power and capability or when a clear disparity exists?

Or, it might well be that the traditional theory overlooks a simple but crucial element: can the invisible hand ever function within so small a population? Certainly a large numerical discrepancy exists between the thousands of buyers and sellers in an economic marketplace and the eighty-two actors in our pre-1945 total system or the one-hundred-twenty–odd ones in the postwar system. It might turn out that hypotheses generated from models of oligopoly or duopoly will stand the empirical test more successfully than those generated by a free and open market model.

Then, again, there is the matter of structural or cultural context. Is it not possible that the structural variable utilized here—alliance aggregation—is in turn responsive to other systemic properties, and that its predictive power is a function of its interaction with such variables? To put it another way, are nations as likely to respond to short- and middle-range security requirements and make alliances on that basis alone, when the diplomatic culture is increasingly ideological or less homogeneous, or when the structure of the system is more rigid or its supra-national aspects are increasing? Similarly, it can be argued that our approach is entirely too formal, and that emphasis might better be placed on other indices of international relationship: diplomatic communication, trade, tourism, or less formal and perhaps unwritten indicators of reciprocal commitment. Though these suggestions would carry us beyond our immediate concern here, they are certainly well taken.

A final concern is that raised in a thoughtful but as yet unpublished critique (Zinnes, 1966) regarding the extent to which this analysis really "tested the balance of power theory." As the title of this paper and its specific sections make clear, we are not testing *the theory*, but only one basic proposition which we believe can be deduced from it; moreover, to grace the conceptual and empirical chaos of the balance of power literature with the label "theory" is much too generous. Within that critique, however, a specific problem of considerable importance *is* raised, and it merits a brief discussion. As we understand the criticism, it concerns the validity of our independent variable, and questions whether our alliance aggregation and alliance involvement indicators really reflect the diminution of cross-pressures as implied in our theoretical argument. Our argument, it will be recalled, is that each alliance commitment undertaken by a nation reduces its interaction opportunities, and thus the interaction opportunities available to the entire system; as these diminish, we reason that the allied nation is now "less free to compete with its new allies and less free to cooperate with non-allies." The randomized cross-pressures on it give way, to some extent, to pressures that are likely to be more discriminatory and systematic. That is, the nation is now less likely to treat all others in a neutral fashion, but will tend to remove some of them from the neutral category and treat them more nearly as friends or as opponents. Given what we know about reciprocity in diplomatic behavior, it follows that those nations which are now treated in a non-random fashion will respond more or less in kind. The original randomized pressures (impinging on it from many directions) will now come in upon the newly-allied nation from more parallel or polarized directions, with a net loss of pluralistic cross-pressures in the system as a whole.

The criticism is that this model, while a reasonable interpretation of the classical formulation, ignores the fact that cross-pressures are *not* reduced unless the "nations belong to one and only one alliance." (Zinnes, 1966, p. 7). It goes on further to contend that in only 22 of our 130 years does that condition hold, and that our various indicators are therefore not theoretically valid. The assertion here, as we understand it, is that multiple alliance commitments do not necessarily diminish the cross-pressures, and may, under some conditions, even increase them. While the question is an empirical one, neither we nor others have yet sought to test it against evidence, and we must therefore fall back on logical analysis. In principle we would expect the assertion to hold in only an extremely limited set of cases: those in which a nation belongs to two alliances which are clearly *directed against one another*. And the only case in our population which clearly satisfies this unlikely condition is that of Italy, which belonged to both the Triple Alliance and the Entente (in a fragile sort of way) during the period leading up to World War I.

Even if there were other cases of such multiple membership in conflicting alliance groupings, however, the criticism would not hold. That is, it would only hold if the international system were composed solely of those two alliance memberships; as long as the system is larger than the five nations hypothesized in the critique, the assertion fails to stand. This is so because the allied nation, in its dealings with nations outside the two conflicting alliances, will not be as free as a non-allied nation would be in dealing with these more remote system members. In sum, we consider our independent and our intervening variables to be valid, and therefore remain satisfied that we have indeed examined a proposition which is central to the classical balance of power paradigm.[22]

These considerations bring us, therefore, back to the points raised at the outset of the paper. In any search for the "causes" of war, the quest for correlates may lead us not only into attributes of the international system, but into attributes of the more war-prone nations, their pre-conflict and pre-war relationships, and their pre-war behavior and interaction. It is our working assumption that any theory of the causes of war will include all four sets of independent variables. But we urge that considerable exploration of systemic properties be given high priority. Unless we understand the environment within which inter-nation conflict occurs, and can ascertain the approximate effect of that environment, there is no meaningful way of establishing the controls which are essential to any experimental inquiry. And if we look upon this quantitative approach to diplomatic history as a sequence of ex post facto, natural world experiment, the importance of such controls cannot be exaggerated.

CHAPTER FIFTEEN

———————— ■ ————————

# Capabilities, Allocations, and Success in Militarized Disputes and Wars, 1816–1976

Frank W. Wayman, J. David Singer,
and Gary Goertz

IT IS OFTEN SUGGESTED THAT power is to the study of politics as wealth is to the study of economics, but that whereas wealth is rather easily measured, power remains a more elusive phenomenon. Nowhere is this more apparent than in the study—and practice—of international politics. We have attended to the concept of power for centuries, built our models and predicted our policies upon it, yet we still remain far from an agreed definition, not to mention a valid and reliable way of measuring it.

This suggests the need for further work in several areas. First, it seems that much conceptual clarification remains to be done, despite the work of a number of scholars (Lasswell and Kaplan, 1950; Shapley and Shubik, 1954; Dahl, 1957; Bachrach and Baratz, 1962; Singer, 1963; March, 1966; Schelling, 1966; Nagel, 1975; Baldwin, 1979). Second is the need for a set of more valid, reliable, empirically vindicated indicators of power and the related concepts of capability and influence, building on previous efforts in this direction (German, 1960; Fucks, 1965; Knorr, 1970; Ferris, 1973; Newcombe and Wert, 1973; Cline, 1977; Nagel, 1975; Hart, 1976; Saaty and Khouja, 1976). Third, and perhaps most important, is the need for research that examines the efficacy of different forms of power as an instrument of political influence. Work of this latter sort is most crucial, inasmuch as careful evaluation of the role of various indicators in the crucible of political struggle can help establish the validity of alternative indicators, while at the same time contributing to greater conceptual clarity.

This chapter originally appeared in the *International Studies Quarterly*, vol. 27 (1983), pp. 497–515. Copyright © International Studies Association. Reprinted by permission.

In this paper our primary concern is with this third focus, and we take up this task by building on the efforts of others (Rosen, 1972; Singer et al., 1972; Mack, 1975; Blechman and Kaplan, 1978; Organski and Kugler, 1979; Bremer, 1980; Bueno de Mesquita, 1980; Cannizzo, 1980; Maoz, 1982; Yengst, 1982) who have made it their concern as well. In particular, we examine one aspect of power that all of these researchers agree is intrinsic to an understanding of its role in international politics: the material capabilities available to the state, and the extent to which these can be brought to bear in the exercise of interstate influence. More specifically, our concern here is with the historical efficacy of material capabilities—especially those that are allocated to the military establishment—in achieving success in military confrontations and in all-out war. Whatever else is subsumed under the rubric of power, the ability of a state to have its way in conflict is an element that must be considered. This point may appear commonplace; the necessity of armed forces in the pursuit of success in conflict is so readily assumed that one must look diligently to find, since the rise of the modern interstate system, that rare state that somehow manages to survive without such forces.[1] Be that as it may, our intent here is to measure as validly as possible—though in no way conclusively—the extent to which the states' armed forces and the industrial-demographic base on which they rest do indeed lead to victory in war and to prevailing in disputes at the brink of war.

Of course, one does not undertake an ambitious empirical investigation merely out of curiosity. One is almost always motivated by some intellectual challenge or ethical concern, and usually certain preconceptions as to the empirical results are brought to bear. We share a general opposition to war as an instrument of national policy, and thus to the establishment of armed forces as the engine of war. Further, as students of diplomatic history and international politics, we find, in both narrative histories and data-based analyses conducted to date, grounds for skepticism regarding the utility of the armed forces as an instrument for avoiding war and prevailing in disputes short of war.

These considerations lead us, in turn, to formulate what might be called the capability-security hypothesis: that there is a curvilinear relationship between a state's level of security and the level of its military capabilities. In an essentially anarchic international system, in which there are always scarcities, especially the scarcity of security, and in which force or the threat of force is the final arbiter, the *absence* of armed forces can be a dangerous temptation to even a moderately armed neighbor, making some modest level of preparedness a useful deterrent. But at the other end of the preparedness spectrum, there is also a serious danger. Excessively *high levels* of militarization can not only provoke an arms buildup and/or adventurous behavior on the part of potential enemies, but become a temptation to a state's own political elites to embark on their own military adventures. This temptation arises partly out of the domestic consequences of over-preparedness, since it usually increases the influence of the pro-military elements while decreasing that of countervailing elements in the society, and reduces the availability of economic, diplomatic, and cultural resources as alternative instruments thereby reducing the range of options likely to be considered when the need for interstate influence is indicated. Externally, over-preparedness tends to stimulate the same within rivals and/ or neighboring societies, further enhancing the escalatory process on both sides.

It is, of course, one thing to posit such a curvilinear relationship and quite another to put it to the empirical test. To be satisfactory, such a test requires: (a) a sufficiently large spatial temporal domain, and (b) the generation of an appropriate data base, including of course indicators of (c) military capabilities and (d) security. While we think we satisfy three of these requirements here, the fourth, an indicator of national security, is satisfied to only a limited extent. The concept of national security is so broad and elusive, and the possible range of indicators so varied, that we must settle for indicators that fall short of tapping the entire range of the concept.

We conceptualize national security in the context of the Correlates of War Project's research foci as a relatively low frequency of *involvement* in wars and military disputes, and a relatively high frequency of *success* when such events occur. Here we consider only the latter. A subsequent paper will examine the relationship of capabilities to frequency of involvement in wars and disputes. While we realize that national security is a more complex and multidimensional concept, and that our definition would be too restrictive for many whose scholarly interests are different than ours (Blechman and Kaplan, 1978:4-12), we believe that measuring success in war and in militarized disputes over 160 years is not a bad way to begin. It is to these procedural matters we first turn.

## EMPIRICAL DOMAIN, DATA, AND INDICATORS

While much of the empirical work in our field suggests otherwise, one can hardly claim to generalize on the basis of a few cases, a brief historical period, or one particular region. Thus, in order to provide a strong basis for generalization we continue in this project's tradition by examining: (a) all interstate wars in the international system from the end of the Napoleonic Wars up through 1976, the last year for which the relevant data base is relatively complete; and (b) all militarized disputes in which there was at least one major power on each side, for the same 160-year period. Elsewhere, we have defended the length (and the brevity!) of our temporal domain, and specified the criteria for inclusion in the interstate system and the major power subsystem, along with the fluctuating membership of both since 1816 (Singer and Small, 1972). Here, we need merely reiterate the states that have constituted the major power grouping, and the years up through 1976 during which each qualified for inclusion:

| | |
|---|---|
| Austria-Hungary | 1816-1918 |
| Prussia/Germany | 1816-1918; 1925-1945 |

| Russia/USSR | 1816-1917; 1922- |
| France | 1816-1940; 1945- |
| United Kingdom | 1816- |
| Italy | 1860-1943 |
| Japan | 1895-1945 |
| United States | 1898- |
| China | 1949- |

## The Population of Cases

For an investigation of the sort proposed here, we need not examine the data for each state and each year that it was in the larger system, or in the more restricted major power subsystem. Since we are concerned only with the states' success or failure in militarized disputes and in interstate wars, we need consider only the data for those particular states and years. This requires, of course, a specification of disputes and wars and their participants.

With respect to wars, we differentiate among three types (omitting, of course, civil wars): (a) interstate; (b) imperial; and (c) colonial. Our concern here is with the first type only. We define interstate war as sustained military combat between the official armed forces of at least two sovereign members of the interstate system which results in at least 1000 fatalities among the combat personnel. (Detailed criteria, justification, and emerging data describing these 69 interstate wars are found in Resort to Arms (Small and Singer, 1982), along with data for the 51 imperial or colonial wars.)

It should be noted that every war is preceded by a militarized dispute, though most such disputes (about 88 percent) end in stalemate, compromise, or capitulation rather than war. How do we recognize these militarized disputes, and how are they differentiated from less serious, non-militarized disputes? Identifying all qualifying interstate disputes, and the candidate cases from which they emerge, was much more difficult than identifying the qualifying wars; the latter have left many more traces, on both the battlefield and in the archives. We can bury our dead, but we cannot bury our wars. Disputes, on the other hand, often leave no corpses, and governments frequently have good reason to either conceal or distort these confrontational events. However, by systematically combing through such compilations as Langer's (1968) Encyclopedia of World History and the Dupuy and Dupuy (1977) Encyclopaedia of Military History, plus the diplomatic and military histories of every state for every year that it was a system member, we believe that our N of 967 (of which 101 had a major power on each side) is very close to complete. For an interstate dispute to qualify as "militarized," one of the protagonists had to have committed one of the following acts: (a) an explicit threat to resort to war; (b) the mobilization of inactive forces; (c) the deployment or redeployment of active forces; or (d) the actual use of force short of war.[2]

In this paper, we examine major-major disputes and all wars. We included only major-major disputes because they are the only ones for which dispute outcomes have been coded to date, because these disputes are usually of greater salience in our field, and because they are the ones that most frequently escalate to war (Gochman and Maoz, 1982).

## Measuring Success in Wars and Disputes

Turning now to our two sets of variables—outcomes and predictor— how do we propose to measure them? While the concepts one thinks of as reflecting national security have seldom been approached in an operational fashion, there are some fairly obvious approaches. Here, we defer the joys of trying to measure security on an interval scale and resort to relatively unambiguous, if not always precise, *nominal* categories. That is, we will classify as successful those states or coalitions that "won" in each dispute and each war, no matter how pyrrhic the victory. Of course, the state that systematically avoids brink-of-war confrontations as well as wars themselves, while still managing to have its way, would score very high on national security. As noted above, a later paper will examine the efficacy of capabilities and allocations in that effort, but here we restrict ourselves to the matter of success (prevailing in a dispute and winning in war) if the state actually gets involved in such an altercation.

In war—at least until World War III—one state or coalition usually emerges victorious in the sense that its forces are sufficiently superior at the close of combat that the other side seeks a cessation of hostilities. The victors may even have suffered greater casualties and loss of more material and/or territory, yet, in the eyes of the participants, contemporary observers, and later historians, one side is the victor and the other the vanquished. Of the 69 interstate wars from 1816 to 1976 studied here, there were only two in which the scholarly consensus ruled the outcome a "draw," and both of them since World War II: the Korean War of 1950 and the Israeli-Egyptian War of Attrition in 1969–1970, leaving a population of 67 for our concerns.

Measuring success in war, while not without its problems (O'Connor, 1969), is simpler than measuring success in a militarized dispute. But despite the uneven quality of knowledge and the ambiguity of interpretation, even when the facts are accurate and fairly complete, we again find a satisfactory consensus among observers.[3] First of all, if a militarized dispute escalates to war (and nine of our 101 major-major ones do),[4] the outcome of the war determines the outcome of the dispute, with military victory coded as success, and defeat coded as failure. By turning to the case histories, we find sufficient evidence to code all of our dispute outcomes as win, lose, or draw for the initiator (i.e. the party making the first move in the interaction sequence). We do this by first identifying the initiator's objectives and intentions in setting the sequence in motion, as expressed in fairly explicit demands and requests. The coding problem arises, however, when we next try to estimate the extent to which the initiator's demands have been met (within six months of the final act in the dispute sequence). We rely on historians' accounts of the extent to which demands were met by opponents and, following Maoz, we code a win for the initiator if:

(1) the balance of demand-satisfaction clearly favors the initiator . . . [or] (2) the balance of victory in military operations clearly favors the initiator . . . If demands were satisfied despite the failure in military operations, but the date in which the political demands were met followed the military operations, [we] code a "win." Similarly, if demands were not met but the following military operations were successful, [we] code "win" (Maoz, 1982:231).

We code a "tie" if the balance of demand-satisfaction or balance of victory in military operations is roughly equal, or if "there are sharp discrepancies between demand-satisfaction and the outcomes of military operations which cannot be resolved" by determining which was the more recent (Maoz, 1982:321). In these terms, nearly half of the cases are classified as a tie or draw. One final problem here is whether to treat only the losses as failure, or to include the "draw" outcomes as well, producing a lower success score. The latter strategy seems reasonable, inasmuch as a failure to win can hardly be classed as a successful outcome for the initiator. Just to be sure, we code our outcomes both ways.

## Measuring Military Capabilities and Allocations

When we shift from our outcome variable of success in disputes and war to our predictors, we can move "up" from nominal to interval scaling, but the use of magnitudes rather than frequencies should not mislead us. As we have noted elsewhere (Singer, 1982), data that are "hand-quarried out of hard rock" are often higher in reliability as well as in validity than numbers that are found more or less ready-made. Again, despite the problems, we have no choice but to move ahead, hoping that each successive study will invest in and produce a yet-better data set.

There are several different ways of getting at national capabilities, military or otherwise. The most obvious and general approach is to consider military expenditure, expressed in some standardized unit of currency, pegged to a given year. Alternatively, one might compare the numbers and types of equipment or personnel in the military inventory. Or, after ascertaining these figures for each state in the population to be studied, that state's share of the total funding, hardware, or personnel in that population at that time could be compared in percentage terms. A second approach would conceive such static indicators in more dynamic terms, looking at the direction and rate of change in one or more of them, and interpreting relative capabilities as the rate at which one or the other rival is closing in, forging ahead, or remaining constant vis-à-vis its rivals. In an earlier paper (Wayman, 1982) we utilized this orientation and found that the greater the rate at which two major powers' material capabilities were converging, the greater the likelihood of war between them. A third variation would consider national capabilities not merely in terms that are relative to another state, but relative to the given state's economic, demographic, or industrial base. Military expenditure as a function of GNP is one of the most widely used of these possible indicators of military burden or allocation, but besides using a denominator reflecting some economic or industrial attribute of the country, one might also use a "softer" attribute, such as political status or diplomatic importance (East, 1972; Wallace, 1973).

Here we will use the two static types of indicator: military and other capabilities at the onset of each dispute and each war, and a number of allocation ratios. This latter type of indicator is not, of itself, an accurate reflection of a state's capability level, but rather of the extent to which the society has deflected resources from other sectors to the military. Referring back to our general hypothesis, we should note that a high allocation ratio, in terms of money vis-à-vis the economic base or personnel vis-à-vis the demographic base, can be as provocative as the *absolute* expenditure or armed forces levels.

We begin with a six-dimensional indicator of each state's material capabilities for each year it was in the system. We use total population and urban population (*not* percent urban) to tap the demographic dimensions, commercial energy consumption and iron/steel production to tap the industrial dimensions, and military expenditures and active duty armed force levels to tap the military dimensions.[5] Our concern here is with the industrial and military capability dimensions, although we also look briefly at the efficacy of the demographic indicators in a state's ability to prevail in disputes and war. In order to compare the capabilities of opposing states or coalitions, we begin with the basic score for each in the year that the dispute or war began, total that score for all of the major powers, and then calculate the percentage share held by each.[6]

We should justify our failure to use Gross National (or Domestic) Product, given the frequency with which it *is* used. First, that type of economic indicator is of relatively recent vintage (i.e., mid-20th century, and even then for only the more developed economies), and has been reconstructed for only a very few countries going back into the 19th century (Kindleberger, 1964; Kuznets, 1966). Second, GNP makes comparison between countries of differing economic types, and at different stages of development, a most dubious proposition. And third, it typically reflects a great deal of economic activity that is either irrelevant or detrimental to a state's capacity to wage or credibly threaten war. For these same reasons, we do not use GNP as the base in calculating the extent to which a country's resources have been allocated to the military sector.

Turning from the measurement of material capabilities we next face the economic policy question of the allocation of national resources to the military sector. We eschew calling these allocations a "burden," partly to avoid the normative connotation and partly because, for some countries at some periods in their early development, the allocation of resources to military preparedness has been economically advantageous rather than burdensome (Benoit, 1973; but see also Russett, 1970). What we seek here

TABLE 1. Military allocation indicators for the major powers, 1970 and 1975.

| | Expenditures/Industrial | | Expenditures/Iron–Steel | | Personnel/Population | |
|---|---|---|---|---|---|---|
| | 1970 | 1975 | 1970 | 1975 | 1970 | 1975 |
| US | 0.75 | 0.85 | 0.97 | 1.06 | 1.90 | 1.48 |
| USSR | 1.31 | 1.25 | 1.18 | 1.03 | 1.85 | 1.73 |
| UK | 0.32 | 0.72 | 0.31 | 0.71 | 0.84 | 0.94 |
| France | 0.74 | 0.91 | 0.37 | 0.75 | 1.26 | 1.43 |
| China | 4.14 | 1.10 | 2.07 | 1.22 | 0.49 | 0.58 |

is an indicator of the fraction of a country's industrial or demographic resources that have been allocated to military preparedness. As suggested in our introduction, many practitioners and observers contend that this, rather than the absolute levels of expenditure, personnel, infrastructure, or hardware, offers a more valid measure of capability inasmuch as it allegedly reflects national will or resolve (Andreski, 1968). Whether that argument is compelling or not, it is clear that allocation ratios *do* tap an important and different aspect of a state's capacity to protect its interests and enhance its security; and as we discuss shortly, there is almost no correlation between allocation and capability scores.

With these considerations in mind, we go on to measure military allocations in three ways. To get at the share of the industrial base allocated in each country each year, we compute the ratio between military expenditures and overall industrial capabilities as reflected in both the energy consumption and iron-steel production figures. Because we have energy figures only since 1870, but need to go back to 1816, we also use the military expenditures to iron-steel ratio alone. As with the absolute estimates, we make our cross-country comparisons by converting both the numerators and denominators into each country's percentage shares. Thus, if a country accounts for 5 percent of the major power system's energy consumption and 5 percent of its military expenditures in a given year, its allocation ratio would have a value of 1; if 10 percent of the major power system's expenditures, the value would be 2.[7] On the demographic side, for our third allocations ratio, we use the same procedures, dividing the active duty armed forces level by the estimated total population of the country that year.

To illustrate the values that result from these data-generation and index-construction procedures, we include in Table 1 the military allocation ratios for the five major powers in 1970 and 1975. If our indicators are indeed valid, we see that the USSR, in order to achieve or maintain military parity with the U.S. (or, as some would contend, gain superiority), had a much higher, though declining, military expenditure to industrial base ratio in both years, while that of the U.S. was increasing. And if GNP were used the Soviet score would be even higher. Note also that the other

Western powers, U.K. and France, showed increases in every one of their military allocation scores between 1970 and 1975, while China (whose economy was a shambles as a result of the Cultural Revolution) registered a sharp decline in the share of its industrial capabilities allocated to the military.

Anyone looking at Table 1 will notice the large changes for which there is not an easy military explanation, and may wonder what non-obvious forces are affecting the allocation scores. Among non-military factors that might explain the changes in allocations, we would note the following: an increasing industrial base may lower the expenditure ratios (as occurred in China in the aftermath of the Cultural Revolution); a decline in the value of the U.S. dollar relative to a national currency will enhance the dollar-value of that state's military expenditures, and thus increase its expenditure ratios; and an increase in other major powers' iron and steel output relative to one's own will decrease their relative military allocation and hence increase one's own relative military allocation.

It might also be useful here if we looked at the extent of covariation of our several indicators of capability and of preparedness/allocation ratios, partly to illuminate the general patterns and partly to address the problem of multi-collinearity in our logit analyses (logit being a regression-like procedure for nominal dependent variables). Thus, in Table 2, we present the product-moment correlation coefficients amongst all of our capability and allocation indicators for the 1870–1976 period. We do so only for those states that were on the initiating side in major vs. major disputes, but the correlations are essentially the same for targets and ratios.[8]

The results are hardly surprising. Quite prominent is the high association between the two industrial capability indicators and the urban population levels, as well as that between military expenditures and these three factors. Equally relevant, but perhaps less expected, are the moderate to high *negative* correlations between these three indicators of industrialization and the military expenditure/steel and energy ratio. That is, one might have expected that the more economically developed a country was, the *more* it would allocate to preparedness, but what we see here is that the less-developed countries tend to put more of their resources into the military sector. Finally, we note the relative absence of any serious multi-collinearity problems between allocation and capability measures. For example, our most-used allocation indicator (expenditures/iron and steel production—because it goes back to 1816) is not significantly correlated with any of the six material capability scores.

## VICTORY AND DEFEAT IN WAR

Having laid out the theoretical considerations guiding this investigation, along with the complexities of our raw and generated data base, we may now turn to our analyses. First, we examine the separate effects of material capabilities and of military allocation ratios on the outcome of interstate

TABLE 2. Correlations among capability and allocation indicators for initiators, 1870–1976.

| | Military personnel | Military expenditures | Iron and steel production | Industrial energy consumption | Urban population | Total population | Military expenditures/ iron and steel production | Military expenditures/ steel and energy |
|---|---|---|---|---|---|---|---|---|
| Military personnel | — | | | | | | | |
| Military expenditure | 0.55 | | | | | | | |
| Iron and steel production | 0.15 | 0.70 | — | | | | | |
| Industrial energy consumption | 0.08 | 0.65 | 0.97 | — | | | | |
| Urban population | 0.33 | 0.49 | 0.67 | 0.68 | — | | | |
| Total population | 0.52 | 0.12 | -0.01 | 0.02 | 0.55 | — | | |
| Military expenditures/ iron and steel production | -0.12 | -0.12 | -0.17 | -0.15 | -0.16 | -0.12 | — | |
| Military expenditures/ steel and energy | -0.04 | -0.26 | -0.52 | -0.52 | -0.50 | -0.15 | 0.71 | — |
| Military personnel/ Population | 0.33 | 0.29 | 0.01 | -0.06 | -0.27 | -0.52 | -0.02 | 0.08 |

$N = 81$; correlations > $|0.17|$ are statistically significant at the 0.05 level. The period 1870–1976 is the time span for which data for all variables are available.

*wars* for the two initial protagonists, and then we do the same for all the participants on both sides. In the second half of the analysis, our focus is on the outcome of militarized *disputes*, again distinguishing between the initial disputants and all who eventually participated.

As noted in our introduction, practitioners have traditionally been attentive to the importance of being able to evaluate the capabilities of rivals and allies and thus predict with some confidence the outcome of some contemplated confrontation or war. But if it is true that states rarely go to war, or the brink of war, without a strong belief in their chances of success, as is often claimed, then leaders—by definition—have been wrong just about half the time. A more sophisticated model would recognize that political and military elites often go to, and over, the brink, even when they are dubious or pessimistic about the likelihood of success.

In any event, given the importance of this calculation, there has been no dearth of efforts to measure the war-making capacity of states; of greater interest here, however, are the efforts to ascertain which factors have actually accounted for success or failure in the past. The first systematic historical effort was that of Quincy Wright, one of the pioneers in the peace science movement. While his 1965 article was primarily concerned with differentiating (within a sample of 45 conflicts out of 160 he identified from 1914 through 1964) among those conflicts that ended in war, militarized dispute, or less, he also coded the outcomes in terms of success or failure. He included actual and potential force in his equation and found them no more important than world opinion, centrality of interests, and legal constraints in affecting the outcomes. There have also been three more recent studies, all published in 1980, of particular relevance here. As part of a larger inquiry, Cannizzo (1980) found that armed forces' size alone had a weak but positive effect on the chances of military victory over the period since 1816. Using GNP, the tax extraction rate, and foreign aid figures, Organski and Kugler (1978) looked at four major wars and found their indicator of tax extraction rate quite satisfactory as a predictor to victory. Working from our own six-dimensional capabilities data base, and adjusting for the protagonists' distance from the site of the dispute, Bueno de Mesquita (1980) found a strong association with victory in wars and in disputes.

Turning to our own effort, we selected four of the six components, leaving out urban population and energy consumption because of missing data on these variables for the minor powers. In Table 3 we look at the association between the four initiator-to-target capability indicators and the distribution of victory and defeat for the initial protagonists in the interstate wars for whose participants we have all the relevant capabilities data.

Worth noting at the onset is that initiators of war are superior to their targets about twice as often as they are equal or weaker. While this may seem impressive, it reminds us that in well over a third of the cases the initiator is weaker than or approximately equal to the target state. The correlation between strength and victory is measured by the ordinal

TABLE 3. Initiator's success in interstate wars as a function of *capabilities* *vis-à-vis* target, 1816–1976.*

| Capability dimension | Initiator is: | N | Frequency of victory (%) | Tau-beta | S.E. | Approximate significance level |
|---|---|---|---|---|---|---|
| Military personnel | Stronger | 28 | 64 | | | |
| | Equal | 12 | 42 | 0.16 | 0.07 | 0.05 |
| | Weaker | 19 | 47 | | | |
| Military expenditure | Stronger | 28 | 57 | | | |
| | Equal | 7 | 57 | 0.16 | 0.07 | 0.05 |
| | Weaker | 14 | 36 | | | |
| Steel | Stronger | 27 | 74 | | | |
| | Equal | 14 | 29 | 0.41 | 0.06 | 0.001 |
| | Weaker | 14 | 29 | | | |
| Total population | Stronger | 30 | 57 | | | |
| | Equal | 6 | 50 | 0.06 | 0.07 | not significant |
| | Weaker | 20 | 50 | | | |

* The $N$s vary for reasons of missing data; these data are not available for all states involved in wars; the major problems are Latin American countries and Turkey during the 19th century.

In devising criteria for 'stronger', 'same', and 'weaker' there are two main considerations: (1) that 'weaker' or 'stronger' represent significant differences between the two parties, and (2) that there should be a large enough $N$ in each cell for the statistical techniques to be valid. The thresholds chosen were a compromise between these two criteria. For example, the thresholds in Table 3 for the four capabilities were

$$A > 3/2B; \; 3/2B > A > 2/3B; \; A < 2/3B$$

for the military and demographic capabilities; and

$$A > 4/3B; \; 4/3B > A > 3/4B; \; A < 3/4B$$

for the iron and steel. Analyses were performed, in the case of all tables, with other values with no significant change in the results.

correlation coefficient, tau-beta. Whenever the absolute value of tau-beta is two (or more) times its standard error, the ordinal association between strength and victory is statistically significant at approximately the 0.05 level (or better). Examining these statistics and the frequencies of victory, we see that industrial strength as reflected in iron and steel output is the most critical of those factors examined, and that armed force size and military expenditure are fairly important elements, followed by total population, which has an effect in the predicted direction but which, unlike the others, is too weak to be statistically significant.

The importance of the industrial factor does not mean, of course, that military expenditures and personnel are negligible. Recall that these capabilities were measured in the year the war started and, as World War II demonstrated, the economic base provides the potential for an effective development of military capabilities *during* the fighting (up to a limit

TABLE 4. Initiator's success in interstate wars as a function of military *allocations* vis-à-vis target, 1816–1976.*

| Allocation dimension | Initiator allocates: | N | Frequency of victory (%) | Tau-beta | S.E. | Approximate significance level |
|---|---|---|---|---|---|---|
| Military expenditure to steel | More | 8 | 50 | | | |
| | Same | 3 | 0 | −0.21 | 0.11 | 0.05 |
| | Less | 10 | 70 | | | |
| Military personnel to total population | More | 17 | 65 | | | |
| | Same | 24 | 50 | 0.16 | 0.07 | 0.05 |
| | Less | 14 | 43 | | | |

* The *N*s vary here for reasons given in the note to Table 3, and the fact that if a country has no steel production (e.g. 19th-century Latin America) the indicator Military expenditure to steel is undefined, hence missing.

discussed by Yengst, 1982). For this reason, the findings reported here, which are related to actual power, are consistent with Alcock and Newcombe (1970), who find that the best predictors of perceived power are economic capability in peacetime and military capability in wartime.

Shifting from basic capabilities to the military allocation indicators for the first participants, major and non-major powers, we turn to Table 4.

Here we find the first of our counter-intuitive results. While a heavy allocation of manpower to the armed forces tends to pay off with moderate frequency in military victory, heavy monetary allocations do not. That is, and bearing in mind the relatively small population of cases here, those initiators which allocate more of their economic and industrial resources to military expenditure on the eve of war emerge victorious in only half the cases, whereas the under-allocators win 70 percent of the time.

Before leaving this discussion, it might be useful to ascertain whether the "determinants" of victory in war are any different if we compare the capabilities of not only the initial combatants, but those of the entire coalition on each side in wars that expand beyond the dyadic. The patterns are remarkably similar, with superiority in military personnel and total population somewhat more critical, expenditure about the same, and iron-steel production somewhat less critical.

Moreover, the unexpected pattern again is uncovered when we compare the ratios of military spending to the industrial base of the coalitions using iron and steel production as the indicator. When the initiating coalition's expenditure allocation is greater than that of the target, it wins 60 percent of the time, but when it is "under-allocating" the success score rises to 78 percent, with a tau-beta coefficient of −0.17 and an 0.09 standard error. To put it another way, initiators have a better win-lose record than targets, in both the dyadic and multi-party cases, but they fare quite a bit better if they are not "over-allocating" funds to the military sector on the eve of war.

## SUCCESS AND FAILURE IN MILITARIZED DISPUTES

While the difference between success and failure in interstate war may mean the survival or extinction of a state or a regime, war remains a relatively rare event: an average of only six per decade throughout the international system since the Napoleonic era. Militarized disputes, on the other hand, occur with much greater frequency: nearly 60 per decade, and, even though their consequences are less dramatic, their cumulative effects can bode as ill or well for the fate of the states. And with the advent of the nuclear-missile era, bringing as it has a profound inhibition against the major powers' resorting to war, the frequency of these brink-of-war confrontations has increased; up to 1945, the annual average of militarized disputes was 0.23 per major power, but since then the figure has doubled to 0.46. Further, given the ominous implications of miscalculation in a nuclear face-down, it behooves us to know much more than we now do regarding the determinants of success in these cases. This section of the paper, then, aims to provide a better grasp of those elements that permit one major power to prevail over another when they find themselves in these ever more ominous brink-of-war situations.

Before examining our own findings, let us briefly look at the results of those few prior empirical efforts. In an important pioneering study, Blechman and Kaplan (1978) examined those 12 cases since World War II in which the U.S. mobilized, displayed, or used force short of war vis-à-vis the USSR. They found that neither regional nor global military superiority was as critical in prevailing as was demonstrating higher resolve or defending a client state where the *status quo* was threatened. Similarly, using more operational criteria, Maoz (1982) found that demonstrating resolve by initiating most of the escalatory moves was more critical than greater military or material capabilities. Worth noting in this connection is Leng's (1983) finding that *success* in one crisis encourages use of the same level of coerciveness in the next one, that *failure* encourages an increase in the effort to show resolve, and that reciprocal pursuit of that effort gives us an increase in the likelihood of war.

Looking at the results in Table 5, note that we not only examine the effects of all six capability dimension ratios but, given the greater frequency with which militarized disputes end up in a draw (as compared to wars), we show that frequency for each of the capability comparisons. Note also (as with the war analyses) that the ratios reflect only the first major power participant on each side if there were more than one on either.

While the associations are not dramatic, the results are quite different from those that turn up in the case of victory in war. Prevailing in these disputes is associated with superiority in the "industrialization" dimensions only: energy, iron and steel, and urban population. When the initiator

TABLE 5. Initiator's success in major-major disputes as a function of *capabilities vis-à-vis* target, 1816–1976.

| Capability dimension | Initiator | $N$ | Frequency of prevailing (%) | Frequency of draws (%) | Tau-beta and S.E. | Approximate significance level |
|---|---|---|---|---|---|---|
| Military personnel | Stronger | 34 | 27 | 53 | − 0.09 | not |
| | Equal | 39 | 26 | 49 | (0.06) | significant |
| | Weaker | 26 | 39 | 50 | | |
| Military expenditure | Stronger | 33 | 21 | 61 | − 0.09 | not |
| | Equal | 34 | 27 | 53 | (0.06) | significant |
| | Weaker | 33 | 39 | 39 | | |
| Industrial energy* | Stronger | 35 | 29 | 60 | + 0.16 | |
| | Equal | 14 | 29 | 50 | (0.06) | 0.05 |
| | Weaker | 36 | 19 | 53 | | |
| Steel | Stronger | 39 | 39 | 49 | + 0.21 | 0.01 |
| | Equal | 25 | 28 | 56 | (0.06) | |
| | Weaker | 35 | 20 | 49 | | |
| Urban population | Stronger | 35 | 31 | 49 | + 0.08 | not |
| | Equal | 40 | 28 | 63 | (0.06) | significant |
| | Weaker | 24 | 29 | 33 | | |
| Total population | Stronger | 32 | 28 | 44 | − 0.08 | not |
| | Equal | 36 | 33 | 53 | (0.06) | significant |
| | Weaker | 22 | 32 | 50 | | |

* There is a decrease of 15 in the $N$ in this case because energy consumption data are available only after 1870.

enjoyed superiority on these three dimensions, success followed more often than failure. But note the very high number of draws; if we treat these as non-success/failure, the advantage of industrial superiority is appreciably muted. More important, however, is the frequency with which superiority on the other three dimensions leads to *failure*. All else being equal, these figures suggest that superiority in military personnel and expenditure, as well as in total population, is actually a *disadvantage* for the initiating power. And, as noted above, the high frequency of draws further weakens the case for superior military strength.

As with the war outcomes, we must attend not only to relative capabilities but the extent to which each of the protagonists is allocating personnel and money to military preparedness. As Table 6 indicates, we find once again that over-allocation to the military is not at all advantageous, but in the case of disputes the costs of higher allocation are even greater than in wars. The initiator prevails twice as often when it is allocating *less* money to the military than when it is allocating more than its adversary, and even in the case of military personnel per capita, such allocation is almost as disadvantageous.

Once again, recognizing that those states that join in after a war or dispute has begun might change the patterns, we compared the figures for

TABLE 6. Initiator's success in major-major disputes as a function of military *allocations* *vis-à-vis* target, 1816–1976.

| Allocation dimension | Initiator is: | N | Frequency of prevailing (%) | Frequency of draws (%) | Tau-beta and S.E. | Approximate significance level |
|---|---|---|---|---|---|---|
| Military expenditure to steel | More | 40 | 23 | 48 | −0.24 | 0.001 |
|  | Same | 24 | 17 | 67 | (0.06) |  |
|  | Less | 35 | 46 | 43 |  |  |
| Military expenditure to steel and energy | More | 40 | 18 | 50 | −0.26 | 0.001 |
|  | Same | 17 | 24 | 65 | (0.06) |  |
|  | Less | 28 | 36 | 57 |  |  |
| Military personnel to total population | More | 27 | 30 | 59 | −0.09 | not significant |
|  | Same | 33 | 21 | 46 | (0.06) |  |
|  | Less | 27 | 44 | 48 |  |  |

the two sides in disputes when there were multiple protagonists. Here the results are much the same, with superiority on the industrial and demographic dimensions advantageous to the initiator, and military superiority again a net liability. Shifting from these capability ratios to the ways in which the major powers allocate their industrial and demographic resources to preparedness, we again find the now familiar pattern: the greater the military expenditures in terms of the iron-steel and the combined industrial base, the lower the frequency of prevailing, and the same holds true for armed forces per capita.

## SUMMARIZING THE RESULTS

Having examined a rather diverse set of bivariate relationships, we find a highly consistent set of results, although they are not sufficiently high in statistical significance to make a conclusive case. In war, it is advantageous to have an overall superiority in industrial and demographic as well as military terms, and it is advantageous to be over-mobilized in terms of armed forces per capita. All of these indicators are associated with victory in interstate war from 1816 to 1976. But those initiators of war who were over-allocating in terms of expenditures vis-à-vis the industrial base were defeated in war more often than they were victorious.

In militarized disputes, we again find that industrial and urban capabilities are associated with prevailing, but that whatever value there is in military superiority in war fades away in disputes; the weaker party in terms of both personnel and expenditure is more frequently the successful protagonist. And if we look at allocation ratios, the counter-intuitive pattern is even more pronounced. Whether for the initial participants or entire coalitions, the side whose resources are more heavily committed to military preparedness prevails less often than the one that is under-allocating. These bivariate

TABLE 7. Summary associations (tau-beta) between selected capability and allocation comparisons and initiator's success in wars and disputes, 1816–1976.*

|  | | Wars | | Disputes | |
|---|---|---|---|---|---|
| 1816–1976 | | Initial parties | Coalition members | Initial parties | Coalition members |
| Capability ratios | Military personnel | 0.16 | 0.30 | −0.09 | −0.08 |
| | Military expenditures | 0.16 | 0.10 | −0.09 | −0.05 |
| | Energy | — | — | 0.16 | 0.19 |
| | Steel | 0.41 | 0.28 | 0.21 | 0.20 |
| | Urban population | — | — | 0.08 | 0.13 |
| | Total population | 0.06 | 0.25 | −0.08 | 0.05 |
| Military allocations | Military expenditures/ steel production | −0.21 | −0.17 | −0.24 | −0.24 |
| | Military expenditures/ steel and energy | — | — | −0.26 | −0.23 |
| | Military personnel/ total population | 0.16 | 0.08 | −0.09 | −0.01 |

* For wars, $N$ equals approximately 67, and correlations over 0.15 are significant at the 0.05 level. For disputes, $N$ equals approximately 101, and correlations over 0.12 are significant at the 0.05 level.

regularities are nicely summarized in Table 7. Examining the correlations in the table, one sees that in past wars the initial party won if it was stronger than its opponent in all four scrutinized material capabilities, especially iron and steel production (tau-beta = 0.41). If the war expanded beyond the two original parties, the initial party fared best by building a coalition that was stronger in military personnel (tau-beta = 0.30), steel production (tau-beta = 0.28), and total population (tau-beta = 0.25). For both the initial parties and coalitions, the winning side was more heavily allocated in military personnel but more lightly allocated in military expenditures.

As for winning disputes (the right side of Table 7), the initial party fared best when stronger in the industrial capabilities (tau-beta = 0.21 and 0.16) and (to a lesser extent) urban population (tau-beta = 0.08). The other capabilities appear counter-productive, as do heavier military allocations of all three sorts. Whereas in war the winner's profile was different for initial parties than for coalitions, in disputes the profile is basically the same for initial parties and for coalitions.

To further consider the stability of these results, we carried out a set of multivariate logit analyses, with the following results. The factor most associated with success in wars and in disputes is the steel production ratio, and the military expenditure ratio is also associated with victory more often than not. The military personnel ratio, however, is associated with defeat most of the time, as are the allocation indicators, especially that reflecting military expenditure as a fraction of the country's industrial base. The general profile of a successful state thus suggested would be one that, when compared with its rival, has a relatively heavy industrial base, moderately high military expenditures, relatively low military personnel preparedness (both absolute and relative to population), and a relatively low military expenditure allocation. The multivariate results are generally consistent with the bivariate results, with, however, the exception of the effect of the personnel figures in wars. Do the multivariate results mean that higher levels of military personnel *in the absence of* higher expenditures and industrial base are more likely to draw one into the vortex of a lost war than to give one a basis for victory? The inconsistencies with the bivariate results could be further examined using causal models to judge whether inferences from the bivariate association between personnel and victory in war are spurious, or whether the multivariate results are misleading because of interaction effects, reduced N or multi-collinearity. The high multi-collinearity of some of the independent variables and the small number of degrees of freedom are reasons to treat the multivariate analyses with considerable caution. While the overall $R^2$ in the logit analysis was often impressive, the coefficients for individual variables were rarely strongly statistically significant.

## CONCLUSIONS

While it is recognized rather infrequently, a few scholars have observed that states arm and spend for a number of reasons beyond the obvious (Singer, 1968; Nincic, 1982). In addition to the pursuit of national security as traditionally defined, we might note some of the other considerations. One of these is that of nation-building, via the mobilization, socialization, and education of military conscripts and volunteers, training of political elites, and the maintenance of domestic order. Another, in more established states, is that of economic growth, redistributing the geographical wealth, pump-priming, and taking up the unemployment slack in depressions. The distribution of beliefs regarding the domestic consequences of military spending, while still mixed and certainly controversial, nevertheless rests on *some* empirical evidence. And that evidence, as we see it, strongly suggests that while certain benefits from military allocations do accrue to the economy, or some sectors thereof, there are also some well-demonstrated disabilities (Scitovsky et al., 1951; Leontief et al., 1965; Melman, 1974; Weidenbaum, 1974; Sivard, 1976; Lindblom, 1977).

But the general expectation is that any economic disadvantages resulting from high levels of preparedness will be more than counterbalanced by the gains in national security. More specifically, it is usually asserted that, at the very least, the state will be secure from domination by the rival of the moment and, in addition, will be able to prevail if involved in a crisis or confrontation, and emerge victorious if drawn into the crucible of war.

As is already evident, this first systematic data-based investigation hardly confirms such expectations. To the contrary, we find that victory in war depends more upon a country's industrial base than on the extremes to which such resources are allocated to the armed forces. As we noted at the outset, this is not to suggest that total disarmament is thus the preferred strategy, but merely to emphasize that a state can be not only under-armed, but over-armed. And this conclusion is even more powerfully indicated by our analysis of militarized disputes between major powers and coalitions thereof. There we find not only that industrial capabilities are more critical than military preparedness, but that those powers that "under-allocate" to the military have, over a span of 160 years, enjoyed a significantly higher rate of success in these brink of war confrontations than those that have "over-allocated." Despite the tentative nature of these findings, and the absence of a fully formulated theoretical model, we now suspect that Frederick the Great was soon to be wide of the mark when he wrote to the Countess Von Gotha in 1760 that "God is always with the strongest battalions."

## ACKNOWLEDGMENTS

We are grateful to the editors of *International Studies Quarterly* and our colleagues on the Correlates of War project for their suggestions, and to the National Science Foundation and the University of Michigan— Dearborn Grants Committee for research support.

We would also like to dedicate this study to the memory of Alexander Mark Wayman.

# CHAPTER SIXTEEN

———————— ■ ————————

# Periodicity, Inexorability, and Steersmanship in International War

## J. David Singer and Thomas Cusack

IN READING, CONVERSING, AND COLLABORATING with Karl Deutsch over the years, one finds certain themes to which he returns again and again. Despite the extraordinary breadth and depth of his conceptual repertoire, there seem to be a few basic concepts that are essential to his over-all paradigm. One of these is that of steersmanship. Borrowed from cybernetics and creatively developed by Deutsch in his frequent conversations with Wiener and others, the steersmanship concept emphasizes that we are not mere ships on the ocean of history. Rather, as our knowledge of the ocean, the vessel, and the self develop, we are increasingly able to estimate which course will bring us to our destination with the greatest facility.

Integral to this notion, of course—and implicit in the very metaphor—is awareness of the limits on our autonomy. The currents and waves of the oceans, not to mention the visibility and positioning of the stars that we steer by, are essentially beyond our control, and the craft in which we travel, be it fragile or sturdy, is largely inherited. But the more we know of geography, the more precisely we can set our objective; the better we comprehend the seas, the more likely we are to stay afloat; and the keener our mastery of navigation, the straighter will be our path.

The ways in which we comprehend and evaluate these limits will inevitably affect our orientation toward coping with them. We can set out on our voyage with an outlook that runs the gamut from the Ancient Mariner and the Flying Dutchman, through Beowulf, to the Owl and the Pussycat; each such orientation helps determine the effort we will make to comprehend

This chapter appeared originally in Richard L. Merritt and Bruce M. Russett (eds.), *From National Development to Global Community: Essays in Honor of Karl W. Deutsch*. Winchester, MA.: George Allen & Unwin, 1981. Reprinted by permission.

and to control. Whether it be the seas, the heavens, the gods, or ourselves, humans have generally tried to make sense of it all. Confronted with what might otherwise be a mysterious conundrum or a vast, buzzing welter, we have devised all sorts of models and metaphors as a means of imposing coherence.[1] Our earlier metaphors, the wheel, the lever, the pyramid, the river—rested largely on observation and experience, but with increasing sophistication we turned to more complex and less directly experienced metaphors of an organic or a cybernetic sort.[2] Further, as our focus shifted from the "natural" to the "artificial world"—to use Simon's unfortunate distinction between physical and social phenomena[3]—these metaphors could be as stochastic as the capricious gods and as deterministic as predestination.

## CYCLES AND THEIR IMPLICATIONS

Whatever model or metaphor one chooses in order to cope with the complexities in our environment, certain assumptions are carried with it, and certain implications inhere. And among these assumptions, one of the most critical is that which reflects our views on the temporal unfolding of human experience. We may, for example, see social history as a long road to ultimate catastrophe, or as an inexorable path of continued progress, or as highly cyclical and perhaps even dialectic, or as a sequence of meaningless perturbations, to name the more obvious possibilities.

Further, each such assumed model carries with it certain notions of appropriate human response, particularly vis-à-vis the questions of predictability and controllability. If we lean toward secular trend models of human history (be they persistently toward or away from the specified conditions), we often accept notions of a teleological sort, assigning some cosmic purpose to it all. While such models may increase our belief in social predictability, the more extreme versions of them seldom encourage efforts to intervene in the process or to control our collective destiny. Similarly, assumptions of a more chaotic sort will probably not encourage efforts to understand or predict, but they need not—depending on the degree of fatalism that lies behind the stochastic model—discourage efforts at control. Again, if one's model of social reality is built around cycles and periodicities, prediction becomes a major preoccupation, but intervention seems less justified.

While most social scientists and some historians see the human experience as an elusive mix of these three—trends, cycles, and perturbations—we would suggest that discovering the nature of that mix is not only intellectually possible, but worth pursuing for pragmatic reasons. That is, the more fully we can ascertain how much of our fate is determined by Fate and how our chances are settled by Chance, the more accurately we can estimate how much control remains in our own hands. This is not, of course, to suggest that all of humanity can readily intervene in a highly co-ordinated fashion to head off one or another type of catastrophe. The plethora of conflicting interests that must be reconciled today is not dramatically different from those that, in years gone by, helped to shape the very state of affairs, be it menacing or benign, that confronts us in the present. But having a reasonable comprehension of the degree of conscious intervention that remains available, as well as which interventions are likely to produce which outcomes, could at least improve the odds. When neither of these is adequately understood, we are apt to become poker players operating in the dark, rather than aware and competent steersmen.

When it comes to war—a type of social event that is clearly the result of complex and interdependent processes—the tendency to fall back on one or another of these simple models is particularly acute. Whether we are practitioners of foreign affairs, scholars, or laymen, we suspect that the road to war is a murky and confusing one, and as a result we are all too prone to embrace one of the above models or metaphors. From among the inexorable trend (toward or away), the cyclical, and the stochastic models, modern man seems to prefer the cyclical. The trend model seems too teleological and the stochastic model seems too nihilistic, whereas the cyclical one has a certain aura of *a priori* plausibility in the twentieth century. After all, who amongst us is eager to embrace the implicit assumption of a largely beneficent, or essentially malevolent, or utterly capricious cosmos? Somehow, the notion that war comes and goes with some regularity seems to be the assumption that is least offensive to contemporary sensibilities.

Turning, then, from ontological speculation to empirical investigation, we will examine here the evidence and the reasoning that might support the assumption of cycles or periodicity in the incidence of international war. At the outset, we note that any such pattern may be sought or identified at several levels of social aggregation. The patterns could obtain at the systemic level, at the regional level, or at the national level, and the evidence found at one need not necessarily obtain at another. Thus, the intervals between the war experiences of the separate nations could be quite random, but when we look at the regional or global system level, there would emerge a clear regularity. That is, if we ignore the identity or location of the nations at war in a given year and ask only whether— somewhere in the system—war will occur at some fixed interval, the answer can be affirmative even though each nation's experiences occur in a highly irregular fashion. For the moment, then, we look only at the nation level, and will return to that of the international system later in the discussion.

Before examining the evidence, however, we might consider several of the possible reasons for expecting the war-peace-war cycle to be a strong and constant one for the nations. Leaving aside those who suspect that it is inherent in human nature or part of the cosmic plan, we find a few macro-social models and a somewhat greater number of micro-social (and essentially social-psychological) reasons for expecting such periodicity. At the macro-social level, perhaps the most familiar argument is that of the business cycle. Whether one proceeds from the perspective of a Ricardo, a Keynes, or a Marx, it is possible to posit the economic connection. That is, we may differ in our explanations of what "causes" the business cycle, but nevertheless agree that it brings war ineluctably in its wake. One school of thought would have wars occurring near the peak,[4] another on the down side,[5] another at the trough,[6] and others on the rising side.[7] For each of these schools of thought, the link between one or another of the business cycles and war is somewhat different, but each tends to view fluctuations in national or global economic activity as a necessary and/or sufficient condition for the onset of war.

Another macro-level argument is the demographic one. Here, we note that wars are fought largely by young males, often in the train of decisions taken by older males. At the close of war, those who ordered it begin to retire or die, and those who fought in it move into positions of some influence. The former no longer *can* order it and the latter *will* not order it, given their experiences. But as memories of destruction are gradually replaced—by memories either of glory and victory, or of humiliation and defeat—and as a new generation of warriors comes of age, the nation once again is ready to resume the deadly cycle.

Then there are the more micro-level models, of which two are illustrative. First, there is David McClelland's "Love and War" model,[8] which begins with the assumption of cycles in the cultural life of nations. These are the familiar need for affiliation, need for achievement, and need for power, whose existence has been demonstrated in several nations during certain periods, recent as well as remote.[9] Put simply, when the need for affiliation is on the rise in a nation, those who experience it most will soon recognize (and try to fulfill) the need for power as a means to domestic social reform. But given the incompatibility of these two norms, power soon dominates affiliative and altruistic concerns, leads to a more restrictive sense of in-group affiliation, and reinforces the concomitant tendency toward out-group hostility. Given the ubiquitousness of foreign provocation and opportunity, this hostility can readily led to war, which leaves in its wake a new series of domestic inequities, thus generating yet another rise in the need for affiliation and thence for power at home, and so on to the next cycle.

Another social-psychological model pointing toward cyclical war involvement patterns is that of Frank Klingberg,[10] focusing on the shifts from isolationist to interventionist foreign policies on the part of the United States. After adducing some historical evidence for the existence of this periodicity, he goes on to suggest the psychological factors that might account for it. The introverted orientation that precedes and is associated with the isolationist period usually succumbs to the need for more action, new experiences and challenges, and a tendency toward national assertiveness. This shift to a more extroverted mood usually brings a more aggressive and interventionist policy in its wake, often culminating in war. But then there is "the reaction to a long period of strain and tension—the need for a period of rest and relaxation"[11] and soon the nation has reverted to a more passive and less war-prone set of policies.

There is, as we might expect, other speculation and some mixed evidence as to why national war experiences should come and go in a cyclical pattern,

Table 1     *The Major Powers and Their War Experience, 1816–1965*

|  | Years as major power | Number of wars | |
| --- | --- | --- | --- |
|  |  | International | Interstate |
| United Kingdom | 1816–1965 | 19 | 7 |
| France | 1816–1940; 1945–1965 | 19 | 12 |
| Russia/USSR | 1816–1965 | 15 | 10 |
| Prussia/Germany | 1816–1918; 1925–1945 | 6 | 6 |
| Austria–Hungary | 1816–1918 | 8 | 6 |
| Italy | 1860–1943 | 12 | 11 |
| United States | 1899–1965 | 5 | 4 |
| Japan | 1895–1945 | 7 | 7 |
| China | 1950–1965 | 3 | 2 |

from sun-spots[12] to grain and livestock cycles, to alternations between liberal and conservative regimes, to surges in technological innovation. But as is all too frequent in the social sciences, much of this speculation and model-building may be premature or worse. That is, should we invest in the effort to account for a particularly intriguing pattern of phenomena when it is not at all clear that such a pattern—however plausible—even obtains? Thus, let us shift now to the effort to ascertain whether or not there is indeed some periodicity in the war experience of the nations.

## EXAMINING THE EVIDENCE

Given the difficulties of comparing, combining, and integrating the results of macro-social research—thanks to the limited and differing empirical domains from which we generalize, as well as the differing and often idiosyncratic ways in which we measure our variables—it might be appropriate to treat these two matters before examining the evidence adduced here.

### The Empirical Domain and the Indicators

As to the temporal domain, we embrace in this study the same 150-year period from the Congress of Vienna up through 1965 that has characterized almost all investigations of the Correlates of War Project, with plans to extend that span up through the 1970s in future investigations. Regarding the nations under study here, we restrict ourselves to the major powers as defined by the consensus of diplomatic historians codified by the project.[13]

As Table 1 makes clear, industrial productivity or large population alone does not suffice for major power status. A variety of diplomatic, political, military, and economic attributes is essential, but the most obvious one is that which concerns us particularly in the study at hand: the ability to wage war frequently, and to win most of those wars. Thus we include in our population here the nations and years listed in the table. To this awesome array of relatively successful warriors, we add the Ottoman Empire/

Turkey for the entire period 1816–1965, even though it was treated neither by the other powers of the time nor by most subsequent historians as a full-fledged member of the club. Although its power was on the wane during most of the period under study, Turkey fought seventeen international wars, of which eleven were interstate and six extra-systemic (colonial or imperial), making her the third most war-prone nation in post-Napoleonic history. This factor alone has led some scholars to classify Turkey as a major power up through the First World War, despite being on the losing side in six of the eleven interstate wars. In any event, all of our analyses have been run both with and without Turkey, and when her exclusion makes a difference in the generalizations we will so indicate.

Shifting from the years and the nations to the events, our population of cases begins with all international wars fought by the major powers when they were in the select class. But we also include the most recent war they experienced prior to moving into major power status, with the *ad hoc* exception of China, since it underwent a dramatic revolution between the close of the Second World War and its achievement of major power status in the crucible of the Korean War.

As to the two types of war, an interstate war is an episode of sustained combat engaging at least one sovereign state member of the system on each side, and leading to at least 1,000 battle-connected fatalities. By extra-systemic wars, we mean those in which the adversary of the major power was not a sovereign state, but a national political entity whose political and legal status was less than that of full sovereignty. The detailed coding rules, rationale, and resulting data are reported in *The Wages of War*.[14] We combine extra-systemic and interstate wars to arrive at the category of all international wars, and once again we will run our analyses both ways: for interstate wars only, as well as for all international wars combined. The results will always be reported for the combined category, but if they differ appreciably when interstate wars only are analyzed, those differences will be noted.

Turning next to the indicators that will be used in our search for periodicities in major power war participation, there are three important variables: (1) intervals; (2) outcomes; and (3) costs. As to intervals, our most frequently used indicator is that of years between the termination of one war experience and the onset of the following one. But as before, it is essential to assure that our findings are not an artifact of our measurement procedures, and we therefore also run our analyses using the longer interval: that which extends from the onset of the prior war to the onset of the subsequent one. If the longer of the two indicators produces appreciably different results, this will be duly reported.

By outcome, we mean simply whether the participant was on the victorious or defeated side; in only one case (the Korean War of 1950–3) was the outcome classified as a draw. While the coding criteria here are "softer" than in most of our variables, the scholarly consensus was most impressive, reflecting a collective judgement as to which side enjoyed the dominant role in negotiating or imposing the terms of the armistice and the peace that allegedly followed.

By costs, we mean the damage sustained, and as one general indicator, we find battle-connected fatalities amongst combat personnel sufficiently valid; we label this the severity of the experience. But since some wars are short but bloody and others are longer but less severe, we also use an indicator of magnitude: the war months invested by the protagonist. Finally, just to be sure, we measure war costs in terms of two intensity ratios. One of these is battle-connected deaths per war month and the other is battle-connected deaths *per capita*, with the denominator reflecting the prewar population of the nation as a whole.

## The Constant Probability Model of War Re-Entry

Having now summarized the empirical domain against which we hope to generalize, and the ways in which our variables are measured, let us return to the substantive questions that concern us here. The first question is that of the intervals between major power war experiences: are they the result of certain probabilities that rise or fall as time passes since the prior war? Or do they occur with more or less equal probabilities in *any* postwar year, regardless of the passage of time? To the extent that subsequent war experiences show a constant relative frequency in the ensuing years, we can infer that the passage of time has neither an enhancing nor a diminishing effect on the likelihood of another war entry. And to the extent that these relative frequencies increase and/or decrease across repetitive fixed intervals with the passage of time, we can infer that some cyclical process is at work.

Among the models that would reflect a constant probability of re-entry into war, regardless of the passage of time, is the exponential model,[15] and the better the fit between the historically observed distribution of interwar intervals and that predicted by the exponential model, the more readily we can reject the hypothesis that some periodicity inheres in the war-to-war histories of the major powers. This particular model is, of course, functionally equivalent to the better-known Poisson model in that the latter would predict (or in this case, post-dict) a random distribution of the interwar intervals, and to get such a distribution, the probability of a given nation entering into a new war would have to be independent of the length of the interval since its prior war. But since our concern is not with discrete phenomena, such as the frequency of each of a given class of events, but with the distribution of continuous temporal distances between those discretely measured phenomena of sequential war experience, the exponential model is most appropriate.

The first step in examining the fit between the predicted and observed number of war entries that occur during successive five-year periods is to calculate the number predicted by the exponential distribution model. The equation used for the calculation of the probability density is: $f(X) = \theta e^{-\theta x}$, if $X \geq 0$, and where $X$ is the time interval between war experiences, e is the base of the natural log, and θ is the estimated parameter of the distribution. But when, as occasionally occurs, X is less than 0 because of the nation's entry into a new war while still engaged in an earlier one, $\int X(X) = 0$. In any event, the value of θ is the inverse of the expected value—that is, the mean—of the *observed* distribution.

The probability that we will find an interval of a length that is greater than or equal to $a$, and less than or equal to $b$, is given by the following formula:

$$P_r\{a \leq X \leq b\} = e^{\theta a} - e^{\theta b}$$

Thus, if we wanted to know the probability that an interval between wars was between one and three years, and our estimate of θ was equal to 0.20, the following would hold:

$$P_r\{1 \leq X \leq 3\} = e^{-(0.20)1} - e^{-(0.20)3} = 0.27$$

So much, then, for the constant probability model, and why we might expect systematic deviations from it. Let us turn now to the empirical evidence and the extent to which such expectations are borne out by the historical patterns.

### Passage of Time and the Probability of War Re-Entry

We turn, then, to the data summaries by which we can examine the validity of the null hypothesis, which states that the distribution of the observed interwar intervals for the major powers will be identical to that predicted by the exponential model, given the number of cases and the average length of these observed intervals. To cover the possibility that our patterns might differ if we look not only at *all* their international war experiences but at their interstate ones only, as well as not only the intervals from termination to onset but also from onset to onset, we need four different tabulations, as shown in Tables 2 and 3.

Looking first at the 101 cases in which a major power went from one interstate or extra-systemic war to another (i.e., all international wars), we find a rather close fit between the distribution of intervals predicted by the exponential model and the distribution that was actually observed. Whether the interval is measured from the *termination* of the first war to the onset of the second, or from one onset to the next, the significance of the chi-square values (0.20–0.10 and 0.50–0.30) indicates that there is little difference between the observed pattern and that predicted by the exponential model. In other words, the passage of time since the prior war experience seems to have little effect on the likelihood that the typical major power will soon find itself at war again; that historical likelihood remained constant, regardless of how long ago the previous war occurred.

Shifting now to the more restricted population of wars—those sixty-six fought against other sovereign states, be they major powers or not—we find a somewhat more ambiguous pattern. In the analysis of interstate war

Table 2    *Distribution of intervals between all international war experiences, compared to those predicted by exponential model (N = 101)*

| Interval from termination to onset | No. of cases observed | No. of cases predicted | Interval from onset to onset | No. of cases observed | No. of cases predicted |
|---|---|---|---|---|---|
| <5 | 58 | 51 | <5 | 50 | 44 |
| 6–10 | 13 | 25 | 6–10 | 17 | 25 |
| 11–15 | 14 | 13 | 11–15 | 13 | 14 |
| 16–20 | 7 | 6 | 16–20 | 10 | 8 |
| 21–25 | 4 | 3 | 21–25 | 4 | 4 |
| 26–30 | 3 | 2 | 26–30 | 4 | 2 |
| >30 | 2 | 1 | 31–35 | 1 | 2 |
|  |  |  | >35 | 2 | 2 |

$\theta = 0.14$;    $x^2 = 8.76$;    $p = 0.20$–$0.10$ || $\theta = 0.12$;    $x^2 = 7.01$;    $p = 0.50$–$0.30$

Table 3    *Distribution of intervals between interstate war experiences, compared to those predicted by exponential model (N = 66)*

| interval from termination to onset | No. of cases observed | No. of cases predicted | Interval from onset to onset | No. of cases observed | No. of cases predicted |
|---|---|---|---|---|---|
| 5 | 31 | 23 | 5 | 25 | 21 |
| 6–10 | 9 | 15 | 6–10 | 9 | 14 |
| 11–15 | 5 | 10 | 11–15 | 8 | 10 |
| 16–20 | 3 | 6 | 16–20 | 5 | 7 |
| 21–25 | 10 | 4 | 21–25 | 6 | 5 |
| 26–30 | 4 | 3 | 26–30 | 8 | 3 |
| 31–35 | 0 | 2 | 31–35 | 1 | 2 |
| 36–40 | 0 | 1 | 36–40 | 0 | 2 |
| 40 | 4 | 2 | 41–45 | 1 | 1 |
|  |  |  | 45 | 3 | 2 |

$\theta = 0.09$;    $x^2 = 22.62$;    $p = 0.01$–$0.00$ || $\theta = 0.08$;    $x^2 = 14.00$;    $p = 0.20$–$0.10$

Note: In this, as well as several other tables, the predicted number of cases appears to increase in the final half-decade, but this is merely a result of combining several such periods at the far end of the scale.

re-entries, when we measure from the *onset* of one war to the onset of the next (in the right hand column), the exponential model again does a fair job of predicting the re-entry rates that were actually observed. That is, the chi-square value of 14 is sufficiently insignificant (0.20–0.10) to justify rejecting the hypothesis that there is a strong difference between the predicted and observed distributions.

But when we return to the more intuitively reasonable cutting-point—from *termination* to onset (as on the left)—the significance level (0.01–0.00) is strong enough to suggest a distribution of observed interwar intervals different from those predicted by the model. Rather, we find a distinct bimodal distribution, with thirty-one re-entries within five years

Table 4   *Distribution of intervals between termination and onset of interstate war experiences, with the eleven First and Second World War cases omitted (N = 55)*

|  | No. of cases observed | No. of cases predicted |
|---|---|---|
| 5 | 27 | 20 |
| 6–10 | 8 | 10 |
| 11–15 | 4 | 6 |
| 16–20 | 3 | 5 |
| 21–25 | 5 | 4 |
| 26–30 | 4 | 3 |
| 31–35 | 0 | 2 |
| 36–40 | 0 | 2 |
| 40 | 4 | 3 |

$\theta = 0.09$;    $\chi^2 = 8.49$;    $p = 0.50-0.25$

after the termination (compared to the twenty-three predicted by the model), then three periods with fewer re-entries than predicted, and then ten in the fifth half-decade, against the four predicted. While the unexpectedly high frequency of quick re-entries offers no support for the periodicity hypothesis, the high frequency during the twenty-one to twenty-five year span *would* seem to support that interpretation. However, a glance at the raw data reminds us that five of these ten re-entries are accounted for by the interval between the World Wars, and one suspects that this one case accounts for much of the belief that wars are cyclical. As a matter of fact, when the analysis is re-run without the eleven World War cases (Table 4), the chi-square value increases to 8.49, further supporting the equal interval hypothesis. In sum, any theoretical proposition that rests so heavily on a single set of outliers is not to be taken too literally.

### Victory, Defeat, and the Probability of War Re-Entry

If the likelihood of getting into war in a month or year is independent of *when* the last war was fought, is it possible that other attributes of the last war might be affecting this likelihood? If not the interval since the prior war, might it be, for example, its outcome in terms of victory or defeat, or its costs in battle fatalities? This certainly seems to be a reasonable question, and the answers are far from obvious. That is, victory in a prior war could certainly be a rewarding and reinforcing experience, making for more adventurous and war-accepting, if not war-seeking, policies in the aftermath of victory. Conversely, defeat could produce national resentment and "revanchism," with early war re-entry again an all-too-likely event. Similarly, if the battle fatalities in the prior war were relatively few, this could reduce the inhibitions that usually follow very high casualty levels. But once more, the greater the losses in one war, the more eager some will be to avenge those losses. And, to complicate things further, a power can experience all possible combinations: victory with low or high fatalities, or defeat with low or high fatalities.

Table 5    *Distribution of intervals between military defeats and next experience in all international and in interstate wars, compared to those predicted by exponential model (N = 27 + 16)*

| Interval from termination to onset, all wars | No. of cases observed | No. of cases predicted | Interval from termination to onset, interstate wars | No. of cases observed | No. of cases predicted |
|---|---|---|---|---|---|
| 5 | 15 | 15 | 5 | 8 | 6 |
| 6–10 | 4 | 7 | 6–10 | 2 | 4 |
| 11–15 | 4 | 3 | 11–15 | 1 | 2 |
| 15 | 4 | 2 | 16–20 | 1 | 2 |
| | | | 20 | 4 | 3 |

$\theta = 0.17;$    $X^2 = 3.18;$    $p = 0.50–0.40$   ‖   $\theta = 0.09;$    $X^2 = 3.42;$    $p = 0.50–0.40$

Table 6    *Distribution of intervals between military victories and next experience in all international and in interstate wars, compared to those predicted by exponential model (N = 71 + 47)*

| Interval from termination to onset, all wars | No. of cases observed | No. of cases predicted | Interval from termination to onset, interstate wars | No. of cases observed | No. of cases predicted |
|---|---|---|---|---|---|
| 5 | 40 | 34 | 5 | 21 | 16 |
| 6–10 | 9 | 18 | 6–10 | 6 | 10 |
| 11–15 | 10 | 9 | 11–15 | 4 | 7 |
| 16–20 | 4 | 5 | 16–20 | 2 | 5 |
| 21–25 | 3 | 3 | 21–25 | 7 | 3 |
| 26–30 | 3 | 1 | 26–30 | 4 | 2 |
| 30 | 2 | 2 | 31–35 | 0 | 1 |
| | | | 35 | 3 | 3 |

$\theta = 0.13;$    $X^2 = 8.99;$    $p = 0.20–0.10$   ‖   $\theta = 0.08;$    $x^2 = 14.56;$    $p = 0.05$

Turning first to the matter of outcome and its effect on the interval until the power's next war experience, we note in Table 5 that suffering military defeat seems to have no effect either way. The closeness of the distribution of war intervals actually observed to those predicted by the exponential, constant probability models tells us that military defeat makes a major power neither more nor less likely to get into another war quickly. Neither the positive nor the negative reinforcement effect arises out of defeat, and the same holds true whether we look at all international war experiences or at interstate wars alone.

As to the effects of victory, the picture is a bit less clear, as Table 6 indicates. While the distribution of intervals between military victory and the next war is relatively close to that predicted by the model, there is— for all such war experiences and for interstate wars alone—a discernible propensity toward early re-entry into war. The model leads us to expect

Table 7    *Differences between interwar intervals of victorious and defeated powers*

|  |  | Victorious | Defeated |  |
| --- | --- | --- | --- | --- |
| Interwar intervals, | mean : | 7·80 | 5·90 | t = 0·93 |
| all wars, | variation : | 90·48 | 56·48 | p = 0·35 |
| termination to onset | N : | 71 | 27 |  |
| Interwar intervals, | mean : | 12·44 | 10·79 | t = 0·43 |
| interstate, | variation : | 177·39 | 172·91 | p = 0·67 |
| termination to onset | N : | 47 | 16 |  |

thirty-four and sixteen such entries respectively, but we actually observe forty and twenty-one cases in which the victorious nation is back at war within five years. Also deviating from the expected is the number of re-entries during the twenty-one to twenty-five year interval following victory in interstate war: seven as against the three that were predicted.

Another way to look at this is to compare (Table 7) the average intervals for the victorious war participants against those for powers that were defeated, and ascertain whether the differences are large enough to have occurred by chance alone. Whether we compare these means for all war experiences or for interstate wars alone, the figures are quite close. As the significance levels show, differences between 7·8 and 5·9 and between 12·4 and 10·8 are sufficiently low to have occurred by chance alone.

### Fatalities, Duration, and the Probability of War Re-Entry

An equally plausible factor, when it comes to predicting the war re-entry patterns of the major powers, is that of the *cost* of the prior war experience. Regardless of which side emerges victorious, each participant engages in combat for some number of months and loses some fraction of its population in the hostilities that ensue, and it is reasonable to expect the duration and casualty levels to affect its propensity to fight again in the near future. But as before, there is no obvious and compelling *a priori* expectation as to the most likely direction of the relationship. If the costs of the war were high, we *could* expect the memory of such devastation and the need to recuperate to have a fairly long delaying effect, but we could also expect the drive for revenge to stimulate rather rapid re-entry into war. And if the costs were low, with no inhibiting memory of devastation, war *could* become an acceptable option early on; but these low costs would also predict a low drive for revenge.

Before checking these equally plausible expectations against the historical evidence, let us recapitulate the indicators of cost that we will use. The most valid one would seem to be that of battle-connected fatalities measured in absolute terms, and the second might be that of war duration. A third and fourth might be the "intensity" of that prior war experience, as measured first by fatalities per capita and secondly by fatalities per month.

Table 8    *Product-moment correlations between indicators of costs of prior war and length of interval to next war*

|  | Intervals for all wars (N = 101) | Intervals for interstate wars (N = 66) |
|---|---|---|
| Battle deaths | 0·07 | 0·05 |
| Battle deaths/capita | 0·12 | 0·10 |
| Nation-months | −0·14 | −0·04 |
| Battle deaths/nation-month | 0·07 | 0·05 |

Table 9    *Product-moment correlations between indicators of costs of prior war ending in victory or defeat, and length of interval to next war*

|  | Victorious in Prior War | | Defeated in Prior War | |
|---|---|---|---|---|
|  | Interval for all wars (N = 71) | Interval for interstate wars (N = 47) | Intervals for all wars (N = 27) | Intervals for interstate wars (N = 16) |
| Battle deaths | 0·04 | 0·03 | 0·40** | 0·20 |
| Battle deaths/capita | 0·08 | 0·09 | 0·29 | 0·12 |
| Nation-months | −0·02 | 0·02 | −0·33* | −0·12 |
| Battle deaths/nation-month | 0·03 | 0·01 | 0·38** | 0·31 |

*Significant at 0·10 level.
**Significant at 0·05 level.

What does the evidence suggest using these four indicators? Very simply, Table 8 contains not a single statistically significant correlation between any of these indicators and the interwar intervals of the powers. Whether we look at all 101 international war experiences, or the 66 interstate wars only, the product-moment coefficients range from 0·5 to 0·12 for the fatality indicators, and from 0·04 to 0·14 when the prior war's duration is used to reflect the war's cost. In other words, battle fatalities have a very slight prolonging effect and nation months had a very slight foreshortening effect on the interwar intervals.

### The Combined Effects of Outcome and Cost

If the separate effects of outcome and cost on interwar intervals are negligible, what about the *combined* effects? As Table 9 shows, the pattern continues to hold when we look at those war experiences that ended in military *victory*; this desirable outcome has little impact upon the effects of either fatalities or duration. But *defeat* in the prior war combines with the costs of that war in a relatively clear fashion. More specifically, we find that the greater the cost in nation-months, the *shorter* the interval until the next war, and the pattern is stronger for all types of war experience than for those associated with interstate wars alone.

Table 10    *Product-moment correlations between the interwar interval and the costs of the subsequent war*

|  | Interval since first war for all powers | Interval since first war, excluding Turkish cases |
|---|---|---|
| Battle deaths | 0·29**** | 0·39**** |
| Battle deaths/capita | 0·25*** | 0·36**** |
| Nation-months | 0·19** | 0·20** |
| Battle deaths/nation-month | 0·21** | 0·36**** |

**Significant at 0·05 level.
***Significant at 0·01 level.
****Significant at 0·001 level.

Conversely, it turns out that the greater the battle fatalities sustained in defeat, the *longer* will be the interval before re-entry into war; again, this relationship is especially clear when we include the colonial and imperial war experiences as well as the interstate wars. Worth noting here is the fact that interwar intervals are especially lengthened by prior war experiences that were both severe and brief. One of the strongest associations in Table 9 is that with our intensity measure of battle deaths per nation-month (0·38), and if we exclude Turkey from the analysis, this coefficient rises to 0·53.

An interesting implication arises out of this finding. If high battle death levels in short wars clearly lengthen the interval until a defeated power again goes to war, it is reasonable to ask whether the length of that interval has—in turn—any effect on the severity, duration, or intensity of that next war when it finally occurs. As Table 10 shows clearly, the answer is affirmative, with the length of the interwar interval correlating 0·29 with the battle death level for the next war and 0·25 with the intensity measure of battle deaths per million population. And if we exclude Turkey, the coefficients again rise, to 0·39 and 0·36 respectively, significant at the 0·001 level.

We now have a rather suggestive chain of relationships, at least for those powers that suffer defeat in a given war. That is, Table 9 indicates that the more intense the costs of that war in battle deaths per nation-month, the greater the interval to the next war, and Table 10 indicates that the greater that interval, the greater the intensity of the *next* war experience.

Thus, one might discern the glimmerings of a slow and long-run secular trend in the war histories of the major powers. When they suffer military defeat, and pay a high price in battle deaths per month of war, they tend to avoid war for a longer time, and the longer they wait, the more intense the next war experience will be. It follows that if we wait long enough and there are more defeated than victorious powers in each successive war, the phenomenon might eventually disappear. While this would be a logical possibility if there are more powers on the losing side, the historical pattern—not surprisingly[16]—shows that the *victorious* side usually is more numerous. In any event, we can hardly pin our hopes on so slender a reed. To do so would be to repeat the naive error of Bloch[17] who—quite correctly—predicted the effects of weapons technology on the conduct of war and on the costs of preparing for war. But, like all too many social scientists from his epoch to ours, he assumed that awareness of these implications would lead us to seek other and more adaptive modes of conflict resolution. Knowledge may be *necessary* for rational human intervention, but the bloody pages of international history remind us that it is hardly *sufficient*.

## ALTERNATIVE INTERPRETATIONS

Having found no discernible periodicity here in the intervals between major power war experiences, may we conclude more generally that there is no periodicity in international war since the Congress of Vienna? Not quite yet. First of all, there may be other and less obvious periodicities in the war experience of these nations, and secondly, it could be that the level at which to look is the systemic rather than the individual states.

Before attending to these possibilities, however, we digress long enough to treat the logical possibility that because our "sample" is not representative, we might have overlooked such a periodicity in the war experience of other classes of nations. But a moment's consideration reminds us that if these particularly war-prone major powers, experiencing an average of 0·95 wars per decade, show no periodicity, there is little likelihood that the minor powers, with an average of fewer than 0·21 per decade, could show any periodicity in as brief a period as a century and a half.

Turning then to other possible periodicities in major power war, four considerations arise. One is that there exists a cyclical pattern, but without the constant length intervals; this could occur if national war experiences occurred in clusters of two or three in close sequence, followed by a much longer interval and then the next cluster. We find nothing in our data to support this surmise. Secondly, it could be that the periodicity being measured should not be the simple *occurrence* of war, but its magnitude or severity. That is, one could hypothesize that armed conflict, above as well as below the war threshold, is a relatively constant characteristic of the major powers' existence, but that peaks of particularly large amounts of war occur at regular intervals. Using spectral analysis and related techniques, we found no evidence for such, whether we looked at the battle death or the nation-month indicators.[18]

A third possibility in this context is that we have defined periodicity in too conventional a manner. Ordinarily, we mean approximately equal time-intervals between peaks and/or troughs of approximately equal magnitude, but one could extend the definition somewhat. And one possibility might be to define the intervals, not in fixed units of time alone, but these units weighted or multiplied by factors such as the outcome or cost of the prior war experience. But since our procedures are functionally equivalent to that sort of measurement, we can pretty clearly rule out such a possibility.

Turning to a fourth possibility, could it be that our search is at the wrong level of aggregation, and that the theoretically interesting question is whether there is a cyclical pattern of warfare when we move up to the systemic level? Somewhat like such physical phenomena as Brownian motion, one finds randomness in the behavior of each component, but a clearly discernible pattern at the aggregated level. In an earlier investigation we looked into this possibility from several perspectives, and found only the weakest suggestion of periodicity in system-level warfare.[19] That is, using spectral analysis and related techniques, we found no cyclical pattern between occurrences (measuring from onset to onset as well as from termination to onset), but a barely discernible one when measuring from peak to peak in terms of nation-months of war under way. Further, the periodicity was sufficiently ambiguous that we could only infer that it ranges between twenty and forty years.

We pursue this question farther than might seem necessary for two reasons. One is the well-understood danger of committing a type II error, in which a latent pattern goes undetected. Social scientists tend to be careful to avoid the type I error, and seldom are guilty of claiming the existence of a meaningful pattern when it could, for example, have occurred by chance alone. But it is equally important that we do not overlook some theoretically significant configuration merely because we used too few instruments of observation or too rigid a strategy of inference.

The second reason—returning to the matter of type I errors—is that a number of researchers claim to have discovered all sorts of periodicities in war, and there is thus a general tendency in our field to accept the proposition that war is indeed a cyclical phenomenon. Since we only presented the reasons for expecting this to be true in our introductory pages, and said little about the prior evidence one way or another, let us summarize that evidence here.

While we are merely the most recent in a long line of researchers to have examined the question, our predecessors have fared little better in their searches for periodicity, despite occasional claims to the contrary. Neither Sorokin[20] nor Richardson[21]—who had better data than the former, but worked in a much shorter time-span—was able to find any strong cyclical patterns at the regional or systemic level. But in a secondary analysis of the above data sets, as well as the data generated by Wright,[22] Denton and Phillips discerned an upswing in the incidence of war about every thirty years since 1680.[23] Similarly, in a secondary analysis of Wheeler's estimates,[24] Dewey claims to find a number of periodicities going back to 600 BC.[25] Another long-range study, but at the national and/or regional level, is Lee's analysis of Chinese internal wars from 221 BC to 1929, indicating a clear 800-year cycle, as well as less evident ones of a shorter duration.[26] And, as already noted, our own investigation—at the system level for the period 1816–1965—also came up with ambiguous, but basically negative, results.[27]

Given the paucity of the evidence at the national level so far, as well as our skepticism regarding much of the methods and data used in the pro-cyclic literature, we find ourselves in agreement with Sorokin's dim view.[28] "These considerations are sufficient," he said, "until real evidence to the contrary is given, to . . . conclude that . . . no regular periodicity, no uniform rhythm, no universal uniformity of the curve of war movement in all of the countries studied are identifiable."

Having addressed the proposition that national war experiences come at regular intervals in tune with some periodicity—foreordained or otherwise— all we have demonstrated is that the probability of the major powers getting into war is independent of when and with what effects they experienced their prior wars. Does this absence of periodicity permit us to infer that there is no underlying regularity, and that war experiences are randomly occurring responses to randomly occurring conditions? Clearly not, since it is quite possible that war requires the concatenation of several conditions, each of whose appearance is cyclical, but with different intervals. This *could* produce a periodicity in the war experiences of nations, but the concatenation of as few as three such cycles, even if they show (for example) three-, ten-, and fifty-year periodicities, would occur only once every 150 years. Thus the war cycle would be so long as to make its occurrence barely visible in the span under scrutiny here. Furthermore, since we know that the mean interwar experience interval is under ten years (depending on the class of nation) we can reject as impossible any fixed interval periodicity that is appreciably greater (or lesser) than that figure.

It follows, then, that whatever periodicities there *may* be in our unspecified predictor variables, these could not be exercising any cyclical effect on interwar experience intervals.

## CONCLUSION

Is there anything in these findings that would strengthen our confidence in one or another of the orientations that we bring to the temporal incidence of war? Clearly the evidence does not support the cyclical view; the intervals are too irregular, and the occurrence of war entries has been virtually indifferent to the passage of time since the prior war. Moreover, when we control for the outcome of the prior war or its duration or its fatality level, we still find that the probability of the next war entry is basically unrelated to the passage of time.

And, of course, if there is no periodicity—as well as no upward or downward secular trend—we can more readily reject any suggestion of historical inexorability. As noted earlier, empirical confirmation of a cyclical pattern or clear secular trend would not demonstrate the existence of one or another of these inexorable historical laws, but the absence of such a pattern comes very close to refuting the proposition. To quote Sorokin[29] once more, "History seems to be neither as monotonous and uninventive as the partisans of the strict periodicities and 'iron laws' and 'universal uniformities' think; nor so dull and mechanical as an engine, making the same number of revolutions in a unit of time. It repeats its 'themes' but almost always with new variations. In this sense it is ever new, and ever old, so far as the ups and downs are repeated."

We close, then, with the proposition that regularity and inexorability are far from identical. As suggested in the introduction, a fully determined and inexorable outcome need not be preceded by a discernible pattern of observed regularities. Just as chaos can mark the most teleologic of historical processes, pattern and regularity can characterize processes whose outcome remains very much in doubt. In sum, the purpose of systematic research into the correlates of war and the conditions of peace is to estimate as closely as we can how much variance in the outcome is explained by the deterministic processes of fate and the stochastic processes of chance, and how much is left for rational human steersmanship. The demonstrated absence of periodicity is no guarantee that we will either arrive at such an estimate or take advantage of the unexplained variance, but its presence would certainly have suggested an even more pessimistic conclusion.

## ACKNOWLEDGMENTS

We are grateful to the volume's editors, to Michael Champion, Melvin Small, and Bradley Martin for their helpful comments, and to the National Science Foundation for research support under grant SOC71-03593 A05.

# CHAPTER SEVENTEEN

— ■ —

# System Structure, Decision Processes, and the Incidence of International War

A QUARTER OF A CENTURY AGO, three young scholars—in an unexpectedly symbiotic fashion—converged to identify and, perhaps, clarify what has come to be called the "level of analysis problem." In *Man, the State, and War* (1959), Waltz carefully articulated the empirical premises that are more or less inexorably associated with the several levels of analysis/aggregation and concluded that most of the variance in the incidence of war and other major events could be accounted for by the characteristics of the international system. While Singer (1960, 1961) concurred with that theoretical judgment, he pursued the question a bit further, suggesting that each level—the individual, the national society, and the international system—had a role to play in shaping the behavior of the nations and the fortunes of their citizens. The third of the new and interdisciplinary breed of scholars central to this discussion was Kaplan (1957), who not only concluded that the international system was "subsystem dominant" in the sense that the more significant aspects of international politics were determined by the properties and behaviors of the nations rather than the properties of the system, but also went on to postulate a set of axiomatic rules that seemed to govern that behavior. Among others, those who participated actively in these exchanges were Rosenau (1969), Haas (1953), Russett (1967), Hoffmann (1965), Liska (1956), Rosecrance (1966), and Deutsch and Singer (1964).

Fortunately for the discipline, this spate of interesting and insightful speculation was gradually followed by a decade or so of empirical-operational investigations, which were characterized by the reasonable assertion that if deductive argument buttressed by selective anecdote could lead to such

This chapter originally appeared in the *Handbook of War Studies* (London: Unwin Hyman, 1989), pp. 1–21. Reprinted by permission of the publisher.

diverse conclusions, it might be time to look at the historical evidence. Much of this work utilized the data sets that were being generated by Singer and Small and their colleagues in the Correlates of War Project (1966a, b, 1970, and 1973), but the findings were far from convergent, reminding us that results arise out of a research design that is, in turn, a consequence of some complex mix that includes the theoretical model, the spatial and temporal domain, the choice of indicators, the data aggregation procedures, and, of course, the choice of data analysis strategies.

Before attempting to summarize and make sense of those empirical investigations into the role of the international system vis-à-vis the incidence of international war, it might be useful to lay out the theoretical question in more precise terms. Thus, this first section will examine and compare two different but convergent arguments as to why the properties of the system might indeed be critical in accounting for the incidence of war in international politics. The metaphor here might be that the properties of the sea affect the behavior of marine life, and those of the community affect the behavior of its residents, but only to some finite extent. Some behavior is largely generated from within animals and people; furthermore, that behavior also helps both to perpetuate and to modify the system itself. In the second section, we address the elusive question of how system properties impinge on the domestic decision process in order to reinforce or modify the behavior of their nations. From there, we go on to examine the more relevant empirical evidence.

## THE THEORETICAL CONTEXT

Many scholars in the field of international politics would, with little hesitation, dismiss the effort to identify the impact of system properties on the incidence of war (or on any other set of phenomena). Their reasons would be of two sorts. First, from the policy perspective, they note that even if the attributes of the system do affect international interactions, it would only be of "academic interest" because of the relatively slow pace at which these properties (to be described shortly) change and because of the corollary that they are largely unresponsive to the policy moves of the nations. If there is little we can do to modify the system in the short term, why worry about its effects? At best, the system's structural, material, and cultural properties are similar to geographical and climatological phenomena: they must be reckoned with, but they cannot be controlled.

A second and more substantial argument is of a theoretical sort: the nations are highly autonomous actors and, while systemic conditions may impose some modest constraints, national behavior is primarily a consequence of the domestically determined objectives and capabilities of each society. This is, of course, an extreme version of the "subsystem dominated" assumption.

While recognizing the partial accuracy of both arguments, those of us who consider the issue an important one proceed from the following perspective. First, there is the by now familiar refrain that "it is an empirical question," one to be settled by examining the historical evidence rather than by some premature premise usually resting on a biased recollection of a handful of cases or periods. That is, although system properties, especially those of a structural and material sort, do appear to be resistant to rapid and conscious change, some of them do seem more volatile, especially those reflecting alliance formation and dissolution on the structural side and those reflecting technological breakthrough on the material side. Widely shared perceptions on the cultural side, as implied, do occasionally shift rapidly, often in response to the policies of one or two major powers. While the empirical question has remained largely rhetorical with few efforts to measure either the rate of change or the stimuli effecting such change, one promising exception is now under way: Wallace and Singer are well along in a data-based analysis of the system's structural dimensions from 1816 to the present; while the results so far tend to support the more "glacial" of the orientations, it is too early to generalize.

The second counter-argument is partly theoretically derived and partly empirical: the system's properties do—or should—affect national behavior regarding war and peace in a discernible fashion. And that is the purpose of this chapter: to examine both the deductive reasoning and the inductive findings that illuminate systemic impact on the military behavior of the component units.

## Definitions

Given the dearth of systematic research as well as the diverse meanings attached to the concepts introduced in the previous section, a brief definitional digression is in order, beginning with the reminder that "systemness" is largely in the eye of the beholder; one can look at or imagine an extraordinarily diverse range of social, biological, or physical entities and assign them to a system. Most (but not all) scientists would agree that systemness requires (1) some degree of comparability among its component entities, (2) a modicum of interdependence among the entities, and, less often, (3) a degree of common fate (Campbell 1958). Once the components and the boundaries of the social system are defined, we can go on to describe it along three sets of attribute dimensions. Ranging in order of tangibility, durability, and observability, these are material, structural, and cultural. The first, *material*, embraces geographical, demographic, and technological features. Even though these cry out for more systematic, data-based attention as determinants of national behavior, little has been done to date. These dimensions will be ignored here.

Next are the *structural* attributes of a system, and these are typically distinguished both on a formal-informal dimension (ranging from legal institutions to loose coalitions, for example) and on a vertical-horizontal dimension. By vertical structure, we mean hierarchy, ranking, status ordering, and so on. Horizontal structure reflects the bonds, links, and associations that allow a system to be examined in terms of the extent to which diplomatic ranking correlates with the number of votes in a formal international organization (vertical), or how clearly bipolar the configuration that emerges out of the nations' alliance bonds is (horizontal). Finally, there are *cultural* attributes, which may also, in turn, be disaggregated into the distribution of perceptions, preferences, and predictions among some or all of the individuals in the system, including those elites who speak and act on behalf of the subsystem groups into which the people are organized. As with the material properties of the international system, these also (1) demand, but have not yet received, much greater research attention and (2) will be largely ignored here.

I cannot leave this brief section without a few general comments on the importance of definitional clarity in the social sciences. Largely because ours are the most recent and least developed of the sciences and, thus, are still heavily influenced by practises in the humanities, we tend to follow an excessively permissive approach. One hears with alarming frequency the following phrase: "I don't care what you call it as long as you define your terms!" This may be pleasantly nondogmatic, but it means that each of us needs to carry around a truckload of dictionaries, one for each scholar's own idiosyncratic vocabulary. The central concept in this chapter and in much of the literature in world politics is "structure," yet the variety of definitions (implicit more often than explicit) is awesome. In addition to the configurations and links and bonds and ranks of the component units in a system as used here, one also finds the word applied to (1) any slowly changing condition, (2) any observed or hypothesized regularity in the behavior of social entities, (3) any observed or hypothesized pattern of statistical associations among any sets of variables, and (4) any regularity, observed or imagined, for which no other word comes to mind! Other examples occur, but space is limited and my point should be clear.

## Interaction Opportunities

With some of the terminological ambiguities removed (for the moment only, I fear), let us turn now to the more general theoretical argument. In the process, I will suggest that there is an unsuspected underlying unity in the apparent diversity, if not chaos, of the relevant literature. As I understand it, there would seem to be two approaches to the connection between system structure and war. One is that of interaction opportunities, and the other is structural clarity; both—quite naturally—exercise their effects (if any) on internation conflict through the national security decision process. Let me address them separately at first.

The interaction opportunity theme is analogous to the "invisible hand" notion associated with Adam Smith and his theoretical descendents, and it assumes that the less constrained the actors in an economic system are, the more fully they can pursue their natural self-interests. Further, the greater this freedom is, the greater the prosperity of the system as a whole and its members in general will be. Conversely, any tendencies toward restraint, via oligopoly, monopoly, or government regulation, will inhibit such pursuit, weaken the efforts of the invisible hand, and thus redound to the collective disadvantage. Similarly, as we hypothesized in previous work (Deutsch and Singer 1964; Singer and Small 1968) and as the classical scholars argued earlier (Gulick 1955; Kennan 1951), the members of the international system are more likely to enjoy autonomy and security when they are free to pursue these interests via interaction with many other nations. Constraints in the form of alliance obligations or relatively permanent hostility or friendship based on dynastic or ideological considerations will inhibit the efficacy of those multiple cross-cutting ties that permit the invisible hand to work as a self-regulating mechanism in the service of peace and stability.

In sum, this theoretical focus makes a virtue of sovereignty, assumes a sense of national restraint and rationality, and predicts a moderately harmonious state of affairs as long as the rules of the game are generally followed. The point of the argument, then, is that national security elites must be sufficiently competent to recognize the interests of their own state as well as the interests of the others. They must also be sufficiently free of parochial domestic interests—as well as the unnatural bonds of enduring alliance and alignment—to pursue the former and, in so doing, preserve the system's basic configuration while adjusting to the inevitable shifts in the capabilities and interests of its most salient members. For peace to prevail, interaction opportunities must be kept to the maximum.

## Structural Clarity

Turning from the theme of interaction opportunity to that of structural clarity, we once again find a not-so-elusive connection between a structural property of the system and the role of the national security elites. But here the emphasis is less on the need for high competence and wide latitude among the decisionmakers than on the extent to which their predictive abilities are enhanced by the state of the system. That is, the greater the structural clarity of the system, the more accurately they can predict who will be on whose side, and with what capabilities, in a confrontation.

This clarity is found along both the horizontal and vertical dimensions. The former reflects the strength and variety of ways that the nations are linked together in coalitions based on alliances, diplomatic bonds, shared membership in international organizations, trade, and the like. The stronger and more numerous these links, and the more discrete, distinct, and reinforcing the groupings produced by them, the greater the structural clarity on the horizontal dimension. Similarly, the nations can be ranked according to their industrial capacity, military capabilities, economic dominance, diplomatic importance, and so forth. And the greater the clarity and isomorphism of these several rank orders at a given moment, the more obvious are their overall strengths, the clearer the pecking order, and the more readily they can be evaluated vis-à-vis one another. From these two sets of dimensions, as noted previously, the decisional elites can estimate, in a crunch, (1) who will line up with whom and (2) with what overall capabilities.

Working from the structural clarity model, the literature contains two competing interpretations relevant to the incidence of war (Midlarsky, 1981). In one of these, the assumption is that high clarity will produce greater decisional certainty, and such certainty as to the lineup will reduce the likelihood of a dispute or confrontation escalating to war. As the cliché says, under such conditions the stronger need not, and the weaker dare not, fight; thus, we would expect a strong, negative correlation between structural clarity and the incidence of war. But like so many of the theoretical models in the field of world politics, there is an equally plausible counter-argument. In this rival version, the hypothesis is that structural clarity is *positively* associated with war because elites are more likely to initiate war when the outcome is relatively clear and, of course, promising. In this version, ambiguity and uncertainty is what inhibits escalatory behavior, and clarity and confidence encourage it on the side of those who enjoy superiority. As should be clear, this is a corollary of the less complex hypothesis on the relationship between parity and war, and as with that long-standing question, the prediction can go either way.

Returning to the interaction opportunity approach, the convergence between these two models should be clear. As such opportunities increase, two consequences allegedly follow. First, as already noted, when there are fewer constraints on the nations from alliances and other bonds, each can more readily pursue its own apparent interests. This produces in turn, the putatively positive effects of the invisible hand, with war that much less likely. But an important and less obvious implication links the theoretical focus quite nicely with the structural clarity/ambiguity focus: when these opportunities are high it is because of the relative absence of clear coalitions that rest on the inhibiting bonds of alignment via unambiguous political and economic association.

In other words, the two dominant foci in the efforts to explain war on the basis of system structure turn out to converge on the theme of decisional certainty at the national level. Interaction opportunities, thus, stem from low levels of structural clarity that result in lower levels of decisional certainty. While making this cross-system convergence evident is a desirable step toward theoretical integration, it nevertheless still leaves us with the elusive empirical question at the national level of analysis: Are nations in conflict more prone to escalation and war under conditions of high certainty and predictability or when configurations are ambiguous, certainty is low, and predictability is more difficult?

Another perspective on this is dyadic. If structural clarity at the global or regional level provides a relatively solid basis for national security elites to estimate the relative aggregate capabilities of the relevant coalitions and, thus, the likely outcome of war (should it come to that), it follows that similar estimates at the dyadic level should have the same effect. That is, if we focus only on the two central protagonists or blocs in a dispute or confrontation and ignore the existence and configurations (commitments and capabilities) of others, we have essentially the same problem facing those responsible for the war/no war decision: How likely are we to win, and at what cost, if the dispute goes to war? Furthermore, this situation poses the same question for the researcher as the analogous situation at the system level, and that is whether the relationship between the predictability of the outcome and the probability of war is positive or negative.

Of course, the simplifying assumption of symmetry that we have been making so far could be misleading. This is because it posits not only that the elites on each side will (1) see the same objective capability and commitment configurations and (2) evaluate it in the same way, but also that they will respond to it in the same way. Such heroic assumptions ignore the differentiating effects of all of those factors that make predicting international events difficult for both the practitioner and the scholarly observer.

Having laid out some of the key concepts and suggested not only the models that rest on these concepts but also the surprising convergence among these models, the next step is to articulate more fully a model of the decision process by which structural properties of the system exercise their alleged effect upon national behavior. More specifically, and despite a massive speculative literature to the contrary, unless one can illuminate the decisional links between environmental conditions and the behavior of the nations making up the system, any model of systemic effects on the incidence of war must remain less than complete. This proposition would seem to hold even if the statistical associations to date between system structure and war were both consistent and robust—which they certainly are not.

And if further justification is necessary, consider the frequency with which we read or listen to arguments about macro-economic policy and come away confused. As I see it, the explanation is simple: the writer or speaker has not made the decisional connection clear because he or she has not considered it, assumes it to be self-evident, or finds it too elusive to address. Let us see whether we can do better in international politics than in the allegedly most advanced of the social sciences.

## THE DECISIONAL CONNECTION

Let me begin with some crucial assumptions of an empirical sort on the premise that my epistemological assumptions are self-evident, while those of an ethical sort can be deferred to the conclusion. The first is what my students often call "Singer's First Law": No individual and no organization ever does anything for one reason alone. And I use *reason* here in both senses of the word: the pull of the future and the push of the past. By the former, I mean preferences for the future, "in order to" reasons; these preferences can be thought of as goals or purposes, but only in the sense that actors are willing to allocate energy and invest resources in their pursuit. This is to distinguish between goals, purposes, and objectives on the one hand and idle dreams and fantasies on the other. Many individuals would like to achieve fame, fortune, and power, but very few invest seriously in the pursuit of such ends. Rather, we typically set more modest goals and then proceed to work toward them; becoming a millionaire, a prime minister, or even a Nobel Prize winner is insufficiently salient for most of us to concentrate our energies toward them. Similarly, those who act on behalf of national or multinational states, political parties, movements, or corporations may well fantasize about global domination and so forth, but rarely in history do we find concerted efforts to realize such dreams. Even granting that Napoleon, Hitler, and Stalin may have been acting on such dreams and were able to mobilize people and resources toward such grandiose ends, one must recognize how small a fraction of the political elites of the last two centuries they represent. Furthermore, individuals and groups must find themselves well along the road to these ends before they begin to pursue them as relevant goals—and that, too, is a relatively rare event.

## The Pull of the Future

Returning, then, to the pull of the future, it is hardly radical to note that governments and their national security elements are inevitably coalitions made up of subcoalitions of individuals. Nor is it surprising, despite the appreciable effects of selection and socialization, that these individuals and groups will have different goal priorities. Their preference orderings will be at variance, as will the utilities and disutilities they assign to conceivable outcomes. These differences not only reflect diverse views of national interest and diverse models of political reality, but they lead to differences in those short term goals that are seen as instrumental means to longer term goals (March 1981).

Equally important, of course, are the more provincial of their interests: the personal and the bureaucratic. Only those who believe in fairy tales would accept the scenario of hundreds of functionaries, from minister of defense down to assistant desk officers, working assiduously (or even competently) in the selfless pursuit of some higher societal purpose. A more realistic scenario might be what I call "doing well while appearing to do good," which is nicely reflected in the recent case of those officers who sought and achieved financial gains while selling U.S. arms to Iran and passing some of the profits along to the "Contra" factions in the Nicaraguan insurrection. And as I have argued for some years (Singer 1972) it is easier to attend to doing well for oneself and one's bureau or faction when there is considerable uncertainty as to which policies are most likely to do good for the country. This uncertainty, in turn, rests on that lethal combination of inadequate research by the scholarly community and the policy community's ignorance, indifference, and disdain for rigorous research findings in those instances when they exist and are publicly available.

## The Push of the Past

Much of the preceding analysis applies equally to the other set of reasons for pursuing and advocating a given national security policy: the "push of the past." Often understood as a learning model in the rational choice literature, the assumption is that decisional elites select those policies and strategies that seemed to have been successful in the past and then utilize them in the pursuit of their goals and objectives. While not unreasonable, this excessively rational assumption is seriously incomplete; we need to incorporate several other types of "pushes" from the past.

That is, in addition to events from the past that are part of the individual and institutional memories of the foreign policy elites, there are several additional components. First, there are those that are incorrectly or incompletely remembered, those from which "lessons" are erroneously drawn. A nice example of this is found in Ray (1987), where we are reminded that, after World War I, scholars and practitioners tended to believe that the polarization of the Triple Entente versus the Central Powers played a key role in converting the pre-1914 crisis into all-out war; the nations involved in the war, therefore, avoided alliance formation during the 1920s and 1930s. But with the close of World War II, the belief that it was the *lack* of alliances that brought on that disaster was instrumental in stimulating the frenzy of alliance building in the 1950s. By generalizing from a single salient case, elites "learned" the wrong thing. Selective recall may represent the push of the past, but it does so hardly in a constructive sense.

Second, and perhaps more potent, is the extent to which the conditions of today are a result of the conditions, events, and decisions taken years, decades, and centuries earlier. The powerful, ever-present hand of the past is instrumental in shaping the structural, material, and cultural context within which the international politics of the present are conceived and executed. While our understanding of those influences remains pitifully inadequate, they are, nevertheless, at work in every aspect of human activity. We may indeed never "step into the river of history at the same place," but step into it we must.

## Rational Choice and Realpolitik

The preceding discussion now permits us to address two issues that are central to any systemic—or other—explanation of international war. One issue is that of rational choice, the other is that of reductionism. Despite suggestions to the contrary (Waltz 1975), they are indeed separable; one need not work from the rational choice model in order to utilize a reductionist approach. Let me explain.

If the preceding interpretation of decision making is a fair statement of the problem, it is clear that the discrepancy between political reality and the rational choice model is profound. The argument cannot be salvaged by distinguishing between collective and individual rationality; the individuals in any organization can indeed be expected to pursue their own parochial goals and priorities in a relatively rational manner, but the collective, runs this line of argument, nevertheless shows rationality in pursuit of the larger entity's goals. The only way that this crutch can work is by falling back on the trivial definition of rationality often used in game theory: we pursue outcomes that we most prefer! While on the question of definition, let me suggest a distinction that would make the concept of rationality more relevant in the social sciences. That is, instead of using the trivial definition noted here or applying the concept to the policy decision or choice that emerges from the process of deciding, rationality should be applied only to the *process* itself. Policies may or may not be successful, prudent, or adaptive, but they should not be evaluated on a rationality dimension; that is reserved for the process alone.

Returning for a moment to the fit between national security decision-making and rational choice in its several incarnations, the preceding discussion should indicate the extent of my skepticism. For a more complete and devastating view, two other sources deserve mention. One is the fascinating article by the Swiss economist Bruno Frey (1983) in which we find a veritable catalog of the assumptions found in the rational choice literature of economics (and other social sciences) set alongside the experimental findings of cognitive and social psychologists. The other, in the context of international politics, is that of Philip Schrodt (1985), a political scientist pursuing the application of "artificial intelligence" to foreign policy decisionmaking. In this refreshingly coherent and explicit discussion, we find not only a treatment of the discrepancies between the assumptions of rational choice models and the empirical evidence, but a rejection of the widely accepted notion that our theoretical assumptions need not be empirically correct as long as they are "useful" in the sense that the models incorporating these assumptions turn out to provide accurate predictions.

Having said all of this, let me now hedge somewhat. If we bear in mind that internation conflict can embrace a rather wide range of behaviors and responses, it follows that much—perhaps most—of that conflict occurs in a routine, low-level, low-intensity mode. In that type of context, the line of argument adduced here would seem to hold in most nations and in most cases. Here, it is not surprising that individual and bureaucratic priorities mingle with poor organization, faulty intelligence, and collective ignorance, giving us a decision process rather close to that suggested previously.

On the other hand, what happens in crisis and confrontation? While the hard evidence may be far from adequate, most of us appreciate that "business as usual" gives way to a rather different mood with a somewhat different set of decision rules. Perhaps the most crucial change is that of priorities: among the world's crisis managers, it is taboo to think of or allude to personal or factional interests. Patriotism is the order of the day and the national interest is the touchstone. Another is that of time frame: with the nation at the brink of disaster or opportunity and the world on the knife-edge of destruction, one does not worry about mealtime or family plans. Too much is riding on our timely judgment.

This, in turn, is a result of one of the better documented generalizations: a rapid contraction of the size of the decision-making apparatus. Senior officials, elected or appointed, step in and take charge of matters ordinarily left to their subordinates, and while they may have inadequate familiarity with the details and history and context of the issue, they also have little patience with the glacial pace and seeming irrelevance they associate with the foreign policy and national security bureaucracy. Among the considerations that now may receive shorter shrift are interagency rivalries, public opinion, or the preferences of other governments, allied or otherwise. In other words, there is less interest in "what will sell" and more in "what will work." These, then, are the rare occasions in which something akin to rational choice might exist (Herek et al. 1987).

Having said all of this, however, the distinction should not be drawn too sharply. There are three considerations. First, as suggested, the evidence is more anecdotal and intuitively reasonable than it is reproducible. Second, people who have succeeded and have been socialized in one set of decision processes are unlikely to shed the habits of a lifetime overnight; the vestiges of personal, factional, and national politics will inevitably be present—and there is a tomorrow when they will once more dominate. And third, not only are the cultural norms regarding the decision process partially carried over into crises, but the entire configuration of the crisis situation is largely the result of that decision process.

## Reductionism and Realpolitik

The line of reasoning to this point provides strong support for those who are skeptical of the realpolitik perspective; other labels that can be used are "realist" or "balance of power," but the former is ideologically self-serving (whether pro or con), and the latter, as Haas (1953) urged years ago, means all things to all people. By realpolitik, we mean nothing more than the assumption that, on the world scene, national policies are (1) driven primarily by the pursuit of national power and (2) in the hands of competent, rational, patriotic officials. While arguing that such an explanatory model is woefully incomplete and, thus, quite misleading, I do not suggest that these considerations are absent or irrelevant. To the contrary, they are always present in the decision process when internation rivalry and conflict are on the agenda, and they exist even when highly collaborative policies are under consideration. But they are so intertwined with and corrupted by the pursuit of individual and bureaucratic-factional power that they provide a poor basis for prediction and explanation. In a later section we will see that this has not always been so; even up to the close of the nineteenth century, one could make a fair case for the realpolitik model. In response to industrialization, urbanization, and democratization, however, these factors began to decline in their analytic potency. One might say that when officials could no longer say or believe with the old French royalty that "l'etat, c'est moi," all sorts of other considerations began to intrude into the decision process.

## Reductionism and Explanation

Enough has been said about the decisional context and process to indicate their importance in examining the effects of system properties on subsystem interactions. It is now time for a brief summary in the context of a crucial epistemological argument. If the goal of scientific research is to explain the variation in some outcome phenomenon across time, places, or cases, we need to distinguish explanation from both prediction and covariation. While neither of the latter is a "piece of cake," they demand much less of the researcher and his or her theoretical model than does the task of explanation. One source of confusion on this score is the oft-heard assertion that the acid test of a theory is its ability to predict, and this is unfortunate as well as incorrect. Think of all the relatively accurate predictions that can be made without fully understanding or being able to explain the connection between input and output or stimulus and response. On the basis of observed or reported covariation alone, most of us can predict that flipping a switch will (usually) turn on a light, that a bicycle's speed will (up to a point) accelerate the longer it coasts downhill, that it takes more strength to get a heavy load moving than to keep it moving, that a small crowd will attract many passersby, that high winds will spread a forest fire, that a baby will cry if its parents scowl at it, and so forth. In other words, it requires relatively modest knowledge to make fairly accurate predictions, but quite a bit more knowledge is needed to explain why the predicted outcome usually results.

This is where reductionism enters the picture. An adequate explanation is one that tells the story, step by step, of how a given event or condition sets in motion a sequence that regularly culminates in a given outcome. That sequence—despite the impression that many social scientists give—is indeed "touched by human hands." While Marxist as well as market-oriented economists think it is self-evident that some macro-phenomenon, such as the spread of automated production, will regularly lead to some other macro-event, such as a fall in worldwide wage levels, it may not be at all self-evident either to the skeptic or to the innocent. Or, to take a more immediate issue in the American economy, the conventional wisdom is that a reduction in the individual tax rate will lead, in short order, to increased savings and investment levels. But in boom periods, this is not exactly what happens. First, most of the beneficiaries of a tax cut may be the less wealthy, but the aggregated monetary "return" is very much in the hands of the wealthy few. And second, the latter have little need or incentive to save; consequently, they invest, not in productivity-enhancing activities, but in speculative ones. Looking at the micro-level links can save us from accepting many a foolish generalization.

Another example is that of operations research, in which some tinkering with a system-level variable, such as an increase in oil prices, culminates in lower life expectancy levels (via more air pollution?), or construction of a highway culminates in lower classroom performance (via higher noise levels?). While observing or predicting such correlations is worthwhile from the perspectives of both science and public welfare, understanding the connection between "cause" and "effect" would be more valuable (and also more difficult).

The point, then, is that a theoretical formulation that ignores, avoids, or obfuscates the human decisions that link stimulus to response will be, at best, incomplete and, at worst, downright wrong. There is, of course, an important counterpoint: Reductionism can be carried too far. While the macro-level social scientist may, as I do, insist on bringing the individual into the model, the psychiatrist might want to disaggregate further down to the ego, superego, and libido. The biochemist might require that we examine the role of brain lipids in individual behavior, and the physical chemist could urge including the cells, neurons, and so on. Ultimately, we might indeed develop a unified and integrated theory of all human behavior (Miller 1976), but for the decades ahead, we can be satisfied with the more limited sort of reductionism advocated here.

We conclude this section, then, by noting that any explanation of war—systemic, dyadic, or national; material, structural, or cultural—must attend to the ways in which the putative explanatory factors impinge upon and are affected by the decision process. And even as we move, however slowly and reluctantly, toward the political equivalent of computer-assisted medical diagnosis (or the more advanced computer-assisted automotive diagnosis), human individuals and groups will be involved in reading and responding to certain stimuli in order to produce certain behavioral events. Without that connecting link, the "causal" association between input and output will remain shrouded in speculation, if not outright superstition.

## THE EMPIRICAL EVIDENCE

Having laid out the theoretical context and some of the key assumptions affecting the possible link between system structure and the incidence of war, we turn next to the very salient question: How strong is the empirical evidence in support of one version or another of the general hypothesis? To put it simply, it is not strong at all, but quite mixed at this point in the unfolding of the data-based research sequence.

Looking first at an earlier effort to evaluate the structural clarity argument, we (Singer and Bouxsein 1975) reexamined a number of prior studies that reflect not only a diversity of theoretical concerns, but also rest on far from identical data bases. One indicator of polarity in the major power subsystem, reflecting the extent to which alliances had increased structural clarity, was related to war negatively in the nineteenth century but positively in the twentieth century, while another indicator of system-wide polarity was weakly but positively related for both centuries. But when the same author (Wallace 1973) weighted the alliance configurations by the size of the signatories' armed forces, he found that greater polarity predicted to *lower* levels of war. Perhaps more compelling were the findings of his follow-up test of a curvilinear model: very high and very low levels of weighted polarity were positively associated with war, while moderate levels preceded periods of a clear decline in war over the two centuries, as was hypothesized by Rosecrance in 1966.

Another way to look at polarity and structural clarity is in terms of the direction and rate of change rather than the degree of polarity at each fixed observation interval. Thus, after finding only the weakest association between several indicators of the latter and war, Bueno de Mesquita (1978) discovered that the greater the change in the tightness and clarity of the alliance configuration (in either direction), the more international war there was in subsequent years. By using a more complex and discriminating model, however, he also found that declining tightness was strongly and *negatively* related to war.

We then turned to another Correlates of War study in which the indicators of clarity were based not on the horizontal configurations produced by formal alliances (or shared memberships in international organizations or diplomatic groupings, which will be alluded to later), but on the vertical configurations produced by the distribution of material capabilities. Here (Singer et al. 1972), the results pointed in yet a different direction, with periods of high clarity—as indicated by a heavy concentration of capabilities in the hands of a very few major powers—predicting higher levels of war in the nineteenth century and lower levels in the twentieth century. Once more, on the assumption that the direction and rate of change might be equally or more relevant, we looked at both the net and the gross change in the concentration of capabilities and found that shifts toward higher concentration had the same "effects" as such a configuration in the static sense: more war in the nineteenth century and less in the twentieth century. And using gross changes, a mere redistribution, we found that less change was associated with more war in the earlier century and less war in the current century.

Given these apparently erratic patterns, we shifted from discrete bivariate analyses to the test of a primitive, multivariate model. Using alliance aggregation, polarity, concentration, and net and gross shifts in concentration (for major powers only), we found additional support for the notion that the indicators of structural clarity are indeed strongly associated with war, but once again the *direction* of that association is far from clear. That is, the coefficients of determination ($r^2$) were rather strong (.74 and .72) for the two centuries, but in opposite directions.

Drawing on those earlier efforts as well as on the research of the following half-decade, we found little to challenge the original conclusion (Singer 1981, 9). In that review article, I concluded that "regardless of the theoretical interpretation, the empirical investigations led once more to inconsistent results." At about the same time, Thompson et al. (1980) published the only other study explicitly using the interaction opportunities concept. This team, which has done some of the best research on the link between long economic cycles and war, attempted to replicate the earliest data-based analysis (Singer and Small 1968). Although they used somewhat different procedures, they also found only the weakest relationship over the 1816–1965 period. As with some earlier work, they did find some interesting—but surprising—cross-temporal differences. Rather than the intercentury break, they uncovered a positive, strong association between interaction opportunities and the onset of war, but only for the period since World War II. Equally inconclusive is a comprehensive examination of the effects of polarity in several forms along with capability distributions, in which a variety of additive and interactional models all failed to account for war and no-war outcomes (Bueno de Mesquita and Lalman 1987).

To further convey the absence of clear evidence, Stiglicz (1981) developed an indicator of structural clarity based on the ratio of balanced to unbalanced triads in the system and found that it is moderately but negatively associated with war in the nineteenth century and strongly positive in its "effect" on war in the twentieth century. Once again, it looks as if we probably have a good idea here, but there are so many diverse ways of measuring it that its scientific usefulness is nil (Bueno de Mesquita and Singer 1973). In this connection, it should be noted that, in addition to the index construction efforts contained in these contributions, there is also a formidable number of excellent articles devoted solely to the problems of defining and measuring a range of potentially useful indicators of system structure, but they cannot be reviewed here.

Dissatisfied with the inconsistency of the previous findings, Stoll and Champion (1985) pursued a different tack and looked to levels of major power satisfaction as a possible explanatory variable. While their indicator relied on the soft judgments of their Correlates of War colleagues, including this variable provided an appreciably better fit between the incidence of war (and disputes) predicted by their model and the amounts actually observed. Briefly stated, by identifying blocs of states in terms of their apparent satisfaction with the international status quo, they came closer than their predecessors in postdicting fluctuations (if not precise magnitudes) in war across both centuries.

A more recent review article (Vasquez 1987), which evaluated the Correlates of War project and, in an imaginative fashion, examined the convergence of other research with ours, discerned a clearer set of results. While he does not invoke such systemic concepts as clarity or interaction opportunities, his interpretation of the data-based research at the national, dyadic, and system levels readily lends itself to such treatment, especially in his summary of the effects of military alliances at all of these levels. Starkly put, Vasquez sees such alliances as not only increasing the frequency of war since 1816, but also increasing their duration, magnitude, and severity.

## RECONCILING THE FINDINGS AND THE MODEL

While these intercentury differences and other inconsistencies are not found uniformly in every investigation that embraces part or most of the 1800s and 1900s, they occur with sufficient frequency to be taken seriously.

Further, they *may* be interpreted as a disappointing reminder that the search for lawlike regularities is a futile task, as many traditionalists with a predilection for the ideographic view of the world do interpret them. But they may also be taken as a valuable reminder that our theoretical models are inadequately specified, which is a pretentious way of saying that we have overlooked an important variable that, once identified, could help explain these apparent anomalies in our findings.

Committed as I am to the nomothetic view that assumes the existence of empirical regularities and recurrent patterns, my tendency is to ask what factor needs to be introduced into our model. If several structural properties of the international system are negatively associated with armed conflict in one century and positively associated with armed conflict in the next century, something must have occurred to "produce" this reversal of effects. In one of the earlier studies to turn up this cross-century shift, we offered a tentative and partial post hoc explanation, which is presented here in a more complete fashion.

With the nineteenth century drawing to a close, the European landscape had begun to change rather dramatically. As the industrial revolution accelerated, so did the rate of urbanization, and along with this came a rise in labor unions and working class militancy. This, in due course, contributed to the rise of the welfare state and, hence, to greater citizen interest and participation in domestic politics along with public education, higher literacy, and wider newspaper circulation. This social mobilization not only gave the political elites greater access to and control over the nation's demographic and economic resources (via, inter alia, conscription, mass education, and taxation), but it also imposed a relatively unfamiliar burden on them. Both the elites and the counter-elites found it necessary to generate popular support for their policies, which required, in turn, the articulation of a more coherent ideological argument. While largely focused on domestic matters, this attention, interest, and awareness gradually extended beyond national boundaries; growing interdependence among the nations and growing appreciation of the reciprocal impact of domestic and foreign policies led inevitably to the rising salience of the latter. Briefly put, foreign policy—long the private domain of a small elite—became more and more politicized.

As a consequence, the arcane complexities and subtleties of diplomatic and military practice were translated increasingly into ideological terms. And while such ideological presentations and justification still contained numerous contradictions, there was a powerful incentive to make them *appear* consistent in both the sense of their internal logic and in terms of compatibility with the more dominant national values. This certainly required some departure from the cynical and Machiavellian decision rules of realpolitik; politicians needed to justify their behavior in increasingly moral terms, even to the point of praising or condemning the domestic policies and putative values of other national governments (Hunt 1987).

It is, of course, easy to imagine the impact of these trends as that epoch gave way to the twentieth century. Cooperating with some governments called forth rather elaborate justifications, as did opposing them, offering or withdrawing diplomatic recognition, taking sides in disputes, entering into alliances or other treaties, and, to some extent, even engaging in commerce or negotiating agreements on immigration, citizenship, licensing, extradition, and copyright. What all of this added up to was the formation of international coalitions that were more responsive to the vagaries of public opinion, interest group pressures, media campaigns, and the whole panoply of domestic politics than they were to the more consistent imperatives of a geopolitical, and strategic kind. To repeat an earlier phrase of mine, alliances and other commitments became less and less "affairs of convenience" and more and more "marriages of passion."

This leads, in turn, to the connection between the structure of the international system and its culture, which provides the context within which national security decisions are made. To continue this line of reasoning, then, in those earlier periods, marked as they were by relatively high levels of tolerance and flexibility among political elites, structural ambiguity worked quite well to keep the peace: deep ideological cleavages, obsession with the struggle between the forces of light and the forces of darkness, beliefs that some domestic political forms are inherently evil and some inherently virtuous—all of these are part of the Manichean culture. And this is the outlook that amplifies the sense of fear in both camps, with the word "both" used advisedly to reflect the pressures on most nations to declare for one coalition or the other. Neutralism is, of course, unacceptable: If you're not *with* us, you're *against* us.

Under these more recent conditions of high cultural clarity, the normal effects of structural ambiguity are unlikely to work. As already suggested, the latter requires—if confrontation and war are to be minimized—the application of middle-run rationality to the foreign policy decision process. And this requires, in turn, a detached calculation of not only our own society's general interests and welfare but, more crucial, the interests, objectives, strategies, and capabilities of the others. Passions of hatred, paranoid fear, and self-righteousness, especially as these passions permeate the society and weaken the potential for rational self-correction from other domestic elites and counter-elites, will clearly inhibit our ability to think clearly about foreign and military policies. Under these conditions, which are highly contagious in the anarchic international system, each society's elites will be increasingly prone to exaggerate the ambitions and the capabilities of those in the "enemy camp." Also inhibiting the efficacy of the invisible hand mentioned earlier will be the tendency for weaker allies to exploit their dominant coalition partners and the willingness of the latter to acquiesce. The effect here will be the evolution of a double standard, with tolerance toward allies and cynicism toward rivals that further erodes our capacity to apply pragmatic and consistent criteria to foreign-policy decisions.

In sum, the beneficent results of the invisible hand rest on the ability of foreign policy elites to "read" the system and its other members accurately and dispassionately, a capacity that is enhanced under conditions of cultural and normative detachment but inhibited when the system's culture is marked by deep feeling and broad belief that there are well-defined camps and coalitions that distinguish between the decent folk and their enemies. Just as "conspiracies in restraint of trade" make it difficult for *Homo economus* to pragmatically interact with the multitude of other actors in the marketplace, coalitions in restraint of diplomacy make it difficult for *Homo politicus* to deal pragmatically with the less numerous, but clearly sufficient, aggregation of other actors in the global system.

## CONCLUSION

Every scholarly article in the social sciences can and should play a number of educational, policy, and scientific roles. Some will open up and clarify a relatively unfamiliar area of knowledge for the reader, others might alert the policymaker or analyst to some pertinent lessons of history, and still others will perhaps theoretically integrate a large fraction of previous research or point toward the most promising research strategy. While I hope that this one will help to illuminate the relationship between system structure and international war—and sensitize the policy-oriented reader to the fact that certain conflictual strategies may be safer under some circumstances and irresponsibly prone to war under others—the main concern has been the scientific one: bridging the gap between what we think we know and what we need to know next. And despite frequent assertions from those who should know better, this is a far cry from "testing the balance-of-power (or any other) theory"; there *is* no such theory, nor will there be one until much more of the work discussed here has been completed (Zinnes 1967; Siverson and Sullivan 1983).

In the case in hand, this is no easy task. On the one hand, we have more than the usual speculative essays based on the selective recall of historical anecdote or, worse yet, based on folkloristic hunches about how individuals allegedly behave (as in much of the literature on strategic deterrence). But on the other hand, as should be abundantly clear, the reproducible findings of the research to date hardly point in one clear direction. Depending on the variables used, the ways in which they were measured, the spatial-temporal domain covered, and the statistical models that were applied to the data, we obtain appreciably different results (Midlarsky 1986a). The task, therefore, is to both reexamine more fully the empirical investigations to date and to construct a theoretical model that best captures what we think we know about the ways in which the structural properties of the system impinge on those who act for nations in conflict. For the moment, while continuing to work on both of these tasks, my bet is on the ultimate ability of the structural clarity-interaction opportunity model—mediated by the changing culture of international politics—to capture the processes by which system structure leads toward and away from the ever-menacing threat of international war.

# PART FIVE

■

# Implications and
# Recapitulation

I have sought, in bringing together these papers of mine from the past three decades, to "make the case for peace research," even though I boggled at the label when it first sullied my ears, and still do. That reluctance arose out of two major concerns. First, by identifying our research too intimately with "peace," we might be perceived as pacifists, which, of course, many of us are; as Chapter 18 makes evident, I did not start my adult life, or even my scholarly career, as a pacifist. My upbringing and later military experiences assured that it would be otherwise. But the longer I taught, thought, read, and conducted research, the more of a skeptic I became. And the more I learned, the more convinced I became that national security elites—in my own country and elsewhere—were not only inherently incapable of dealing with matters of war and peace in a competent way but were so situated that the security of their people would rarely be, in any consistent fashion, their primary priority. And as it became increasingly evident that nations arm for a multiplicity of reasons and that arms act not only to deter, but also to provoke, it was inevitable that I would move closer to the pacifist position. Today, I would describe my position as 90 percent pacifist, suggesting not only a very limited set of conditions under which war would be ethically and pragmatically legitimate but also a steady response set opposed to arms acquisitions and in favor of arms reductions. Although one must differentiate between and among types and quantities of armaments, it can safely be said that one can show Singer few weapon systems that he likes!

But returning to my opening observation, I may be perfectly comfortable, as a citizen of my nation and the world as well as a social scientist, with the pacifist label. But how about my compatriots and colleagues? Because my career so far has spanned that grim and menacing period of history known as the cold war, it has been no more socially legitimate for me than for my Soviet or British or Chinese or French colleagues to question my nation's policies and oppose their mindless stockpiling of genocidal weap-

257

ons. Thus, one can appreciate my concern that our research would be dismissed as lacking in both virility and objectivity. My thought then was that, regardless of one's ideological position on the dove-owl-hawk dimension, one ought to do: (a) the most rigorous research on (b) such big questions as the causes of war.

But it soon became clear that the incentives lay elsewhere—hence that insidious growth industry of "arms control" research. One can convey a repugnance of war, treat armaments as morally neutral, and try to make a case for certain types, levels, and deployments of weapons, and against others. More alarmingly, one can do all of this, find considerable financial and social support, and work exclusively in the prescientific mode. As my papers in Part Two make clear, I am not opposed to arms control, but as I say in moments of excessive frankness, "one can knock off that sort of writing over the weekend"; it is, in other words, not serious political science! Thus, I feared that the "peace" label would make one's research less acceptable, less publishable, and less fundable, while making one's self less promotable, less marketable, and more suspect in the political and academic climate of the post-World War II (or pre-World War III?) era. As suggested, those fears were exaggerated, but not by much.

If the "peace" label has been a source of grief from the conventional right, the "research" label (my second concern) has been a source of grief from the alienated left. What I mean by this surprising comment is that all too many people working under this rubric seem to have no better an understanding of scientific research than the "objective" fence-sitters and the apologists for their respective governments, parties, and factions around the world. While lamenting the stupidities and callousness of most nations' policies, especially those of the industrial "capitalist" sort, my more politically progressive friends have been as prone to loaded analysis and careless reasoning as the most ardent bolshevik-basher in the West or anti-imperialist in the East. Although my ideological biases are certainly in the direction of my progressive friends, my epistemological biases make them uncomfortable bedfellows—and many of them express similar reservations toward me.

Finally, there was a period, largely from the mid-1960s to the mid-1970s and now far less evident, when a fair number of the left-oriented peace researchers not only eschewed research as I define it here, they also eschewed peace! That is, embracing justice as a higher value than nonviolence and confronted with the incredible amount of injustice in the world, they tended to endorse, if not agitate for, violent efforts to destroy those apparently responsible for those intolerable conditions. Again, I shared then, and still share, that sense of outrage and fury at the exploitation—and the complacency—that pervades the global village, but nevertheless believe that violent and bloody revolt is not a promising strategy. There are more powerful and less corrupting options, but I have neither the space nor the expertise to develop them here.

Be all of this as it may, we—and I—are stuck with the label; all we can do now is try to make it a badge of honor. In this final part of the book I hope to move a step closer to that goal. Chapter 18, then, tries to link together several of the themes developed in the first four parts. Prepared for the Nobel Prize Commission's conference in Norway in 1985, the chapter was designed to inform my colleagues about my type of research while focusing on its applicability to the contemporary human condition; my hope, so far unmet, was also that they might better appreciate the significance of this sort of enterprise and thus give that prestigious award, in due course, to a real peace researcher. Chapter 19 was originally my presidential address to the International Studies Association in 1985 and is perhaps best described as an intemperate critique of the discipline coupled with a fair amount of gratuitous advice, and, as the careful reader will note, some repetition of earlier points, including the research queries suggested in the proposed "Manhattan Project" for war prevention (Chapter 9). Although it was not hailed with enthusiasm, no impeachment proceedings were initiated nor have I yet been read out of the profession.

———— ∎ ————

# CHAPTER EIGHTEEN

# Research, Policy, and the Correlates of War

IN THE FORMULATION OF NATIONAL policies, what is the role of the scholarly community? In making decisions in the national security sector, what contributions can be expected from those of us who conduct research into matters of war and peace? Are we primarily there to write learned essays on the wisdom and virtue of our own foreign policy elites? Conversely, is it to provide lively polemics, questioning that wisdom and challenging that virtue? Or, alternatively, is it our mission to identify and advocate options other than those likely to emanate from the decisional apparatus?

Readers of the scholarly journals and books in many parts of the world could be forgiven for inferring that most of us do little more than speak either for the elites, the counter-elites, or for some third force in our respective nations. To the extent that these impressions are correct—and they seem all too correct to me—we may well be failing in our mission and derelict in our duty. Is there a different way to define the scholar's mission in the field of war and peace? Might our countrymen not expect more from us than the role of cheerleader, critic, or pundit? I suspect that there *is* a different mission, and will address it in the introductory section before turning to matters more substantive.

## THE ROLES FOR RESEARCH IN NATIONAL SECURITY POLICY

### Explanatory and Correlational Knowledge

Perhaps the dominant role is that of generating explanatory knowledge such that the dangerously high error rate in the policy process might be

This chapter originally appeared in *Studies of War and Peace*, Øyvind Østerud, ed. (Oslo: Norwegian University Press, 1986), pp. 44-59, 251-253. Copyright © 1986. Reprinted by permission of Det Norske Nobelinstitut.

reduced. As our knowledge regarding the regularities and patterns of international conflict dynamics becomes more cumulative and more integrated, we should increasingly be able to identify the key characteristics of the case at hand, classify it into the proper and more general class of historical cases to which it belongs, and indicate which behavior patterns on the part of which protagonists led to which particular outcomes, and why, given the contextual conditions that characterize that class of cases. This is, of course, a tall order, and one that we are unlikely to satisfy until our research becomes far more systematic, theoretically coherent, and methodologically reproducible.

This is not, however, the only contribution that we might make in our efforts to reduce the menacingly high frequency with which governments make incorrect predictions as to the consequences of their conflict behavior. A *second* task, somewhat more modest and quite appropriate to the current stage of development in our discipline, is that of generating correlational-predictive knowledge resting on empirical evidence. To generate predictions in which we can have high confidence, resting on a solid mix of both explanatory and correlational knowledge, may still be some years into the future. But to generate more limited knowledge which can be used not only for making contingent forecasts, but for debunking the folk wisdom of the moment and indicating that certain propositions are *not* historically accurate, or are accurate only for an earlier epoch, a different region of the world, or another class of cases, can be quite helpful.[1] Foreign policy elites and their apologists are very fond of invoking the "lessons of history" but it will require a great deal of assistance from the research community before they begin to draw the correct lessons with greater frequency. As May reminds us, most policy-makers "use history badly. When resorting to an analogy they tend to seize upon the first that comes to mind. They do not search more widely. Nor do they pause to analyze the case, test its fitness, or even ask in what ways it might be misleading."[2]

A few illustrations should suffice. First, there has been this tendency to ransack the historical record or personal memory in search of the self-serving analogy. One of the more egregious cases was that of the U.S. foreign minister, Dean Rusk, who argued that the situation facing the democratic powers in Indochina twenty years ago was highly similar to that which faced us at the time of the Munich crisis. Nor was he effectively challenged as to the class of cases to which it belonged, the distinguishing characteristics of that class of cases, the other cases in that class, and the extent to which the alleged policy consequences obtained in that population of cases. The same may be said of Anthony Eden's equation of the Suez crisis of 1956 with Munich, leading to equally unfortunate results. Then there is the recurrent phenomenon to which Ray alludes, in which successive generations of policy-makers learn the "opposite mistake" lesson.[3] Persuaded, for example, that the First World War was virtually guaranteed by the ubiquitous defense pact commitments in the European system (88 percent of the major powers were so committed from 1903 to 1914), statesmen consciously avoided them during most of the inter-war period (with none at all until 1935), and then persuaded that it was the *absence* of such pacts that brought us the Second World War, the post-war generation turned to allliance making with a vengeance, such that all major powers were in one or more defense pacts by 1950.[4]

## Conceptual Precision and Operational Indicators

Yet a third role for the research community is that of demanding, encouraging, and providing conceptual precision. While obvious to the point of embarrassment, it nevertheless seems necessary to not only emphasize the importance of such precision but to note its relatively infrequent appearance. Whether describing the putative priorities of one's own or another nation, comparing their capabilities, characterizing systemic conditions or trends, or classifying the behavior of a given regime, there is considerable room for improvement.

The researcher in this field can, of course, do more than call attention to lapses in precision and suggest more accurate verbal labeling. He or she can also devise, test, and apply operational indicators of many of the concepts used in international intercourse.[5] For example, there are several extant indicators in the literature by which we can more precisely measure the polarity, alliance aggregation, capability concentration, or structural clarity, of the international system or its regional subsystems.[6] Similarly, we can distinguish among—and then enumerate the frequency of—militarized disputes, civil wars, inter-state wars, etc., after which we can describe such events in terms of their magnitude, severity, intensity, and so forth.[7] Other indicators that come to mind are political integration, economic interdependence, international tension, and inter-state behavior patterns.[8] These efforts at the construction of indicators that can validly capture and reliably measure some of our more widely-used concepts are, then, not only essential to the development of a body of cumulative evidence, but to greater clarity and lower error rates in the description and prediction of international phenomena.

## Broadened Horizons in Time and Space

Then there is a role for the research community that is as much an ethical as it is a scientific one. Reference is to the need for a broader and longer perspective on the nations' foreign policies. It is all too natural that political elites will tend towards a relatively short-run outlook, giving much greater emphasis to the time horizon that more or less coincides with their expected tenure in office, and less to the consequences that may unfold later on. "Not on *my* watch" is often the focus, and scholars could be helpful by identifying and making more salient the middle- and long-run implications of policy, even when the forecasts rest on a less than solid scientific foundation.

Equally natural is the tendency toward geographical myopia, cultural chauvinism, and xenophobic interpretations of world affairs. Even when foreign and defense ministries are partially isolated from domestic politics, those who shape the larger policy orientation are preoccupied with the need for support from a variety of interest groups, regions, professions, and social strata, and thus give close attention to how a policy will sit with the army and "how it will play" in Marseilles, Manchester, and Middletown. While recognizing the fact that elites must operate in both the domestic and the global contexts, researchers can remind us that the keys to success in these two settings are often incompatible, and that "bashing" another government will not only cause difficulties with those foreigners but will also reinforce exactly those domestic tendencies that set such devastating constraints on foreign policy rationality the next time around. By reminding the elites, the counter-elites, and the opinion-makers that, to the citizens of each nation all the others are foreigners, and that their perceptions and priorities may well be different than ours, the scholar might play yet another constructive role.

## DATA-BASED RESEARCH FOR POLICY PURPOSES

Needless to say, several of the intellectual tasks outlined in the previous section need not be assigned to the research community alone; several of them might be well taken on or shared by a variety of world affairs specialists. But there is one task that can only be assumed by scholarly researchers, and unfortunately, only a small fraction of that small community. While scholars from a range of methodological orientations can play (and already have played) a valuable ancillary role, the bulk of this task must fall to that lamentably limited sub-set of researchers who work in the explicitly scientific mode. Without the more traditional scholars, our conceptual repertoire would be less rich, our mastery of historical detail less complete, and our range of explanatory hypotheses far less adequate. Having been trained in that tradition long before the scientific orientation resurfaced in the world politics field—and I say resurfaced in deference to the monumental pioneering efforts of Bloch, Richardson, Sorokin, and Wright—I take second place to no one in my appreciation of the value of traditional scholarship.[9] But honesty requires me to distinguish between the necessary and the sufficient. As Deutsch and others have reminded us, without concepts we cannot recognize patterns and organize facts, and without the historical facts we cannot even begin to search for regularities and explanations.[10] But as necessary as these activities may be, they are not and never will be sufficient if we aim to describe, predict, and explain with an adequate degree of competence.

All too many years ago, several of us began to exchange views on the relative merits of the "classical" and the "behavioral" orientations, and in the years since have merely agreed to disagree.[11] Were we students of art history or comparative literature, or even of molecular biology or astrophysics, it would be quite seemly for advocates of different epistemologies to carry on a genteel academic debate, full of tolerance and good humor. Not very much is really at stake, and whether a certain pigment came to Verona from the Moors or the Persians, or whether Tolstoy or Dostoyevskii best captures the Russian culture, or even whether DNA really contains the essence of the genetic code, or whether the "big bang" model best explains the origins of our universe is not central to the survival of the human race. These are exciting, important, and engaging controversies, and it would be satisfying to arrive at answers. But if it takes another decade or another century to do so is of minor consequence to most of the inhabitants of the global village.

On the other hand, it matters greatly whether major powers typically back down or escalate under certain classes of threat, or whether negotiations are more likely to succeed when the agenda is a broad or a narrow one. More specifically, it matters greatly that we—those of us who make or shape policy—*know* which of these pairs of hunches is more correct; it is not merely a matter of academic interest, individual hunch, or idle curiosity. For example, American national security elites believe that the way to deal with confrontations vis-à-vis their major rival is—time after time—to stand firm, hang tough, and pursue escalation dominance while providing the Soviets with a face-saving capitulation, when the evidence is that this strategy only works—and not as well as believed—for the first two or three confrontations.[12] Acting on this ill-founded proposition, we could lay waste to most of the Northern Hemisphere in less than a day.

In other words, strategies of world politics are so pregnant with real consequence that we just cannot afford to continue treating such questions as "matters of opinion." To use a crude analogy, if a scuba diver subscribes to—and acts upon—the belief that a high calcium diet permits him to ascend at more than the prescribed number of meters per minute, he will die or spend the rest of his life as a vegetable. Or if, to go further back in history, a surgeon believes that 200 leeches will cure a certain infection, he will kill a good many patients, or if (to take a recent example), an engineer believes that 5/32" steel plates will hold the girders of a bridge together, dozens of motorists will die in disconfirming his belief. To put it bluntly, it is time for us to get serious, turn professional, and begin to treat matters of war and peace as if human survival—rather than mere academic reputation—is at stake.

Having argued, perhaps too energetically, for "the importance of being scientific," let me reiterate the need to be modest about our accomplishments to date. Given the complexity of the problem, the multiplicity of rival models, the paucity of the data base, and the difficulty of validly measuring our concepts—not to mention the limited number of scientifically educated scholars and the inadequate resources that go to this small band—it comes as no surprise that nothing worthy of the name has yet emerged in the way of a compelling theory of war. Space limitations preclude any effort here to describe, compare, or evaluate some of the contenders (and pretenders), but one can, in my judgment, indicate certain of the characteristics of what that theory will most probably look like.

First, its central variables will almost certainly be those already used by the many scholars and practitioners who work, explicitly or otherwise, with one or another version of the *realpolitik* model. Over-stated, our theory will revolve around capabilities, commitments, and contiguities, and the ways in which these three sets of phenomena both drive and constrain those who act—and have acted since the Napoleonic Wars—on behalf of the territorial state. But, second, our theory will be far more attentive to the internal-external interface and the processes by which the external interactions of nations impinge on domestic politics, shape the internal configurations of power and beliefs, and thus help to modify and/or reinforce external behavior in relatively long cycles of policy orientation. And, third, our theory will give greater emphasis to the role of extra-rational (as distinct from ir-rational) considerations in that messy, multi-level, cross-pressured process that passes for foreign policy decision-making.[13]

Fourth, and not surprising in light of the above observations, such a theory will postulate a high degree of uniformity in the internal-external relationship, downgrading the putative importance of political-economic regime type and national culture while recognizing the role of material capabilities and the fluctuating levels of militarization and economic activity in the respective societies. Another way to express this theoretical orientation is to point out the remarkable—and alarming—similarity in the national security/foreign policy decision rules of such dissimilar societies as Russia, America, and Israel in today's world, or England and Germany at the beginning of the century. This theoretical model and the inductive and deductive premises behind it will be spelled out in greater detail in a later work.

If it is correct to say that we have no adequate theory as yet, what sorts of advances *have* we made? Let me devote the balance of this essay to an illustrative summary of two sets of empirical findings from the Correlates of War project, accompanied by a cursory overview of their implications for the policies of nations as they stagger—like the three Norwegian trolls with only one eye among them[14]—along the highways and byways of the international system, often managing to reconcile and coordinate their policies, but all too frequently getting themselves trapped into dysfunctional interaction patterns that bring them again and again to the brink of war.

## System Properties and the Incidence of War

Let me begin with a discussion of what we call the "structural clarity" model, in which it is postulated that the vertical and horizontal configurations of the international system impinge on the decisional elites in such a way as to increase or decrease their ability to predict changes and continuities in the environment in which a given rivalry occurs. On the *horizontal* dimension are those inter-nation bonds and links that affect governments' ability to predict who will line up with whom if a rivalry or conflict approaches the brink of war: alliances, diplomatic recognition, shared memberships in international organizations, trade, and geographical contiguities. On the *vertical* dimension are the indicators that reflect the capabilities of the relevant nations in the system: industrial, military, demographic, and diplomatic. Looking out on the systemic setting, these two sets of indicators should enhance or reduce the elites' capacity to predict who will be on which side in a "crunch" and with how much "clout."

At this juncture, however, we find two contradictory models. One says that war will be less likely if there is a high degree of vertical and horizontal *clarity* in the system structure, on the premise that such clarity makes it relatively easy to predict the outcome of a militarized dispute or war. As the cliché has it, the weaker coalition *dare* not fight, and the stronger side *need* not; such predictability is said to preclude the need to go to, or over, the brink of war since the outcome is almost foreordained. There is also a counter-hypothesis, equally plausible. This is that war will be less likely under conditions of *ambiguity*, inasmuch as elites tend to be more cautious and prudent when it is difficult to predict the commitment-capability lineup. Unsure of the configuration, they will be reluctant to press the adversary for concessions and will be more amenable to compromise.

Faced with these incompatible models—each finding considerable support in the classical literature—of the consequences of structural clarity, it seemed worthwhile to construct the relevant indicators, generate the appropriate data sets, and then go on to examine the resulting evidence. Given the modest tone in my evaluation of our research findings to date, one need not be astonished to hear that the results were far from complete or consistent. As in any scientific enterprise during its very early stages, results will initially be inconsistent and inconclusive; this does not justify a sense of failure, but rather a realization that much remains to be done.

Returning to the matter at hand, what *did* turn up? We found that neither model was successful in post-dicting the incidence of war for the century and a half from 1816 to 1965, and this led us in turn to see whether one or the other model offered a strong fit to the historical data for one or more of the familiar epochs during the full period. Interestingly enough, the conventional inter-century division did produce the best fit, but with divergent results. That is, for the current century, war was consistently less frequent and/or less severe following periods of *high* structural clarity, but for the nineteenth century, *low* levels of clarity (i.e., high ambiguity) led to a diminished incidence of war.[15]

While we have yet to follow up these anomalies in a systematic way, despite the excellent suggestions of Zinnes and others, several other studies tend to point in the same direction.[16] For example, one might look at a more limited aspect of structural clarity such as the extent to which military and industrial capabilities are highly concentrated in the hands of one or two of the major powers or more equally distributed among all of them. Interpreting high concentration as one indicator of structural clarity, we found even stronger confirmation of the inter-century difference. That is, for the nineteenth century, fluctuations in the concentration indicators alone accounted for as much as 73 percent of the variance in war, with low concentration scores making for less war, whereas the relationship was a negative one in the twentieth century. Not only did *high* concentration make for less war in this epoch, but less clearly so, with no more than 46 percent of the variance attributable to these systemic properties, suggesting that the *realpolitik* variables are, in general, less dominant in recent decades than during the earlier ones.[17]

## National Attributes, Behavior, and the Incidence of War

Moving abruptly from a couple of studies designed to tell us what sorts of configurations in the *system* tend to make war more probable, and thus prudence in the conduct of disputes more crucial, let me turn briefly to some tentatively ascertained effects of *national* attributes and behavior on the incidence of militarized disputes and war. While most major wars tend to settle certain structural ambiguities and to produce a fairly clear vertical hierarchy among the major powers, this pattern of status consistency rarely endures. As the nations at the top begin to decline (objectively and subjectively) on various capabilities or influence dimensions, they typically try to correct that decline by looking to their alliances and by increasing their military allocation ratios. The trouble with this recurrent strategy is that it tends to make them more likely to get into militarized disputes. Our data show unambiguous positive relationships between military capabilities and dispute-proneness for the major powers since 1815; 17 percent of the nation-years with high military expenditures and personnel were followed by militarized disputes, as opposed to only 10 percent for the medium scorers and 7 percent for those in the lowest grouping.[18]

Not quite as compelling, but equally suggestive, is the effect (statistically speaking) of the military allocation ratio, calculated by dividing each major power's percentage share of the subsystem's combined industrial capabilities each year into its share of the military expenditures. Here we see that the very high nation-year allocations have as low a frequency of dispute involvement as the very low ones (6 percent), whereas the medium range ratios are five times more likely (31 percent) to be followed by involvement in a militarized dispute. We have not yet examined the effect of the *rate* of increase or decrease, but one plausible inference from the results is that the most dispute-prone phase occurs as major powers gain momentum in their efforts to put larger and larger shares of their resources into preparedness programs. Perhaps it is in this phase that they are allocating too little to deter but more than enough to provoke their rivals.

But this propensity to become *involved* in militarized disputes is only part of this menacing scenario. Our next set of findings is considerably more dramatic and points to the sort of misreading of the lessons of history that May warns against.[19] Shifting from the propensity to become embroiled in militarized disputes to that of being able to "prevail" and walk away with more gains than losses while avoiding war, we find that the major power whose military expenditures are *lower* than the protagonist's prevail in 39 percent of the disputes, while the higher prevails only 21 percent of the time; in terms of military personnel, the figures are 39 percent and

27 percent. What helps to accentuate these figures is that they are virtually reversed when *industrial* capabilities are examined. Here we find that the stronger power prevails 39 percent of the time as opposed to only 20 percent for the weaker, using iron and steel production as the indicator, and nearly identical figures of 29 percent and 19 percent emerge when industrial energy consumption is the indicator of industrial strength.

If this is not enough to make us look again at the conventional wisdom, let us turn now from capabilities to allocation ratios. Once again the relationship between "strength" and success is a negative one, but even more so. Whereas the major power whose military expenditure to industrial capacity (iron/steel and energy combined) ratio is higher prevails only 18 percent of the time, the putatively under-prepared protagonist comes away successful in 36 percent of the militarized disputes since 1816.[20]

While there is no reproducible evidence to date, one plausible interpretation of those findings might be drawn from the works of Schumpeter and Lasswell dealing with the idea of the militarized society and the garrison state.[21] As a society begins to allocate resources to the military sector above and beyond some "normal" threshold, we can expect that those who advocate and stand to gain by that allocation will indeed become slightly more numerous and influential than prior to that allocation, and as the process continues, that influence will expand.[22] Necessarily believing that the military instrument is there to be used, and that it will be effective, elites with such orientations will tend to bring their nations into militarized disputes more frequently.[23] Moreover, as this process goes forward, the tendency will not only be to escalate from mild to militarized disputes more often, but to manage them less skillfully; belief in the efficacy of the more blunt instruments of international intercourse leads to a narrowing of the diplomatic repertoire, while the more appropriate instruments tend to be neglected.

Thus, we find a self-amplifying process in which higher allocations to the military are followed by increases in the frequency of involvement in these brink-of-war disputes, additional increases to the military, further militarization of the nation's foreign policy, more failures in the management of the disputes, and yet additional resource allocation. If force, and the threat of force, was not successful, perhaps it was because there was an insufficient level; like those addicted to gambling or alcohol, one more iteration should make things turn out better next time!

The historical evidence suggests otherwise. In an earlier study, we found for the period 1816–1964 strong positive correlations (from 0.51 to 0.63) between the military capabilities of nations and their tendency to become involved in—and to initiate—war.[24] Looking only at the major powers, this same pattern holds, with the nation-years of high capabilities followed by war three times more frequently (0.035 to 0.013) than the low capabilities years. Less dramatically, but in the same direction, the high allocators among the major powers are also more war-prone than those at the low end of the military allocation scale, with comparisons of 0.018 to 0.013,

0.018 to 0.016, 0.027 to 0.013, and 0.018 to 0.010, depending on the indicators used.

Just to add to the evidence, it is worth noting that victory in war, when it comes, is indeed associated with higher military capabilities, but much more influential in determining that outcome are the industrial capabilities of the opposing sides. Military expenditure "superiority" led to victory by 57 percent to 36 percent, whereas higher steel production led to victory by 74 percent to 29 percent. But when it comes to allocation ratios, the earlier pattern obtains, with the low allocators winning their wars 70 percent of the time while the high allocators emerged triumphant in only 50 percent of their war experiences.[25]

These, then, are just a few of the data-based historical investigations from a single research team on the extent to which we can account for, if not fully explain, variations in the incidence and outcome of militarized disputes and international war. The literature is of course considerably larger, suggesting that we are at least on the way to being able to show which conditions and events have in the past, and might in the future, lead toward or away from confrontation.

## CONCLUSION

Enough has been said to suggest that the social science community may already be far from irrelevant to the policy process and the ways in which the nations navigate the murky waters between war and peace. While it remains true, in my judgment, that foreign policy elites are still likely to do better relying on intuitive judgments than on data-based research alone for making their contingent forecasts in the national security sector, a prudent mix would probably be better than either by itself.

But as already indicated, the research community has *several* roles to play and contributions to make while we move—all too haltingly—toward development of the sort of data-based and deductively tight theories from which predictions of high reliability (but not total certainty) could be expected. First, there is the simple post-dictive/pre-dictive contribution, in which we can make reasonably solid predictions, but only the most tentative explanation as to *why* a given sequence of events in a given type of context culminates in a certain outcome with great regularity. Hence the interim importance of early warning indicators.[26]

Then there is the ability to move toward increasing verbal and quantitative precision in our descriptions of events and conditions that affect outcomes and determine destinies, and considerable progress has already been registered. And, third, because of our familiarity with a long historical span, a wide geographical area, a complex variety of cases, and an awareness of the findings of related disciplines, we should be able to help the decisional elites see their problems in a more complete context: less parochial, self-righteous, and short-sighted.

All of these could be—and to a very modest extent, already have been— of considerable help in reducing the error rate in the international security field. Without denying for a moment the significance of all those other factors—a badly organized international system, a weak sense of global ethics, centuries of accumulated bad habits, the destabilizing effects of technological innovation, the unsettling impact of non-state groups, the incompatibility of internal and external incentives, and of course, the genuine clash of security interests—ignorance must nevertheless be recognized as a critical variable in the onset and escalation of disputes and wars. Rigorous social science research can help to ameliorate the effects of that ignorance.[27]

But even if the members of the scientific community were to increase their number by ten-fold, their creativity by twenty-fold, and their resources by a hundred-fold, the policy impact could remain marginal. Those who make, shape, modify, evaluate, and execute policy in national agencies, legislatures, international organizations and secretariats, private institutions, and the media, may have a great many conflicting interests and incompatible priorities. Yet, in light of the current weapons technology, they do have one strong interest in common: reducing the frequency of civil or international war. Even the most Clausewitzean bureaucrats in the most revisionist of nations must recognize that armed conflict at that level of violence is ultimately disadvantageous to their interests and far from the most functional of outcomes for their nations. And if, as this analysis suggests, war is more often than not a consequence of faulty diagnosis and erroneous prediction, the practitioner should also have a preference for greater rigor in the analysis of international politics.

Thus, the practitioner must also become more sophisticated in both the substantive and methodological sense. To make use of research results, the practitioner needs to be equipped to identify, comprehend, and evaluate the quality and relevance of those results, yet few of them are so equipped to date. Whereas medical and legal practitioners in most societies receive three or four years of professional training after university, foreign policy and national security specialists rarely do. And when such post-graduate training *is* utilized, it is far less rigorous than it needs to be, looking all too similar to that offered to teachers, journalists, or social workers.

Post-graduate preparation of high quality is, of course, not enough; intellectual preparation needs to begin at the undergraduate level, or better still, in secondary school. The more adequately prepared the advanced student is, the more rigorous and sophisticated the later training can be, and if, as at present in the West (and elsewhere, one suspects), much of the post-graduate program is devoted to "remedial" work in logic, philosophy of science, statistics, and measurement, there is less opportunity for the student to move on to more challenging work in which substance and method are brought together.

Another obstacle here is the questionable notion that since the potential world affairs specialist will not be expected to *conduct* scientific research, there is no need for that to be included in the curriculum. Whether the premise is correct or not, it strikes me as irrelevant. If the practitioner is to read, comprehend, and apply scientific research findings, he/she must know how it is, and should be, done; there are all too many examples of decision-makers looking at incompetent studies that rest on inappropriate analyses of invalid indicators, and then making destructively inept policy judgments (such as in the U.S. Department of Defense during the Vietnam War). And as the unhappy practice of contract research by "beltway bandits" for federal agencies in America (and perhaps elsewhere) continues, we can expect more examples of counter-productive policy decisions emanating from inadequate understanding of research results.

Finally, even if both the scholarly community and the policy elites do begin to move toward the generation and application of first-rate research, a serious problem would still remain. That is, the journalists who report and interpret the news, as well as the citizens who ultimately acquiesce in or endorse certain policy decisions (and the arguments in support of them) can continue to do great mischief. Hence the above suggestion that a systematic and scientific approach to matters of public policy needs to begin in the undergraduate university curriculum, if not earlier.

In sum, the sort of research—and teaching, and consulting—that is reflected in the Correlates of War project and others like it needs to be more carefully examined, considered, and perhaps emulated. To reiterate, there is more involved than academic curiosity or the desirability of scholarly tolerance and open-mindedness. The physical and biological sciences no longer operate on the assumption that one person's opinion is as good as another's; there are procedural standards and there are stringent criteria for the evaluation of evidence. And given how much more is at stake in the area of international politics, continued acquiescence in pre-scientific analysis and shifting intellectual fashions may well qualify as the ultimate in war crimes, not only because of the destruction it may visit on humanity, but also because it would take so little to correct our ways!

CHAPTER NINETEEN

■

# The Responsibilities of Competence in the Global Village

MUCH IS AT STAKE, OUR TALENTS are many, yet so little has been done. Worse yet, so little has been attempted. World affairs specialists in most countries lead a rather privileged existence, largely insulated from danger, oppression, poverty and boredom. To be sure, most of us earn these privileges, working diligently and even creatively at our tasks as teachers, researchers, and writers, but perhaps we define these tasks too narrowly.

Many of us, too often, are fine organization men and women, but is our constituency that limited? Is our responsibility that circumscribed? At the risk of furthering my reputation as a modern Don Quixote, let me suggest that those are *not* windmills out there. They are, rather, towers of indifference, ignorance and incompetence, and if we have not helped to erect them, we have done much too little to bring them down. Until we do, the global village remains in great jeopardy. Since most of us believe that our efforts—whether in the academic, governmental, journalistic or commercial vineyards—do and should have some impact on the human condition beyond our immediate circles, I address here the question of what these efforts might be. But it would be naive to assume that we also share identical priorities, loyalties and policy preferences; thus, in offering one man's reflections on our proper professional roles, a frank statement of his normative-theoretical point of departure is in order.

I begin with the premise that beyond our individual, professional and national self-interests we do need to give higher priority to the welfare of the entire human race, including those global citizens yet to be born. This requires that we demand higher standards of competence and compassion from our governments, parties and associations before lending our support. This also requires us to attend more carefully to the legitimate interests

This chapter originally appeared in the *International Studies Quarterly*, vol. 29 (1985), pp. 245-262. Copyright © 1985 International Studies Association. Reprinted by permission.

of other groupings, and perhaps most important, to recognize that "the national interest" may often be contrary to the very real and human interests of those diverse groups that make up our own society. Another normative premise needs to be made clear: too many of us, eager to be of service to the state—especially service that is well rewarded—are willing to suppress our own professional judgments so as to avoid being denied that privilege. Sometimes, we even go so far as to acquiesce in the dubious proposition that our decisionmakers know more than we. *None* of us knows enough about the dynamics of world affairs, but surely those of us who devote our professional lives to the subject need not be too quick to defer to provincial political elites recently come to their nation's capital. Nor need we be unduly impressed with the functionary who assures us that if *we* had access to *his* top-secret information, we would readily endorse his views; those of us who have worked with classified information in most governments know that it rarely changes the overall picture and often serves purposes other than those that are claimed.

Before leaving this topic, a less conventional but equally important assumption needs to be articulated: many propositions about world affairs that we regard as purely normative—and thus beyond the reach of logic or evidence—can be translated to some extent into *empirical* propositions. For example, some of us may believe that it is immoral for a government to lie or mislead another in international negotiations, or to threaten force against their civilian population, while others would assert that the national interest represents a higher morality, demanding leaders who have the stomach to lie or murder. While I know of no systematic research on the empirical efficacy of dishonesty to date, one could imagine a study designed to put the proposition to the test. Similarly, the efficacy of the threat of force (without discriminating between civilian populations and other targets) has already received some scholarly attention, and the research problem is far from insoluble, unless of course we accept the foolish fatalism of the post-behavioural syndrome which too often eschews systematic empirical research entirely.

## THE PRIORITIES: POVERTY AND WAR

It is one thing to assert that knowledge can make a difference, and that our responsibilities extend beyond ourselves and our own nations, and quite another to identify those responsibilities and then go on to suggest some sort of priority among them. Let me attempt that, but in a very restricted fashion. As I see it, the human race has an extraordinary array of problems, some physical and some emotional, some more menacing than others, some closer in time, and many of them falling quite unequally upon different regions, races, genders, classes and political groupings. In the short run, two of these problems seem overwhelmingly critical, and though I focus on them here, this is not to suggest that all others are insignificant.

Simply put, these are the global security problem and the global development problem, and merely by so labelling them we emphasize their interdependence. We must put an end to war and we must put an end to poverty and starvation. Some of us believe that we cannot solve the development problem until we solve the security problem, and vice versa, and all too often one's view depends on which of them is most immediately threatening. Those who experience (or, more precisely, speak for those who experience) the tragedies of poverty, whether in the Third and Fourth Worlds or in the First and Second Worlds, tend to give highest priority to the development problem. And those for whom an adequately high material quality of life is no longer a concern tend to give higher priority to the security problem. As the immediate threat of death or disablement from grinding poverty begins to recede, one can begin to attend to the threat of death and disablement from war, civil or international.

But there may be more to the question than the immediate situation of the observer. Many analysts accept the proposition that poverty is a major "cause" of domestic and international conflict, much of which ultimately escalates to war. And while one can make a plausible argument as to why this *should* be so, the empirical evidence reveals a *negative* correlation between the poverty levels of nations (aggregated as well as per capita) and their war-proneness. Even if we look at civil war, there tends to be a curvilinear relationship, with very few cases occurring in the extremely poor or extremely rich societies; the very poor are too weak, physically as well as politically, nor do they have the incentive for violent change that typically requires both the hope based upon a small taste of economic progress and the aggressiveness based on a frustration of that hope. The rich, of course, have even fewer incentives.

If poverty seldom leads to war, it follows that its elimination or amelioration will have little effect on the incidence of war: we may want to give development the highest priority for normative or ideological reasons, but not because we expect it to reduce the incidence of international war.

Recognizing the possibility that, as a white male, middle class and middle aged, well-fed and healthy, in a relatively prosperous society, my concern for the poor and starving might not be as strong as it should be, let me nevertheless summarize the counter-arguments. A useful point of departure is an itemization of the ways in which the search for security among the industrial powers inhibits and corrupts the search for development among the pre-industrial societies. The most obvious, of course, is the deflection into military preparedness of funds that might have gone into development assistance programs. While there is no assurance that the annual world military spending (nearly 600 billion dollars in the 1980s) that could meet the essential food and health needs of the developing countries for two decades would indeed go to that purpose, it is clear that the funds that do go to the military cannot go to development.

But military preparedness programs mobilize more than money; they mobilize the minds of their citizens in a way that is destructive both at home and abroad. As the financial resources of a major power go to the military sector over a long period of time, two important consequences develop. One is the incremental shift in political power away from those who might be fairly cosmopolitan, farsighted and humane, and toward those who seldom give high priority to such considerations. The policies of that nation become increasingly militarized, and with that shift, the resources that *could* have gone to economic development assistance go instead to military buildups, arms transfers and other military assistance programs.

The second consequence of this mobilization is an ethical and emotional one. Governments, however centralized, cannot milk the public economically, intrude into their political freedom, conscript their sons, and poison their environment with weapon tests, unless there is a sufficiently widespread and strong belief among mass publics and elites in the legitimacy of these depredations. That requires a propaganda and socialization program of some magnitude and duration, and the more successful that program, the more xenophobic the public and the opinionmakers will become; with these cognitive and affective trends, we should not be surprised to find two attendant shifts. One is the obvious shift toward greater belief in the importance of military force as an instrument of national security; for even in the most autocratic of societies, cognitive dissonance is uncommon. The other is an increasing indifference to those whom Franz Fanon called "the wretched of the earth." Persuaded of the threat to the nation from enemies at home and abroad, and acquiescing in the threat or use of mass murder as a legitimate instrument of national survival, there is little room for concern, altruism or generosity, not to mention far-sighted self-interest. (For the present, I am ignoring the effects of military preparedness programs on the domestic scene and on the moral integration of the citizens and their society.)

Another dysfunctional linkage between the major power rivalry and economic development is found in their struggle for influence in the underdeveloped regions, and while less obvious, the effects of these rivalries may be equally pernicious. First, there is the eagerness to put and to keep friendly regimes in power, and it seems that—along with economic and military aid—no ploy is beneath these powers: from bribery and subversion to assassination and insurgency, all are used by the leaders of the "free world" and the "socialist camp" to depose less-than-friendly regimes. And to maintain these staunch supporters of democracy and/or socialism, no amount of terrorism, torture, repression and intimidation seems excessive. Without suggesting that these instruments of political influence are entirely the creation of Washington and Moscow, Paris and Prague, the initiative, the training and the resources typically originate north of the equator. That it is easy to find indigenous elites and counter-elites to carry out these unsavory deeds should come as no surprise. How many political leaders and their opponents in the Third World have come to power or to opposition without outside support? And even when the struggle for power in the developing countries is not violent, brutal and evil, it is heavily burdened by East-West rivalry. This is not to say that essentially domestic issues are of no consequence in Third World local politics, but that the superpower rivalry is so pervasive that the money, the men and the methods can usually be traced back to the Soviets, the Americans or their allies.

This corruption of the political process in the southern hemisphere's underdeveloped nations has, in turn, a disquieting effect on their economies and their foreign policies. Given the ubiquitousness of the fluctuating standoff between East-leaning and West-leaning regimes in most regions, the high incidence of rivalry, conflict and war in these areas is virtually foreordained; all too often, these are proxy wars between regimes and armies that are financed, trained, equipped and sometimes even led by the superpower rivals. Such externally stimulated conflict not only leads to death, devastation, brutality, flight and famine, and to a steady drain on the financial resources of the regional economies, but to the incurring of high opportunity costs as well. External funds that might have gone to development go to the military. Occasional surpluses in the balance of payments that might have gone to investment in agricultural infrastructure often go to pay for training military personnel in overseas war colleges and military academies. In addition, military expenditures typically (not always) inhibit economic growth, generate inflationary pressures, enhance the rate of debt accumulation, exercise an upward push on interest rates, mortgage the nation's economic future, and encourage more attention to short-run considerations.

Then there is the competition for human resources; Third World economies need a fairly large cadre of trained public administrators, foreign ministry personnel, commercial managers, industrial technicians, mining engineers, harbor pilots, agricultural specialists and health-care professionals, to name but a few. But if the educational facilities are limited, offshore training expensive, and armed forces' salaries (not to mention related personal and political perquisites) high, it should come as no surprise that there will be insufficient talent for development purposes. Further, because the resources are greater, the recruiting incentives less idealistic, and the role of the military often more of a domestic constabulary than a national defense force, one typically finds rather higher levels of corruption in the military than in other sectors of developing societies, and the larger the military the more pervasive its corrupting influence.

Closely related is the problem of negotiating equitable terms of trade or reasonable roles for their nationals in the multinational corporations resident in their countries. Addiction to military 'preparedness' and dependence on the supplier are hardly conducive to a strong bargaining stance.

There are other ways, more political, in which the militarization of these nations, through cold-war incentives and blandishments, turns out to hamper development. One is the increasing boldness of major power interference in the domestic political process: those who pay the piper *expect* to call the tune, and in order to ingratiate themselves with donor nations, local parties and factions are inclined to put domestic issues into the terms of their patrons to the north, often distorting and submerging bona fide issues in a sea of ideological rhetoric. One extension of this pressure, of course, is in the foreign policy realm. Rather than address the very real security and economic interests of their nations vis-à-vis regional neighbors, eagerness for funds and equipment along with dependence on the donors for spare parts and technical support, all too frequently makes these regimes inclined to do their master's bidding.

This arraignment should suffice. As long as the East-West rivalry continues, the possibilities for highly symbiotic relations between local elites and one or another of the major powers are extraordinary. And to the extent that these possibilities are exploited, misallocation of material, demographic and psychic resources will be endemic, and the processes of economic, social and political development will be stultified. Short-run considerations will overwhelm those of long-run health and welfare.

## THE CALCULUS OF MILITARY PREPAREDNESS

In the preceding section, I outlined a number of ways in which the Soviet-American rivalry intrudes upon the nations of the Third and Fourth Worlds, strongly suggesting that a dramatic amelioration and reorientation of that contest must occur before any appreciable progress can be achieved on the development front. It follows, of course, that those of us who are committed to the independence and evolution of the nonindustrial societies have a powerful incentive to do what we can to slow and reverse the superpowers' arms race, and to direct the associated competition into less costly and destructive channels.

Let me shift now to the incentives that should be, but seldom are, at work in the nations more directly caught up in an armed rivalry. What are some of the calculations that might lead those of us in the two dominant coalitions to take a harder look at the policies of our governments? To what extent are world affairs specialists, East and West, contributing to or acquiescing in policies that make little sense in either ethical or pragmatic terms?

To begin, if nuclear deterrence should fail, we in the northern hemisphere are even more vulnerable to mass destruction, widespread devastation and horrible death than our neighbors to the south. One can understand why people in Third and Fourth World countries might underestimate the damage they might sustain in the event of nuclear war, but for those in the First and Second Worlds such denial is literally a death-defying act. Before identifying the many costs, economic and otherwise, of military preparedness, let us try to look objectively at the alleged benefits.

First, preparedness is supposed to provide the basic ingredient of national security, which can be thought of as a simple two-dimensional concern.

Primarily, it is to *minimize* the extent to which the rival can control, dominate or influence one's own external behavior or domestic processes. Secondarily, it is to *maximize* one's own ability to influence and shape the external behavior and domestic processes of the other. Power, we might say, is the ability to both exercise and to inhibit influence. The extreme case, to which the elites refer obliquely and infrequently, would see American troops parading through Red Square or Soviet forces marching up Pennsylvania Avenue. These scenarios are so outlandish as to be relegated to the fantasy life of the deranged and the misinformed. More serious, for some, is a disarming strategic assault so devastating that no nuclear retaliation is possible. Given the technologies of delivery and destruction today and in the decades ahead, this must be classed as an equally improbable event, even though the Dr. Strangeloves on each side may dream and work in terms of such an obsession.

Somewhat more realistic, and thus more objectively dangerous, is the scenario in which one of the rivals is able to launch a nearly disarming first strike and, with an extraordinarily massive mix of active and passive defenses, keep the retaliatory damage low enough to be politically "acceptable." This obscene hope or psychotic fear must rest on a nearly inconceivable combination of worst-case and best-case analysis, defying the calculations of virtually all who are not either at the public trough or well nourished on the more exotic hallucinogens. Of course, the possible credibility of such a scenario is what drives the American and, to a lesser extent, the Soviet investment in one or another version of the "strategic defense initiative." Staying with the strategic problem and the more exotic weapons, the feasibility—and thus the possibility—of a bacteriological, chemical or radiological attack on the U.S.A., USSR or their European allies cannot be quite as readily dismissed. Nevertheless, the inadequacy of any known or projected delivery systems, the near-certainty of retaliation in one form or another, and the limitations of potential defensive measures all suggest strategic use of BCR weapons as sufficiently suicidal to rule out as a viable threat to major-power security.

Remaining for the moment with the threats to security via intentional attack, we next examine the non-strategic scenarios, meaning primarily the use of nuclear, exotic or conventional forces within the European theatre. Here, of course, the Soviet-American symmetry breaks down because the USSR is for the relevant future much more geographically vulnerable than is North America. On the other hand, the NATO allies, in whose security the Americans have invested heavily in the military, political and psychological senses, are about as vulnerable as the Soviet Union or its Warsaw Pact allies. But the first use of nuclear or BCR weapons on the Continent in either direction is so pregnant with sure retaliation, regionally and intercontinentally, as to be hardly more credible than the original strategic scenarios.

We come, then, to the purely conventional (or more accurately subexotic) weapons case, in which tactical air, massed armor and mobile infantry could conceivably be employed in Europe. But despite the numerical superiorities of the Soviet bloc in some categories and the NATO forces' superiority in others, military analysts are nearly unanimous in agreeing that neither side has anything approaching a preponderance sufficient for an offensive assault against the other. And if extra-conventional forces are introduced to provide the necessary preponderance, we are back to the stalemate described earlier. In other words, given the character of today's military technology, combined with the force levels on both sides, the likelihood of a calculated attack in either direction must be considered extremely low.

This brings us, then, to the oft-heard argument that it is not so much the *objective* threat to basic security on each side, but the *perceived* threat. Of course, in a sane world there would be a fairly close relationship between the objective and the subjective threats, but if we lived in a sane world, no one would have permitted the arms race to proceed to such mutually destructive and destabilizing heights. In the insane and obscene world of military analysts and national security elites, this discrepancy need not surprise us. Those who seek to generate perceptions of missile and bomber gaps, asymmetric windows of vulnerability, and impending enemy breakthroughs in weapons technology, for purposes of budgetary and political mobilization or career advancement, have little difficulty doing so. A press corps that is ill-trained and easily seduced—if not indistinguishable from those who shape, make, and enunciate security policy—is usually all too ready to provide such a service.

Once the legitimacy of such misperceptions has been established, the case for military preparations against them can more easily be made. Sometimes the perceived threat is a current one, as when Americans were being told that their nation's land-based missiles were in jeopardy via a window of vulnerability, but more typically, the alleged threat is a *projected* one. For recent examples, there is the U.S. argument that a strategic defense initiative is essential to defend against a dramatic buildup in Soviet land-based ICBM forces, or the Soviet argument that the further deployment of SS-20 or SSX-28 Euro-missiles would be necessary to "counter" the NATO deployment of Pershing II missiles.

In these and other cases that come to mind, one might wonder whether the alleged perception is not only intentionally generated, but a self-fulfilling one—in two senses—as well. The first sense is the more immediately dangerous in that it could conceivably lead the adversary to *believe* such statements of its superiority and then seek to exploit it. For decades, the Western line has emphasized a critical Warsaw Pact superiority in conventional capabilities, but fortunately, Moscow has either not accepted such an appraisal or has, at least, not sought to exploit it in an effective way. The second is more remote in time, but it is also more dangerous, as the earlier examples suggest. In the East-West arms race, the worst-case analysis, anticipating the rival's intention *and* capability to develop and deploy a given offensive or defensive weapon system, typically provides the justification for going ahead on the next available system of its own; with the exception of ABM (so far), one is hard-pressed to identify any case in which the worst case did not thus come to fruition.

To return to the basic question of genuine military threats to either superpower or its European allies, we have so far been unable to identify a single compelling example. The qualities of the weapons and, to a lesser extent, the quantities are more than adequate to deter all but the most ill-advised attack. This is not to say that the military deterrent is always sufficient, nor is it to say that it is always necessary; as already noted, misperception of capabilities or intentions or both are by no means rare in history. Similarly, there may well be less costly and more reliable instruments of national security.

This then leaves us with only two sectors in which a case might be made in today's world (or that of the past three decades) for a continuing buildup of the superpowers' military capabilities. The first, already alluded to, is that of intimidation via the brandishing of military force. But as already seen, if the threat of force is far from credible, there is little political mileage in seeking to exploit it. The second is, however, a more legitimate concern, and reference is to the so-called gray areas: regions outside North America and Europe. Most salient is North Asia, where both China and Japan are relatively vulnerable to the USSR. As to China, its conventional forces are probably sufficient to deter a non-nuclear threat, and even its limited "force de frappe" should be adequate to head off a nuclear threat. The Japanese case, along with that of Taiwan, the Philippines, and the Koreas, could be more troublesome, but local capabilities and superpower commitments should probably suffice to keep the peace, at least in the short run.

As we cross the equator, however, the military configurations are considerably more ambiguous. But the relative tenuousness of that state of affairs should raise two important questions for the U.S. and the USSR. One concerns the centrality of these regions to the vital security interests of the superpowers, and the evidence is that both sides are, wisely, increasingly inclined to recognize both the marginality of their interests in the Third and Fourth Worlds (especially if the Western hemisphere is excluded) and the volatility of their dominance at a given time and place. The ability to keep commitments limited in these regions would, on balance, serve to enhance the security of both. The other question, closely related, is whether military force, be it deployed rapidly or slowly, is indeed the appropriate instrument of superpower security or influence in the Third and Fourth Worlds. By converting their struggle for influence in these regions into a non-military one, with heavier reliance on diplomatic, psychological, economic and other political instruments, the U.S. and the USSR could not only enhance their own security, but that of the peoples over whom they now seek to establish some degree of hegemony.

Having gone into considerable detail regarding the possible relevance of high levels of military preparedness to the security of the superpowers, and concluding that the *benefits* are probably much lower than we tend to believe, let me shift briefly to the *costs*. First are the obvious economic opportunity costs: government revenues that might go to constructive activities at home or abroad are diverted instead to the creation, growth and maintenance of the military machine. To arouse the slumbering sensibilities that often accompany professional involvement, let me be more specific as to where those funds could be used: prenatal care of a welfare mother, adequately educated teachers in adequate school buildings, public transport that does not foul the human nest, programs in health maintenance, including sex, drug and alcohol education, adequate housing for poorer families, job retraining for the potentially unemployed, enforcement of laws against exploitation, pollution and all the myriad forms of abuse that the strong impose on the weak, legal aid for those so abused, economic development programs to put an end to poverty at home and abroad and— of particular concern to our profession—funds for research and education on the correlates, causes and possible cures for war, poverty and the other indignities and deprivations that humans continue to inflict upon one another.

A second cost—less immediate and less uniform—is the weakening of the nation's economic, industrial and agricultural foundations. In most economies at most stages of development, military spending can sometimes serve as a pump-primer, but more often it tends to reduce gainful employment, inhibit sound investment, deflect innovation away from constructive activities, encourage stockpiling of "strategic materials," exacerbate protectionist tendencies, discourage sound agricultural practices, and generate inflationary pressures. To the extent that these generalizations are correct, we perpetuate all those deprivations and indignities noted above.

A third set of costs are those associated with what Lasswell called "the garrison state," in which we mobilize and misallocate not only our material resources but our moral and psychic resources as well. We even allocate resources to propaganda production, so that those who benefit from these misallocations can help persuade us to continue feeding the war machine: a classic example of the self-amplifying mechanism. We go on to acquiesce in government and party intrusion into our lives; the press, usually with adequate incentives, typically accepts and/or embraces censorship in one form or another, and the educational system becomes increasingly integrated into the national security apparatus, turning students into technically skilled but politically eviscerated adults. And, eagerly or reluctantly, these adults tolerate governmental secrecy (often more helpful in concealing incompetence than in protecting information), and security clearances (as useful in isolating the responsible non-conformist as in preserving legitimate secrets) along with mail covers, 'security risk' files, and the other appurtenances of domestic spying and informing.

A collateral cost, less obvious but no less lethal to humane existence, is in the moral degeneracy and schizophrenia that often goes with the garrison state. Citizens—even those who are trained and educated to know better—applaud or acquiesce in assertions that are empirically absurd and logically inconsistent. We learn not only to be discreet in what we say and write, lest we be thought naive, soft on enemy-ism, or actually an agent or lackey of the rival regime and its perfidious ideology, but also we give our assent to the intellectual rape of those who do dare to question. We use the climate of national security conformity to gain acceptance, to aggrandize ourselves, and to settle old scores; just as "partisan" groups under enemy occupation often justify vilification and murder on the grounds of collaboration with the enemy, citizens at all levels invoke national security to isolate, weaken or destroy those whom they fear or dislike for rather different reasons. Worse yet, we come to acquiesce in duplicity, assassination, bullying and mass murder as legitimate instruments of national security. In sum, we encourage in our children and accept in our contemporaries an erosion of morality, integrity and intellectual autonomy. It should be little wonder that our students and our children become more egocentric, hedonistic, cynical and dishonest, lose hope in their futures and trust in their societies, and cop out on drugs and alcohol.

Before leaving this itemization of the costs of preparedness for war, let me note three more immediate, politically salient and self-amplifying costs. One of these is the stifling of political creativity at home and amongst our allies. Because it is considered naive if not unpatriotic to come up with ideas that might help ameliorate the rivalry, make it less costly and dangerous, or enhance the security of both one's own and the adversary nation, we put a premium on fatalism. A standard refrain from our political elites and their all-too-pliable allies is "What else can we do? We have no choice! The arms race is imposed on us by our enemies!" Yet any effort to take our destiny out of the hands of the adversary and restore some degree of control over our national fate is often dismissed, ridiculed, and condemned.

This psychological deterioration is, quite naturally, part of a larger and more menacing process: the incremental redistribution of economic power, ideological legitimacy and political clout away from the thoughtful, competent and independent-minded people, and toward the super-patriots, the atavistic cheerleaders, the bloodthirsty, the profiteers and those who get an emotional high out of psychological mobilization and hard-nosed crisis management. This not only makes for a less humane and dignified society, but for a far less competent national security policy. When we turn power over to the primitives, we need not be astonished that we get primitive policies. The competents are replaced by the claque, and those capable of subtlety and differentiation give way to the Manicheans, dividing the world into those who are with us and those who are against us.

Second, there are the destructive and self-amplifying consequences abroad. Those who would prefer non-alignment will frequently be pushed into the camp of our rival, and those who might serve as honest brokers are insulted into indifference. Clearly, the more militarized a major power's policies become, the less goodwill and support it will get from allies and neutrals; even when the U.S. or the USSR have their way in the short run, the seeds of secession become more firmly planted.

But the real damage is to the *rival* society, and the greatest cost is in the policy behavior that one's own policies generate. The process should be self-evident, given the frequency of its occurrence over the past century or so, and given our awareness of the relationship between domestic power distribution and the main outlines of a major power's foreign policy. That is, when one of the rivals begins to increase its military preparedness, there will typically be two fairly short-run consequences. First, there will be, as noted above, a small change in the distribution of power at home toward the more hawkish elements, given the resources and legitimacy that are allocated to those elements. Second, the rival will, in fairly short order, respond in kind, if it has not already anticipated the first's buildup and begun its own. This will in turn have similar effects of a modest degree within *its* domestic power configuration, and if the reactive process between the rivals continues for several years, the domestic consequences tend to become less trivial. Before too long, most of the self-correcting mechanisms in both societies will become too frail to resist the reciprocal dynamics between and within them; in their place will appear a variety of self-amplifying social and psychological mechanisms, and a bona fide arms race has begun.

There is, of course, a third class of phenomena at work in major power rivalries that are accompanied by an arms race, and that is the appearance of an increasingly bellicose foreign policy. This bellicosity is stimulated by the lethal interaction between one side's continuing arms buildup and the hawkishness of the other's political elites; merely anticipating or countering the other's buildup is not sufficient. One must confront, challenge, counter, and deter the rival on all fronts; the alleged "lesson of Munich," learned and overlearned decades ago, remains in good odor in all too many centers today, despite its fit to a very small fraction of modern international disputes.

Let me conclude this section, then, by suggesting that the costs of military preparedness for most major powers are far higher than we often recognize, even if the preparedness program does *not* culminate in war. Many of these costs are less than obvious, and some of the bills come due long after those who incurred them have departed, leaving it to the next generation to make the payments. And when we compare these costs to the benefits that actually accrue, one must wonder at the frequency with which nations enter into this Faustian bargain. While one can readily think of several alternative strategies by which a nation's security might be preserved, ranging from a more sophisticated diplomacy, through more effective supra-national institutions, to such unilateral measures as non-violent civilian defense, our knowledge base is far too modest to tell us which strategies are most likely to be effective under a given set of circumstances. While the evidence *against* the standard strategy of military buildup (with or without alliance building) is relatively compelling, the evidence *for* the various alternatives barely exists, as the following section makes all too clear.

## WHAT WE THINK WE KNOW AND NEED TO KNOW

In concluding the previous section, I suggested that while we have a moderately solid basis for doubting the efficacy of sustained military buildup as an instrument of national security, we have considerably less evidence on the relative efficacy of *alternative* instruments or substitute strategies. This is not merely a scholarly misfortune, nor can we write it off as the inevitable by-product of a relatively new discipline. It is a bona fide failure— one among many—of our profession, with ominous human consequences. This is not to say that systematic historical and empirical research could readily show us the most adaptive paths to national security, or that governments will jump eagerly to put into practice the results of high-quality research. The path from knowledge to practice is a long one, strewn with many obstacles, cognitive, emotional, ethical, epistemological and tactical; but *without* relevant knowledge, the likelihood of adaptive national security policies in the nations of the world is menacingly close to zero.

Why should this be so? I begin with the premise that all political decisionmaking is a form of collective and incremental behavior. It involves individuals who, despite a sharing of some basic ideological tendencies and perhaps even some relatively similar experiences and social origins, nevertheless have diverse interests and often incompatible priorities. The participants, while ostensibly employed to identify, choose and carry out policies that are supposed to enhance the security of the nation and maximize the interests of the society as a whole, tend to be equally if not more concerned with the maximization of their factional, bureaucratic and individual interests.

Then there is the above-noted inadequacy in our knowledge base; the amount, quality, and relevance of our research to date is far from adequate. And even if this were not the sad case, would that knowledge be adequately understood and applied? Not if our foreign policy elites are recruited from among those who are pre-scientific or, worse yet, anti-scientific in their outlook, incapable of evaluating conflicting evidence and comparing incompatible analyses. While we would hardly seek finance ministry officials from the ranks of shopkeepers or health ministry staff from among those who write advertising copy for patent medicines, we do almost as poorly when we recruit for ministries of defense and foreign affairs. If we have yet to provide for the training of enough scientifically oriented practitioners, it should not surprise us to find so few in positions of policy influence. But that merely pushes the problem back one step; we have so few fully prepared decisionmakers because we have too few universities that provide a sufficiently rigorous education, and too few professors sufficiently prepared to properly staff our universities.

How do we break out of this vicious circle? There are several ways of going about this, but let me—to emphasize that neither the problem nor its possible solutions have gone unnoticed in the past—merely list some recommendations made to the U.S. National Academy of Sciences panel on the state of the social sciences in 1967. We might provide for: (a) traditionally trained scholars to "tool up" on their own through postdoctoral or retraining grants; (b) undergraduate and graduate students to train at those institutes and universities around the world at which the more systematic and rigorous preparation is offered; and (c) expansion of the curriculum at the more traditional schools to include more teaching in the social science mode. There are, of course, other possibilities by which to increase the competence of the teachers, researchers and practitioners (as well as journalists) in the world affairs field. When, and if, such a program were instituted—perhaps via a UN diplomatic academy—we could expect a gradual improvement in teaching and research, followed in due course by improvement in the formulation and execution of policy. With such a development, the case for going with the extra-rational considerations of self and faction—because there is no way to tell which policies would produce the best outcome for the nation as a whole—would be seriously weakened. The practitioners, their critics, and the journalists will not only have more solid knowledge available, but will also be more able to evaluate and apply that knowledge.

In principle, this may sound interesting, but precisely what do we think we already know, what do we not yet know, and what is it that we need to know? First, let us distinguish between knowledge and belief, noting that we often confuse the two; many of us *believe* certain generalizations to be empirically true, but since these beliefs vary widely from nation to nation, class to class, faction to faction, time to time, and even from page to page in the writings of the same analyst, beliefs would be better treated as hunches or hypotheses, to be examined against the relevant evidence. Second, let us recognize that even systematically generated knowledge is often tentative and far from final. In all scientific disciplines, there may be a strong consensus that a certain proposition or theoretical model is indeed correct and yet have it overturned by subsequent research. This is less true of empirical generalizations than of explanations and theories, but it does happen, and we need therefore to be somewhat tentative in accepting research findings—and, more specifically, explanatory inferences from them— as if they were eternal verities.

Third, we might want to distinguish among existential, correlational and explanatory knowledge. Students of historical cases often absorb large bodies of existential knowledge, but seldom do so in a self-aware and comparative fashion such that a set of *data* might emerge. Rather, they tend to focus on one or a few cases in a non-operational manner, generating bits of existential knowledge, rather than a coherent set of data, not to mention correlational or explanatory knowledge. Existential knowledge of a scientifically useful sort is, then, a series or string of observations produced by the same classificatory criteria, and correlational knowledge is a succinct, precise and operational statement of the extent to which two or more bodies of existential knowledge go together across some population of cases. Whereas the existence of existential and correlational knowledge is relatively objective and unambiguous, explanatory knowledge tends to be more subjective or, in the philosophy of science vernacular, intersubjective. That is, any one of us might look at a theoretical model and at the correlational knowledge and deductive reasoning that allegedly support the model, and then conclude that the goodness-of-fit between the model and the evidence is sufficiently compelling. But unless a reasonable fraction of the specialists concur, it is difficult to say that explanatory knowledge has been provided.

Having suggested some oft-unnoticed distinctions amongst types of knowledge and belief, let me return to the question of what we know, do not know, and need to know. To begin, we do not know very much about the dynamics of world affairs, and of that, little has been catalogued and codified; even less has passed into the professional culture to replace the folk beliefs and conventional wisdom that have contributed so much to the world's grief and mayhem. Just as an athletic team will be quite unsuccessful if its coaches are ignorant of the principles of the sport, mountain-climbers will fail if they do not know the laws of friction and gravity, and teachers will perform badly if unaware of the psychology of learning, foreign policy elites will have an abysmal track record if the regularities—and exceptions—of global politics are relatively unknown. A summary of what is "known" about world affairs and about international conflict will be found in recent review articles in the *Journal of Conflict Resolution* and the *Journal of Peace Research*.

Let me, then, list a series of questions, all of which seem relevant to the question of war and peace, and none of which has been examined with sufficient rigor and creativity. At the national and system levels, the following might be of interest:

1. Which behaviors create structural and cultural conditions in the system that make war more likely five or ten years later?
2. Which behaviors generate predictions and perceptions in the adversary that make intelligent crisis management more difficult ten, five, or two years later?
3. Which behaviors generate political processes in the adversary's society that strengthen the hawkish elements and weaken the more prudent factions?
4. Under which systemic or regional conditions is it essential to avoid confrontation or crisis, given that war is more likely then?
5. Given the apparent fluctuations in inter-nation tension during long rivalry, are war prevention efforts more likely to be successful during the high-tension, low-tension, upside, or downside periods? Which types of efforts are most successful at which stage? Which decisional structures are most efficacious or most dangerous at which phases of the process? Is secrecy more essential to war prevention at certain phases?
6. Under which conditions, and vis-à-vis which types of adversary, are different behaviors most destabilizing? When to use threats, promises, rewards, punishments? When to increase military preparedness, when to decrease, and when is it essential not to change?

7. If the adversary is suffering losses of influence elsewhere in the system, is it more prudent to press him hard or to ease up? Similarly, when his regime is facing dissension or strong opposition at home or in satellite nations.

8. When your relative capabilities vis-à-vis the adversary are declining in the region or globally, is it more prudent to be aggressive or conciliatory or merely passive? When increasing? When stable?

9. If one of the rivals has, and expects to continue, a steady and clear superiority in weapons technology, is it more prudent to *offer* arms control and reduction concessions, to *demand* such concessions, or to avoid negotiation on this question?

10. Are there certain optimal levels of hostility, fear, etc., that rival regimes should strive to maintain at home? Can these levels get too low? Too high? Which tension-generating and tension-reducing tactics are most effective, most reversible, etc.?

11. When formal negotiations have been agreed to, are the chances of overall agreement enhanced by a broad agenda or by a narrow one? Is it better to deal with one problem at a time?

12. During periods of rivalry, is it safer to keep certain ideological or personality types out of power? If so, which types, and how do we identify and isolate them politically?

13. During long rivalries is it safer to form countervailing alliances, coalitions, trade blocs, etc., or to perpetuate a more polycentric and/ or flexible system structure?

And at the individual and sub-national levels:

1. To what extent does the education process in most nations make for greater or lesser war-proneness? Would more knowledge of social science methods and greater epistemological sophistication reduce the error rate in decisionmaking, would the news media become more competent, and would the general public become less gullible?

2. How effective could cultural exchange, language training, and awareness of others' histories be in making a population less xenophobic and chauvinistic?

3. Is the childhood socialization of boys, in home, school, youth organizations, etc., a major contributor to war-proneness by perpetuating primitive notions of masculinity, courage and intrepidity?

4. Do regimes that differ economically and politically "produce" citizens who systematically differ in their epistemological criteria, moral preferences and priorities, and problemsolving competence?

5. To what extent do ethnic, religious and linguistic discrimination in a society increase the likelihood that the victims (and children of the victims) of such discrimination will behave in such a way as to increase their nations' war-proneness. Does discrimination lead to an

exaggerated need to demonstrate excessive patriotism or, alternatively, create a subconscious desire to see the society suffer or be destroyed?
6. Would widespread knowledge of the consequences of nuclear or conventional war affect the tendency of the public or opinionmakers to acquiesce in provocative weapon systems and military strategies?
7. Would solid research and dissemination of the results regarding economic conversion and the feasibility of phasing out military production and service help increase public support for more prudent security policies?
8. To what extent do the definition and treatment of disease, mental illness, delinquency and crime correlate with a nation's security policies and/or war-proneness?

This list could, of course, be expanded, and it certainly could be modified in several directions, but the point should be clear. While we will "never" be able to acquire, codify and apply *all* the knowledge needed, a major increase in it could certainly serve to reduce the potency of those extra-rational considerations that so badly contaminate the decision process, make practitioners and their critics more competent, and reduce the menacingly high error rates of the past century before it is too late.

This should not, however, be taken as a call for nothing more than barefooted empiricism and an endorsement of the principle that well-founded empirical generalizations are easily aggregated into a powerful explanatory theory. While I think that the inductive search for the lessons of history has taken more criticism than it deserves in recent years, it will not do to put all our reliance on that strategy. Rather, it must be coupled with the search for and development of a theoretical model that can do two very important things: (a) help account for the sequence of processes and conditions that has brought the international system to this current dismal pass; and (b) identify the moves that can undo that sequence and move us with all deliberate speed toward a safer, more prosperous, and dignified human condition.

While some of us have labored in that theoretical vineyard, in the empirical one, or in both, we seem to have a long way to go to bring evidence and our models into powerful juxtaposition. In several of my own papers one finds the crude outlines of such a model built around the cybernetic concepts of self-correcting and self-amplifying feedback while attending to the intimate links among the individual, sub-national, and extra-national actors in world politics, but its convergence with the historical evidence remains all too fragile. Having said this, however, let me underline the implications of the phrase above: models that are so vague, ahistorical and preoperational as to defy empirical disconfirmation just will not suffice. We can no longer afford the luxury of that unproductive division of labor in which too many of us sit in our armchairs and conjure up elegant but irrelevant "theories," and others laboriously generate correlational knowledge that recognizes no theoretical parent.

## AN EXCESS OF TOLERANCE

There should be little ambiguity about the line of reasoning followed here. The human condition is, on balance, morally unacceptable. Too many of our fellows continue to die prematurely from war, terrorism, assassination, poverty, starvation, disease, and even more of them suffer untold misery, pain and degradation en route to the grave. Nor is this unsavory state of affairs restricted to the people of the Third and Fourth Worlds. In the First and Second Worlds, we not only have intolerable levels of violence and misery, but, equally sad, a degree of incompetence, corruption and indifference that no civilized society need accept, and whose continuation is an affront to any self-respecting human group. Moreover, we in the North have brought the entire family of man all too close to the brink of extermination by our acquiescence, if not active participation, in this costly, immoral and destructive struggle to the death between the military leviathans and their supine allies.

Despite the lateness of the hour and the monumental grief that has already been inflicted, there may still be time. But the little time that remains will not be used effectively if we continue business as usual. We have in this Association, and in the ranks of other professions, the talent, the numbers and, yes, the potential clout to turn the world around. We represent, if I may use the cliché, humanity's last, best hope: political elites, counter-elites, researchers, teachers and publicists—a good fraction of the taste-makers and opinionmakers—and a small but critical fraction of the decisionmakers as well. Yet we remain impotent while the wheel of destiny moves us ever closer to the brink of unmitigated disaster.

Despite the good fortune of our intellect, education, institutional support, relative autonomy and vista of opportunity, we seem to be caught up in a social trap of ominous proportions. As scholars, too many of us have overinterpreted the doctrine of tolerance. In our reluctance to impose our own standards (a commendable characteristic if not carried to excess) we accept research that is conceptually imprecise, methods far inferior to those available, empirical premises (implicit as well as explicit) that fly in the face of existing evidence, and ideological predispositions so shortsighted and self-centered as to discredit all but the most parochial. As teachers, we again are much too tolerant: rather than encourage and reinforce those students who are most concerned, motivated, autonomous and gifted, we often enfeeble them in our tolerance of intellectual sloth and ethical indifference. And in the name of objectivity and our repugnance for indoctrination, we typically help to legitimize the assertions of our tribal shamans and the policies of those who have climbed to power over the bodies of their less ruthless countrymen.

As journalists, we are again guilty of inordinate tolerance: we accept and repeat, as objective news, statements that all too often fail even the mildest standards of accuracy and logic, honesty and even-handedness. For reasons outlined below, we eschew the role of a countervailing force, enter into immoderately symbiotic relations with our sponsors and our sources, and often convert what could be an honourable profession into another arm of the entertainment industry or a transmission belt of the ruling elites. In the West, this tendency has gone so far that we now refer to the exception as "investigative journalism"!

One might well point out that what passes for tolerance in intellectual circles is really little more than a fig leaf behind which we conceal acquiescence in the dominant views of our particular time, place and social niche, and intolerance of alternative views. Too many of us seem bent on authenticating Karl Mannheim's dictum that an objective and rigorous social science is impossible because none of us can rise above and detach ourselves from the blinders of class, culture and nationality.

Let me conclude, then, by urging a reconsideration and a redefinition of the various roles taken on by international studies specialists. Much needs to be done if our research, teaching and practice is to be turned to the benefit of the global village. Our responsibilities in scientific, pedagogical, journalistic and policy analysis terms are great, and the need is apparent. But there are obligations of competence in *ethical* terms as well, and these may be even more difficult to meet. Leaving aside the inadequate knowledge base and the ambiguity of the evidence as to which policies are most likely to produce which consequences, we must recognize that the problems of human survival are not purely scientific. They are to an appreciable extent ethical as well. In the face of limited, contradictory and inconclusive evidence, we cannot afford to remain immobile and acquiescent; an integrated human being acts, and must act, day by day, on the basis of inadequate evidence; political passivity while waiting for all the evidence is hardly the mark of a mature scholar-citizen.

Worse yet, these empirical and theoretical inadequacies often serve as camouflage for less savory explanations. To put it indelicately, too many of us find all too many temptations to "go with the flow" in our nations' policies. For the *academic*, East or West, North or South, challenging the conventional wisdom can be costly. At the least, we can suffer loss of credibility in the eyes of the establishment, exclusion from professional groups, conferences, committees, and diminished financial support for our research, our travel, and our students' stipends. At the most, we pay an even higher price for dissidence: underemployment, unemployment, expulsion and even incarceration. When we conform, we and our professional allies, however mediocre, tend to be recognized, rewarded, reinforced and lionized. Even greater rewards typically go to those with that supreme skill of deviating just enough from the party line to appear innovative and original, but not far enough to appear subversive or naive.

For the *journalist* in many societies, the incentives and constraints can be equally awesome. The reporter and columnist "who goes along, gets along." To illustrate from recent American experience, an intelligent and knowledgeable military affairs reporter for the *New York Times* turned out so many articles that were incomplete, inaccurate and misleading that he had to be—or soon hoped to be—in the employ of the establishment. He is now an Assistant Secretary of State. Another case is that of an equally capable television analyst specializing in foreign affairs, whose long and successful career was marked by a less obvious but equally distorted interpretive pattern. He is now senior spokesman for the Department of State. These two obvious cases could easily be augmented by scores of others in the West, and in other parts of the world this symbiosis is so prevalent as to be morally uninteresting. Less dramatic, but far more pervasive, are the temptations that afflict the more junior members of the fifth estate. The reporter with too many assignments who finds it easier to write up his or her story on the basis of a governmental press release will receive a friendly welcome at that agency, and those whose columns rest on interviews with key officials but not with readily located critics often find themselves invited for voyages on aircraft carriers or luncheon at the Foreign Office. Conversely, how often are the national security "naysayers" in the media invited to select briefings and not-for-attribution "backgrounders"?

Moving from academic and media circles to those directly involved in the *policy* process, the incentives and constraints are even more formidable and the temptations more excruciating. Whether serving full-time in a governmental agency or as a temporary or part-time consultant, we have little difficulty discovering the main configurations of the establishment line, but the decision to deviate in other than a minor and tactical fashion is particularly painful. To do so is to court professional disaster; and if one is not actually dismissed, the same treatment is always meted out in the universities, research institutes, and the media: isolation, ridicule, suspicion, and all the instruments of coercive conformity. Nor is it only the incentive of advancement and survival in one's career. There is also the more noble motivation of serving one's nation and perhaps of acquiring sufficient seniority and credibility to help deflect the regime away from a course that seems pregnant with disaster and into more adaptive channels. As a consultant, I have been often astonished to hear a colleague agree with an official position that he or she has previously questioned or rejected. On discussing the matter in private, the explanation has all too often been the familiar strain of credibility-enhancement: "If I go against the consensus now, who will listen to me later?"

While admitting the strength of that temptation, we ought not to overlook the counter-arguments. First, such calculated acquiescence strengthens the clout and legitimacy of the dominant line. Second, it helps to delegitimize and reduce the credibility of the colleague who *does* take an honest stand, whether sound or not in terms of the policy problem. Third, such going along could make the difference between choosing a more adaptive policy or getting one's nation into serious trouble, and given the frequency with which the conventional view—reinforced by the vagaries of domestic politics, group dynamics and bureaucratic gamesmanship—turns out to be ill-founded, it is dangerously wrong.

In sum, there are many reasons, some of them all too persuasive, why international studies specialists fail in their responsibilities. Nevertheless, we have as a profession done so much damage, brought humanity so much grief, and helped us drift so much closer to the abyss of World War III that it is now time to take a fresh look at our past performances and our current responsibilities. We have it in our power to go along with the post-1945 policies and thus accelerate the momentum toward disaster, or to step back, pull up our socks, shoulder our intellectual and ethical obligations, and perhaps slow down and reverse these ominous trends.

*Editor's note:* J. David Singer was president of the International Studies Association during 1985–1986. This chapter is an edited version, without footnotes, of his presidential inaugural address following the Annual Business Meeting of the International Studies Association on Thursday, March 7, 1985, at the 26th Annual Convention in Washington, D.C.

---
■
---

# Notes

## CHAPTER ONE

1. Singer, J. David, *The Correlates of War I: Research Origins and Rationale*, New York: Free Press, 1979.

2. _____, *The Correlates of War II: Testing Some Realpolitik Models*, New York: Free Press, 1980.

3. _____, *Explaining War*, Beverly Hills, Calif: Sage, 1979.

4. Bloch, Jean de, *The Future of War*, New York: Doubleday and McClure, 1896.

5. Angell, Norman, *The Great Illusion*, London: Allen and Unwin, 1910.

6. Gochman, Charles, and Maoz, Zeev, "Militarized Interstate Disputes, 1816–1976," *Journal of Conflict Resolution* 28/4 (December 1984) 585–616.

7. Leng, Russell J., "When Will They Ever Learn?" *Journal of Conflict Resolution* 27/3 (September 1983) 379–419.

8. Singer, J. David, and Cusack, Thomas, "Periodicity, Inexorability, and Steersmanship in Major Power War," In Merritt and Russett (eds.) *From National Development to Global Community*, Herts, England: George Allen and Unwin Ltd. (1981) 404–425.

9. Singer, J. David, op. cit., 1981.

10. _____, "Confrontational Behavior and Escalation to War, 1816–1980: A Research Plan," *Journal of Peace Research*, 19/1 (1982) 37–48.

11. Leng, Russell J., op. cit.

12. Etheredge, Lloyd S., *Can Governments Learn?* New York: Pergamon Press, 1985.

13. Wright, Quincy, "Project for a World Intelligence Center," *Journal of Conflict Resolution* I/1 (March 1957) 93–97.

14. Singer, J. David, and Wallace, Michael (eds.), *To Augur Well: Early Warning Indicators in World Politics*, Beverly Hills, Calif: Sage, 1979.

15. Singer, J. David, and Stoll, Richard (eds.), *Quantitative Indicators in World Politics: Timely Assurance and Early Warning*, New York: Praeger, 1984.

## CHAPTER TEN

1. See J. David Singer (ed.), *Human Behavior and International Politics* (Chicago, 1965) "Introduction," 1–20; and "The Behavioral Science Approach to International Relations: Payoff and Prospect," *SAIS Review*, Vol. 10 (Summer 1966), pp. 12–20.

2. Reference is to Charles Burton Marshall's "rejoinder" to my paper cited above; for his soliloquy on etymology, eternal verities, and primitive magic see "Waiting for the Curtain," *SAIS Review*, ibid., 21–27.

3. A valuable exception is Hayward Alker's response to Hoffmann; see his "Long Road to International Relations Theory: Problems of Statistical Nonaddictivity,"

*World Politics*, Vol. 18, No. 4 (July 1966), pp. 623–55; and Stanley Hoffmann "International Relations: The Long Road to Theory," *World Politics*, Vol. 11, No. 3 (April 1959), pp. 346–78.

4. If Anatol Rapoport's *Fights, Games, and Debates* (Ann Arbor, 1960), had only come out earlier, the struggle could have been much more genteel, since readers in both camps would have learned there that in a fight one seeks to destroy the adversary, in a game one seeks to outwit him, and in a debate one seeks to convert him. My strategy here falls somewhere between the game and the debate as—and I record this with pleasure—does Professor Bull's.

5. In another paper stemming from the Bailey Conference on the University Teaching of International Relations (for which Bull's was originally prepared), Michael Banks uses the "behavioral" label, but in a sympathetic fashion; see his "Two Meanings of Theory in the Study of International Relations," *Yearbook of World Affairs*, 1966, 220–40.

6. There are some purists, mostly among *philosophers* of science, who argue that there is no such thing as verification or confirmation, and insist that we must always set up a "null" hypothesis and then proceed to disconfirm it. They may be the characters who give the rest of us more flexible people the reputation for rigidity! See, for example, Karl Popper, *The Logic of Scientific Discovery* (New York, 1959), 40–42 and *passim*. A preoccupation with this sort of formalism at the present stage of social science would be an unnecessary affectation, in my judgment, even though I agree with Popper's logical argument.

7. An inconclusive statement is, of course, a probabilistic one—referring to either past or future—and all of empirical science rests to a large extent on probabilistic statements. Thus, the best we can do in science is to develop propositions whose probability of being true gets closer and closer to 1.0, or certainty. A provocative analysis of this point of view (and his differences with Popper) is in Hans Reichenbach, *Experience and Prediction* (Chicago, 1938).

8. Arnold Wolfers, *Discord and Collaboration* (Baltimore, 1962), 236–37.

9. This is perhaps as good a place as any for an obiter dictum on the many uses of "empirical." In medical practice, it suggests a wallowing about in observed facts with no theoretical anchor, and quackery is still vaguely associated with it. In most sciences, however, it implies nothing more than the inductive approach, in which sensory observations—aided by instruments or not—are put together to form generalizations. When empirical observations are systematic, explicit, visible, and replicable by other researchers, we call them "operational." Thus, the issue is not between the pro- and the anti-empiricists here, but between those who work only at the impressionistic end of the spectrum and those who use operational procedures and thereby generate useful data or evidence.

10. For details, plus data on the annual variations in alliance distributions, see J. David Singer and Melvin Small, "Formal Alliances, 1815–1939: A Quantitative Description," *Journal of Peace Research*, 1966 (1), pp. 1–32.

11. Fuller details and procedures are outlined in Singer and Small, "The Composition and Status Ordering of the International System, 1815–1940," *World Politics*, Vol. 18 (January 1966), pp. 236–82. A more refined measure will be available in a forthcoming study on the effect of status, its distribution, and its rate of change upon the frequency and magnitude of war. For a scathing, but misguided, attack on the original paper, see "Column," *Encounter* (July 1966), 29–30.

12. These and a variety of other results are reported in two recent papers by Singer and Small: "National Alliance Commitments and War Involvement, 1815–1945," *Peace Research Society Papers*, Vol. 5 (1966), pp. 109–40, and "Alliance

Aggregation and the Onset of War, 1815-1945," in Singer (ed.) *Quantitative International Politics* (New York: Free Press, 1968), 247-86. The amount of war is measured in terms of the frequency of different types of war, the number of military fatalities they produced, the number of nations participating, and the duration.

13. A useful exercise for such skeptics would be to tease out (since few of them are made explicit) all the propositions in the classical literature, and then check them for consistency and compatibility—even *within* a single author's work.

14. Extremely relevant here is the extent to which subjective estimates and beliefs may be radically distorted by the social milieu of the observer. In the famous experiments of Asch and of Sherif, the highly erroneous, but prearranged, majority views, when expressed, were able to induce equally striking errors in the perceptions of the subjects. Had the subjects used explicit and standard measuring devices, such influence would have been negligible. For more recent research on the malleability of subjective and non-operational estimates (physical and social), see section E-3 in Singer (ed.), *Human Behavior and International Politics* (Chicago, 1965), 274-87.

15. The final point, regarding the effect of findings and concepts on the very world under examination is by no means trivial, but neither is it compelling. Space precludes a treatment of the "contamination" problem here, but the reader will find helpful discussions in Ernest Nagel, *The Structure of Science* (New York, 1961), and Abraham Kaplan, *The Conduct of Inquiry* (San Francisco, 1964).

16. An excellent introductory article on factor analysis in international politics is Rudolph J. Rummel, "Understanding Factor Analysis," *Journal of Conflict Resolutions*, Vol. 11, No. 4 (December 1967), 444-80. The technique is effectively demonstrated in a number of Rummel's articles and in such other studies as Raymond Tanter, "Dimensions of Conflict Behavior Within and Between Nations," *Journal of Conflict Resolutions*, Vol. 10, No. 1 (March 1966), 41-64, and Hayward Alker and Bruce Russett, *World Politics in the General Assembly* (New Haven, Conn., 1966); of course, one requires a great deal of data to make factor analysis worthwhile, and it is recommended only when such data are readily available, as in opinion surveys, roll-call records, government yearbooks, and the like.

17. While any scholar in our field who has finished graduate work in the past five years should demand a refund if these methods are unfamiliar, those who are relatively untutored may learn enough about data analysis to conduct first-class empirical research via a patient colleague, an advanced student, a variety of basic textbooks, and those few published research reports that make clear their statistical procedures. Among the more useful texts are: M. Ezekiel and K. Fox, *Methods of Correlation and Regression Analysis* (3rd ed., New York, 1959); William Hays, *Statistics for Psychologists* (New York, 1963); and B. Phillips, *Social Research: Strategy and Tactics* (New York, 1966).

18. See J. David Singer, "Data-Making in International Relations," *Behavioral Science*, Vol. 10 (January 1965), pp. 68-80, for a delineation of the weaknesses in the interpersonal simulation of international policies.

19. An excellent and witty compendium of ideas on how we might measure a variety of allegedly intangible phenomena in the natural (as distinct from the laboratory) setting, and without affecting those phenomena, is in Eugene Webb et al., *Unobtrusive Measures: Nonreactive Research in the Social Sciences* (Chicago, 1966).

20. One reason for the skepticism, of course, is the fact that very little of the scientific work in international politics is published yet, and that which is available to the entire scholarly community is often in journals that have not yet found their way to the traditionalists' desks. In a quick survey, I found that as of June 1967, there were still fewer than 100 English language articles which—in my

judgment—fall in the scientific, data-based category, and of these, four were in *World Politics*, and five in *American Political Science Review*, while the rest were in *Journal of Conflict Resolution*, *Journal of Peace Research*, *Peace Research Society Papers*, and *General Systems*. Moreover, with the time lag between submission and publication of an article, we rely increasingly on the exchange of preprints and other informal communication.

21. A perceptive discussion of various forms of validation is in Charles Hermann, "Validation Problems in Games and Simulations with Special Reference to Models of International Politics," *Behavioral Science*, Vol. 12 (May 1967), pp. 216–31.

22. While our critic does note, in his opening and closing sections, the diversities within the scientific school, the concentration of his fire upon Kaplan's work suggests that he is really not conversant with that diversity. There is, indeed, a painful similarity here to the myopia evidenced in another attack on American political science from across the waters. I refer to the sadly misinformed polemic by Bernard Crick on *The American Science of Politics* (Berkeley, Calif., 1959).

23. These are some of the bivariate relationships which have already been demonstrated or are now under investigation in various research centers. Even if an operational measure turns out to have little or no predictive or explanatory power, it may be a useful descriptor, and that, too, is a step toward further knowledge.

24. There is, of course, no *certainty* that bias can be eliminated from the research design, the sampling scheme, the measurement techniques, the statistics employed, or the interpretations made. There is some evidence that the scientist—physical or social—does occasionally see only what he wants to see; on the other hand, since scientific method requires that *every* step be visible, explicit, and replicable by others, the odds are considerably better for us than for the prescientific scholars.

25. One might even argue that these efforts to remain "value-free" in the classroom or the public forum turn out to be political acts, inasmuch as they increase the relative influence of parochial or ignorant forces, and thus affect the policy outcome.

26. For an excellent statement on behalf of a more modern approach in history, see Committee on Historiography, *The Social Sciences in Historical Study* (New York: Social Science Research Council, 1954).

27. Almost all of Richardson's papers on international politics are brought together in *Statistics of Deadly Quarrels* and in *Arms and Insecurity* (Chicago, Ill., 1960).

28. In preparation is a volume in which all such articles will be abstracted, along with an extensive bibliography of data-based research that lies at the margin of international politics.

29. There may actually be a great many more latent quantifiers among the traditionalists than is recognized. Note, for example, the frequency with which numbers (admittedly, Roman) are used in place of words at the beginning of each section in articles written for *Foreign Affairs*, *International Organization*, *International Journal*, and other favorites of the self-confessed anti-quantification fraternity!

## CHAPTER TWELVE

1. J. David Singer, "Knowledge, Practice, and the Social Sciences in International Politics," in Norman Palmer, ed., *A Design for International Relations Research*, Monograph 10 of the American Academy of Political and Social Science (October

1970), 137–49; and "The Peace Researcher and Foreign Policy Prediction," *Peace Science Society Papers*, 21 (1973), 1–13.

2. J. David Singer, "Cumulativeness in the Social Sciences: Some Counter-Prescriptions," *PS*, 8:1 (Winter, 1975), 19–21.

3. Karl Pearson, *The Grammar of Science* (New York: 1957) [originally published in 1892]; Ronald A. Fisher, *Statistical Methods for Research Workers* (London, 1925); Ronald A. Fisher and Ghuean T. Prance, *The Design of Experiments* (London, 1935); Samuel A. Stouffer, *Social Research to Test Ideas* (New York, 1962); Hubert M. Blalock, Jr., *Causal Inferences in Nonexperimental Research* (Chapel Hill, 1961); and Donald T. Campbell and Julian Stanley, *Experimental and Quasi-Experimental Designs for Research* (Chicago, 1966).

4. For example, Samuel J. Eldersveld, "Experimental Propaganda Techniques and Voting Behavior," *American Political Science Review*, 50 (March 1956), 154–65; Herbert Simon and Frederick Stern, "The Effect of Television upon Voting Behavior in Iowa in the 1952 Presidential Election," *American Political Science Review*, 49 (June 1955), 470–77; and Heinz Eulau, "Policy Making in American Cities: Comparisons in a Quasi-Longitudinal, Quasi-Experimental Design" (New York, 1971).

5. Representative of that view is Amitai Etzioni, *Political Unification* (New York, 1965), on page 88: "There probably will never be a science of international relations as there is one of physics or chemistry, if for no other reason than experiments are practically impossible and the number of cases is too small for a rigorous statistical analysis." And even so creative and catholic a scholar as Paul Lazarfield in "The American Soldier—An Expository Review," *Public Opinion Quarterly*, 13 (Fall 1949), 377–404 alleges on page 378 that survey methods "do not use experimental techniques." On the other hand, on page 155 in "The History of Human Conflict," in Elton B. McNeil, ed., *The Nature of Human Conflict* (Englewood Cliffs, 1965), Ole R. Holsti and Robert C. North actually allude to the possibility of transforming history "into something approaching a laboratory of international behavior." A similar point is made by Richard C. Snyder in "Some Perspectives on the Use of Experimental Techniques in the Study of International Relations," in Harold Guetzkow *et al*, eds., *Simulation in International Relations* (Englewood Cliffs, 1963), 1–23. In sociology, two of the early proponents of the experimental mode were Ernest Greenwood, *Experimental Sociology: A Study in Method* (New York, 1945) and F. Stuart Chapin, *Experimental Designs in Sociological Research* (New York, 1947).

6. Elsewhere, I have spelled out in greater detail my views on the more promising strategies for explaining war in general (J. David Singer, "Modern International War: From Conjecture to Explanation," in Albert Lepawsky *et al*, eds., *The Search for World Order* [New York, 1971], 47–71), as well as the strategy being pursued in the Correlates of War project in particular (J. David Singer, "The Correlates of War Project," *World Politics*, 24 [January 1972], 243–70).

7. Anatol Rapoport, "Methodology in the Physical, Biological, and Social Science," *General Systems*, 14 (1969), 179–86.

8. Some would differentiate between these two versions of the field experiment. When the researcher merely waits for a condition or event that is probably coming anyway, we refer to a "natural" field experiment; illustrative is the Herbert Simon and Frederick Stern study on the effects of TV upon voter turnout. When the researcher consciously injects the stimulus condition, we refer to a "contrived" field experiment.

9. Campbell and Stanley, *Experimental and Quasi-Experimental Designs*.

10. Eugene Webb *et al*, *Unobtrusive Measures: Non-Reactive Research in the Social Sciences* (Chicago, 1966).

11. Jean Laponce, "Experimenting: A Two-Person Game between Man and Nature," in Jean Laponce and Paul Smoker, eds., *Experimentation and Simulation in Political Science* (Toronto, 1972), 4–5.

12. Jean Laponce, "An Experimental Method to Measure the Tendency to Equibalance in a Political System," *American Political Science Review*, 60 (December 1966) 982–93.

13. Anatol Rapoport and Melvin Guyer, "The Psychology of Conflict Involving Mixed-Motive Decisions," Final Research Report NIH-MH 12880-02, 1969.

14. Robert Freed Bales, "A Set of Categories for the Analysis of Small Group Interaction," *American Sociological Review*, 15 (1950), 257–63; and Timothy Leary, *Interpersonal Diagnosis of Personality* (New York, 1957).

15. S. J. Hutt and Corinne Hutt, *Direct Observation and Measurement of Behavior* (Springfield, Illinois, 1970).

16. Eldersveld, "Experimental Propaganda Techniques."

17. On the detailed procedures of observation, measurement, and index construction in the Correlates of War project, see: Melvin Small and J. David Singer, "Formal Alliances, 1816–1965: An Extension of the Basic Data," *Journal of Peace Research*, 3 (1969), 257–82; Melvin Small and J. David Singer, "Diplomatic Importance of States, 1816–1970: An Extension and Refinement of the Indicator," *World Politics*, 25 (July 1973), 577–99; J. David Singer and Melvin Small, *The Wages of War, 1816–1965: A Statistical Handbook* (New York, 1972); Michael D. Wallace and J. David Singer, "Inter-Governmental Organization in the Global System, 1816–1964: A Quantitative Description," *International Organization*, 24 (Spring 1970), 239–87; and James Lee Ray and J. David Singer, "Measuring the Concentration of Power in the International System," *Sociological Methods and Research*, 1 (May 1973), 403–37.

18. As a matter of fact, the laboratory experimenter must face several problems that need not concern those of us who conduct historical experiments. Perhaps foremost among these is the problem of experimenter bias. As Robert Rosenthal, in "On the Social Psychology of the Psychological Experiment," *American Scientist*, 51 (June 1963) 268–83; and *Experimenter Effects in Behavioral Research* (New York, 1966), and others have demonstrated, the theoretical biases of the researcher—or laboratory assistants—constitute a recurrent source of distortion in the experimental work of physical and biological, as well as social scientists. In small group experiments, for example, the way in which the stimulus is presented can induce systematic bias in the behavior of the subjects. Similarly, the observation and measurement of human or animal responses to a stimulus can be systematically distorted by the expectations of the observer.

19. Fred Kort, "Regression Analysis and Discriminant Analysis," *American Political Science Review*, 67 (June 1973), 555–59.

20. Campbell and Stanley, *Experimental and Quasi-Experimental Designs*.

21. Hayward Alker, "Causal Inference and Political Analysis," in Joseph Bernd, ed., *Mathematical Applications in Political Science* 2 (Dallas, 1966), 7–43.

22. Campbell and Stanley, *Experimental and Quasi-Experimental Designs*, 5.

23. These are: "*History*, the specific events occurring between the first and second measurement in addition to the experimental variable; *Maturation*, processes within the respondents operating as a function of the passage of time per se (not specific to the particular events), including growing older, growing hungrier, growing more tired, and the like; *Testing*, the effects of taking a test upon the scores of a second testing; *Instrumentation*, in which changes in the observers or scorers used may produce changes in the obtained measurements; *Statistical regression*, operating where groups have been selected on the basis of their extreme scores; *Biases* resulting in

differential selection of respondents for the comparison groups; *Experimental mortality*, or differential loss of respondents from the comparison groups; *Selection-maturation interaction*, etc., which in certain of the multiple-group quasi-experimental designs, such as Design 10, is confounded with, i.e., might be mistaken for, the effect of the experimental variable."

24. A reasonable position on this issue is that taken by Blalock (*Causal Inferences*, 5): "There appears to be an inherent gap between the languages of theory and research which can never be bridged in a completely satisfactory way. One *thinks* in terms of . . . causes . . . but one's *tests* are made in terms of covariations, operations, and pointer readings."

25. Neil J. Smelser, *Essays in Sociological Explanation* (Englewood Cliffs, N.J., 1968) distinguishes between "parameter variables" and "operative variables" to emphasize this distinction.

26. We should, of course, make clear that History—like all disciplines—contains a wide range of epistemological viewpoints. Illustrative of the growing trend toward greater rigor in that discipline are: Don K. Rowney and James Q. Graham, Jr., eds., *Quantitative History* (Homewood, Illinois, 1969); Val. R. Lorwin and Jacob M. Price, eds., *The Dimensions of the Past* (New Haven, 1972); and Charles M. Dollar and Richard J. Jensen, *Historian's Guide to Statistics* (New York, 1971).

27. One problem with this comparative case method, however, is the likelihood of ending up with too few cases and too many variables, giving us a poor N:K ratio; see Karl W. Deutsch, J. David Singer, and Keith Smith, "The Organizing Efficiency of Theories," *American Behavioral Scientist*, 9 (October 1965), 30-33.

28. The theoretical model is articulated in considerable detail in Karl W. Deutsch and J. David Singer, "Multipolar Power Systems and International Stability, *World Politics*, 16 (April 1964), 390-406.

29. Samuel H. Beer, "The Comparative Method and the Study of British Politics," *Comparative Politics*, 1 (October 1968), 19.

30. Arend Lijphart, "Comparative Politics and the Comparative Method," *American Political Science Review*, 65 (September 1971), 684.

31. Ernest Nagel, *The Structure of Science* (New York, 1961), 452.

32. While this is an imaginary experiment, simplified for illustrative purposes, a fair number of "real" ones have been conducted within the Correlates of War project at Michigan. See, for example, J. David Singer and Melvin Small, "Alliance Aggregation and the Onset of War, 1815-1945," in J. David Singer, ed., *Quantitative International Politics* (New York, 1968), 247-86; J. David Singer, Stuart Bremer, and John Stuckey, "Capability Distribution, Uncertainty, and Major Power War, 1816-1965," in Bruce Russett, ed., *Peace, War, and Numbers* (Beverly Hills, 1972), 19-48; and Michael D. Wallace, *War and Rank Among Nations*, (Lexington, Massachusetts, 1973). For another imaginary one, see J. David Singer, *On the Scientific Study of Politics* (New York, 1972). I am indebted to John Stuckey for the illustrations used here.

33. John R. Platt, "Strong Inference," *Science*, 146 (October 1964), 347-53.

34. Guetzkow *et al.*, *Simulation in International Relations*.

35. Thomas H. Naylor, *Computer Simulation Experiments with Models of Economic Systems* (New York, 1971).

36. For an excellent example of a simulation that combines empirical and logical components, see Stuart A. Bremer, *Simulated Worlds: A Computer Model of National Decision Making* (Princeton, 1977).

# CHAPTER FOURTEEN

1. This study is part of a larger project on the correlates of war, supported by the Carnegie Corporation of New York and the Center for Research on Conflict Resolution at the University of Michigan. We are also grateful to Anatol Rapoport and Keith Smith with whom we consulted often on conceptual as well as methodological problems. For his efficient aid in data analysis, our thanks go also to Wen Chao Hsieh.

2. Almost all textbooks in the field devote some space to an effort to systematize balance-of-power concepts, with varying degrees of success. In addition, there are several theoretical efforts, among which are Claude (1962), Gareau (1962), Haas (1953), Kaplan (1957), Liska (1962), Deutsch and Singer (1964), and Waltz (1964). Three important efforts to examine the international system in the historical context are Gulick (1955), Langer (1931), and Rosecrance (1963).

3. A recent statement which explicitly expresses these restraints is that by Secretary Rusk in regard to Soviet-American arms control negotiations: "Of course, anything that involves our NATO allies would have to be discussed fully with our NATO allies. We could not, for example, make arrangements ourselves, nor even could the four NATO members now sitting at Geneva be able to make arrangements on control posts throughout the NATO alliance without fullest consideration in NATO."

4. One admittedly intuitive analysis concludes, for example, that "decision to wage war precedes by one to five years the outbreak of hostilities" (Abel, 1941).

5. For a full description of the operations by which nations were coded and classified, see Singer and Small (1966a).

6. There are, of course, a fair number of additional German and Italian states, but they fail to meet our population threshold of 500,000; the classification criteria are discussed below.

7. The population threshold of 500,000 was only established after a fairly exhaustive list of political entities was compiled and it then became evident that almost no nation of a lesser population revealed itself as an active participant. As to recognition, we found that Britain and France almost invariably led the way to recognition by a majority of members of the European state system. Thus, we get a parsimonious criterion which produces almost exactly the same results as would one requiring, let us say, 50 percent of the major power members of the European system to serve as legitimizers; actually these two constituted 40 percent of that group until 1860 and from then until 1895 they constituted 33 percent. Moreover, only Britain and France had sufficiently strong interest in Latin America to justify extending diplomatic recognition to nations in that area. By recognition we mean the accreditation of a representative at or above the rank of chargé d'affaires; neither the consul nor the diplomatic agent qualifies under this scheme.

8. Moreover, there were only three Latin American alliances (Ecuador-Peru, 1860–1861; Colombia-Ecuador, 1864–1865; and Bolivia-Peru, 1873–1883) which met our criteria of formality, population of the signatories, and consummation in peace time. In general, see Burr (1955).

9. This is a very simple and a-theoretical presentation of such distributions. For an indication of the theoretical implication of "mere" distributions, see Horvath and Foster (1963), Weiss (1963), Smoker (1964), and Denton (1966).

10. There is a rapidly burgeoning literature on the subject and it reminds us that very few civil wars remain purely internal for any length of time. See Rosenau (1964), Modelski (1961), and Eckstein (1963).

11. This figure permits us to eliminate many border skirmishes, brief interventions, punitive expeditions, blockades, and bombardments of marginal interest to the international relations student, yet excludes no international war. Where our confidence levels were low and the deaths were estimated to be nearly 1,000, we did, however, include the wars. Three examples of such an occurrence were the French invasion of Spain in 1823, the conquest of the Papal States in 1860, and Spain versus Peru, Chile, and Ecuador in 1866.

12. Some might quarrel with our use of the historians' consensus on the classification of nations into major and minor. One significant point of assurance is found in Morgenthau where approximately the same major-power listing as ours is used (1956, p. 324).

13. As to civilian and military deaths from non-battlefield engagements, the major possible source is the siege. During the period under study, however, there were few sieges which led to an appreciable number of deaths; see Hargreaves (1948).

14. Elsewhere, we not only spell out the coding rules in greater detail and with illustrations, but give the voluminous bibliography from which our basic information was drawn; see Singer and Small (1966b).

15. Though some scholars tend to differentiate between an alliance and a coalition, the distinction seems unimportant. Gulick, for example, defines an alliance as a "bilateral or trilateral agreement for offensive or defensive purposes," and then defines a coalition as "a similar agreement signed by four or more powers or a conjunction of several alliances directed toward the same end" (1955, p. 78). He alludes to other distinctions, but they make the difference no clearer.

16. We also gathered data for neutrality pacts and ententes, but further refinements of those measures is called for in order to handle the problem of which alliance commitment takes precedence when a nation belongs to alliances of different classes. Findings based on those measures will be reported subsequently.

17. An interesting point emerges when these various time lags are examined carefully. In the nineteenth century, the effects are seldom fully evident until five years have elapsed, whereas three years suffice in the twentieth century. This pattern strongly suggests that, in contrast to "real" time, "diplomatic" time has indeed speeded up in more recent years. In a subsequent paper, we will report a number of other indications of this time compression tendency. A suggestive treatment of this problem in social science is Moore (1963).

18. A statistical note is in order here. We recognize that our observations do not satisfy the requirements which most statisticians would demand in order to speak of levels of significance. First, we are not sampling here, but are observing the entire population of events. Second our indices—annual readings of alliance aggregation and war onset—obviously are not independent of one another from year to year. Third, the distributions are not "normally" distributed, and any normalizing transformation would have distorted a perfectly satisfactory scale. However, one must use some objective and quantitative benchmark by which "strong" relationships may be differentiated from "weak" ones, and by which one may classify these observed relationships as compelling or not. Thus, we have used the Pearson product-moment correlation as our measure of the strength of the observed relationships and gone on to scrutinize each such correlation value ($r$) to ascertain whether or not we might call it strong or weak. For that purpose, we use Fisher's exact test of statistical significance (two-tailed to allow for negative correlations) and treat all $r$'s that exceed the requirements for an .01 level of significance with a given $N$ as strong. For the nineteenth century and an $N$ of 85, that threshold is .25, and for the twentieth and an $N$ of only 45, the threshold

requirement goes up to a coincidental .45; values meeting these levels are italicized. Note that r's are rounded off to only two places and that the decimal point is omitted.

19. To be doubly sure, we also ran these correlations *without* the World War years, with only a minor reduction in the coefficients resulting.

20. Another way of saying this is to reiterate that bivariate analyses can seldom explain (account for) highly complex and obviously multivariate social phenomena.

21. See, for example, Harary (1961), Coleman (1964), Rapoport (1963), Rapoport and Horvath (1961), Berge (1962), and Flament (1963).

22. Furthermore, even though our alliance aggregation index is not responsive to multiple memberships, the alliance *involvement* index presented in an earlier paper *is*, and the correlations between the two indicators when applied to all nations in any alliances and to all in defense pacts are .90 and .87 respectively (Singer and Small, 1966b, p. 20).

# CHAPTER FIFTEEN

1. Today, of nearly 160 independent territorial nation-states, only a few (such as Iceland and Costa Rica) are so bereft. As sympathetic observers of the glacial movement toward strategies of non-violent, but active, civilian defense, we do not applaud this ubiquity; we merely recognize it.

2. Detailed coding rules and the resulting data may be found in Gochman and Maoz (1982).

3. The coding rules will be found in *Paths to Conflict* (Maoz, 1982).

4. The dispute analyses in the present paper include these nine cases that erupted into, and are thus also coded as, wars. We performed analyses both with and without the nine cases, and the results each time were essentially as reported in the tables.

5. While this is one data set from the Correlates of War project whose coding rules, rationale, and emerging scores have not yet been published in great detail, a fairly complete summary may be found in Bremer (1980).

6. There are, of course, alternative routes to the measurement of a state's overall material capabilities or its military strength alone, and in due course we hope to publish not only our data set for each state in the entire system since 1816, but a full discussion of the theoretical, empirical, and methodological reasons for our decisions. For our purposes here, let us merely refer to those other efforts cited in our introduction, and state that one of our primary objectives was to generate a set of indicators that would be valid for comparing countries of widely varying levels of economic development covering the period from the Congress of Vienna to the present.

7. A critic might object that we should directly compare state 1's military effort (e.g., its expenditures, A, divided by its industrial base, P) to state 2's military effort (its expenditures, B, divided by its industrial base, Q). Such a change is needless, however, because the alternative proposed is mathematically equivalent to our own approach. In our approach, we divide each state's capabilities by the total capabilities of the major powers, so that state 1's military allocation is

$$\frac{A/A+B+\ldots+D}{P/P+Q+\ldots+S,}$$

and state 2's military allocation is

$$\frac{B/A + B + \ldots D}{Q/P + Q + \ldots + S,}$$

where $A + \ldots + D$ equals the military expenditures of the great powers, and $P + \ldots + S$ equals the industrial base of the great powers. We then compare the two allocations to see if they are equal or not. But if

$$\frac{A/A + B + \ldots + D}{P/P + Q + \ldots + S} = \frac{B/A + B + \ldots + D}{Q/P + Q + \ldots + S,}$$

then, multiplying both sides by

$$A + B + \ldots + D/P + Q + \ldots + S,$$

$A/P = B/Q$, which is exactly what the hypothetical critic had proposed that we compute. While our approach of computing major power shares may in this light seem unnecessarily complex, we prefer it for certain purposes because it expresses each state's allocations in standard units, with a score of 1.0 indicating a typical burden.

For our analyses of wars involving minor powers, the denominators (the sum of major power capabilities) remain the same, but in the numerators we substitute $E$ and $F$ (the military expenditures of the minor powers in question) for $A$ and $B$, and substitute 7 and 1 (the industrial base of the minor powers in question) for $P$ and $Q$.

8. The exact strength of association among the indicators of capabilities and allocations varies with the unit of analysis (major and/or minor powers; states or coalitions), the time span (1816-1976; 1870-1976), the states included (the initiating side, the target side, or the ratio between the two sides), and other factors. The general patterns as seen in Table 2, however, are broadly consistent across all combinations of the above factors.

## CHAPTER SIXTEEN

1. Jacob Bronowski, *Magic, Science, and Civilization* (New York: Columbia University Press, 1978); and Karl W. Deutsch, "Some notes on research on the role of models in the natural and social sciences," *Synthèse*, vol. 7 (1948), pp. 506-33.

2. Norbert Wiener, *Cybernetics; or, Control and Communication in the Animal and the Machine* (Cambridge, Mass.: MIT Press, 1948); Walter Bradford Cannon, *The Way of an Investigator: A Scientist's Experiences in Medical Research* (New York: Norton, 1945); and Karl W. Deutsch, *The Nerves of Government: Models of Political Communication and Control* (New York: The Free Press, 1963).

3. Herbert A. Simon, *The Sciences of the Artificial* (Cambridge, Mass.: MIT Press, 1969).

4. Slavko Šećerov, *Economic Phenomena Before and After War: A Statistical Theory of Modern Wars* (London: Routledge; and New York: Dutton, 1919).

5. Miller Pontius, *A Study of the Recurring Economic Pattern Surrounding Major Wars* (New York: mimeo, 1958).

6. Niels Lindberg, "The conflict theory and economic depressions, with some views on various political aspects of an anti-depression programme as supplementary to armaments cuts" (Stockholm, Sweden: mimeo., 1967).

7. A. L. Macfie, "The outbreak of war and the trade cycle," *Economic History* (supplement of *Economic Journal*), vol. 3, no. 13 (February 1938), pp. 89–97; and Ragnar Frisch, *Noen Trekk av Konjunkturlaeren: Med et Tillegg om Levestandard og Prisindeks* (Oslo, Norway: Aschehoug, 1947); summarized by Nils Petter Gleditsch, "The causes of war: a research proposal" (Ann Arbor, Mich.: mimeo., 1966).

8. David C. McClelland, "Love and power: the psychological signals of war," *Psychology Today*, vol. 8, no. 8 (January 1975), pp. 44–48.

9. David C. McClelland, *Power: The Inner Experience* (New York: Irvington, distr. Halstead Press, 1975).

10. Frank Klingberg, "The historical alternation of moods in American foreign policy," *World Politics*, vol. 4, no. 2 (January 1952), pp. 239–73.

11. Ibid., p. 262.

12. Norman Z. Alcock and Christopher Young, "Evidence of an epochal cycle," *Peace Research*, vol. 5, no. 4 (April 1973), pp. 17–20.

13. J. David Singer and Melvin Small, "Diplomatic importance of states, 1816–1970: An extension and refinement of the indicator," *World Politics*, vol. 25, no. 4 (July 1973), pp. 577–99; and Charles Gochman, "Status, conflict, and war: The major powers, 1820–1970," PhD dissertation, University of Michigan, 1975.

14. J. David Singer and Melvin Small, *The Wages of War, 1816–1965: A Statistical Handbook* (New York: Wiley, 1972).

15. Cyrus Derman, Leon J. Gleser, and Ingram Olkin, *A Guide to Probability Theory and Application* (New York: Holt, Rinehart & Winston, 1973).

16. Bruce Bueno de Mesquita and J. David Singer, "Alliances, capabilities, and war: a review and synthesis," in *Political Science Annual: An International Review*, ed. Cornelius P. Cotter (Indianapolis, Ind., and New York: Bobbs-Merrill, 1973), Vol. 4, pp. 237–80.

17. Ivan S. Bloch [Ivan Stanislavovich Bliokh], *The Future of War in Its Technical, Economic, and Political Relations: Is War Now Impossible?* tr. R. C. Long (New York: Doubleday & McClure, 1899).

18. Singer and Small, *The Wages of War*.

19. Ibid., ch. 9.

20. Pitirim A. Sorokin, *Social and Cultural Dynamics* (New York: American Book Company, 1937–41), Vol. 3, *Fluctuation of Social Relationships, War, and Revolution* (1937).

21. Lewis F. Richardson, *Statistics of Deadly Quarrels*, ed. Quincy Wright and C. C. Lienau (Pittsburgh, Pa: Boxwood Press; and Chicago: Quadrangle Books, 1960).

22. Quincy Wright, *A Study of War*, 2 vols (Chicago: University of Chicago Press, 1942).

23. Frank H. Denton and Warren Phillips, "Some patterns in the history of violence," *Journal of Conflict Resolution*, vol. 12, no. 2 (June 1968); pp. 182–95.

24. Raymond H. Wheeler, *War, 599 BC–AD 1950: Indexes of International and Civil War Battles of the World* (Pittsburgh, Pa.: Foundation for the Study of Cycles, 1951).

25. Edward R. Dewey, *The 177-Year Cycle in War, 600 BC–AD 1957* (Pittsburgh, Pa: Foundation for the Study of Cycles, 1964).

26. J. S. Lee, "The periodic recurrence of internecine wars in China," *China Journal*, vol. 14, no. 3 (March 1931), pp. 111–15; and vol. 14, no. 4 (April 1931), pp. 159–63.

27. Singer and Small, *The Wages of War.*

28. Sorokin, *Social and Cultural Dynamics,* Vol. 3, *Fluctuations of Social Relationships, War, and Revolution,* p. 359.

29. Ibid., pp. 359-60.

## CHAPTER EIGHTEEN

1. J. David Singer and Melvin Small, "Foreign Policy Indicators: Predictors of War in History and in the State of the World Message," *Policy Sciences* 5/3 (September 1974), pp. 271-296.

2. Ernest R. May, *Lessons of the Past: The Use and Misuse of History in American Foreign Policy* (New York: Oxford University Press, 1973), p. xi.

3. James Lee Ray, *Global Politics* (Boston: Houghton Mifflin, 1983).

4. J. David Singer and Melvin Small, "National Alliance Commitments and War Involvement, 1815-1945," *Peace Research Society Paper,* 5 (1966), pp. 109-140; Melvin Small and J. David Singer, "Alliance Aggregation and the Onset of War, 1815-1945" in J. David Singer (ed.). *Quantitative International Politics: Insights and Evidence* (New York: Free Press, 1968).

5. James Lee Ray, "The Measurement of System Structure" in J. David Singer (ed.), *Correlates of War II: Testing Some Realpolitik Models* (New York: Free Press, 1980).

6. For polarity indicators, see Bruce Bueno de Mesquita, "Measuring Systemic Polarity," *Journal of Conflict Resolution* 19/2 (1975), pp. 187-216; for alliance aggregation indicators, see J. David Singer and Melvin Small, "National Alliance Commitments," op. cit., 1966; for structural clarity indicators, see J. David Singer and Sandra Bouxsein, "Structural Clarity and International War: Some Tentative Findings" in Murray (ed.), *Interdisciplinary Aspects of General Systems Theory,* 1975, pp. 126-135. (A useful collection will be found in Paul Diehl and J. David Singer, eds., *Measuring the Correlates of War* [Ann Arbor, Michigan: University of Michigan Press, 1990].)

7. Charles Gochman & Zeev Maoz, "Militarized Interstate Disputes, 1816-1976: Procedures, Patterns, and Insights," *Journal of Conflict Resolution* 28/4 (December 1984), pp. 585-616; Melvin Small and J. David Singer, *Resort to Arms* (Beverly Hills, California: Sage, 1982).

8. For political integration indicators, see Quincy Wright, "The Mode of Financing Unions of States as a Measure of their Degree of Integration," *International Organization* XI (Winter 1957), pp. 30-40; for economic interdependence indicators, see Karl Deutsch & Alexander Eckstein, "National Industrialization and the Declining Share of the International Economic Sector, 1890-1959," *World Politics* 13 (1961), pp. 267-299; for international tension indicators, see Kjell Goldmann, *Tension and Detente in Bipolar Europe* (Stockholm: Scandinavia University Press, 1974); and for inter-state behavior patterns, see Russell Leng & J. David Singer, "Toward a Multi-Theoretical Typology of International Behavior," in Bunge, Galtung & Mulitza (eds.), *Mathematical Approaches to International Relations* (Bucharest: Romanian Academy of Social and Political Sciences, 1977).

9. Jean de Bloch, *The Future of War* (New York: Doubleday & McClure, 1899); Lewis F. Richardson, *Mathematical Psychology of War* (London: UK Copyright Library, 1919; Pitirim Sorokin, *Social and Cultural Dynamics* 3 (New York: American Book Co., 1937); Quincy Wright, *A Study of War* (Chicago: Chicago University Press, 1942).

10. Karl Deutsch, *The Nerves of Government* (New York: Free Press, 1963).

11. Klaus Knorr and James Rosenau (eds.), *Contending Approaches to International Politics* (Princeton, N.J.: Princeton University Press, 1968).

12. On these points, see Zeev Maoz, *Paths to Conflict: International Dispute Initiation, 1816–1976* (Boulder, Colorado: Westview, 1982); Russell J. Leng, "Coercive Bargaining in Recurrent Crises," *Journal of Conflict Resolution* 27 (1983), pp. 379–420; and "Reagan and the Russians: Crisis Bargaining Beliefs and the Historical Record," *American Political Science Review* 78 (June 1984), pp. 338–355.

13. J. David Singer (ed.), *Human Behavior and International Politics: Contributions from the Social-Psychological Sciences* (Chicago: Rand McNally, 1965).

14. P. C. Asbjornsen & J. Moe, *Norwegian Folk Tales* (Oslo: Dreyers Forlag, 1960).

15. J. David Singer and Sandra Bouxsein, op. cit., 1975.

16. Dina Zinnes, *Contemporary Research in International Relations* (New York: Free Press, 1976).

17. J. David Singer, Stuart Bremer, and John Stuckey, "Capability Distribution, Uncertainty, and Major Power War, 1820–1965" in Bruce Russett (ed.), *Peace, War, and Numbers* (Beverly Hills, California: Sage, 1972).

18. J. David Singer, "Military Preparedness, National Security, and the Lessons of History," in Huldt (ed.), *Swedish Yearbook of International Affairs* (Stockholm: 1985).

19. On this point, see Will Durant and Ariel Durant, *The Lessons of History* (New York: Simon & Schuster, 1968) and Ernest R. May, op. cit., 1973.

20. Frank Wayman, J. David Singer & Gary Goertz, "Capabilities, Allocations, and Success in Militarized Disputes and Wars, 1810–1976," *International Studies Quarterly* 27 (1983), pp. 497–515.

21. Joseph A. Schumpeter, *Imperialism and Social Classes* (New York: Kelley 1919 and 1951; Harold Lasswell, "The Garrison State," *American Journal of Sociology* 46 (1941), pp. 455–468.

22. Paul Diehl & Gary Goertz, "Trends in Military Allocations Since 1816" (Athens, Ga: University of Georgia, mimeo, 1985).

23. Leon Festinger, *Conflict, Decision, and Dissonance* (Stanford, California: Stanford University Press, 1964).

24. Stuart Bremer, "National Capabilities and War-Proneness" in J. David Singer (ed.), *The Correlates of War II: Testing Some Realpolitik Models* (New York: Free Press, 1980).

25. Frank Wayman, J. David Singer, and Gary Goertz, op. cit., 1983.

26. Quincy Wright, "Project for a World Intelligence Center," *Journal of Conflict Resolution* I (1957), pp. 93–97; J. David Singer & Michael Wallace, *To Augur Well: Early Warning Indicators in World Politics* (Beverly Hills, California: Sage, 1979); J. David Singer & Richard Stoll, *Quantitative Indicators in World Politics: Timely Assurance and Early Warning* (New York: Praeger, 1984).

27. For a badly organized international system, see Hedley Bull, *The Anarchical Society* (New York: Columbia, 1979); also F. H. Hinsley, *Power and the Pursuit of Peace* (Cambridge: Cambridge University Press, 1963) and Kenneth Waltz, *Man, the State, and War* (New York: Columbia, 1959); for a weak sense of global ethics, see Michael Howard, *The Causes of War* (Cambridge, Mass.: Harvard University Press, 1984), also Michael Walzer, *Just and Unjust Wars* (New York: Basic Books, 1979).

# References

## INTRODUCTION

Bloch, Jean de (1899) *The Future of War*. New York: Doubleday and McClure.
Feyerabend, Paul K. (1975) *Against Method: Outline of an Anarchistic Theory of Knowledge*. London: Verso.
Richardson, Lewis F. (1919) *Mathematical Psychology of War*. Oxford, U.K.: William Hunt.
Singer, J. David (1989) "The Making of a Peace Researcher," in Joseph Kruzel and James Rosenau (eds.), *Journeys Through World Politics*. Lexington, MA: Lexington Books.
———. (1990) "One Man's View," in Charles Gochman and Alan Sabrosky (eds.) *Prisoners of War? Nation-States in the Modern Era*. Lexington, MA: Lexington Books.
Sorokin, Pitirim A. (1937) *Social and Cultural Dynamics: Fluctuations of Social Relationships, War, and Revolution*, Vol. III. New York: American Books.
Wright, Q. (1942) *A Study of War*. Chicago: University of Chicago Press (1st edition); 1965 (2nd ed.).

## CHAPTER SEVEN

Habermas, Jurgen. *Toward a Rational Society*. Boston: Beacon Press, 1970.
Kelman, Herbert. *A Time to Speak*. San Francisco: Jossey-Bass, 1968.
Sanford, Nevitt, and Comstock, Craig, eds. *Sanctions for Evil*. Boston: Beacon Press, 1971.
Singer, J. David. *Correlates of War I: Research Origins and Rationale*. New York: Free Press, 1979.

## CHAPTER ELEVEN

Alker, H., and B. Russett (1964) "On measuring inequality." *Behavioral Science* 9 (July): 207–218.
Alger, C. (1966) "Interaction and negotiation in a committee of the United Nations general assembly." *Peace Research Society (International) Papers*: 141–169.
Allport, G. (1955) *Becoming*. New Haven, CT: Yale Univ. Press.
Banks, A. (1971) *Cross-Polity Time Series Data*. Cambridge, MA: MIT Press.
——— and R. Textor (1963) *A Cross-Polity Survey*. Cambridge, MA: MIT Press.
Bell, W. (1954) "A probability model for the measurement of ecological segregation." *Social Forces* 32 (May): 357–364.
Berelson, B. (1952) *Content Analysis in Communication Research*. Glencoe, IL: Free Press.
Blalock, H. (1968) "The measurement problem: the gap between the language of theory and research," in H. Blalock and A. Blalock (eds.) *Methodology in Social Research*. New York: McGraw-Hill.

_____ (1961) "Theory, measurement, and replication in the social sciences." *Amer. J. of Sociology* 66 (January): 342-347.

Bueno de Mesquita, B. (1975) "Measuring systemic polarity." *J. of Conflict Resolution* 19, 2: 187-216.

Campbell, D. and D. W. Fiske (1959) "Convergent and discriminant validation by the multitrait-multimethod matrix." *Psych. Bull.* 56: 81-105.

Clark, R. (1971) *Einstein: The Life and Times.* New York: T. Y. Crowell.

Cutright, P. (1967) "Inequality: a cross-national analysis." *Amer. Soc. Rev.* 32 (August): 562-578.

Deutsch, K. W. (1969) "On methodological problems of quantitative research," in M. Dogan and S. Rokkan (eds.) *Quantitative Ecological Analysis in the Social Sciences.* Cambridge, MA: MIT Press.

_____ (1966) "The theoretical basis of data programs," in R. Merritt and S. Rokkan (eds.) *Comparing Nations.* New Haven, CT: Yale Univ. Press.

_____ J. D. Singer, and K. Smith (1965) "The organizing efficiency of theories: the N/V ratio as a crude rank order measure." *Amer. Behavioral Scientist* 9 (October): 30-33.

Duncan, O. D. and B. Duncan (1955) "A methodological analysis of segregation indexes." *Amer. Soc. Rev.* 20 (April): 210-217.

Gini, C. (1912) *Variabilita e Multabilita.* Bologna.

Greenberg, J. (1956) "The measurement of linguistic diversity." *Language* 32: 109-115.

Gurr, T. (1974) "The neo-Alexandrians: a review essay on data handbooks in political science." *Amer. Pol. Sci. Rev.* 68 (March): 243-252.

_____ (1972) *Politimetrics.* Englewood Cliffs, NJ: Prentice-Hall.

Guttman, L. (1968) "A general non-metric technique for finding the smallest coordinate space for a configuration of points." *Psychometrica* 33: 469-506.

Hall, M. and M. Tideman (1967) "Measures of concentration." *J. of the Amer. Statistical Association* 61: 162-186.

Harmon, H. (1976) *Modern Factor Analysis.* Chicago: Univ. of Chicago Press.

Holsti, O. (1969) *Content Analysis of the Social Sciences and Humanities.* Reading, MA: Addison-Wesley.

Kerlinger, N. (1973) *The Foundations of Behavioral Research.* New York: Holt, Rinehart & Winston.

Leng, R. and J. D. Singer (1970) "A multi-theoretical typology of international behavior," pp. 71-93 in Bunge, Galtung, and Malitza (eds.) *Mathematical Approaches to International Relations.* Bucharest: Romanian Academy of Social and Political Sciences.

Lieberson, S. (1969) "Measuring population diversity." *Amer. Soc. Rev.* 34 (December): 850-862.

Lingoes, J. C. (1973) *The Guttman-Lingoes Non-Metric Program Series.* Ann Arbor, MI: Mathesis Press.

McClelland, C. (1972) "Theoretical problems," in J. N. Rosenau, V. Davis, and M. A. East (eds.) *The Analysis of International Politics.* New York: Free Press.

Merritt, R. (1966) *Symbols of American Community, 1735-1775.* New Haven, CT: Yale Univ. Press.

Moll, K. (1974) "International conflict as a decision system." *J. of Conflict Resolution* 18, 4: 555-577.

Morgenstern, O. (1963) *On the Accuracy of Economic Observations.* Princeton, NJ: Princeton Univ. Press.

Morrison, D. et al. (1972) *Black Africa: A Comparative Handbook.* New York: Free Press.

Moul, W. (1973) "The level of analysis problem revisited." *Canadian J. of Pol. Sci.* 6, 3: 494-513.

Namenworth, J. Z. and H. Lasswell (1970) *The Changing Language of American Value.* Beverly Hills: Sage.

Naroll, R. (1962) *Data Quality Control.* New York: Free Press.

Nelson, C. R. (1973) *Applied Time Series Analysis.* San Francisco: Holden-Day.

North, R. et al. (1963) *Content Analysis: A Handbook with Applications for the Study of International Crisis.* Evanston, IL: Northwestern Univ. Press.

Pool, I. de S. [ed.] (1959) *Trends in Content Analysis*. Urbana: Univ. of Illinois Press.

Rae, D. and M. Taylor (1970) *The Analysis of Political Cleavages*. New Haven, CT: Yale Univ. Press.

Ray, J. and J. D. Singer (1973) "Measuring the concentration of power in the international system." *Soc. Methods & Research* 1 (May): 403-437.

Rummel, R. (1972) *The Dimensions of Nations*. Beverly Hills: Sage.

Russett, B. et al. (1964) *World Handbook of Social and Political Indicators*. New Haven, CT: Yale Univ. Press.

Simon, H. (1954) "Spurious correlation: a causal interpretation." *J. of the Amer. Statistical Association* 49 (September): 467-479.

Singer, J. D. (1977) "The historical experiment as a research strategy in world politics." *Social Science History* 2 (Fall): 1-22.

———— (1968) "Man and world politics: the psycho-cultural interface." *J. of Social Issues* 24 (July): 127-165.

———— (1965) "Data-making in international relations." *Behavioral Science* 10 (January): 68-80.

———— (1963) "Media analysis in inspection for disarmament." *J. of Arms Control* 1 (July): 248-260.

———— (1961) "The level of analysis problem in international relations." *World Politics* 14: 77-92.

———— and M. Small (1972) *The Wages of War*. New York: John Wiley.

———— (1966) "The composition and status ordering of the international system, 1815-1940." *World Politics* 18 (January): 236-282.

Singer, J. D., S. Bremer, and J. Stuckey (1972) "Capability distribution, uncertainty, and major power war, 1820-1965," in B. Russett (ed.) *Peace, War, and Numbers*. Beverly Hills: Sage.

Small, M. and J. D. Singer (1973) "Diplomatic importance of states, 1816-1970: an extension and refinement of the indicator." *World Politics* 25 (July): 577-599.

Stone, P. et al. (1966) *The General Inquirer*. Cambridge, MA: MIT Press.

Taylor, C. L. and M. Hudson (1972) *World Handbook of Political and Social Indicators*. New Haven, CT: Yale Univ. Press.

Wallace, M. (1973) "Alliance polarization, cross-cutting, and major power war, 1816-1965." *J. of Conflict Resolution* 17, 4: 575-604.

Webb, E. et al. (1966) *Unobtrusive Measures: Non-Reactive Research in the Social Sciences*. Chicago: Rand-McNally.

## CHAPTER FIFTEEN

Bueno de Mesquita, Bruce. "Systematic Polarization and the Occurrence and Duration of War," *Journal of Conflict Resolutions* 22/2 (June 1978) 241-67.

Bueno de Mesquita, Bruce, and Lalman, David. "Empirical Support for Systemic and Dyadic Explanations of International Conflict." Stanford, Calif: Hoover Institution, 1987 (mimeo.).

Bueno de Mesquita, Bruce, and Singer, J. David. "Alliances, Capabilities, and War: A Review and Synthesis," in Cotter, Cornelius (ed.) *Political Science Annual* Vol. 4 (1973) 237-80.

Campbell, Donald T. "Common Fate, Similarity, and Other Indices of the Status of Aggregates of Persons as Social Entities," *Behavioral Science* 3/1 (1958) 14-25.

Deutsch, Karl W., and Singer, J. David, "Multipolar Power Systems and International Stability." *World Politics*, Vol. 16 (1964), 390-406.

Frey, Bruno. "The Economic Model of Behavior: Shortcomings and Fruitful Developments." Zurich, Switzerland: Institute for Empirical Research in Economics, 1983 (mimeo).

Gulick, Edward V. *Europe's Classical Balance of Power*. New York: Norton, 1955.

Haas, Ernst B. "The Balance of Power: Prescription, Concept, or Propaganda," *World Politics* 5/3 (April, 1953) 442-77.

Herek, Gregory M., Janis, Irving L., and Huth, Paul. "Decision Making During International Crises" *Journal of Conflict Resolution* 31/2 (June 1987) 203–226.

Hoffman, Stanley. *The State of War*. New York: Praeger, 1965.

Hunt, Michael H. *Ideology and U.S. Foreign Policy*. New Haven: Yale University Press, 1987.

Kaplan, Morton. *System and Process in International Politics*. New York: Wiley, 1957.

Kennan, George F. *American Diplomacy, 1900–1950*. Chicago: Univ. of Chicago Press, 1951.

Levy, Jack. "Alliance Formation and War Behavior: An Analysis of the Great Powers, 1495–1975" *Journal of Conflict Resolution* 25/4 (December, 1981) 581–613.

――――. "The Polarity of the System and International Stability: An Empirical Analysis" in Alan Sabrosky (ed.) *Polarity and War: The Changing Structure of International Conflict*. Boulder, Colorado: Westview, 1985.

Liska, George. *International Equilibrium*. Cambridge: Harvard, 1956.

March, James G. "Decisions in Organizations and Theories of Choice" in A.H. Van de Wen and W.F. Joyce (eds.) *Perspectives on Organization Design and Behavior*. New York: Wiley, 1981.

Midlarsky, Manus. "A Hierarchical Equilibrium Theory of Systemic War" *International Studies Quarterly* (1986) 77–105.

――――. "Equilibrium in the Nineteenth Century Balance of Power System," *American Journal of Political Science* (1981) 270–96.

Miller, James G. *Living Systems*, New York: McGraw-Hill, 1976.

Ostrom, Charles, and Aldrich, J. "The Relationship Between Size and Stability in the Major Power International System," *American Journal of Political Science* 22 (1978) 743–771.

Ostrom, Charles W., and Hoole, Francis W. "Alliances and Wars Revisited: A Research Note." *International Studies Quarterly*, Vol. 22 (1978), 215–236.

Ray, James Lee. *Global Politics*. Boston: Houghton Mifflin, 1987.

Rosecrance, Richard. "Bipolarity, Multipolarity, and the Future" *Journal of Conflict Resolution* 10/3 (September 1966) 314–27.

Rosenau, James (ed.). *Linkage Politics: Essays on the Convergence of National and International Systems*. New York: Free Press, 1969.

Russett, Bruce. *International Regions and the International System*. Chicago: Rand-McNally, 1967.

Sabrosky, Alan (ed.) *Polarity and War: The Changing Structure of International Conflict*. Boulder, Colorado: Westview, 1985.

Schrodt, Philip A. "Adaptive Precedent-Based Logic and Rational Choice: A Comparison of Two Approaches to the Modeling of International Behavior" in Luterbacher, U. and Ward, M. (eds.) *Dynamic Models of International Conflict*. Boulder, Colorado: Lynne Rienner, 1985, 373–423.

Singer, J. David. "Accounting for International War: The State of the Discipline" *Journal of Peace Research* 18/1 (1981) 1–18.

Singer, J. David, and Bouxsein, Sandra. "Structural Clarity and International War: Some Tentative Findings," in Thomas Murray (ed.) *Interdisciplinary Aspects of General System Theory* (1975) 126–35.

Singer, J. David, Bremer, Stuart, and Stuckey, John. "Capability Distribution, Uncertainty, and Major Power War, 1820–1965." In Bruce Russett (ed.) *Peace, War and Numbers*. Beverly Hills: Sage, 1972.

Singer, J. David, and Small, Melvin. "Alliance Aggregation and the Onset of War, 1815–1945," in J. David Singer (ed.) *Quantitative International Politics*, New York: Free Press, 1968.

Siverson, Randolph, and Sullivan, Michael. "The Distribution of Power and the Onset of War," *Journal of Conflict Resolution* 27/3 (September, 1983) 473–494.

Stiglicz, Robert. *Structural Clarity, Polarity, Power Concentration, and War*. Minneapolis, MN: University of Minnesota Press. Thesis, 1981.

Stoll, Richard. "Bloc Concentration and Dispute Escalation Among the Major Powers, 1830–1965," in *Social Science Quarterly* 65/1 (March 1984) 48–59.

Stoll, Richard, and Champion, Michael. "Capability Concentration, Alliance Bonding, and Conflict Among the Major Powers," in Alan Sabrosky (ed.) *Polarity and War: The Changing Structure of International Conflict.* Boulder, CO: Westview Press (1985) 67–94.

Thompson, William, Rasler, Karen, and Li, Richard. "Systemic Interaction Opportunities and War Behavior," *International Interactions* 7/1 (1980) 57–85.

———. "Polarity, the Long Cycle, and Global Power Warfare," *Journal of Conflict Resolution* 30/4 (December 1986) 587–615.

Vasquez, John A. "The Steps to War: Toward a Scientific Explanation of Correlates of War Findings," *World Politics* (October 1987) 108–145.

Wallace, Michael D. "Alliance Polarization, Cross-Cutting, and International War, 1815–1964: A Measurement Procedure and Some Preliminary Evidence," *Journal of Conflict Resolution*, Vol. 17 (1973), pp. 575–604.

Wallace, Michael D., and Singer, J. David. *A Structural History of the International System.* Columbia, S.C.: University of South Carolina Press (forthcoming, 1991).

Waltz, Kenneth N. "Theory of International Relations," in Fred I. Greenstein and Nelson W. Polsby (eds.), *Handbook of Political Science: International Politics*, Vol. 8. Reading: Addison-Wesley, 1975.

Wayman, Frank. "Bipolarity and War: The Role of Capability Concentration and Alliance Patterns Among Major Powers, 1816–1965," *Journal of Peace Research* 21/1 (April 1984) 61–78.

Zinnes, Dinna. "An Analytical Study of the Balance of Power Theories," *Journal of Peace Research* 4/3 (1967) 270–288.

## CHAPTER SIXTEEN

Note: The brevity of this list is due to the fact that most of the sources used in the development of our data are listed in the two basic descriptive papers (Singer, Small, and Kraft, 1965; and Small and Singer, 1965). The archival and monograph sources are voluminous and there is no point in listing them again here.

Abel, Theodore. "The Element of Decision in the Pattern of War," *American Sociological Review* 6 (December 1941), pp. 853–59.

Berge, Claude. *The Theory of Graphs.* London: Methuen, 1962.

Bodart, G. *Losses of Life in Modern Wars.* Oxford: Clarendon Press, 1916.

Burr, Robert N. "The Balance of Power in Nineteenth Century South America: An Exploratory Essay," *Hispanic American Historical Review* 35 (February 1955), pp. 37–60.

Claude, Inis L. *Power and International Relations.* New York: Random House, 1962.

Coleman, James. *Introduction to Mathematical Sociology.* New York: The Free Press of Glencoe, 1964.

Deutsch, Karl W., and J. David Singer. "Multipolar Power Systems and International Stability," *World Politics* 16 (1964), pp. 309–406.

Dumas, S., and K. O. Vedel-Peterson. *Losses of Life Caused by War.* Oxford: Clarendon Press, 1923.

Eckstein, Harry (ed.). *Internal War: Basic Problems and Approaches.* New York: The Free Press of Glencoe, 1963.

Falk, Richard. "International Jurisdiction: Horizontal and Vertical Conceptions of Legal Order," *Temple Law Quarterly* 32 (1959).

Flament, Claude. *Applications of Graph Theory to Group Structure.* Englewood, N.J.: Prentice Hall, 1963.

Gareau, Frederick H. *The Balance of Power and Nuclear Deterrence: A Book of Readings.* Massachusetts: Houghton Mifflin, 1962.

Gulick, Edward V. *Europe's Classical Balance of Power.* Ithaca, N.Y.: Cornell University Press, 1955.

Haas, Ernst B. "The Balance of Power: Prescription, Concept, or Propaganda," *World Politics* 5 (1953), pp. 442–77.

Harary, Frank. "A Structural Analysis of the Situation in the Middle East," *Journal of Conflict Resolution* 5, No. 2 (1961), pp. 167–78.

Hargreaves, Reginald. *The Enemy at the Gate: A Book of Famous Sieges, Their Causes, Their Progress, and Their Consequences.* Harrisburg, Pa.: Stackpole, 1948.

Holsti, Ole R., Richard A. Brody, and Robert C. North. *Theory and Measurement of Interstate Behavior: A Research Application of Automated Content Analysis.* Stanford University Studies in International Conflict and Integration, 1964.

Horvath, William J., and Caxton C. Foster. "Stochastic Models of War Alliances," *Journal of Conflict Resolution* 7, No. 2 (June 1963), pp. 110–16.

Kaplan, Morton. *System and Process in International Politics.* New York: Wiley, 1957.

Klingberg, Frank L. *Historical Study of War Casualties.* Washington, D.C.: War Department, 1945.

Liska, George. *Nations in Alliance: The Limits of Interdependence.* Baltimore: Johns Hopkins Press, 1962.

Modelski, G. *The International Relations of Internal War.* Princeton, N.J.: Center of International Studies, 1961.

Moore, W. E. "Predicting Discontinuities in Social Change," *American Sociological Review* 29 (June 1964), pp. 331–38.

Morgenthau, Hans J. *Politics Among Nations.* New York: Knopf, 1956.

Rapoport, Anatol, and W. J. Horvath. "A Study of a Large Sociogram," *Behavioral Science*, 6 (1961), pp. 279–91.

Rapoport, Anatol. "Mathematical Models of Social Interaction," in R. Duncan Luce, Bush and Galenter (eds.), *Handbook of Mathematical Psychology* 2. New York: Wiley, 1963, pp. 494–579.

Richardson, Lewis F. *Statistics of Deadly Quarrels.* Pittsburgh: Boxwood Press, 1960.

Rosecrance, R. *Action and Reaction in World Politics.* Boston: Little, Brown, 1963.

Rosenau, James N. *International Aspects of Civil Strife.* Princeton, N.J.: Princeton University Press, 1964.

Singer, J. David, Melvin Small, and George L. Kraft. "The Frequency, Magnitude, and Severity of International War, 1815–1945." (forthcoming)

Singer, J. David, and Melvin Small. "The Composition and Status Distribution of the International System, 1815–1945." (forthcoming)

Small, Melvin, and J. David Singer. "Inter-Nation Alliance Commitments and Performance, 1815–1939." (forthcoming)

Smoker, Paul. "Fear in the Arms Race: A Mathematical Study," *Journal of Peace Research* 1 (1964), pp. 55–63.

Sorokin, Pitirim A. *Social and Cultural Dynamics.* New York: American Book Company, 1937.

Urlanis, Boris T. *Volny i Narodonaselenie Evropy.* Moscow: 1960.

Waltz, Kenneth N. "The Stability of a Bipolar World," *Daedalus* 43, No. 3 (1964), pp. 881–909.

Weiss, Herbert K. "Stochastic Models for the Duration and Magnitude of a 'Deadly Quarrel,'" *Operations Research* 11, No. 1 (January-February 1963), pp. 101–21.

Weiss, Herbert K. "The Ending of a War Considered as a Markoff Process," *Proceedings of the Military Operations Research Symposia*, Fall 1961.

Wright, Quincy. *A Study of War.* 2 vols. Chicago: University of Chicago Press, 1942.

# CHAPTER SEVENTEEN

Alcock, N., and A. Newcombe (1970) "Perception of National Power." *Journal of Conflict Resolution* 14: 335–343.

Andreski, S. (1968) *Military Organization and Society.* Berkeley: University of California Press.

Bachrach, P., and M. Baratz (1962) "The Two Faces of Power." *American Political Science Review* 56: 947–952.

Baldwin, D. (1979) "Power Analysis and World Politics." *World Politics* 31: 161–194.

Benoit, E. (1973) *Defense and Economic Growth in Developing Countries*. Lexington: Lexington Books.

Blechman, B., and S. Kaplan (1978) *Force Without War*. Washington, D.C.: Brookings.

Bremer, S. (1980) "National Capabilities and War Proness" in J. D. Singer (ed.) *The Correlates of War: II*. New York: The Free Press.

Bueno de Mesquita, B. (1981) *The War Trap*. New Haven: Yale University Press.

Cannizzo, C. (1980) "The Costs of Combat" in J. D. Singer (ed.) *Correlates of War: II*. New York: The Free Press.

Cline, R. S. (1977) *World Power Assessment: A Calculus of Strategic Drift*. Boulder: Westview.

Dahl, R. (1957) "The Concept of Power." *Behavioral Science* 2: 201–15.

Dupuy, R. E., and T. N. Dupuy (1977) *Encyclopedia of Military History*. London: Macdonald and Jane's.

East, M. (1972) "Status Discrepancy and Violence in the International System" in J. N. Rosenau et al. (eds.) *The Analysis of International Politics*. New York: Free Press.

Ferris, W. (1973) *The Power Capabilities of Nation States*. Lexington: Lexington Books.

Fucks, W. (1965) *Formeln zur Macht*. Stuttgart: Deutsch Verlags-Anstalt.

German, C. (1960) "A Tentative Evaluation of World Power." *Journal of Conflict Resolution* 4: 138–144.

Gochman, C., and Z. Maoz. (1982) "Serious Interstate Disputes, 1816–1976: Empirical Patterns and Theoretical Insights." Pittsburgh: University of Pittsburgh, August (unpublished mimeo).

Hart, J. (1976) "Three Approaches to the Measurement of Power in International Relations." *International Organization* 30: 289–305.

Kindleberger, C. (1964) *Economic Growth in France and Britain*. New York: Simon and Schuster.

Knorr, K. (1970) *Military Power and Potential*. Lexington: Heath.

Kuznets, S. (1966) *Modern Economic Growth*. New Haven: Yale University Press.

Langer, W. (1968) *An Encyclopedia of World History*. Boston: Houghton Mifflin.

Lasswell, H., and A. Kaplan (1950) *Power and Society*. New Haven: Yale University Press.

Leng, R. (1983) "When Will They Ever Learn? Coercive Bargaining in Recurrent Crises." *Journal of Conflict Resolution* 27: 379–420.

Leontief, W., A. Morgan, K. Polenske, D. Simpson and E. Tower (1965) "The Economic Impact—Industrial and Regional—of an Arms Cut." *Review of Economics and Statistics* 47: 217–222.

Lindblom, C. E. (1977) *Politics and Markets*. New York: Basic Books.

Mack, A. (1975) "Why Big Nations Lose Small Wars: The Politics of Asymmetric Conflict." *World Politics* 27: 175–200.

Maoz, Z. (1982) *Paths to Conflict: International Dispute Initiation, 1816–1976*. Boulder: Westview.

March, J. (1966) "The Power of Power" in D. Easton (ed.) *Varieties of Political Theory*. Englewood Cliffs: Prentice-Hall.

Melman, S. (1974) *The Permanent War Economy*. New York: Simon and Schuster.

Nagel, J. (1975) *The Descriptive Analysis of Power*. New Haven: Yale University Press.

Newcombe, A. G., and J. Wert (1973) "The Use of an Inter-Nation Tensiometer for the Prediction of War." *Peace Science Society Papers* 23: 73–83.

Nincic, M. (1982) *The Arms Race*. New York: Praeger.

O'Connor, R. (1969) "Victory in Modern War." *Journal of Peace Research* 4: 367–385.

Organski, A. F. K., and J. Kugler (1978) "Davids and Goliaths: Predicting the Outcomes of International Wars." *Comparative Political Studies* 11: 141–180.

Rosen, S. (1972) "War Power and the Willingness to Suffer" in B. Russett (ed.) *Peace, War and Numbers*. Beverly Hills: Sage.

Russett, B. M. (1970) *What Price Vigilance?* New Haven: Yale University Press.

Saaty, T., and M. Khouja (1976) "A Measure of World Influence." *Journal of Peace Studies* 2: 31–48.

Schelling, T. C. (1966) *Arms and Influence*. New Haven: Yale University Press.

Scitovsky, T. et al. (1951) *Mobilizing Resources for War: The Economic Alternatives*. New York: McGraw-Hill.

Shapley, L., and M. Shubick (1954) "A Method for Evaluating the Distribution of Power in a Committee System." *American Political Science Review* 48: 787–792.

Singer, J. D. (1963) "Inter-Nation Influence: A Formal Model." *American Political Science Review* 57: 420–430.

―――― (1968) "Disarmament." *International Encyclopedia of the Social Sciences*. New York: Macmillan.

―――― (1982) "Variables, Indicators, and Data: The Measurement Problem in Macro-Political Research." *Social Science History* 6: 181–217.

Singer, J. D., and M. Small (1972) *The Wages of War*. New York: Wiley.

Singer, J. D., S. Bremer, and J. Stuckey (1972) "Capability, Distribution, Uncertainty and Major Power War, 1820–1965" in B. Russett (ed.) *Peace, War and Numbers*. Beverly Hills: Sage.

Sivard, R. L. (1976) *World Military and Social Expenditures*. Leesburg, Va.: WMSE Publications (annual).

Wallace, M. (1973) *War and Rank Among Nations*. Lexington: Lexington Books.

Wayman, F. (1982) "War and Power Transitions during Enduring Rivalries." Paper presented to the meeting of the Institute for the Study of Conflict Theory and International Security, Champaign-Urbana, Illinois, 22–24 September.

Weidenbaum, M. (1974) *Economics of Peacetime Defense*. New York: Praeger.

Wright, Q. (1965) "The Escalation of International Conflicts." *Journal of Conflict Resolution* 9: 434–449.

Yengst, W. (1982) "War Termination and How Much Is Enough." Presentation for the 3rd Working Meeting on the Theory of Combat and Philosophy of War, U.S. Army War College, Carlisle Barracks, Pa., June.